# IT IS WRITTEN: SCRIPTURE CITING SCRIPTURE

Barnabas Lindars, SSF

[Photo: Invicta Studio, Manchester]

# It is Written:
# Scripture Citing Scripture

## ESSAYS IN HONOUR OF
## BARNABAS LINDARS, SSF

EDITED BY

### D. A. CARSON

AND

### H. G. M. WILLIAMSON

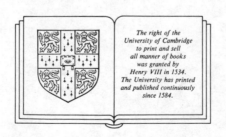

The right of the
University of Cambridge
to print and sell
all manner of books
was granted by
Henry VIII in 1534.
The University has printed
and published continuously
since 1584.

## CAMBRIDGE UNIVERSITY PRESS

CAMBRIDGE

NEW YORK    NEW ROCHELLE

MELBOURNE    SYDNEY

Published by the Press Syndicate of the University of Cambridge
The Pitt Building, Trumpington Street, Cambridge CB2 1RP
32 East 57th Street, New York, NY 10022, USA
10 Stamford Road, Oakleigh, Melbourne 3166, Australia

© Cambridge University Press 1988

First published 1988

Printed in Great Britain by
The University Press, Cambridge

*British Library cataloguing in publication data*
It is written: scripture citing scripture:
essays in honour of Barnabas Lindars.
1. Bible–Commentaries
I. Carson, D. A. II. Williamson, H. G. M.
III. Lindars, Barnabas
220.7   BS491.2

*Library of Congress cataloguing in publication data*
It is written.
Includes indexes.
1. Bible. O. T.–Criticism, interpretation, etc.
2. Bible. N. T.–Relation to the Old Testament.
3. Lindars, Barnabas. I. Lindars, Barnabas.
II. Carson, D. A. III. Williamson, H. G. M. (Hugh
Godfrey Maturin), 1947–
BS1171.2.185   1988   220.6   87–20954

ISBN 0 521 32347 9

# Contents

# Contents

## THE OLD TESTAMENT IN THE NEW TESTAMENT

# Contents

# Preface

AMONGST those who devote their lives to biblical and cognate study, few achieve the range of mastery displayed by Barnabas Lindars. Most aim to specialise in only one of the two Testaments, or perhaps some smaller corpus; they are at home in Hebrew but not in Greek, or the reverse; they can quote Philo with some authority, but have no sympathy for apocalyptic literature. But from the beginning of his writing and teaching career, what has characterised Barnabas Lindars is the breadth of his competence. While lecturing primarily on the Old Testament at Cambridge, he produced his well-received commentary on John. Many of his students and colleagues look forward to reading his forthcoming commentary on Judges in the prestigious ICC series. Although several of his essays revolve around these two poles, others testify to his interest in the Son of Man, Enoch, biblical criticism, the purpose of law, and various aspects of christian ethics. Few scholars achieve academic distinction and gain administrative responsibilities in both *Studiorum Novi Testamenti Societas* and the Society for Old Testament Study, along the way delivering lectures at the International Organization for Septuagint and Cognate Studies.

His membership in the Society of St Francis testifies to his theological, ecclesiastical and pastoral commitments. Initially these commitments kept him from pursuing advanced theological education. Assignment to the chapter in Cambridge allowed him to combine his interests and produce his first major work, *New Testament Apologetic: The Doctrinal Significance of the Old Testament Quotations* (1961). Academic recognition followed, capped by his elevation to the prestigious Rylands Chair in the University of Manchester, a position which, appropriately enough, is not exclusively tied to Old Testament or New Testament studies, but to biblical literature.

Those who have worked closely with him in his present position, in his earlier appointments in Jesus College and in the Faculty of Divinity at Cambridge University, and in the professional societies, can testify to his energy and considerable administrative gifts. His research students remember him as a *Doktorvater* who read their papers with great attention to detail. Some of them at the beginning of their work might remark that Barnabas Lindars was not as easy to get to know as some other mentors; they would soon be heard to give thanks for the privilege of studying under a scholar who offered ready access to his study, astonishingly prompt and thoughtful criticism of all written work, sufficient pressure to get on with the task and enough freedom to make mistakes. Friendship might not be easily won; once won, it was cherished the more.

One of the two editors of this volume wrote his doctoral dissertation under the supervision of Barnabas Lindars, and can testify to two other features that made tutorials enriching. The first was firm intellectual integrity: Barnabas Lindars never bluffs, or pretends to know what he does not. The second virtue is unknown in some parts of the academic world. Though quintessentially British, it is particularly well displayed in Barnabas Lindars: he is not interested in building a 'school' of thought but in teaching his students to think, and therefore is quite happy to allow them to reach decisions rather different from his own.

The world of biblical scholarship will make its own assessment of Barnabas Lindars's contributions; the present editors are happy to collaborate with the scholars who have joined us to produce this volume as a small token of esteem and appreciation for the many ways in which Professor Lindars has enriched our lives. Presented to him on the occasion of his sixty-fifth birthday, St Barnabas' Day, 1988, this book, we hope, will be a satisfying reminder of the honour in which he is held, and an incentive to continue to write challenging and thought-provoking essays and books.

It may be helpful to include a brief note of explanation on the present volume. Following the recent pattern of some *Festschriften*, this book is not a disparate collection of essays but a tightly organised unity. The central theme – the manner in which Scripture uses antecedent Scripture – reflects the breadth of interests in the writings of Professor Lindars, and mirrors the focus of his first book. At the same time, these essays bring together a great deal of material that helps the reader better to grasp that the use of Scripture in Scripture is part of a process that extends beyond any one corpus. To look at the entire subject is to bring to light patterns and continuities that might otherwise be missed.

The limitations on space meant that we did not include any treatment of the use of early New Testament traditions in later New Testament books. Because one cannot responsibly treat the use of the Old Testament in the New without considering how the Old Testament is handled in other sources and the extent to which the New Testament writers depend on these mediating influences, considerable space was devoted to the so-called 'intertestamental' writings. Allotting these writings to particular chapters was not easy. The classification finally adopted attempts to reflect the material itself, and avoids too much overlap. In consequence, some important texts remain unmentioned, but it is hoped that all types of material and all the major exegetical techniques will have been illustrated.

Each contributor was asked to devote the majority of the allotted space to a survey of the field, before going on to make fresh or innovative proposals. The volume can therefore serve as a textbook for the theological student who is just beginning to explore this subject, as well as a stimulus for more mature scholars. Contributors nevertheless enjoyed considerable freedom as to how to develop their own chapters, some choosing to provide a comprehensive survey and others preferring to focus more narrowly on fewer but exemplary texts.

The plan of the book to some extent determined who the contributors would be. It was early decided not to ask only former students of Professor Lindars to contribute, or only his current colleagues at Manchester, or some other narrow group, but to cast the net as widely as his professional associations. We have therefore included colleagues from Cambridge and Manchester, former students, members of SNTS and SOTS in the UK and abroad. Many more could have been approached; but each one who has contributed writes out of a specialist knowledge of the assigned area. The essays and any revisions were completed by the autumn of 1986.

Finally, it is a pleasure to thank all who have helped to produce this book: the contributors, who in some cases set aside other responsibilities to meet pressing deadlines, and in every case worked under the strictures of space and format necessary to an integrated volume, Mr Gerald Peterman and Mrs Tammy Thomas for compiling some of the indexes, and the Syndics and staff of the Cambridge University Press for the various ways they have encouraged and helped forward the publication of what we hope will be a worthy tribute to a distinguished scholar.

# Biographical Note

FREDERICK CHEVALLIER LINDARS
(Barnabas Lindars, SSF)

Born: 11 June 1923
Educated at Altrincham Grammar School
Rogerson Scholarship to St John's College, Cambridge, 1941
BA 1945 (Class 1 in Oriental Languages Tripos, Part I, 1943; Class 1, Theological Tripos, Part I, 1946; Class 2, Part II, 1947)
MA, 1948
BD, 1961
DD, 1973
War service, 1943–5
Westcott House, Cambridge, 1946–8
Deacon, 1948
Priest, 1949
Curate of St Luke's, Pallion, Sunderland, 1948–52
Member of the Society of St Francis from 1952
Assistant Lecturer in Divinity in Cambridge University, 1961–6
Lecturer in Divinity in Cambridge University, 1966–78
Fellow and Dean of Jesus College, Cambridge, 1976–8
Canon Theologian of Leicester Cathedral from 1977
T. W. Manson Memorial Lecturer in Manchester University, 1974
Member: *Studiorum Novi Testamenti Societas* (Assistant Secretary, 1962–75); Society for Old Testament Study (President, 1986)
Ethel M. Wood Lecturer in the University of London, 1983
Rylands Professor of Biblical Criticism and Exegesis in Manchester University, 1978–

Publications

1958   'Matthew, Levi, Lebbaeus and the Value of the Western Text', *NTS* 4, 220–2.
1960   'The Holy Spirit in Romans', *Church Quarterly Review* 161, 410–22.
1961   *New Testament Apologetic: The Doctrinal Significance of the Old Testament Quotations* (SCM/Westminster Press).
         'The Composition of John xx', *NTS* 7, 142–7.

Biographical Note

1964 'Second Thoughts – IV. Books of Testimonies', *ET* 75, 173–5.

1965 'Ezekiel and Individual Responsibility', *VT* 15, 452–67.

'Elijah, Elisha and the Gospel Miracles', in C. F. D. Moule (ed.), *Miracles: Cambridge Studies in their Philosophy and History* (Mowbray), pp. 61–79.

1966 'Gideon and Kingship', *JTS* n.s. 16, 315–26.

1967 'Is Psalm ii an Acrostic Poem?', *VT* 17, 60–7.

1968 *Words and Meanings: Essays Presented to David Winton Thomas*, ed. Peter R. Ackroyd and Barnabas Lindars (Cambridge University Press).

'Torah in Deuteronomy', in *Words and Meanings* (Cambridge), pp. 117–36.

*Church Without Walls: Essays on the Role of the Parish in Contemporary Society*, ed. Barnabas Lindars (SPCK).

'Professors, Priests and People', in *Church Without Walls*, pp. 63–77.

'The Perils of Biblical Preaching', in *Church Without Walls*, pp. 79–92.

1969 'New Books on John', *Theology* 72, 153–8.

1970 'Two Parables in John', *NTS* 16, 318–29.

'Δικαιοσύνη in Jn 16.8 and 10', in Albert Descamps and André de Halleux (eds.), *Mélanges bibliques en hommage au R. P. Béda Rigaux* (Duculot), pp. 275–85.

1971 *Behind the Fourth Gospel* (SPCK).

'Some Septuagint Readings in Judges', *JTS* n.s. 22, 1–14.

1972 *The Gospel of John*, New Century Bible (Oliphants/Attic Press).

1973 *Christ and Spirit in the New Testament: In Honour of Charles Francis Digby Moule*, ed. Barnabas Lindars and Stephen S. Smalley (Cambridge University Press).

'The Son of Man in the Johannine Christology', in *Christ and Spirit in the New Testament*, pp. 43–60.

'The Bible and Christian Ethics. Duty and Discernment, 3', *Theology* 76, 180–9. Reprinted in G. R. Dunstan (ed.), *Duty and Discernment* (SCM, 1975).

'Imitation of God and Imitation of Christ; Duty and Discernment, 7', *Theology* 76, 394–402. Reprinted in G. R. Dunstan (ed.), *Duty and Discernment* (SCM, 1975).

'Jotham's Fable: a New Form-critical Analysis', *JTS* n.s. 24, 355–66.

1974 *Témoignage de l'évangile de Jean: Pour une histoire de Jésus V*, Barnabas Lindars and Béda Rigaux (Desclée de Brouwer, 1974).

'Parola e Sacramento nel quarto Vangelo', in *Chiesa per il mondo: miscellanea M. Pellegrino I* (EDB [Bologna]), pp. 105–9.

1975 'The Apocalyptic Myth and the Death of Christ', *BJRL* 57, 366–87.
'Re-Enter the Apocalyptic Son of Man', *NTS* 22, 52–72.

1976 'Word and Sacrament in the Fourth Gospel', *SJTh* 29, 49–63.
'A Bull, a Lamb and a Word: I Enoch xc.38', *NTS* 22, 483–6.

1977 'The Passion in the Fourth Gospel', in J. Jervell and Wayne A. Meeks (eds.), *God's Christ and His People: Studies in Honour of Nils Alstrup Dahl* (Universitetsforlaget [Oslo]), pp. 71–86.
'The Place of the Old Testament in the Formation of New Testament Theology: Prolegomena and Response', Barnabas Lindars and Peder Borgen, *NTS* 23, 59–75.

1978 'Traditions behind the Fourth Gospel', in M. de Jonge (ed.), *L'Evangile de Jean*, BEThL 44 (Duculot), pp. 109–24.
'Jesus and the Pharisees', in E. Bammel, C. K. Barrett and W. D. Davies (eds.), *Donum Gentilicium: New Testament Studies in Honour of David Daube* (Clarendon), pp. 51–63.
*Il messaggio di Geovanni: Tradizione e teologia*, by Barnabas Lindars and Béda Rigaux (Vita e Pensiero [Milan]).

1979 '"Rachel Weeping for her Children" – Jeremiah 31:15–22', *JSOT* 12, 47–62.
'The Israelite tribes in Judges', in J. A. Emerton (ed.), *Studies in the Historical Books of the Old Testament*, SVT 30 (Brill), pp. 95–112.
'The Irony of Jesus', *The Franciscan* 21, 27–33.

1980 'Jesus as Advocate: A Contribution to the Christology Debate', *BJRL* 62, 476–97.

1981 'John and the Synoptic Gospels: A Test Case', *NTS* 27, 287–94.
'Enoch and Christology', *ET* 92, 295–9.
'Discourse and Tradition: The Use of the Sayings of Jesus in the Discourses of the Fourth Gospel', *JSNT* 13, 83–101.
'The New Look on the Son of Man', *BJRL* 63, 437–62.
'The Persecution of Christians in John 15.18–16.4*a*', in W. Horbury and B. McNeil (eds.), *Suffering and Martyrdom in the New Testament: Studies Presented to G. M. Styler* (Cambridge), pp. 48–69.

1982 'Salvation Proclaimed: VII. Mark 10:45: A Ransom for Many', *ET* 93, 292–5.
'The Use of Scripture in Theological Debate and in Debate on Moral and Ethical Issues: a Discussion Paper' (General Synod, London).
'Bible and Church', in M. Santer (ed.), *Their Lord and Ours* (SPCK), pp. 1–19.
'Christ and Salvation', *BJRL* 64, 481–500.

1983 *Jesus Son of Man: A Fresh Examination of the Son of Man Sayings in the Gospels in the Light of Recent Research* (SPCK). Eerdmans, 1984. (Italian edition: *Credi tu nel Figlio dell'Uomo?*, Milan, 1987).

'Deborah's Song: Women in the Old Testament', *BJRL* 65, 158–75.
'Miracle', in A. Richardson and J. Bowden (eds.), *A New Dictionary of Christian Theology* (SCM), pp. 370–2.
*Interpreting Judges Today*, The Ethel M. Wood Lecture (London).

1984 'The Bible and the Call: The Biblical Roots of the Monastic Life in History and Today', *BJRL* 66, 228–45. Reprinted in G. Rowell (ed.), *Tradition Renewed* (DLT, 1986), pp. 199–213.
'The Spiritual Interpretation of Scripture', *The Franciscan* 26, 126–31.
'Slave and Son in John 8:31–36', in *The New Testament Age: Essays in Honor of Bo Reicke*, ed. W. C. Weinrich, 2 vols. (Mercer) vol. 1, pp. 271–86.

1985 'Old Testament Quotations in the New Testament', in P. J. Achtemeier (ed.), *Harper's Bible Dictionary* (Harper and Row), pp. 723–7.
'The Sound of the Trumpet: Paul and Eschatology', *BJRL* 65, 766–82.

1986 'Jesus Risen: Bodily Resurrection but No Empty Tomb', *Theology* 89, 90–6.
'Good Tidings to Zion: Interpreting Deutero-Isaiah Today', *BJRL* 68, 473–97.

1987 '*Joseph and Asenath* and the Eucharist' in B. P. Thompson (ed.), *Scripture: Meaning and Method. Essays presented to Anthony Tyrrell Hanson* (Hull University Press), pp. 181–99.
'Jesus Christ Yesterday, Today and For Ever', The Peake Memorial Lecture 1986, *Epworth Review* 14, 70–80.
'The Apostle Paul', *Encyclopedia Britannica*, 1987 edition, vol. 25, pp. 456–60.
'The Old Testament and Universalism in Paul', *BJRL* 69, 511–27.
'A Commentary on the Greek Judges?', *VI Congress of the International Organization for Septuagint and Cognate Studies*, ed. Claude E. Cox (SCS 23; Scholars Press).

### In the Press:

'The New Testament', in P. Avis (ed.), *The History of Christian Theology*.
Untitled volume on the history and study of the Bible, in the series *History of Christian Theology*, 5 vols., ed. Barnabas Lindars (Part III: The New Testament), John Rogerson (Part I: The Old Testament), and Christopher Rowland (Part II: The Apocrypha).
*Law and Religion: Essays on the Place of Law in Israel and Early Christianity*, ed. Barnabas Lindars (Cambridge: James Clarke & Co., 1988).
'All Foods Clean: Jesus and the Law', in *Law and Religion*.
'Paul and the Law in Romans 6–8: an Actantial Analysis', in *Law and Religion*.
'The Structure of Psalm cxlv', *VT*.

# Abbreviations

| | |
|---|---|
| AB | Anchor Bible |
| AGSU | Arbeiten zur Geschichte des Spätjudentums und Urchristentums |
| ALGHJ | Arbeiten zur Literatur und Geschichte des hellenistischen Judentums |
| *ALUOS* | *Annual of the Leeds University Oriental Society* |
| AnBib | Analecta Biblica |
| *ANET* | J. Pritchard, *Ancient Near Eastern Texts Relating to the Old Testament*, 3rd edition (Princeton, 1969) |
| ANRU | Aufstieg und Niedergang der römischen Welt |
| ASNU | Acta Seminarii Neotestamentici Upsaliensis |
| *ASTI* | *Annual of the Swedish Theological Institute in Jerusalem* |
| ATD | Das Alte Testament Deutsch |
| *AUSS* | *Andrews University Seminary Studies* |
| *BA* | *The Biblical Archaeologist* |
| BBB | Bonner Biblische Beiträge |
| BET | Beiträge zur biblischen Exegese und Theologie |
| BEThL | Bibliotheca Ephemeridum Theologicarum Lovaniensium |
| BEvTh | Beiträge zur evangelischer Theologie |
| BFChrTh | Beiträge zur Förderung christlicher Theologie |
| *Bib* | *Biblica* |
| *BibOr* | *Bibbia e Oriente* |
| *BJRL* | *Bulletin of the John Rylands Library* |
| BKAT | Biblischer Kommentar, Altes Testament |
| BNTC | Black's New Testament Commentaries (= HNTC) |
| *BSac* | *Bibliotheca Sacra* |
| BU | Biblische Untersuchungen |
| *BVC* | *Bible et Vie Chrétienne* |
| BWANT | Beiträge zur Wissenschaft vom Alten und Neuen Testament |
| *BZ* | *Biblische Zeitschrift* |
| BZAW | Beihefte zur Zeitschrift für die Alttestamentliche Wissenschaft |
| *CBQ* | *Catholic Biblical Quarterly* |
| CBQMS | Catholic Biblical Quarterly Monograph Series |
| ConB | Coniectanea Biblica |

# Abbreviations

| | |
|---|---|
| CT | Cahiers Théologiques |
| *DBSup* | *Dictionnaire de la Bible, Supplément* |
| DSS | Dead Sea Scrolls |
| *ED* | *Euntes Docete* |
| EKK | Evangelisch–Katholischer Kommentar |
| ET | English translation |
| *EThL* | *Ephemerides Theologicae Lovanienses* |
| *ExT* | *Expository Times* |
| FG | Fourth Gospel |
| FRLANT | Forschungen zur Religion und Literatur des Alten und Neuen Testaments |
| HAT | Handbuch zum Alten Testament |
| HNT | Handbuch zum Neuen Testament |
| HNTC | Harper's New Testament Commentaries (= BNTC) |
| HSM | Harvard Semitic Monographs |
| *HTR* | *Harvard Theological Review* |
| HTS | Harvard Theological Studies |
| *HUCA* | *Hebrew Union College Annual* |
| ICC | International Critical Commentary |
| *IDB* | *The Interpreter's Dictionary of the Bible* (4 vols., and supplementary vol., Nashville and New York, 1962, 1976) |
| *Int* | *Interpretation* |
| *JBL* | *Journal of Biblical Literature* |
| JBLMS | Journal of Biblical Literature Monograph Series |
| *JETS* | *Journal of the Evangelical Theological Society* |
| *JJS* | *Journal of Jewish Studies* |
| *JNES* | *Journal of Near Eastern Studies* |
| *JQR* | *Jewish Quarterly Review* |
| JSHRZ | W. G. Kümmel et al., *Jüdische Schriften aus hellenistisch–römischer Zeit* (Gütersloh, 1973–) |
| *JSJ* | *Journal for the Study of Judaism* |
| *JSNT* | *Journal for the Study of the New Testament* |
| *JSOT* | *Journal for the Study of the Old Testament* |
| JSOTSS | Journal for the Study of the Old Testament Supplement Series |
| *JSS* | *Journal of Semitic Studies* |
| *JTS* | *Journal of Theological Studies* |
| LD | Lectio Divina |
| LXX | Septuagint |
| *MDB* | *Le Monde de la Bible* |
| MeyerK | *Kritisch-exegetischer Kommentar über das Neue Testament*, begr. von H. A. W. Meyer |

| | |
|---|---|
| *MGWJ* | *Monatschrift für Geschichte und Wissenschaft des Judentums* |
| MM | J. H. Moulton and G. Milligan, *The Vocabulary of the Greek New Testament* (London, 1930) |
| MT | Masoretic Text |
| NA[26] | The Greek New Testament, Nestle-Aland 26th edition |
| NCB | New Century Bible |
| NF | Neue Folge |
| NICNT | New International Commentary on the New Testament |
| NIGTC | New International Greek Testament Commentary |
| *NKZ* | *Neue Kirchliche Zeitschrift* |
| *NovT* | *Novum Testamentum* |
| *NRTh* | *Nouvelle Revue Théologique* |
| n.s. | new series |
| NT | New Testament |
| *NTS* | *New Testament Studies* |
| OT | Old Testament |
| *OTS* | *Oudtestamentische Studiën* |
| *RB* | *Revue biblique* |
| *RevQ* | *Revue de Qumran* |
| *RivistBib* | *Rivista Bíblica* |
| *RömQ* | *Römische Quartalschrift* |
| *RThL* | *Revue Théologique de Louvain* |
| SANT | Studien zum Alten und Neuen Testament |
| SBL | Society of Biblical Literature |
| SBLDS | Society of Biblical Literature Dissertation Series |
| SBLMS | Society of Biblical Literature Monograph Series |
| SBLSCS | Society of Biblical Literature Septuagint and Cognate Studies |
| SBT | Studies in Biblical Theology |
| SCS | Septuagint and Cognate Studies |
| SJLA | Studies in Judaism in Late Antiquity |
| *SJTh* | *Scottish Journal of Theology* |
| SNT | Supplements to *Novum Testamentum* |
| SNTSMS | Society for New Testament Studies Monograph Series |
| SPB | Studia Post-Biblica |
| *ST* | *Studia Theologica* |
| SUNT | Studien zur Umwelt des Neuen Testaments |
| SVT | Supplements to *Vetus Testamentum* |
| *TDNT* | *Theological Dictionary of the New Testament* |
| *ThLZ* | *Theologische Literaturzeitung* |
| *ThZ* | *Theologische Zeitschrift* |
| *TRE* | *Theologische Realenzyklopädie* |
| *TS* | *Theological Studies* |

## Abbreviations

| | |
|---|---|
| TTS | Trier Theologische Studien |
| TU | Texte und Untersuchungen |
| *TWNT* | *Theologisches Wörterbuch zum Neuen Testament* |
| *TynB* | *Tyndale Bulletin* |
| *VC* | *Vigiliae Christianae* |
| *VT* | *Vetus Testamentum* |
| WBC | Word Biblical Commentary |
| WMANT | Wissenschaftliche Monographien zum Alten und Neuen Testament |
| WUNT | Wissenschaftliche Untersuchungen zum Neuen Testament |
| *ZAW* | *Zeitschrift für die alttestamentliche Wissenschaft* |
| *ZNW* | *Zeitschrift für die neutestamentliche Wissenschaft* |
| *ZThK* | *Zeitschrift für Theologie und Kirche* |

*Note:* When an author's bibliography cites both a foreign-language work and its English translation, the latter is referred to in the text of the chapter.

# 1 · An assessment of recent developments

## I. HOWARD MARSHALL

THE distinguished scholar in whose honour this volume has been compiled has placed on record his view that 'the Old Testament is the greatest single influence in the formation of New Testament theology' (Lindars, 1976, p. 60). The point is one that needs to be made and to be defended, since it is not certain that it would be universally accepted. The contents of some of the essays which follow in this book will demonstrate the pervasiveness and the variety of the use of the OT in the NT. It should thus constitute both an elucidation and a defence of the position which Professor Lindars has stated and which he has done so much to commend as a scholar whose expertise stretches widely, though never superficially, over both fields.

The scope of this volume has admittedly been defined rather more broadly by its editors as the use of Scripture within *Scripture*; that is to say, it discusses not only the use of the OT in the various parts of the NT but also the use of earlier parts of the OT in later parts. But since the use of Scripture in the so-called intertestamental literature throws a flood of light on the NT use of the OT, it is inevitable that this topic is also considered. However, the use of Scripture within Scripture in the sense of the use of earlier texts of the NT or of NT traditions within the NT is excluded from consideration.

This limitation of scope means that the book is not primarily concerned with such topics as the subsequent history of the christian use of the OT or how Christians today should understand and use the OT, although it may be presumed that a study of how the NT writers used the OT is of significance in answering these questions (Longenecker, 1970; Hanson, 1974, pp. 225ff; 1983, pp. 178ff). Nor is the book primarily concerned with elucidation of the theological relationship between the two Testaments (Baker, 1976). Nevertheless, the scope that remains is enormous, and there is no way in which this introductory essay can hope to cover all the ground, embracing as it does a vast body of literature both primary and secondary. Indeed it would not be appropriate to attempt to do so when one bears in mind that the succeeding contributors will each bring a more microscopic attention to bear on each of the several parts of the literature. Between them the contributors will in fact consider all the various areas of the Bible in which Scripture is used. Indeed, their activity might seem to make this introductory essay totally superfluous, were it not that a broad view of the field may help to alert the reader to the several problems which may arise and prevent him from losing the main issues in a wealth of detail. There is also the possibility that the structure of the remainder of the book may prevent the contributors from considering those general problems raised by the topic which are the concern of everybody and hence the concern of nobody. Our task therefore in this essay will be to look at some of the general problems which arise in the study of the use of Scripture by Scripture. We shall, however, steer clear of one problem which is the subject of the first major section of the book, namely the use of the OT in the OT, which is the field of OT specialists.

There have been several recent surveys of the whole field. These can be divided into two kinds. First, there are the works which survey the actual topic of the use of the OT in the NT, usually advancing the author's own view of the subject but manifestly not without some attention to the work of other scholars. Here we may mention the works of Tasker (1946), Barrett (1970), Shires (1974), Longenecker (1975), Hay (1976), Ellis (1978), Vermes (1976), and Hanson (1983). Second, there are the works which survey recent scholarship on the subject rather than the subject itself. Here we have particularly the work of Smith (1972). Our discussion will fall more into this second pattern, and it will confine itself for the most part to study since 1946.

The questions to which we shall attempt to devote some attention include the following: to what extent is it correct to say that the use of the OT was the decisive influence in the creation of christian theology? What led the early Christians and the NT writers to specific texts in the OT? To what extent did they pay respect to the meaning of these texts in their context? In what kind of church situation did the christian use of the OT develop? What kind of exegetical methods were used, and how far were these methods adopted from contemporary Judaism? In what ways did the use of the OT shape the content and structure of the NT?

## The place of the OT in NT theology

The first major contribution to the study of the use of the OT in the NT in the last forty years was that of Dodd (1952). The book has an importance out of all proportion to its brevity, and has been the starting point for a fair amount of discussion. Dodd's basic concern was with the process by which theology developed in the NT church. If it is correct to say 'In the beginning was the kerygma', how did the early church move on to the development of a theology? He argued that the kerygma was understood in the light of the OT, but this then raises the question of how the church used the OT to elucidate the kerygma. He rejected the theory of Harris (1916, 1920) that it was done by the creation of an apologetic testimony book in the early days. Instead he argued that the appearance of the same OT texts independently in different writers but often with the same peculiarities of wording suggested the use of a common stock of textual materials, and that these texts appeared to have been drawn from various specific areas or 'fields' in the OT which were systematically exploited for what they might yield, due attention being paid to context. So the principles of exegesis were established, and the way in which certain doctrines were developed was expounded. It will thus be apparent that Dodd was really concerned to answer three questions:

1 In what way did the early church develop a theology? It understood the kerygma in the light of the OT.

2 How did the early church find its way round the OT? It recognised certain fields which were of particular theological significance.

3 How did the early church use the material from these fields? On the one hand, it recognised the presence of common themes in the various fields and therefore drew materials from them with a certain regard for the context. On the other hand, it developed its theology by the incorporation of teaching that sprang from the OT.

Dodd's first point, which is of major importance, is that the roots of the early church's theologising lie in the illumination of the kerygma by the prophecies of the OT (Dodd, 1952, p. 135).

What might be regarded as a criticism of this hypothesis has come from Wilcox (1979) and has recently been taken up by Black (1986, pp. 7f). He insists that the procedures followed by the early Christians imply a common ground between them and their partners in discussion, namely a set of accepted exegetical traditions for understanding the OT on the basis of which Christians could argue that the traditions found their correct interpretation and fulfilment in Jesus. It was, then, out of debates within the context of 'messianic Judaism' that the kerygma emerged.

However, it is doubtful whether this is really a criticism of Dodd's position or the presentation of an alternative to it. Rather it is a reminder of an important factor in the process, namely that when the early Christians went to the Scriptures for evidence in favour of their view of Jesus it was necessary that their methods of interpretation should follow the accepted procedures of the time. But at the same time the point should be made that it was the use of the OT which helped to shape the kerygma – a fact that Dodd would surely not have denied. Thus when the early summary of the kerygma in 1 Cor. 15:3 declares that 'Christ died for our sins according to the Scriptures', the fact that Christ died is a 'given', and probably also the fact that his death had a significance of some kind. But did the early church go to the Scriptures to find evidence that he died 'for our sins' or was it study of the Scriptures that led to the realisation that he died 'for our sins'? The effect of Wilcox's argument is to remind us that the latter process went on alongside the former, and we

3

may add that many times we must envisage a dialectical process with the influences going in both directions. Again, in 1 Cor. 15:4 the event of the resurrection is probably primary – unless we are to assume that the phenomena of the empty tomb and the appearances of Jesus were interpreted by a category drawn from the OT – and the scriptural backing either for the resurrection itself or for 'on the third day' will have come later. Thus it seems that Wilcox has offered a refinement of Dodd's case rather than an alternative to it.

Dodd developed his theory in express contradiction to the view that Paul based his theology on religious experience, whether visions and revelations or even his conversion experience. Nor was theology based on speculation influenced by and incorporating the religious ideas of Hellenism; its fundamental content and way of thinking are biblical. In saying this Dodd was not arguing for an early church theology which was based purely on the 'Word', but rather for one in which 'the mighty acts of God' in history are understood in the context which is provided by the OT.

Dodd's view may seem at first sight to stand in contrast to that of Kim who argues that the origins of Paul's gospel lie in his Damascus road experience with its vision of Jesus as the image of God (Kim, 1981). But it seems rather that Kim is showing how Paul came to a realisation of the truth of the kerygma, and nothing that he says contradicts the possibility that the development of early church theology and of Paul's own theology took place 'according to the Scriptures'.

The really important question which arises is whether Dodd is justified in his claim that it was the study of the OT which formed the substructure of NT theology. I take 'substructure' to mean the basic underlying presuppositions of thought which supply the basis or structure of the gospel. Is the influence of the OT so far-reaching, or does it merely supply the background for a few aspects of the kerygma, the real and central impetus to the categories in which it is formulated coming from somewhere else? Is it possible to conceive of a different substructure? In order to do so it would be necessary to disprove the claim that the essential vocabulary and conceptualisation and the basic structure of NT theology are drawn from the OT. It is true that the theology of the NT approaches the OT wearing the spectacles of Judaism, but this does not affect the basic fact that it was to the OT and to the traditions inspired by it that the church turned when it began to do theology.

Dodd's view thus stands in sharp contrast to the view of Käsemann, for example, that the mother of christian theology was apocalyptic (Käsemann, 1969, pp. 82–107). Käsemann appears to mean that its structure of thought was determined basically by the near expectation of the parousia and also that its content consisted of the kind of thoughts expressed in the jewish apocalyptic literature. But this view is unacceptable, for, as various scholars have observed, it is the kerygma of the death and resurrection of Jesus which

4

figures in the earliest expressions of the church's theology (Lohse, 1971, p. 58).

Dodd's view that it was the OT which was the inspiration of NT theology stands over against the view that we should look for another source in the Hellenistic world. We should not expect to find much influence from Hellenism in general. It is significant that, when Knox wrote on *Some Hellenistic Elements in Primitive Christianity* (1944), it was a remarkably slim volume which resulted, and there is no doctrine of central importance which can be shown to have been derived from Hellenism. Earlier, of course, Bousset (1921) had tried to show that the understanding of Jesus as Lord was derived from Hellenism, but it is quite clear that his attempt was a failure. A much greater challenge has come from attempts to derive essential elements of early christian doctrine from Gnosticism (Bultmann, 1952; cf. Schmithals, 1971a; 1971b; Schottroff, 1970), but these seem to me to be equally dubious. Nevertheless, there is here a field for continuing discussion.

## THE PROBLEM OF TEXTUAL 'FIELDS' IN THE OT

The second part of Dodd's thesis was concerned with the way in which the early Christians found specific textual 'fields' in the OT.

The discovery of collections of texts at Qumran has made the alternative possibility of a testimony book more plausible than it was when Dodd advanced his thesis. These parallels certainly show that a testimony book was a possibility, but we have still to ask whether the internal evidence of the NT confirms that the texts are most plausibly to be explained in this way. The existence of an actual testimony book and of a set of 'fields' side by side is of course quite possible, and the question is rather whether there is decisive evidence for the existence of either. Subsequent discussion has tended on the whole not to go back to the testimony book theory (Lindars, 1961, pp. 14, 23f).

Dodd's own theory has been strongly criticised by Sundberg, Jr. (1959). Against Dodd's concept of exegetical 'fields' Sundberg argued, first, that the NT authors appear to draw their biblical citations from such a wide area of the OT as to make it seem unlikely that they were following a tradition which directed attention to specific, limited fields. He also claimed, second, that the particular fields which Dodd isolated do not seem to be used particularly often in the NT.

Sundberg's arguments, however, must be tested. The statistics which he produced to prove his point are dubious. He worked from the list of 'citations' in the index to the 1948 edition of Nestle's text, and was able to claim that out of 929 chapters in the OT no less than 423 are cited in the NT. But the latter figure covers far more than express citations of OT texts, and in this respect the figures in the index to the third edition of *The Greek New Testament* furnish a better guide. They show that texts from 162 chapters are cited in the NT. The books which show the greatest number of chapters from which citations are drawn relative to their size are Genesis, Exodus, Leviticus, Deuteronomy, Isaiah, the Twelve, and Psalms. Dodd's own list of fields included Genesis, Deuteronomy, Psalms, Isaiah, Daniel and the Twelve. Only Exodus and Leviticus figure in the revised Sundberg list, which may suggest not that Dodd's list is wrong in principle but that it needs revision in detail. Sundberg then went on to list the relative importance of the various OT books in terms of the number of 'citations' from each (again using the Nestle list). But here in fact Sundberg's figures appear to support Dodd, for the books with the highest ratings are Genesis, Exodus, Deuteronomy, Isaiah, the Twelve, Psalms, Proverbs and Daniel.

Sundberg next tries to establish his point by considering the relative usage of the different NT authors, but fails to observe that the different purposes and characters of the various writings make such a comparison futile. Nor does he recognise adequately that what Dodd was discussing was the fields used in the *earliest* stage of the church's study of the OT. It is reasonable to assume that at the literary stage of composition of the NT the writers would not be tied to the specific fields and would feel free to explore more widely and to ignore materials that had earlier been of greater importance. This point may be relevant in dealing with the further objection that a study of the repetition of *allusions* to specific texts (rather than just the occurrences of actual citations) indicates that a larger area of material was being tapped; again the point may be made that the allusions are more of a literary phenomenon. Nevertheless, the point should be made that Dodd's theory need not require that the early church turned *only* to a limited list of fields. His view was that these fields developed in the earliest days of the church's theologising rather than that they imposed limits throughout the NT period and prevented NT authors from looking outside them, especially to any well-known passages which were not in the fields.

Here we may take up Sundberg's next point which is that Dodd supposed that there was 'a traditional method of exegesis of Old Testament passages' in the church which governed the meaning (Sundberg, 1959, p. 278). Sundberg takes this to mean that the same OT passage should have received the same interpretation whenever it was cited in the New, and he cites examples to show that this did not happen. But these examples are not wholly convincing, as when he finds texts that are applied both to Jesus and to his followers, and ignores the way in which what is true of Christ is also often true of his followers. There is no change in meaning here, only a shift in application. In any case jewish exegesis was quite capable of finding multiple meanings in any one text (Brooke, 1985, 354f).

## An assessment of recent developments

Sundberg (1959, p. 279) argues further that some doubly cited passages refer to 'manifestly developed positions of the church', e.g. the jewish rejection of Jesus which cannot have existed from the beginning. But surely the evidence goes the other way and suggests that this was a problem to the church from an early date (1 Thess. 2:14–16).

Finally Sundberg argues that such a collection as Dodd presupposes should have been preserved in the NT canon. The reasons for this statement are not obvious, especially if the list of passages was oral and so short as to be easily memorable; one cannot see that such a list would be regarded as Scripture in the same way as the actual NT writings.

Sundberg's case against Dodd thus stands open to criticism at every point, and I judge that it is not successful in refuting his case. The hypothesis that the early church turned to specific fields in the OT and used them can still be used as a starting point for investigation (Lindars, 1961, p. 14). What still needs to be determined is how the church used the material from the OT once it had found it.

### THE PROBLEM OF ATTENTION TO THE OT CONTEXT

A further problem is whether the NT writers pay attention to the context in their use of OT materials. Certainly Dodd did not deny that there was what he called 'a certain shift, nearly always an expansion, of the original scope of the passage' (Dodd, 1952, p. 130), and he argued that great literature contains the potential of more meaning than the original author explicitly intended.

Again Sundberg attempts to contradict Dodd. He argues that the meanings given to the citations are not dependent upon the context of the original passages. There seem in fact to be two possible points here. One is whether there is an intended reference to the larger context in which the citation is found; the other is whether the meaning is related to that context. But is either of these quite what Dodd had in mind? He argued that the finding of an appropriate text in part of the OT led the Christians to look in the same context for further appropriate texts, and that in some cases the choice of a text was dependent upon the assumption that the larger passage is christologically oriented. Thus, for example, the quotation of Ps. 69:25 with reference to the defection of Judas presupposes the belief that the Psalm had already been seen to be christological and that therefore this text is relevant to the rejection of Christ. Now over against this Sundberg argues that the majority of texts are cited atomistically. But Sundberg's examination of cases where the NT authors cite several different texts from the same OT passage does not disprove the fact that having found christological significance in one text the NT authors kept coming back to the same area. It is not a case so much of *understanding* the citation that is at issue (Sundberg, 1959, p. 277) but of

7

tracing how the Christians came to use it. In the broader sense all that was needed was a recognition that the passage was christological, so that the use of a text from within it was not arbitrary. This has not been disproved by Sundberg. The general question of whether respect for context in a narrower sense is preserved is a separate issue and deserves further investigation. The point may be made that the NT authors *thought* that they were respecting the context and original meaning, since they would have argued that the meaning which they found was the meaning which God intended.

## THE CONTEXT OF THE USE OF THE OT IN THE NT

But before we discuss the question of how the early Christians determined the meaning of the OT we must comment on the situation in which they did so and the effect which this had on their interpretation. The study of this aspect of our topic received a fresh impetus with the publication in 1961 of Professor Barnabas Lindars's book on *New Testament Apologetic*. Basically Lindars is arguing for two positions. The first is that we can trace shifts in the application of the OT passages in different parts of the NT, and the second is that the starting point of this process lies in the apologetic activity of the early church. The early church was particularly concerned to answer jewish objections to the messiahship of Jesus, and where such a concern can be detected we come up against the earliest uses of the texts in question. Lindars begins with the resurrection of Jesus and then turns to passion apologetic. He then moves on to a secondary development in the application of Scripture to events in the life of Jesus before the passion and to the question of his origins. Finally, he looks at developments in these lines of thinking by Paul.

The discussion is acute and full of penetrating observations. The apologetic use of Scripture by the early church is clearly documented. Nevertheless, it is open to some criticisms. These have been presented by Gundry (1967, pp. 159–63) who lists six objections to Lindars's view before coming to his major point, which is that Lindars's case hangs on detecting *Tendenz* in the varied text forms which are used, whereas the evidence shows the existence of 'mixed text-forms in the untendentious material of many allusive quotations throughout the synoptics'. This is essentially the same objection as that which Gundry raises against the validity of Stendahl's discussion of the material in Matthew, and it is clear that much hangs or falls with the correctness of his interpretation of the material.

It seems to me that Lindars tends to make two assumptions in his work which need greater justification than he provides. One is the assumption, to which Gundry also draws attention, that the earliest use of OT texts was apologetic rather than anything else. This is assumed rather than argued. Obviously much use of the OT would be apologetic, and this need not be denied, and where texts were used apologetically Lindars has much that is helpful to say about them. But are we justified in assuming that in the earliest days there was no other type of use? There is a firm tradition that Jesus used the OT to throw light on his mission, and there is no good reason to reject it (France, 1971). Moreover, the NT shows clearly that the early church used the OT in an explanatory manner as well as in a definitely apologetic and hence somewhat polemical context. We can also observe how the early church went to the OT for the still-valid teaching which it gave and for the responsive material which it took over and used to provide the form and content of its own praise and prayer to God. There is a good deal of use of the OT in the NT which can be labelled 'liturgical', and this usage stems from the life of the church in its early days. Hence the field of use seems to be much wider than Lindars suggests.

Second, Lindars argues that it is probable that the very earliest apologetic would be concerned with the resurrection of Jesus, and he then attempts to find a putative resurrection-application as the starting point for the development of the use of any and every text. This begs the question of Jesus' own use of the OT, to which we have already referred, and it further begs the question of the actual use of specific texts in the early church. Granted what lies beyond dispute, namely that resurrection-apologetic was an early phenomenon in the church, it was by no means the only form of apologetic, and it is a strange assumption that every text used in the earliest days of the church must have had an initial reference to the resurrection. Although Lindars's assumption at this point is thus a puzzling one, he has rendered an important service in stimulating further explorations of the kind of use, or rather the purposes for which use was made, of the OT in the early church.

## TYPES OF USE OF THE OT

We come now to the question of how the NT writers made use of the OT and what understanding they had of it. If anything is clear, it is that a variety of types of use must be recognised. It may be helpful to offer a list of them before considering one or two of them in greater detail:

1   The influence of the language of the OT on the diction of the NT authors, with the result that they write a 'biblical Greek' distinguished by its secondary Semitisms (i.e. Semitisms which have been transmitted through the LXX).

2   The influence of the style of the OT. This emerges specifically in the case of Luke whose use of a LXX style must raise the question whether he thought of himself as writing a work of the same kind and thus continuing the 'salvation historical' story which he found in it.

3 The use of the OT in a straightforward 'literal' manner when reference is being made to events described in it. This use is so 'obvious' that it is often passed over without comment, and yet it may demand further attention.

4 The use of the OT again in a 'literal' manner to refer to the divine commands, etc., which are found in it and which are believed to be still valid (or which may be cited in order to be brought up to date or even abrogated).

5 The use of the OT yet again in a 'literal' manner to refer to passages which were understood as prophecies and which found their literal meaning in the events now taking place. 'About whom does the prophet say this?' Then Philip 'told him the good news of Jesus' (Acts 8:34f).

6 The use of the OT typologically to show a correspondence between a contemporary event and an event in the OT so that understanding of the former (and sometimes of the latter) may be enhanced.

7 The use of the OT allegorically to draw parallels between an OT story and a contemporary situation or piece of teaching.

The lines between these types of use are not always easy to draw. Our attention will centre on the problems of prophecy and typology in the light of jewish usage.

## EXEGESIS IN THE DEAD SEA SCROLLS

In their dialogue on 'The Place of the Old Testament in the Formation of New Testament Theology' Lindars (1976) and Borgen (1976) list between them six areas of jewish interest in, and exegesis of, the OT which are relevant for understanding the use made in the NT. These are: jewish liturgical forms; the rabbinic literature; the targums; the Qumran sect; apocalyptic literature; and Philo. Each of these will receive due attention later in this book. For our present purpose it may suffice to open up the question of jewish influence on the NT use of the OT by looking at some of the issues as they are raised by a consideration of the Qumran documents.

The first important work to show the influence of the Scrolls was Stendahl's book, *The School of St Matthew* (1954; 2nd ed. 1968), of which the author has been known to comment that people tended to quote the title rather than read the book. The thesis was concerned (obviously) with one limited area, namely the use of a specific set of quotations in the gospel of Matthew, which appeared to stand out from the others for formal and textual reasons, and it had two main parts.

First, Stendahl argued that the character of these quotations and the implied interpretation of them resembled the kind of thing found in the use of Scripture at Qumran and specifically in the Habakkuk commentary; in particular, he drew attention to the use of variant readings in the text to promote a particular interpretation, and he labelled the kind of exegesis which was going on as 'midrash pesher'. The name was coined by analogy with midrash halakah and midrash haggadah which designate two other types of midrashic activity (Stendahl, 1968, p. 184), and it is important to bear this fact in mind in view of later discussions of the suitability of the term. In all cases midrash refers to a manner of exegesis of the text which aims to bring out its contemporary significance, for instance by showing how the precepts of the torah still apply in the commentator's own time. In the case of Qumran the type of midrash consists in a technique of quoting the text in a form appropriate to the meaning which is deemed to lie hidden in it and then explaining it in accordance with a set of principles of interpretation, thirteen of which are listed from Brownlee (1951); thus the interpretation lies partly in the text cited and partly in the interpretative comments in which it is embedded.

This led to the second part of the thesis which was that the activity thus demonstrated suggested the work of a 'school' rather than of one specific individual.

The thesis was important for two reasons. First, there was the suggestion that some kind of corporate study of the OT Scriptures developed in the early church. The question whether we should speak of 'school' activity in this connexion was raised with specific reference to the phenomena in Matthew, and it is not necessarily implied that all early christian exegesis was carried out in such a setting. Nevertheless, the character of the NT activity suggests the development of communally known and practised methods of understanding, which it may be appropriate to call 'school' activities. The activity of scriptural interpretation was not confined to a few individuals but was fairly widespread in the church and occupied a position of great importance.

But we must concentrate our attention on Stendahl's other claim, namely that in certain quarters at least the early church practised a form of scriptural exegesis hitherto unknown but now shown to be paralleled in one area of contemporary Judaism. The character of this so-called 'pesher' interpretation deserves some critical comment since it has become something of a catch-phrase in subsequent study. The principles of 'pesher' interpretation cited by Stendahl (1968, pp. 191f) may be listed as follows:

1  What the prophets wrote has a veiled, eschatological meaning.
2  Since the meaning is veiled, the meaning may be discerned by what may appear to be a forced interpretation.
3  One may observe textual or orthographical peculiarities.
4  One may also make use of textual variants (for the light they shed on the text or to replace the text).

5　One may note analogous circumstances.
6　The text may be allegorised in an appropriate manner.
7　One may find more than one meaning in the words.
　　One may assume that the author has hidden the meaning he intended in
　　various ways and 'undo' his techniques:
8　by substituting synonyms for the intended words,
9　by using anagrams,
10　by substituting similar letters for the ones he really intended,
11　by running words together, which must be split to get the meaning,
12　and by using abbreviations which must be spelled out in full.
13　One may find that other passages of Scripture illuminate the meaning of
　　the text.

It is clear that a series of assumptions are operative here. The first is that the prophet's message has a meaning which is 'eschatological'. That is to say, it applies to a future period which the sect identified with its own time and the immediate future. It found its own activities prophesied and it looked forward to whatever else God would do in the future. The question whether the passage had a meaning for the prophet's own time is ignored. Thus the first of the thirteen principles is a statement about the nature of prophecy rather than a method for finding its meaning. It defines the kind of meaning that is presumed to be there.

The second assumption is that this eschatological meaning is often (but not always) 'hidden' and needs to be recovered by suitable procedures which involve going beyond the apparent message of the text to a hidden meaning which can be detected by noting abnormalities in the text. In other words the abnormalities represent a deliberate coding of the message which must now be decoded. Principles 3-13 are in effect methods for apprehending this hidden meaning. The procedures were presumably justified by their 'results'. Some of them are more justifiable than others, such as recourse to analogous circumstances or to other passages of Scripture.

The question whether the method of 'decoding' can be called charismatic seems to have more relevance to the self-understanding of the Qumran interpreters than to an objective assessment of their actual procedures. It seems probable that the Qumran interpreters did claim to have special insights given by revelation into the hidden meaning of Scripture, but there is no necessary tension between this consciousness and the view that there was a 'science' of exegesis, by which a set of rules was applied to get at the meaning of the text. Indeed a cynic might suggest that the rules were so arbitrary that some kind of sense of 'inspired interpretation' was necessary to justify the use of any particular rule at any given time.

Many scholars have suggested that we can find a kind of 'pesher' exegesis in parts of the NT. But the recent discussion by Brooke (1981) makes some cogent criticisms against a slipshod use of this category. He draws attention to the fascination which the term 'pesher' exerts upon scholars and complains that it is used loosely, and that it really means nothing different from midrash, which is the art of bringing the application of the Scriptures up to date. However, this does not necessarily rule out the useful application of the term. The special meaning, if the term has one, can be applied to the kind of exposition which takes up a text and proceeds to quote it in sections and to comment on each phrase in turn using the term *pišrô* to introduce the identification of each significant element in the text and a justification or explanation of the identification – in short the method exemplified in the Habakkuk commentary. The ways in which the comments are 'worked out' is found elsewhere in Qumran in discussions of brief texts grouped around themes rather than simply of continuous texts, but the actual method of commenting with the 'pesher' formula remains distinctive, and it seems appropriate to recognise it as a specific genre of interpretation.

A further point made by Brooke (1985, chap. 1) is to ask whether the 'rules' of the game at Qumran are any different from those of midrashic exegesis among the rabbis. This leads him into a discussion of the antiquity of the middoth, and to argue that while the formulations of them may be late, the practice of them is early. In point of fact there does not seem to be any great distinction between Qumran and rabbinic exegesis so far as methods are concerned. This means that the Qumran methods were not confined to Qumran and were presumably more widespread – so they could perhaps have influenced the early Christians all the more readily. It should be remembered that the formulated middoth are very general and do not necessarily reflect the precise methods that were followed.

## QUMRAN AND THE NT

It follows from what has been said that we need to distinguish between the presence of the more specific characteristics of pesher in the NT and the presence of the kinds of exegetical technique which were used at Qumran in pesher exegesis but which were broadly characteristic of jewish midrash. The presence of the latter has been helpfully discussed by Doeve (1954), but the presence of what can strictly be called 'pesher' is dubious. Even the language of 'pesher' is absent, and the parallels which have been observed by Ellis (1978, p. 160f) are not exact. Nevertheless, we can certainly say that the use of text in an appropriate textual form and the writing of the interpretation into the text are visible (Ellis, 1957).

With regard to the actual methods used at Qumran we saw that they were in reality part of the general approach which has come to be called 'midrashic'.

We can discover many parallels between Qumran and rabbinic methods of exegesis and the methods utilised in the NT. Ellis (1957) claims that the same Qumran-like method of exegesis, for which he took over the label 'midrash pesher' from Stendahl, is to be found in some of the Pauline material. Thus the choice of appropriate wording among variant readings of a text or the deliberate alteration of the wording of a citation to fit a syntactical context or to make a theological point is easily demonstrated. However, many of the devices used at Qumran and listed by Brownlee simply do not function in the NT: the assumption that the OT text has a hidden meaning and must be decoded by what may seem to us to be rather arbitrary procedures in order to reveal it is not present, and this marks a decisive difference between Qumran and NT interpretation of the OT.

From their techniques we move to the first of the assumptions made by the Qumran sect, namely that the Scriptures were seen as having relevance to their own day, so that contemporary events formed a key to the understanding of passages taken to be prophetic. They also regarded their own days as being the last days, so that we can designate their interpretations as 'eschatological' (in the sense of 'having reference to the last days'). The NT writers share the view that at least some prophecy looks forward to the last days and that the coming of Jesus and the establishment of the church are part of the events of the last days (indeed the most significant events) and are the object of prophecy. This means that both groups regarded themselves as having a 'key' to understanding the OT: they 'know' that the text *must* apply to their own situation in the last days, and therefore they use their techniques to get at this meaning. The Qumran sect lived in the conviction that the life of their sect was prophesied in the prophets and Psalms. Consequently, when they came to an obscure passage the method was to ask: Granted that this text must refer to something in our recent history, can we identify a plausible event, and then see the text as a prophetic description of it? So when some genius decides that in one verse of Habakkuk there is a prophecy of the wicked priest, it is natural to look in other verses for further references and to clear away obscurity or lack of message by assuming that the verse must have something to say within this frame of reference. Thus light is thrown both on the career of the wicked priest and also on the problems of the text of Habakkuk by this means.

NT interpretation works in the same way by assuming that prophecy finds its fulfilment in the coming of Jesus and the history of his followers. A familiar way of putting this is: 'Jesus as the Christ opens up the true meaning of the OT' (Hay, 1976, p. 443). But what does this mean? And does it apply to the whole of the OT? Presumably the point is that to the early Christians it was 'obvious' that some passages prophesied the coming of Jesus. Thus Jesus could be seen as, say, the Servant of Yahweh. The next step was to ask whether obscure verses about the Servant could make sense when seen as prophetic of him. Thus a 'key' had been found, but the way in which the Scriptures were interpreted in the light of this conviction that they prophesied Jesus had still to be worked out. But how far can this method be applied throughout the OT? Clearly it will work for passages that can be regarded as prophecy (but not necessarily for all prophecies). It will work for passages that can be interpreted typologically. It will also work for much of the OT teaching, regarded as valid and still true for the church, because written for it (we are the true Israel). It works for praise and other appropriate materials for human address and prayer to God (Hay, 1976, p. 444).

The use of this and other methods helps to draw out the continuity felt by the NT writers between the work of God in their own day and in OT times and hence between themselves and the ancient people of God. But there is also the consciousness of differences, and it may be interesting to work out how far the early christian use of the OT as a court of appeal was affected by their readiness to do away with some of its teaching. Did they see themselves as abrogating it or rather as reinterpreting it to suit their own situation?

Finally, a question arises concerning the purpose of the Qumran exposition. Granted that we know something of the context in which it was carried on, we have still to ask why the sect did it? Was the purpose apologetic or controversial? Was it to mount a reasoned defence of themselves to others or to encourage themselves by showing that they were God's people and that what was happening to them was part of a plan that would not be thwarted? It is not obvious that the question should be answered with a simple either/or, and this should be borne in mind as we come to consider the aims and purposes of early christian use of the Scriptures.

Space forbids discussion of the study of other jewish exegesis of the time. In particular, recent study of the targums is of great importance in throwing light on Christian exegesis as regards both the methods used and some of the interpretations which were reached (Chilton, 1984; Hanson, 1974, 1980).

### THE PROBLEM OF TYPOLOGY

However, some consideration must be given to the question of typology. Ellis in particular drew the attention of English-speaking scholars to the fact that a major element in Paul's interpretation of the OT was typology, where a comparison is made between events in the NT and events in the OT which are historical, which happened in accordance with a divine plan and which may have 'a dispensational or economic relationship to the corresponding NT fact' (Ellis, 1957, p. 128).

Ellis was here taking up the lead given by an earlier work which, strictly speaking, falls outside our period for comment, Goppelt's book *Typos*. Although it was published in 1939, it did not appear in English translation until 1982, and one hopes that from now on it will have a wider influence. Much has been written loosely and inexactly about typology, but it is Goppelt who gives the topic the careful study that it demands and who shows that typology is of central importance in the NT use of the OT. Typology may be defined as the study which traces parallels or correspondences between incidents recorded in the OT and their counterparts in the NT such that the latter can be seen to resemble the former in notable respects and yet to go beyond them. Redemption in Christ shows an analogy to the deliverance of Israel from Egypt but goes beyond it. Thus we see that God works on the same principles in both eras. The OT incident can thus be said to point forward to the NT one, but it does not lose its own significance in and for its own time.

What remains uncertain is whether the OT incident was thought to have been deliberately planned as a type for its antitype, so that a full exposition of the OT passage recording it would have to say 'and God did this *in order that* it would serve as a type for his later redemption of the world in Christ'. It may serve as a type merely because God works consistently in OT and NT times. That is to say: the fact that it points forward to the NT antitype is not part of the meaning of the type. Or, put otherwise, the fact that the NT sees an OT event as a type does not throw light on its interpretation in its OT context.

Or does it? Certainly the type is used to throw light on the NT incident by providing a frame of reference or a metaphorical expression which helps to illuminate the NT incident. We can say: if you want to understand what happened in Christ, it was like what happened at the Exodus. Thus we may be given what can border on an allegorical framework for understanding: just as the people of Israel were slaves in Egypt, so we were slaves to sin. Just as God delivered them by a mighty act, so now the death of Christ is the mighty act by which he delivers us. Just as at that time God made a covenant with his people and sealed it with the blood of a sacrifice, so too he has made a covenant with us and sealed it with the blood of Jesus. But does the NT use the method in the opposite direction: just as we were slaves to sin, so too the Israelites were slaves in Egypt, and so on? Does the NT claim that certain OT incidents happened *in order* to teach *us* lessons? In 1 Corinthians 10 we are told that certain things happened typically to the Israelites and were written for our instruction and as a warning. Here Paul appears to be saying that God caused the incidents in the wilderness to be recorded with the deliberate intent that we might profit from the record. Compare how he says that the commandment about not muzzling the ox was written for us. So we must ask whether typology is a means of interpreting both OT and NT or just NT. Goppelt appears to be uncertain:

Typology begins and ends with the present salvation. NT typology is not trying to find the meaning of some OT story or institution. It compares Jesus and the salvation which he has brought with the OT parallels in order to discover what can be learned from this about the new and then perhaps, what can be learned also about the old. (Goppelt, 1982, p. 201)

Ellis, as we have noted, holds that 'Divine intent is of the essence both in their occurrence and in their inscripturation', so that 'although the "type" has its own historical value, its real significance typologically is revealed only in the "anti-type" or fulfilment' (Ellis, 1957, pp. 127f). Similarly, Walter Kaiser has argued that a passage of Scripture has only one meaning, that given it by God speaking through the original writer, and that consequently when a NT writer sees a passage in a given way, that way must correspond to the divinely-intended meaning. He insists that 'there should be competent evidence of the Divine *intention* in the correspondence between it and the Antitype' (Kaiser, 1985, p. 121, citing Van Mildert, 1815, p. 239; see further the full discussion in Davidson, 1981). On this view, it follows that the meaning detected by the NT author is the original meaning of the passage. The question is whether this view was that of the NT writers themselves.

## THE STRUCTURE OF NT ARGUMENTATION IN THE LIGHT OF THE OT

An interesting feature of recent study has been the search for rabbinic patterns of argument in the NT. Research has been done on the way in which jewish midrashic material, especially in the form of synagogue sermons, was structured in terms of its relation to the seder and the haftarah, and it has been claimed that similar structures can be found in the NT. We may refer particularly to the suggestions of Bowker and Ellis in this regard (Bowker, 1967; Ellis, 1978) who have discovered material of this kind in Acts, the Pauline epistles and Jude. The view that some of the material in John derives from christian sermons is especially associated with Lindars (Lindars, 1971; 1972), but some of this sermon material is based on OT texts, e.g. John 6 (Borgen, 1965), and it is worth asking how far early christian sermons followed jewish patterns.

The question of jewish patterns influencing the structure of the NT has been raised in a more far-reaching way. On the Dodd hypothesis the earliest Christians concentrated their attention on certain specific 'fields' in the OT. We may presume, however, that they extended their search into 'all the Scriptures', as Luke suggests, for material about Jesus. If they attended the synagogue, they would be familiar with some kind of regular pattern of reading the OT which took them through the torah and the prophets section by section. Earlier scholars, among whom Guilding (1960) must especially be mentioned, argued that traces of the synagogue readings appropriate to specific occasions can be detected behind passages in the NT which are linked to such occasions (e.g. the various festivals mentioned in John). The claim that a lengthy section in Luke could be regarded as reflecting the content of successive pericopae in Deuteronomy was made by C. F. Evans (1954).

But the major contribution developing this approach is that of Goulder who has argued that much of the NT, especially the synoptic Gospels, can be shown to have been inspired, pericope by pericope, by the seriatim readings of the Scriptures in the synagogue (Goulder, 1974; 1978). Goulder further argues that the gospels themselves were composed in order to function as christian lectionaries, a use to which they were put at later dates, as the section divisions in certain MSS would indicate. If this theory can be sustained, it indicates that the structure of parts of the OT exercised an important influence on the structure and the content of much of the NT.

But can it be sustained? Reviewers in general have been content to marvel at Goulder's *tour de force* without attempting to evaluate his conclusions in a largely uncharted area of study. It seems to have been left largely to Morris and Hooker to challenge his hypothesis (Morris, 1983; Hooker, 1980; cf. Blomberg, 1983). Goulder's work is in fact open to considerable criticism, but he has drawn attention to an important area where further research is required.

## CONCLUSION

If this survey has demonstrated anything, it has shown the breadth of the field that will be traversed in much greater detail in the remaining chapters of this book. Even so we have not been able to discuss all the topics that might be raised, in particular the question of the kind of understanding of the OT as Scripture which animated the minds of early Christians. In their dialogue, to which reference has already been made, Professor Lindars and Professor Borgen have suggested that the OT may be regarded in some ways as servant and in some ways as master in the process of formation of NT theology. The paradox emerges that the Scriptures 'have an authority which is unquestioned', and yet 'the place of the Old Testament in the formation of New Testament theology is that of a servant, ready to run to the aid of the gospel whenever it is required' (Lindars, 1976, pp. 59, 66). Granted that Jesus Christ is the new master, we may perhaps remind ourselves that to be 'a slave of Jesus Christ', as Paul so frequently called himself, is to occupy a position of humble service which is at the same time one of high authority and dignity.

BIBLIOGRAPHY

D. L. Baker *Two Testaments, One Bible : A Study of Some Modern Solutions to the Theological Problem of the Relationship between the Old and the New Testaments* (Leicester, 1976).

C. K. Barrett 'The Interpretation of the Old Testament in the New', in *The Cambridge History of the Bible*, vol. 1 (Cambridge, 1970), pp. 377–411.

M. Black 'The Theological Appropriation of the Old Testament by the New Testament', *SJTh* 39 (1986), 1–17.

C. L. Blomberg 'Midrash, Chiasmus, and the outline of Luke's Central Section', in R. T. France and D. Wenham (eds.), *Gospel Perspectives : Vol. III. Studies in Midrash and Historiography* (Sheffield, 1983), pp. 217–61.

D. L. Bock 'Evangelicals and the Use of the Old Testament in the New', *BSac* 142 (1985), 209–93, and 143 (1985), 306–19.

P. Borgen *Bread from Heaven*, SNT 10 (Leiden, 1965).
'The Place of the Old Testament in the formation of New Testament Theology', *NTS* 23 (1976–7), 67–75.

W. Bousset *Kyrios Christos* (Göttingen, 1921).

J. W. Bowker 'Speeches in Acts: A study in Proem and Yellammedenu form', *NTS* 14 (1967–8), 96–110.

G. J. Brooke 'Qumran Pesher: Towards the Redefinition of Genre', *RevQ* 10 (1979–81) (Dec. 1981), 485–503.
*Exegesis at Qumran : 4QFlorilegium in its Jewish Context* (Sheffield, 1985).

W. H. Brownlee 'Biblical Interpretation among the Sectaries of the Dead Sea Scrolls', *BA* 14 (1951), 54–76.

R. Bultmann *Theologie des Neuen Testaments*, 9th ed. (Tübingen, 1953); ET *Theology of the New Testament* (London, 1952).

B. Chilton *A Galilean Rabbi and his Bible : Jesus' own Interpretation of Isaiah* (London, 1984).

R. M. Davidson *Typology in Scripture. A Study of Hermeneutical* τύπος *Structures* (Berrien Springs, 1981).

C. H. Dodd *According to the Scriptures* (London, 1952).

J. W. Doeve *Jewish Hermeneutics in the Synoptic Gospels and Acts* (Assen, 1954).

E. E. Ellis *Paul's Use of the Old Testament* (Edinburgh, 1957).
*Prophecy and Hermeneutic in Early Christianity* (Tübingen/Grand Rapids, 1978).

C. F. Evans 'The Central Section of St Luke's Gospel', in D. E. Nineham (ed.), *Studies in the Gospels* (Oxford, 1955), pp. 37–53.

R. T. France *Jesus and the Old Testament* (London, 1971).

L. Goppelt *Typos: Die typologische Deutung des Alten Testaments in Neuen* (Gütersloh, 1939); ET *Typos: The Typological Interpretation of the Old Testament in the New* (Grand Rapids, 1982).

M. D. Goulder *Midrash and Lection in Matthew* (London, 1974).
*The Evangelists' Calendar: A Lectionary Explanation of the Development of Scripture* (London, 1978).

A. Guilding *The Fourth Gospel and Jewish Worship* (Oxford, 1960).

R. H. Gundry *The Use of the Old Testament in St Matthew's Gospel with Special Reference to the Messianic Hope*, SNT 18 (Leiden, 1967).

A. T. Hanson *Jesus Christ in the Old Testament* (London, 1965).
*Studies in Paul's Technique and Theology* (London, 1974).
*The New Testament Interpretation of Scripture* (London, 1980).
*The Living Utterances of God: The New Testament Exegesis of the Old* (London, 1983).

R. Harris *Testimonies: Part I* (Cambridge, 1916), *Part II* (Cambridge, 1920).

D. Hay 'Interpretation, History of. C. NT Interpretation of the OT', in *IDBSup*, pp. 443–6.

M. D. Hooker review of M. D. Goulder, *The Evangelists' Calendar*, in *Epworth Review* 7 (1980), 91–3.

E. Käsemann *Exegetische Versuche und Besinnungen*, 2nd ed. (Göttingen, 1965); ET *New Testament Questions of Today* (London, 1969).

W. C. Kaiser, Jr. *The Uses of the Old Testament in the New* (Chicago, 1985).

S. Kim *The Origin of Paul's Gospel* (Tübingen, 1981).

W. L. Knox *Some Hellenistic Elements in Primitive Christianity* (London, 1944).

B. Lindars *New Testament Apologetic* (London, 1961).
'The Place of the Old Testament in the Formation of New Testament Theology: Prolegomena', *NTS* 23 (1976–7), 59–66.

E. Lohse 'Apokalyptik und Christologie', *ZNW* 62 (1971), 48–67.

R. N. Longenecker 'Can we reproduce the Exegesis of the New Testament?', *TynB* 21 (1970), 3–38.
*Biblical Exegesis in the Apostolic Period* (Grand Rapids, 1975).

L. Morris 'The Gospels and the Jewish Lectionaries', in R. T. France and D. Wenham (eds.), *Gospel Perspectives: Vol. III. Studies in Midrash and Historiography* (Sheffield, 1983), pp. 129–56.

W. Schmithals *Die kirchliche Apostelamt: Eine historische Untersuchung*, FRLANT 81 (Göttingen, 1961); ET *The Office of Apostle in the Early Church* (London, 1971) (= 1971*a*).
*Die Gnosis in Korinth: Eine Untersuchung zu den Korintherbriefen*, 2nd ed.

(1965); ET *Gnosticism in Corinth: An Investigation of the Letters to the Corinthians* (Nashville, 1971) (= 1971*b*).

L. Schottroff *Der Glaubende und die feindliche Welt* (Neukirchen-Vluyn, 1970).

H. M. Shires *Finding the Old Testament in the New* (Philadelphia, 1974).

D. M. Smith, Jr. 'The Use of the Old Testament in the New', in J. M. Efird (ed.), *The Use of the Old Testament in the New and Other Essays: Studies in Honor of William Franklin Stinespring* (Durham, N.C., 1972), pp. 3–65.

K. Stendahl *The School of St Matthew and its Use of the Old Testament* (Lund, 1954; second edition, Philadelphia, 1968; the second edition published at Lund at about the same time is undated).

A. C. Sundberg, Jr. 'On Testimonies', *NovT* 3 (1959), 268–81.

R. V. G. Tasker *The Old Testament in the New Testament* (London, 1946).

G. Vermes 'Interpretation, History of. B. At Qumran and in the Targums', in *IDBSup*, pp. 438–43.

W. Van Mildert *An Inquiry into the General Principles of Scripture-Interpretation* (Oxford, 1815).

M. Wilcox 'On investigating the Use of the Old Testament in the New Testament', in E. Best and R. McL. Wilson (eds.), *Text and Interpretation: Studies in the New Testament Presented to Matthew Black* (Cambridge, 1979), pp. 231–243.

# The Old Testament in the Old Testament

# 2 · History

## H. G. M. WILLIAMSON

THERE are two principal ways in which the historical books of the Old Testament make use of earlier scriptural material. One is the interpretation and application of the law of Moses, attested especially in the books of Ezra and Nehemiah, but not lacking from Chronicles or even the Deuteronomic History. The other is the Chronicler's use of Samuel and Kings. In these two areas is to be found a major stimulus towards both the halakhic and the haggadic readings of Scripture which became so pervasive in later centuries, and we shall therefore concentrate on these in the present chapter. Of the many other topics which clamour for attention, none is of greater theological interest than the use of prophetic sayings in late Old Testament historical writing, so that a third brief section has been devoted to them. Needless to say, for reasons of space it has been necessary severely to limit the number of examples adduced in each case.

### 1 THE LAW

The books of Ezra and Nehemiah refer to the book of the law under an astonishing variety of titles: the law of Moses (Ezra 3:2; 7:6; cf. 2 Chron. 23:18; 30:10); the book of Moses (Ezra 6:18; Neh. 13:1; cf. 2 Chron. 35:12); the law of the Lord (Ezra 7:10, and popular also in Chronicles; cf. 1 Chron. 16:40; 2 Chron. 31:3, 4; 35:26); the law of your God (Ezra 7:14, 26); the book of the law of Moses (Neh. 8:1); the book of the law (Neh. 8:3; cf. 2 Chron. 34:15); the book (Neh. 8:5, 8); the law (Ezra 10:3; Neh. 8:2, 7, 9, 13, 14; 10:35, 37; 13:3; cf. 2 Chron. 34:19); the book of the law of God (Neh. 8:18); the book of the law of the Lord (Neh. 9:3; cf. 2 Chron. 17:9; 34:14); and the law of God (Neh. 8:8; 10:29, 30. 2 Chron. 34:30 also speaks of the book of the covenant). It is clear from the interchange of titles in passages such as Nehemiah 8 that these all refer to one and the same law. This is further confirmed by Neh. 10:30 and 2 Chron. 34:14, where the law of God is said to have been given through Moses, and by 2 Chron. 25:4, where 'that which is written in the law, in the book of Moses' is substituted for 'that which is written in the book of the law of Moses' in 2 Kgs 14:6.

Discussions about the extent to which this work should be identified with the Pentateuch as we know it were intensified by the development of a consensus of critical opinion that Moses was not directly responsible for the first five books of the Bible. During the past two centuries, Ezra's law book has been associated with P, with D, with an unknown collection of laws which lies behind the Pentateuch as well as with the Pentateuch itself (cf. the surveys of research by Mowinckel, 1965; Kellermann, 1968; Klein, 1976; and Houtman, 1981). Because there appear to be references to most major strands of the Pentateuch both in passages concerned with the law (e.g. Nehemiah 10) and with the early history of Israel (e.g. Nehemiah 9), the majority of scholars have continued to associate the book of the law with the Pentateuch. It is true that in recent years Kellermann (1968, and cf. In der Smitten, 1973, pp. 124–30) has argued that Ezra's law book was a form of the deuteronomic law, but this is the result of his limiting what can be known of the historical Ezra to the edict of Artaxerxes in Ezra 7:12–26. On similar grounds, Rendtorff (1983, p. 71 = ET 1985, p. 68, and 1984) has denied any connexion between Ezra's law (Aramaic *dāt*) and the torah, the law of the Lord; again, however, this is an historical conclusion relating to Ezra's mission, and Rendtorff does not extend it to the books of Ezra and Nehemiah as a whole.

Quite different, however, is the radical proposal of Houtman (1981). After surveying the prescriptions in Ezra and Nehemiah which purport to come from the book of the law, he concludes that this cannot have been the Pentateuch but must rather have been some quite separate law book which has not been transmitted to us. He cites the recently published Temple Scroll as an analogy. Clearly, if Houtman is right we cannot learn anything from these books about the inner-biblical use of Old Testament law.

General considerations lead to the conclusion that Houtman's hypothesis is improbable. Being in the form of a first-person address by God (and so never called 'the law of Moses' or equivalents), the Temple Scroll cannot be cited as evidence for the view that 'there were circles of men who held themselves entitled to promulgate existing laws anew in the name of Moses' (p. 110). In any case, we are not dealing in Ezra and Nehemiah with a breakaway group, like the people of Qumran, nor is there any evidence that the latter had doubts about the supreme authority of the Pentateuch, despite the existence of the Temple Scroll. It is thus very difficult to believe that a document which was, *ex hypothesi*, a major formative influence in the development of post-exilic Judaism should have been lost without trace whilst the Pentateuch, unmentioned in these books on Houtman's view, should have risen silently to its position of supreme authority.

That Houtman has been able to formulate such a theory at all, however, alerts us to the fact that the citation and application of pentateuchal laws were already displaying a sophisticated hermeneutic at that time. Awareness of this should help explain the difficulties which Houtman has exposed. Two recent studies in particular call for attention.

First, in a brief but illuminating article on Nehemiah 10, Clines (1981, and cf. 1984, *ad loc*.) has argued that although all the particular stipulations listed in vv. 31–40 include novel material, they nevertheless are 'the result of exegetical work upon previously existing laws' as known to us from the Pentateuch. The basic exegetical principles at work are much as we should expect: being authoritative and considered to be comprehensive, the law can be harmonised to supply clear directives. This may require supplementary laws or reinterpretation along the lines of the law's intention rather than explicit requirement. Five types of legal development are then observed to follow from this basis, namely (i) creation of facilitating law, enabling earlier regulations to be carried out; (ii) revision of facilitating law; (iii) 'creation of a new prescription from a precedent in Pentateuchal law'; (iv) 're-definition of categories, always in the direction of greater comprehensiveness'; and (v) the integration of separate legal prescriptions. To give but one simple example of the first category, Lev. 6:5–6 prescribes that the fire on the altar of sacrifice must be kept burning continually. In the wording of Neh. 10:35, it is clearly to this that the phrase 'as it is written in the law' refers. In earlier times it had been the responsibility of the Gibeonites to provide the necessary wood (cf. Josh. 9:27), but that no longer obtained after the exile. Consequently, there was now a need to establish a 'wood offering' on a rota basis in order to facilitate obedience to the pentateuchal law. As with the other stipulations in this passage, it was a perfectly intelligible first step towards what later became known as *sĕyāg lattôrâ*, 'a hedge for the torah'.

If Clines's essay is brief and programmatic, the other recent study in this field – that of Fishbane (1985) – is lengthy and detailed. Indeed, Fishbane makes so bold as to conclude his book with the claim that it is 'the first comprehensive proof and analysis' of inner-biblical (i.e. Old Testament) exegesis. Of particular relevance for our immediate concerns are his chapters on legal exegesis in historical sources (pp. 107–62) in which he divides his analysis into two parts. In the first, he examines examples of what he calls 'legal exegesis with verbatim, paraphrastic, or pseudo-citations' (principally 2 Chronicles 35; Ezra 9; Neh. 8; 10:30–1; 13; Jer. 17:19–27 and Ezekiel 44) and in the second 'legal exegesis with covert citations' (principally Josh. 5:10–12; 1 Kgs 6:7; 2 Chron. 7:8–19; 30).

Not surprisingly, Fishbane is able to demonstrate a wide variety of exegetical techniques not far from the surface of these texts. Most of his examples have been observed piecemeal by previous commentators, and many of the principles which he sees to have been at work are those which Clines has also catalogued. Thus, to give a simple and well-known example of Clines's fifth category – the integration of separate legal prescriptions – Fishbane rightly defends the widely-held view that 2 Chron. 35:13, 'they boiled the Passover in fire, according to the ordinance (*kammišpāṭ*)', can only be

27

understood as an attempt to harmonise the apparently contradictory stipulations in Deut. 16:7 and Exod. 12:8–9. Thus much of the value of Fishbane's work lies in the collecting, ordering and re-evaluating of this wealth of material, even if a number of obvious examples, such as some other clauses of the pledge in Nehemiah 10, receive no mention.

Interaction with Fishbane's work will not, therefore, be at the level of major disagreement in principle, but rather of detail and the specific interpretation of particular passages. So here we may take just one area of relevance to our present concern which perhaps deserves further examination. In several of the passages with which Fishbane deals there is the comment that something was done *kakkātûb*, 'as prescribed' (or equivalents). Fishbane seems to take this as a rather broad qualification of the preceding context, and since there is often mention of practices for which there is no direct pentateuchal warrant, he finds here evidence for the process by which exegetical conclusions became an authoritative part of the law itself. Houtman too based his argument on some of the same passages, but drew the more radical conclusion which we have already noted. Thus, as well as modifying Fishbane's position, our discussion should also help to cast further doubt on Houtman's hypothesis.

Examination of all the passages where this word and its equivalents occurs points to a different explanation. It may be suggested that *kakkātûb* is used to qualify only the word or phrase which immediately precedes it,[1] and that such a word or phrase is thus *distinguished* from its prevailing context. By stating that some specific act was in accordance with *tôrâ*, the writers acknowledge that other matters may not have been.

We have already argued above that this is so at Neh. 10:35 – 'as it is written in the law' qualifies only the continually burning fire on the altar, not the (non-pentateuchal) wood offering. Similarly two verses later, 'as it is written in the law' relates 'the firstborn of our sons and of our cattle' to the law of Num. 18:15 (note the unusual use of *bĕhēmâ* in both cases) in contrast to the (non-pentateuchal) 'first-fruits of every kind of fruit tree' in the previous clause (cf. Williamson, 1985, p. 337 for fuller detail). In 2 Chron. 23:18 'as it is written in the law of Moses' obviously qualifies only 'to offer the burnt offerings of the Lord' immediately before, since the disposition of the Levites earlier in the verse is explicitly attributed to David. At 2 Chron. 35:26 no one can suppose that 'the rest of the acts of Josiah' were all 'according to that which is written in the law of the Lord'; rather, that phrase qualifies only the word *hăsādâw* which immediately precedes it, explaining in what sense Josiah's deeds were good or pious.

Space precludes a full survey of every relevant passage; we must therefore be content, now that some clear examples have established the principle, to look briefly at those passages which directly affect Fishbane's interpretation before concluding this section with a more detailed analysis of Nehemiah 8. At

2 Chron. 35:12, Fishbane appears to suppose that 'as it is written in the book of Moses' refers to the whole passage in which the paschal slaughter, originally a lay performance, is now the duty of the Levites. In our view, however, it qualifies only *lĕhaqrîb lyhwh*, which even in the present context can be regarded as conforming to pentateuchal law (cf. Rudolph, 1955, p. 327). The situation is similar in v. 6 of the same chapter, where 'to do according to the word of the Lord by the hand of Moses' again does not relate to the Levites killing the passover lambs, but to their 'preparing for their brethren' with reference forward to v. 13 (cf. Williamson, 1982, p. 406). Finally, in 2 Chron. 30:5, 'as it is written' should be taken closely with the observation that the Passover had not been celebrated before 'in great numbers'. When we ask why, we are directed to v. 3, where a similar concern is expressed in relation to the people's coming to Jerusalem. Here, then, there is a specific allusion to Deut. 16:1–8 as the written text to which reference is made.[2]

It should be emphasised that in these and comparable texts which could be cited we are not for one moment denying that in the passages as a whole there is much of the type of exegesis which Fishbane patiently unravels. Our concern rather is to emphasise that in this exercise the writers were perhaps more aware of the distinction between text and interpretation than Fishbane gives them credit for. In other words, so far as the law is concerned it is by no means inappropriate to talk in terms of 'the use of Scripture' for this later post-exilic period.

An instructive example to which we may now give a little more detailed attention is found in Nehemiah 8. The first half of the chapter, vv. 1–12, recounts the reading and explanation of the law in a general way to the people. Then we are told:

On the second day the heads of families of all the people, together with the priests and the Levites, gathered around Ezra the scribe in order to study the words of the law which the Lord had commanded through Moses, that the Israelites should live in booths during the feast of the seventh month, and that they should proclaim the following words and spread them throughout their cities and Jerusalem: 'Go out into the hill country and bring branches of olive and of oleaster, of myrtle, palm and leafy trees in order to make booths as it is written.'
(Neh. 8:13–15, author's translation)

The difficulty which this passage poses is that it includes material which does not appear to have pentateuchal warrant. However, this is less than is generally supposed (e.g. by Houtman) and the remainder may be deduced from the law by the kind of techniques which Clines and Fishbane have described. Nevertheless, in the present case it is simpler than Fishbane perhaps realises, and thus we do not accept that this passage justifies some of the more elaborate conclusions which he draws from it.

The first point to notice is that the primary text under consideration is Lev. 23:39–43, because of all the passages in the Pentateuch which deal with the feast of Tabernacles this is the only one to stipulate that the Israelites should dwell in booths during its celebration (cf. v. 42). The significance of this for the occasion under discussion is apparent not only from the verses cited above ('They found written in the law...that [ʾăšer] the Israelites should live in booths...'), but also from the continuation in vv. 16–17 which relates how the people made their booths and lived in them during the festival, 'something', we are told, 'that the Israelites had not done from the time of Jeshua the son of Nun until that day' (v. 17). Indeed, so great is the concentration on this new aspect of the celebration that we learn very little about what else happened, warning against the dangers of an argument from silence in this regard. We may conclude from this first point that *kakkātûb* at the end of v. 15 probably qualifies only the clause which immediately precedes it, namely 'to make booths'.[3] This would fit well with our study of the use of this word earlier as well as with the emphasis of the present passage in particular. It also alerts us to the possibility that the writer may be aware that some of the other material in the context is not directly cited from the law.

Second, however, our passage states that more than just the dwelling in booths was 'found written in the law'. An additional indirect clause, also introduced by ʾăšer, speaks of a proclamation to be made. Commentators have usually passed this over in silence or used it as evidence for differences between Ezra's law book and the Pentateuch. The suggestion may rather be advanced, however, that it derives from the introduction to the whole calendar in Leviticus 23, which states, 'These are the set feasts of the Lord...which you shall *proclaim* in their appointed season' (v. 4; see also v. 37). Admittedly, Lev. 23:4 uses a different verb (*qrʾ*) from Neh. 8:15 (hiph. of *šmʿ*), but that is not an insuperable difficulty. Naturally, the question will have been raised as to what precisely the proclamation should include, and it is at *this* point, we submit, that 'exegesis' played its part, and that in two ways: (i) concentrating on the discovery of the importance of living in booths during the festival, the leaders told the people to bring materials suitable for the purpose – another example of 'facilitating law' (Clines's first category). Some of the types of tree listed coincide, not unnaturally, with the types that were to be brought in any case for *other aspects* of the festivities (cf. Lev. 23:40), but the remainder are types more generally available. However, the legal prescription of Lev. 23:40 for one aspect of the festival is not to be confused with this facilitating law, as the lack of reference to the bringing of fruit further demonstrates. As a harvest celebration, Tabernacles had been observed regularly before (cf. Ezra 3:4, to go no further); the present description dwells exclusively on the new (or renewed) aspects of the celebration. There is thus no need to follow Fishbane in his less plausible suggestion that it was by way of etymological speculation on the root *skk* that they arrived at the idea of bringing branches. (ii) Though not explicitly stated in so many words, it is clearly implied that the proclamation summoned the people of Judah to Jerusalem for the festival. Though denied by Fishbane, this is the probable implication of v. 16: the residents of Jerusalem built their booths on their roofs or in the courts of their houses, whilst those who came in from the surrounding districts did so in the temple courts or other open spaces in the city. Furthermore, the implication of v. 18 is that the festival was celebrated by all the people together. In that case, we may see the influence of Deut. 16:13–15 on the framing of the proclamation – an example of Clines's fifth category, the integration of separate legal prescriptions.

We may conclude, therefore, from this and other examples that could be mentioned[4] that on close examination the post-exilic historians appear to have been remarkably self-conscious in their use of legal Scripture and that they drew a sharper distinction than has generally been recognised between text and exegesis. They were well aware of the difficulties of applying the written law in situations for which it had not been originally intended, and they quickly developed a wide range of exegetical tools to help them in their task. It seems clear, however, that they took pains to distinguish between the letter and the spirit of the law, and generally left clear lexical markers to prevent confusion in this regard. What we must now turn to investigate is the use they made of narrative rather than legal material.

## 2  NARRATIVE

Although narrative material from earlier biblical sources is used by citation or allusion in a variety of later works (cf. Nehemiah 9, for example, and the typological use of the exodus in various parts of Ezra), it is inevitable that our attention in this section should be directed primarily towards the Chronicler's use of Samuel and Kings. After a period of relative neglect, the books of Chronicles have been the subject of renewed interest during the last fifteen or twenty years, and much of this activity focuses precisely on the topic in hand.

A preliminary point that has to be made concerns the form of the text of Samuel and Kings which the Chronicler used. Despite warning signs to the contrary from the LXX, it was assumed until comparatively recent times that the MT of the respective works could be compared without difficulty. The discovery of the Qumran scrolls – and especially the still unpublished 4QSam[a] – has shown, however, that this is by no means always justified. In a string of publications, Cross and his pupils who have had access to this material have demonstrated that not infrequently the Chronicler followed a text of Samuel which was markedly closer to his own than the MT (cf. Cross, 1964; Lemke, 1965; Ulrich, 1978. McCarter, 1980 and 1984, provides further valuable information). Great caution must therefore be exercised when undertaking detailed comparative study not to confuse theological or tendentious issues with purely textual matters.

Despite this warning, there are several mitigating factors which enable us to proceed, albeit with caution. First, in what is probably the most valuable part of his controversial thesis, McKenzie (1985, pp. 119–58) has shown that the situation in Kings differs from that in Samuel in this regard. Where the Chronicler is following Kings, it appears that his text was after all closer to MT. Secondly, as work on the LXX of Samuel and of Chronicles develops, so comparative work may be put on a sounder footing even in the absence of corroborative Hebrew sources such as 4QSam[a]. Finally, as we shall see, there is a great deal that can usefully be said which is based upon far broader considerations than intricate synoptic comparisons alone.

There is one recent work whose thesis, if correct, would render further discussions more or less otiose, and that is the study already referred to by McKenzie (1985). Briefly stated, McKenzie works on the basis of material found only in Chronicles to isolate a few well-known characteristics which represent the writer's *Tendenz*. Looking then at the passages where Chronicles runs parallel with Samuel and Kings, he allows differences which can be explained by this *Tendenz* to be due to the Chronicler himself. Otherwise, however, he argues that the Chronicler followed his *Vorlage* quite slavishly; the exegetical techniques which others have claimed to find do not come into the picture at all. On this basis, he then advances his view that the Chronicler used Cross's $Dtr_1$ as his source and that Chronicles is therefore of some value in disentangling $Dtr_2$ from $Dtr_1$.

McKenzie's work raises a host of questions which cannot be discussed here (cf. my review, 1987). It must suffice to say for the moment that he has not, in my opinion, done justice to the many ways – some delicate and some quite radical – in which the Chronicler handled his *Vorlage*. In referring to some of these below we shall already be indicating areas where his initial analysis needs far greater refinement before his overall theory can be taken more seriously.

A number of studies, both old and new, which have broached the subject of the Chronicler's use of Scripture have tried to subsume all the evidence under a single rubric as though this contained the clue to the Chronicler's 'purpose' as a whole. Of these, by far the most impressive is that of Willi (1972), who seeks to explain all the material as 'exegesis'. With a prodigious compilation of detail, he marshalls the differences between Samuel–Kings and Chronicles into nine categories which move from such minor matters as textual, orthographic and grammatical differences through more important minor omissions and additions to significant interpretative devices including recension and the use of typology. Whilst inevitably scholars will differ on this or that detail, no one can work through Willi's comparative study without learning a very great deal about the methods which the Chronicler used in his composition.

Despite this positive evaluation, it remains questionable whether Willi's theory is adequate to account for the books of Chronicles as a whole. We must agree that no appraisal of Chronicles which does not take the synoptic passages fully into account can be considered adequate and further that the general shape and order of the Chronicler's work is largely dependent upon the earlier composition. Nevertheless, these passages alone are not sufficient to explain the whole: the Chronicler's selective use of Samuel–Kings shows that he regarded them as a source rather than as a text; there are occasions such as 1 Chronicles 14 and 2 Chronicles 1 where he alters the order of his *Vorlage* for purposes of his own; the considerable amount of additional material which he includes (even if it is reduced by following Noth's 1987 (German original, 1943) literary-critical surgery) cannot be explained on this basis either; and finally the Chronicler used techniques which go far beyond the exegetical, particularly the paradigmatic patterning of his material in terms of 'exilic' and 'restoration' situations (cf. Mosis, 1973; Ackroyd, 1973 and 1977).

In my view, it is therefore preferable not to seize on any one aspect of the Chronicler's use of earlier scriptural material as the key to his method and purpose. Rather, his aim in writing should be sought elsewhere, leaving us free to observe the very considerable range of techniques which he presses into service as he makes use of antecedent material. As well as all those discussed by Willi, they also include adumbrations of much that was later to be developed in the midrashim and targumim (cf. Seeligmann, 1953; Bloch, 1957; Fishbane, 1985, pp. 380–440).

Sketchy as this survey has been, it should be clear by now that the Chronicler's treatment of his narrative *Vorlage* differs to a certain extent from what we saw earlier with regard to the law. There, the few examples which we drew from his work (2 Chronicles 30 and 35) show no appreciable difference in approach from that of Ezra and Nehemiah, where the distinction between text and interpretation seems already quite advanced. It is true that if style is a valid criterion, then the Chronicler exercised greater freedom with respect to his extra-biblical sources than he did with Samuel–Kings. This may indicate that the latter was in some way more 'authoritative' in his estimation, if only because it was undoubtedly the familiar version of his people's history. He was thus in no position to deal with it so freely. Equally it must be remembered, however, that this material had already been subjected to a deuteronomic redaction and was thus *ipso facto* more amenable to the Chronicler's own outlook. Even so, he frequently finds it necessary to draw out the compatibility of the narrative with the pentateuchal law (cf. von Rad, 1930) whilst his use of typology and paradigm seeks to draw from the historically bound narratives of the Deuteronomic History a number of timeless theological values and lessons which he has learned from elsewhere, namely the prophets. Thus in terms of religious authority, the law and the prophets ranked higher for the Chronicler than the narrative history. The latter illustrated and explained the former and could be retold to drive home the lessons which they taught. The lessons themselves, however, derived from these other sources. It is thus appropriate that we should turn in conclusion to the use of the prophetic books in his work.

## 3 THE PROPHETS

The Chronicler's treatment of prophecy and the prophets has been the subject of several recent studies (Westermann, 1960 = ET 1967, pp. 163–8; Petersen, 1977; Seeligmann, 1978; Japhet, 1977, pp. 154ff; Micheel, 1983). Our concern here, however, is with just one aspect of this subject, namely the citation of prophetic 'texts' in the so-called Levitical sermons.

It was von Rad (1966; German original, 1934) who first dealt with this material from a form-critical perspective. He noted that at a number of places in his narrative the Chronicler included a 'sermon' on the lips of a prophet, Levite or king, and that it generally included the following elements: 'the conditions on which God is prepared to give his help – i.e. the doctrine'; application of that principle to some aspect of Israel's history; and an exhortation to faith on the part of the hearer. This influential classification has been accepted by many, and in some cases further refined (e.g. Newsome, 1975). More recently, however, there have been signs of a growing dissatisfaction with aspects of von Rad's theory (e.g. Braun, 1979, p. 54 n. 11; Throntveit, 1982, p. 163), and Mathias (1984) has now published a full-scale attempt at a rebuttal. Whilst many of the points Mathias raises are apposite, they do not empty von Rad's work of all significance. Thus, we may agree that the title 'Levitical' is too specific, that no sure *Sitz im Leben* for this genre can be established, and that the material which we now have probably derives from the Chronicler himself rather than being, as von Rad thought, independent summaries clumsily worked into his narrative by the Chronicler. Despite all this, however, these passages have characteristics in common which are suggestive of sermonic style, even if in imitation. Though they should not be forced into a rigid form-critical mould, Mason (1984) has described the features which they have in common (appeal to an agreed authority; proclamation of some theological teaching about God; and call for response) as well as the literary devices which they regularly use (rhetorical questions; play on words; and illustrations from past history).

Even on Mason's more flexible analysis, it is clear that the use of citations from the prophets remains a fundamental feature. This marks a significant divergence from the speeches in the Deuteronomic History. A probable explanation is that the deuteronomists, who were also responsible for much editorial work on the pre-exilic prophetic corpus, incorporated the insights of the prophets directly into their work. In his much later situation, however, the Chronicler was conscious of standing in a quite different relationship to the writings of the prophets: he derived his theology of history from them at second hand and he could appeal to them as an authority shared both by himself and by his readers. To some extent, therefore, the debate about whether he regarded them as already 'canonical' is beside the point. The use he makes of them in his work shows that within his community they had already been accepted as authoritative religious texts. The Chronicler understood the prophets to be teaching such central doctrines as God's righteousness (Zeph. 3:5 at 2 Chron. 19:7), his universality and omniscience (Zech. 4:10 at 2 Chron. 16:9), the importance of repentance (Jeremiah and Zech. 1:2–6 at 2 Chron. 29:5–11 and 30:6–9), the need for faith (Isa. 7:9 at 2 Chron. 20:20), and the fact of divine response to human initiative (Jer. 29:13–14 at 2 Chron. 15:2). Though this list by no means exhausts the Chronicler's use of the prophets, it shows the extent to which they gave shape to the characteristic parameters of his thought. Indeed, it may not be too much to say that they provided him with the theological context within which to read – and hence retell – his people's history. Since they are never marked out by the formula *kakkātûb*, the writings of the prophets were not to be put on a level with the law so far as religious practice was concerned; but as a resource for broader theological awareness, it appears that the prophets had already attained pre-eminence.

## NOTES

1 An apparent exception to this rule might be claimed for Bar. 2:2, especially if Tov's translation (1975, p. 19) is followed, for there *kakkātûb* refers forward to the following clause. Bar. 2:2, however, is clearly related to Dan. 9:12–13, where the relevant words (also referring forward) are *ka'ăšer kātûb bĕtôrat mōšeh*, and it would have been better if Tov had followed this lead. (The LXX renders *kakkātûb* in a variety of ways, so that there is no reason to prefer this form to that of Dan. 9:13.) Although there is no other OT parallel for the use of this construction in relation to the pentateuchal law, it does not seem impossible that the differences in phraseology and in usage are related.
2 The strongest case for an exception to this consistent pattern is Ezra 6:18 (Aramaic), to which Fishbane makes no reference. Here, it looks as though the system of priestly and Levitical courses and divisions is being ascribed to 'the book of Moses'. If so, we should note (i) that this is not a widely-held position, because elsewhere these arrangements are carefully ascribed to David (e.g. 1 Chron. 23–4); (ii) that the reference to 'Jerusalem' makes clear that this cannot be intended as a direct citation from the

Pentateuch; (iii) that the author of this verse is likely to have worked long after Ezra, Nehemiah and the Chronicler (cf. Williamson, 1983). By this time Houtman's suggested explanation by way of a book quite separate from the Pentateuch is even less plausible; and (iv) that his position is a further development of that already taken by a later reviser of the Chronicler's work in 1 Chron. 24:1–2. An alternative explanation should not be ruled out, however, namely that the phrase qualifies only 'the service of God'.

3 Strictly speaking, Lev. 23:42 speaks only of 'dwelling' in booths, so that we must allow that there is a minimum of obvious interpretation involved in the use of *laᶜăśōt*.

4 Perhaps the most involved passage from the point of view of legal exegesis is Ezra 9:1–2, treated independently by Williamson (1985, *ad loc.*) and Fishbane (1985, pp. 114–23). Together with some shared conclusions we also both include some material not considered by the other, pointing to the complexity of the exegetical process.

## BIBLIOGRAPHY

P. R. Ackroyd *I & II Chronicles, Ezra, Nehemiah* (London, 1973).

'The Chronicler as Exegete', *JSOT* 2 (1977), 2–32.

R. Bloch 'Midrash', *DBSup* 5 (Paris, 1957), cols. 1263–81.

R. L. Braun 'Chronicles, Ezra, and Nehemiah: Theology and Literary History', SVT 30 (1979), 52–64.

A.-M. Brunet 'Le Chroniste et ses sources', *RB* 60 (1953), 481–508, and 61 (1954), 349–86.

D. J. A. Clines 'Nehemiah 10 as an Example of Early Jewish Biblical Exegesis', *JSOT* 21 (1981), 111–17.

*Ezra, Nehemiah, Esther* (London and Grand Rapids, 1984).

F. M. Cross 'The History of the Biblical Text in the Light of Discoveries in the Judean Desert', *HTR* 57 (1964), 281–9.

M. Fishbane *Biblical Interpretation in Ancient Israel* (Oxford, 1985).

C. Houtman 'Ezra and the Law', *OTS* 21 (1981), 91–115.

W. Th. In der Smitten *Esra: Quellen, Überlieferung und Geschichte*, Studia Semitica Neerlandica 15 (Assen, 1973).

S. Japhet *The Ideology of the Book of Chronicles and its Place in Biblical Thought* (Jerusalem, 1977).

D. Kellermann 'Erwägungen zum Esragesetz', *ZAW* 80 (1968), 373–85.

R. W. Klein 'Ezra and Nehemiah in Recent Studies', in F. M. Cross, W. E. Lemke and P. D. Miller (eds.), *The Mighty Acts of God: In Memoriam G. Ernest Wright* (Garden City, 1976), pp. 361–76.

W. E. Lemke 'The Synoptic Problem in the Chronicler's History', *HTR* 58 (1965), 349–63.

P. K. McCarter *I Samuel*, AB 8 (Garden City, 1980).

*II Samuel*, AB 9 (Garden City, 1984).

D. J. McCarthy 'Covenant and Law in Chronicles-Nehemiah', *CBQ* 44 (1982), 25–44.

# History

S. L. McKenzie *The Chronicler's Use of the Deuteronomistic History*, HSM 33 (Atlanta, 1985).

R. Mason 'Some Echoes of the Preaching in the Second Temple? Tradition Elements in Zechariah 1–8', *ZAW* 96 (1984), 221–35.

D. Mathias '"Levitische Predigt" und Deuteronomismus', *ZAW* 94 (1984), 23–49.

R. Micheel *Die Seher- und Prophetenüberlieferungen in der Chronik*, BET 18 (Frankfurt am Main, 1983).

R. Mosis *Untersuchungen zur Theologie des chronistischen Geschichtswerkes*, Freiburger theologische Studien 92 (Freiburg, 1973).

S. Mowinckel *Studien zu dem Buche Ezra-Nehemia III: Die Ezrageschichte und das Gesetz Moses* (Oslo, 1965).

J. D. Newsome 'Toward a New Understanding of the Chronicler and his Purposes', *JBL* 94 (1975), 201–17.

M. Noth *The Chronicler's History*, JSOTSS 50 (Sheffield, 1987) (English translation of *Überlieferungsgeschichtliche Studien* (Halle, 1943), pp. 110–217).

D. L. Petersen *Late Israelite Prophecy: Studies in Deutero-Prophetic Literature and in Chronicles*, SBLMS 23 (Missoula, 1977).

G. von Rad *Das Geschichtsbild des chronistischen Werkes*, BWANT 54 (Stuttgart, 1930).

'The Levitical Sermon in I and II Chronicles', in *The Problem of the Hexateuch and Other Essays* (Edinburgh and London, 1966), pp. 267–80 (English translation of 'Die levitische Predigt in den Büchern der Chronik', in *Festschrift Otto Procksch* (Leipzig, 1934), pp. 113–24 = *Gesammelte Studien zum alten Testament* (Munich, 1958), pp. 248–61).

R. Rendtorff *The Old Testament: an Introduction* (London, 1985) (English translation of *Das Alte Testament: eine Einführung* (Neukirchen, 1983)).

'Esra und das "Gesetz"', *ZAW* 96 (1984), 165–84.

W. Rudolph *Chronikbücher*, HAT 21 (Tübingen, 1955).

I. L. Seeligmann 'Voraussetzungen der Midraschexegese', SVT 1 (1953), 150–81.

M. A. Throntveit *The Significance of the Royal Speeches and Prayers for the Structure and Theology of the Chronicler* (unpublished dissertation, Union Theological Seminary, Richmond, 1982).

E. Tov *The Book of Baruch*, SBL Texts and Translations 8; Pseudepigrapha Series 6 (Missoula, 1975).

E. Ulrich *The Qumran Text of Samuel and Josephus*, HSM 19 (Missoula, 1978).

C. Westermann *Basic Forms of Prophetic Speech* (Philadelphia, 1967) (English translation of *Grundformen prophetischer Rede*, BEvTh 31 (Munich, 1960)).

T. Willi *Die Chronik als Auslegung. Untersuchungen zur literarischen Gestaltung der historischen Überlieferung Israels*, FRLANT 106 (Göttingen, 1972).

H. G. M. Williamson *1 and 2 Chronicles* (London and Grand Rapids, 1982).
'The Composition of Ezra i–vi', *JTS* n.s. 34 (1983), 1–30.
*Ezra, Nehemiah*, Word Biblical Commentary 16 (Waco, 1985)
Review of McKenzie (1985) in *VT* 37 (1987), 107–14.

# 3 · Prophecy

JOHN DAY

THE Old Testament prophets (i.e. the latter prophets) are rich in inner-biblical interpretation. Sometimes they allude to actual biblical texts but in other cases they take up themes from the tradition which was later to become embedded in the biblical text. In considering this large topic I shall discuss first the prophets and the law, then go on to a consideration of the creation and other primeval traditions, historical and legendary traditions, the prophets and the Psalms, and prophets quoting earlier prophets, and finally I shall deal with the subject of *relectures*.

## I  THE PROPHETS AND THE LAW

Traditionally the law was understood as something which preceded the prophets and which was presupposed in the prophetic proclamation. With the rise of critical scholarship in the nineteenth century, as exemplified in the work of Wellhausen, the order was reversed so that the written law came to be seen as a development subsequent to the work of the pre-exilic prophets. Accordingly, the originality of the prophets became emphasised. In the present century, however, there has been a general acceptance that, though the final form of the Priestly legislation is relatively late, the tradition of law in ancient Israel antedates the prophets. Although the prophets were not constantly quoting the letter of the law, it does appear that they were indebted to the tradition of law. Hosea, for example, could declare, 'Were I to write for him my laws by ten thousands, they would be regarded as a strange thing' (Hos. 8:12).

As for the decalogue, there are only two passages in the prophets which appear to contain a direct echo of it. The first is in Hos. 4:2, where the prophet declares, 'there is swearing, lying, killing, stealing, and committing adultery', which seems to echo the third, ninth, sixth, eighth and seventh commandments respectively. (Cf. too Hos. 12:10 [ET 9] and 13:4.) Those, however, who date the decalogue later than Hosea will naturally not see an allusion to it here. The second apparent allusion to the decalogue is in Jer. 7:9, where we read, 'Will you steal, murder, commit adultery, swear falsely, burn incense to Baal, and go after other gods you have not known...?' We find here echoes of the eighth, sixth, seventh and either the third or ninth commandments, in addition to words which presuppose the first commandment. This verse is part of a chapter which has undergone deuteronomic redaction, but it is still possible, as Nicholson believes (1970, p. 69), that authentic words of Jeremiah underlie it.

Condemnation of social injustice and inhumanity is particularly prominent in the preaching of Amos, Isaiah and Micah. It is likely that the laws of social righteousness in the Book of the Covenant lie, at least in part, behind their preaching. This is particularly clear in the case of Amos, who condemned the practice of taking a man's garment in pledge (Amos 2:8), which is the subject of a specific law in Exod. 22:25-7. It is to be noted that this law is in casuistic form, thus refuting the claim of Bach (1957) that Amos only appealed to apodictic law. Bach was able to maintain his position only by supposing that Amos was dependent on apodictically formed laws in Deuteronomy – manifestly later than Amos – rather than on casuistic formulations in the Book of the Covenant (cf. Exod. 22:25-7 and Deut. 24:17). Bergren's claim (1974) that, not only Amos, but the prophets as a whole, appealed to apodictic rather than casuistic law, is also dubious.

The influence of the book of Deuteronomy is, of course, most marked in the book of Jeremiah, a work which has clearly undergone deuteronomic redaction in its prose sermons and probably in its prose narratives. This seems unlikely to have occurred if the prophet himself was known to be anti-deuteronomic. Whatever the famous crux in Jer. 8:8f is saying, it is therefore probably not to be construed as an attack on the book of Deuteronomy *per se*. Moreover, it is interesting that Jer. 3:1 appeals to the deuteronomic law on divorce, which is taken up to illustrate Yahweh's relationship with Israel. Since this is a poetic piece it may well be an authentic word of Jeremiah.

Other prophets who appear to allude to Deuteronomy are Trito-Isaiah and Malachi. In Isa. 56:3-8 we find the view opposed that eunuchs and foreigners have no role in temple worship, which may be contrasted with Deut. 23:2ff (ET 1ff), where eunuchs and certain foreigners are specifically singled out for exclusion from the sanctuary. Mal. 4:4 (ET 3:22) declares, 'Remember the law of my servant Moses, the statutes and ordinances that I commanded him at Horeb for all Israel'. It seems that he had the law of Deuteronomy particularly in mind. Not only are the terms 'law, statutes and ordinances' and 'Horeb' characteristically deuteronomic, but we find in Mal. 1:8 a condemnation of the offering of blemished animals to the Lord couched in terms reminiscent of Deut. 15:21 rather than the Priestly legislation of Lev. 22:22. Also, Mal. 3:5 commends justice to the widow, orphan and sojourner (cf. Deut. 14:29; 16:11; 24:17, etc.), and there are a number of other deuteronomic features.

For a prophet showing clear contacts with the Priestly tradition we need to turn to Ezekiel. In particular there are many parallels with the Holiness Code

(Lev. 17–26). Although the Holiness Code in its final form is surely later than Ezekiel, knowing as it does the Aaronite priesthood and the high priesthood (unlike Ezekiel), it is probable that, as a priest, Ezekiel drew on the priestly tradition which was to be embodied in the Holiness Code.

## 2 CREATION AND OTHER PRIMEVAL TRADITIONS

There are, of course, a number of references in the prophets to Yahweh as creator. Only Jeremiah and Deutero-Isaiah, however, show evidence of familiarity with the P tradition which became embodied in Genesis 1. In Jer. 4:23 the prophet describes the reversal of the process of creation, and included are the words 'I looked on the earth, and lo, it was waste and void' (*tōhû wābōhû*), which recalls the description of primeval chaos in Gen. 1:2. According to Fishbane (1985, p. 321) Jeremiah is directly dependent on Genesis 1. However, in view of the widely accepted evidence that P did not attain its final form before the sixth century BC, I incline to see here an allusion to the tradition behind the P account of Genesis 1 rather than to Genesis 1 itself.

Weinfeld (1968) has plausibly argued that Deutero-Isaiah rejected some of the ideas about creation attested in the P account. Thus, whereas Deutero-Isaiah questioned the idea that God needed assistance when creating the world (Isa. 40:13f; cf. 44:24), Gen. 1:26 has God say, 'Let *us* make man', which is usually thought to refer to his addressing the heavenly council. Again, Deutero-Isaiah opposed the notion that Yahweh had a physical image (Isa. 40:18; 46:5), but in Gen. 1:26f we read that God made man in his own image, a term which surely includes a physical likeness, even if this does not exhaust its meaning (cf. Gen. 5:3). Further, Deutero-Isaiah rejected the idea that Yahweh needed rest (Isa. 40:28), which may be contrasted with Gen. 2:2f, where God is stated to have rested on the seventh day after all his labours. Moreover, Deutero-Isaiah declared that Yahweh did not create the world a waste (*tōhû*, Isa. 45:18), which may be contrasted with Gen. 1:2. However, whereas Weinfeld believes that Deutero-Isaiah was polemicising against the creation account in Gen. 1:1–2, 4a, I think that he was opposing certain ideas in the priestly tradition underlying it, since Isa. 40:13f implicitly (cf. v. 12) and Isa. 44:24 explicitly, are rejecting the notion that God needed to consult his divine council when creating the world as a whole, not man in particular (cf. Gen. 1:26). If this understanding is correct, it becomes necessary to reject Whybray's claim (1971) that there is no known tradition in Israel of Yahweh's needing assistance in creation, and his postulation that Deutero-Isaiah was polemicising against Babylonian concepts is rendered questionable (cf. Day, 1985, pp. 54–6).

A variant tradition of the expulsion of the first man from Eden recounted by J in Genesis 2–3 is preserved in Ezekiel 28, where the imagery is applied to the king of Tyre in an oracle proclaiming judgment on him. The points of comparison are as follows: in both we have a human figure who dwells in the garden of Eden, in both he is at first perfect but sin leads to his expulsion from the garden, and in both reference is made either to a cherub (Ezek. 28:14, 16) or cherubim (Gen. 3:24). Scholars dispute whether the king of Tyre is equated with or distinguished from a cherub in Ezekiel 28. On the former view we should read in v. 14 *ʾatt kĕrûb* ('you were a cherub') with MT but on the latter view *ʾet kĕrûb* ('with a cherub') with LXX and Pesh. The parallel in Genesis 3 enables one to decide in favour of the latter alternative, since the cherubim are there clearly set over against the first man, not equated with him. Interestingly Eden is set on a mountain in Ezek. 28:14, 16, which is unattested in Genesis 2–3. It seemes likely that Ezekiel was indebted to a tradition similar to, but not identical with, our J account.

There is no other reference to the first man in the prophets. It is true that the MT of Hos. 6:7 reads 'But like Adam (*kĕʾādām*) they transgressed the covenant', but it is now generally agreed that, with a very slight emendation, we should read 'But *at* Adam (*bĕʾādām*) they transgressed the covenant', since the next line goes on '*there* they dealt faithlessly with me' (Day, 1986, pp. 2ff).

There are, however, other allusions to Eden in the prophets but they are in the nature of passing references (Isa. 51:3; Ezek. 31:9, 16, 18; 26:35; Joel 2:3). In addition, we find paradisiacal imagery employed in the prophets in a typological sense in descriptions of the coming eschaton (Isa. 11:6–8; Ezek. 47:1–12; Zech. 14:8).

There are two passages in the prophets which make explicit mention of Noah, namely Isa. 54:9 and Ezek. 14:14, 20. Ezekiel cites Noah, alongside two other non-Israelites Job and Daniel, as a righteous man who, were he to be alive in the prophet's own time, would save but his own life by his righteousness. Doubtless the prophet was familiar with the story of the flood in which Noah did deliver his life by his righteousness, just as the righteous Job was eventually delivered from his suffering, and some comparable deliverance for the Ugaritic Daniel may be presumed (Day, 1980*a*). In Isa. 54:9 Deutero-Isaiah makes a typological comparison between the exile and Noah's flood and declares that, just as God had promised never to bring such a flood on the earth again, so now he promises never again to bring judgment on the nation. Interestingly, the next verse refers to Yahweh's 'covenant of peace', which suggests that the prophet was familiar with the Noachic covenant of the P tradition (Gen. 9:11) and not simply with J's version (Gen. 8:21), which contains Yahweh's promise without expressing it in covenantal terms. Gunn has attempted to find other implicit Noachic allusions in Deutero-Isaiah (Isa. 44:27; 50:2; 51:10a; 55:13b) but, as I have argued elsewhere, these are unconvincing (Day, 1985, p. 93).

There are, however, two implicit Noachic allusions in the 'Isaiah apocalypse', in Isa. 24:5 and 18. The former verse declares that the inhabitants of the earth 'have...broken the everlasting covenant'. The universal context suggests that it is specifically the covenant with Noah which is in mind here (referred to as 'the everlasting covenant' in Gen. 9:16, cf. v. 12). This conclusion is further borne out by Isa. 24:18, which reads 'for the windows of heaven (lit. on high) are opened' (kî ʾărubbôt mimmārôm niptāḥû), thus echoing the words of the flood story in Gen. 7:11, 'and the windows of heaven were opened' (waʾărubbôt haššāmayim niptāḥû). Since the words of Isa. 24:18 describe the judgment which follows the breaking of the everlasting covenant, it would appear that the writer of Isaiah 24 regarded it as appropriate that the breaking of the Noachic covenant should result in a punishment like that of Noah's flood. This is contrary to the idea found in Genesis 9 and Isa. 54:9f.

## 3  HISTORICAL AND LEGENDARY TRADITIONS

We turn now to the patriarchs. The most extended patriarchal references in the prophets are the verses about Jacob in Hos. 12:3ff, 13 (ET 2ff, 12), where a whole series of parallels with pentateuchal traditions may be found. Hosea does not cite the allusions in the same chronological sequence as in Genesis, but this need not be significant as his purpose was something other than to provide a narrative account. The series of parallels suggests that Hosea knew a tradition similar to, though not identical with, our pentateuchal narratives. Verse 4a (ET 3a), for instance, contains a play on the name of Jacob, 'In the womb he supplanted (ʿāqab) his brother', which recalls the play on words in the birth story in Gen. 25:26 (J), 'Afterward his brother came forth, and his hand had taken hold of Esau's heel (ʿāqēb)'. However, it is clear that in the Hosea passage the meaning of ʿāqab is 'supplant, deceive, cheat' and not 'take by the heel', because the verb is not attested with the latter meaning; consequently the parallel with Gen. 25:26 is not exact. On the other hand, the verb ʿāqab 'supplant, deceive, cheat' is used in connexion with Jacob's taking Esau's birthright and blessing in Gen. 27:36 (J). In Hos. 12:4b–5a (ET 3b–4a) Jacob is said to have striven with God or an angel, and in Gen. 32:22–32 (J) we read of the incident of Jacob's striving with God or a man at Penuel. Hosea's allusion to Jacob's weeping and seeking God's favour in Hos. 12:5a (ET 4a) is unparalleled in our Genesis account, and must reflect some tradition not recorded there. The attempt by Holladay (1966) to see here rather a reference to Jacob's weeping before *Esau* and seeking his favour (cf. Gen. 33:4, 8, 10, 15) does not seem the most natural way of construing the Hebrew text. God's meeting Jacob at Bethel in Hos. 12:5b (ET 4b) presumably refers to the story in Gen. 28:10–22 (J) rather than the later P version in Gen. 35:9–15. The point of the reference in Hos. 12:13 (ET 12) to Jacob's fleeing to Aram and there doing service for a wife (cf. Gen. 28:5 [P]; 29:15–30 [J]) is not entirely clear. The most likely explanation is that it has reference to Israel's subservience to foreign powers, which is contrasted in the following verse Hos. 12:14 (ET 13) with Moses' deliverance of Israel from slavery in Egypt.

There is no universally held view about these verses. There seem no convincing grounds for supposing that the verses should be rearranged (*contra* Ginsberg, 1961) or that a dialogue is taking place between prophet and people (*contra* Vriezen, 1942). The dominant view is that in these verses Jacob is presented in a critical light, Israel's current deceitfulness and striving against God being regarded as of a piece with the behaviour of its ancestor. A number of scholars, however, especially Ackroyd (1963), suppose that Jacob is being presented in a positive light, and that we have here a depiction of God's providential guidance comparable to the famous passage in Deut. 26:5ff about Jacob as 'a wandering Aramean'. Ackroyd claims that we should not suppose that Jacob's deceitfulness was necessarily viewed in a bad light. However, this interpretation does not seem the most natural one. The allusions to Jacob are introduced in v. 3 (ET 2) by the words, 'The Lord...will punish Jacob according to his ways, and requite him according to his deeds.' In the light of this introductory reference to Jacob we expect negative, not positive, things to be said about the patriarch. Verse 4a (ET 3a) surely bears this out, for the allusion to Jacob's cheating his brother must be taken as a negative comment, *contra* Ackroyd, since deceit (*mirmâ*) is specifically singled out for criticism in connexion with Israel in nearby verses, Hos. 12:2 (ET 1) and 12:8 (ET 7). Although it might seem surprising for Israel's national ancestor to be presented in a negative light, it may be noted that this attitude is not unparalleled in the prophets. Jer. 9:3f (ET 4f) seems to be alluding to the Jacob tradition: note especially the word-play in v. 3a (ET 4a), 'Let every one beware of his neighbour, and put no trust in any brother: for every brother is a supplanter (*ʿāqōb yaʿăqōb*)', as well as the reference to *mirmâ* 'deceit' in v. 5 (ET 6; cf. Gen. 27:35). In addition, Isa. 43:27, 'Your first father sinned', is generally agreed to be referring to Jacob (cf. v. 28). The prophetic attitude to Jacob appears therefore to be remarkably negative. We do find a positive reference, however, in Mal. 1:2f, 'Yet I have loved Jacob but I have hated Esau...'. There are also favourable allusions in Ezek. 28:25 and 37:25 (secondary, according to Zimmerli, 1969); cf. too Jer. 33:26 and Mic. 7:20.

Unlike Jacob, the prophetic allusions to Abraham are uniformly positive. He is referred to in Isa. 29:22; 41:8f; 51:2; 62:16 and Ezek. 33:24 (cf. Jer. 33:26 and Mic. 7:20), all of which are exilic or post-exilic. The reference in

Isa. 29:22 to 'the Lord, who redeemed Abraham' is not easy to identify with any particular event, but the other allusions all cohere well with Genesis. Thus, Abraham's call is known in Isa. 41:8f and 51:2, and his coming from a distant country may be referred to in Isa. 41:9. His wife's name Sarah is attested in Isa. 51:2, as is Yahweh's blessing Abraham and granting him many descendants (cf. Jer. 33:26; Mic. 7:20). Similarly, Ezek. 33:24 knows of Abraham's taking the land in possession. In this last verse, however, there is a negative note, not against Abraham himself, but against the false confidence of the people: the prophet implies that, since the people are guilty of manifold sins, they do not have the automatic right to take possession of the land like their ancestor Abraham.

An incident from the Abraham cycle which is frequently alluded to in the prophets (though no patriarchal name is mentioned) is that concerning Sodom and Gomorrah. The prophets clearly knew of them as cities of exemplary wickedness which God overthrew, and they are usually cited as an object lesson for Israel (Isa. 1:9f; 3:9; Jer. 23:14; Ezek. 16:46, 48f, 53, 55f; Amos 4:11; also note Admah and Zeboiim in Hos. 11:8) but also for Babylon (Isa. 13:19; Jer. 50:40), Edom (Jer. 49:18), and Moab and Ammon (Zeph. 2:9). In Genesis (J) the cities are clearly regarded as wicked generally (Gen. 13:13, 18:20) but special attention is drawn to the homosexual rape with which the Sodomites threaten the angels; cf. Gen. 19:5, where the Sodomites say to Lot, 'Bring them out to us, that we may know them'. That 'know' is here being used in its sexual sense is strongly supported by Gen. 19:8, where Lot replies to the Sodomites, 'Behold I have two daughters who have *known* not man...', and these he offers in lieu of the angels. It is therefore surprising that none of the prophetic references indicates awareness of Sodom's propensity to homosexuality. Rather, such indications as we have point in the direction of social injustice (cf. Isa. 1:10ff; Ezek. 16:49f), and, although there are sexual innuendoes in Jer. 23:14 and throughout Ezekiel 16, these are of a heterosexual nature. This should not be used as an argument against the homosexual interpretation of Sodom's sin in Gen. 19:5, as some apologists suppose (e.g. Bailey, 1955, chap. 1). Rather we should suppose that the prophets were familiar with a version of the Sodom story in which homosexuality was not emphasised.

We turn now to the Exodus, which is frequently mentioned in the prophets, but it is not necessary to discuss every occurrence (cf. Isa. 10:24, 26; 63:11; Jer. 7:22, 25; 32:20f; Hos. 12:14 [ET 13]; Amos 2:10; 4:10; 9:7; Mic. 6:4, in addition to passages discussed below.) All the allusions are clearly paralleled in the Pentateuch, with the exception of the reference in Ezekiel to the idolatry practised by the Israelites in Egypt (Ezek. 20:7f). Fishbane (1985, p. 365) is wrong, however, in saying that this reference is 'thoroughly unique', since, as a matter of fact, Israel's idolatry in Egypt is clearly alluded to in Josh. 24:14. There is also possibly a hint of it in Lev. 18:3 (interesting in view of the evident connexion between Ezekiel and the Holiness Code).

In addition to the references to the historic Exodus, the prophets also make allusion to the Exodus in a typological sense, i.e. Exodus imagery is employed to describe the future deliverance. This is the case in Hos. 2:16ff (ET 14ff), Mic. 7:14f, Jer. 16:14f (= 23:7f), and Ezek. 20:33–44. But it is, of course, Deutero-Isaiah who is most renowned for his use of Exodus typology. The importance of the motif for this prophet is underlined by the fact that it occurs both at the beginning (Isa. 40:3–5) and at the very end of his prophecy (Isa. 55:12f), as well as in a considerable number of passages in between (Isa. 41:17–20; 42:14–16; 43:1–3, 14–21; 48:20f; 49:8–12; 51:9f; 52:11–12). For Deutero-Isaiah it seems that the future Exodus from Babylon is going to surpass the Exodus from Egypt (Isa. 43:16–19; cf. Jer. 16:14f = 23:7f). As well as in Isa. 43:16f, the deliverance at the Sea of Reeds is also mentioned in Isa. 51:9f, where it is fused with imagery drawn from Yahweh's conflict with chaos at creation. There is no explicit reference to the Plagues or Passover in Deutero-Isaiah, but in Isa. 52:12 we read, 'For you shall not go out in haste (běhippāzôn)...', the Hebrew expression being found elsewhere in the OT only in connexion with the Exodus, when the Hebrews did leave Egypt in haste (Exod. 12:11; Deut. 16:3). We thus have here an anti-type of the Exodus. Finally we read in Deutero-Isaiah that in the wilderness wanderings water will flow from the rock (Isa. 48:21; cf. 43:19f), which of course recalls the first Exodus (cf. Exod. 17:2–7; Num. 20:8).

Joshua is never mentioned by name in the prophets, but there are two allusions to the dispossession of the Amorites (Amos 2:9; Isa. 17:9, cf. LXX). A few scholars (e.g. Sparks, 1949, p. 135; Tournay, 1965, p. 428) have seen a further reference to the Joshua traditions in Hab. 3:11, where we read that 'The sun and moon stood still in their habitation...', which has been taken to refer to the standing still of the sun and moon during the battle of Gibeon in Josh. 10:12b–13a. This, however, is improbable, for just two verses later, in Hab. 3:13, we read of Yahweh's saving his anointed (i.e. the king) as part of the same course of events. This indicates that the description does not refer to the time of Joshua. There is, admittedly, an interesting verbal similarity between Hab. 3:11 and Josh. 10:12b–13a, suggesting that similar phenomena may be being described here. In Hab. 3:11 the reference seems to be to the blotting out of the sun and moon by the brightness of Yahweh's theophany in the lightning. This may lend support to the view that Josh. 10:12b–13a originally referred to the disappearance of the sun and moon as a result of an early morning storm, which would cohere with the allusion to the hail-storm in Josh. 10:11.

There are a few references in the prophets to events of the periods of the

# Prophecy

Judges and early monarchy (cf. Isa. 9:3 [ET 4]; 10:26; 28:21; Jer. 51:1; Hos. 9:9; 10:9; Amos 6:5; Zech. 12:8), in addition to well-known passages anticipating an ideal future Davidic ruler (cf. Isa. 9:1–6 [ET 2–6]; 11:1–9; Jer. 23:5f; Mic. 5:1–5 [ET 2–6]; Zech. 9:9f), a concept democratised in Isa. 55:3–5, but it is not my intention to discuss these here.

## 4  THE PROPHETS AND THE PSALMS

That the prophets were indebted to the tradition of psalmody in ancient Israel is clear enough. Isaiah, for example, had a theology that was firmly rooted in the Zion Psalms (e.g. Ps. 46 is echoed in Isa. 7:14 and 17:12–14) and Jeremiah's 'Confessions' are clearly modelled on the Individual Lament Psalms. For reasons of space, however, I shall confine myself to Deutero-Isaiah and that genre of hymn known as the Enthronement Psalms (Psalms 47; 93; 95–9), which both have a number of theological themes and linguistic traits in common.

One question that has been discussed is whether Deutero-Isaiah was dependent on the Psalms or whether the Psalms were dependent on Deutero-Isaiah. An earlier generation of scholars believed that the Enthronement Psalms were post-exilic and dependent on Deutero-Isaiah. While there are a few scholars who still follow this view, the majority upholds the priority of the Psalms, or at the very least of the Enthronement Psalm form. In support of this view a number of points may be made. First, Deutero-Isaiah was explicitly monotheistic, whereas the Psalms assume the existence of other gods (Pss. 95:3; 96:4; 97:7). After the ringing declaration of Deutero-Isaiah that no God existed apart from Yahweh, it would be surprising for these Psalms to be dependent on him. Secondly, as Johnson has pointed out (1967, p. 61, n. 1), the theme of Yahweh as *gōʾēl* 'redeemer', which is important in Deutero-Isaiah, is absent from these Psalms, suggesting that they were not dependent on the prophet. Thirdly, Ps. 99:1 refers to the cherubim and Ps. 47:6 (ET 5) appears to presuppose the ark, neither of which existed in the post-exilic temple.

Theological echoes of the Enthronement Psalms may be detected in the declaration 'Your God reigns (or has become king)' (Isa. 52:7; cf. Ps. 47:8 [ET 7], etc.), in the theme of Yahweh's victory over the chaos waters (Isa. 51:9f; cf. Ps. 93:3f), of Yahweh's exaltation over all other gods (Isa. 45:21f; 46:9; cf. Ps. 95:3; 97:9), his creation of the world (Isa. 40:12, 28; cf. Ps. 95:4f), and the appeal to nature to join in the song of praise to Yahweh (Isa. 44:23; 49:13; cf. Ps. 96:11f). There are also many linguistic echoes of the Enthronement Psalms in Deutero-Isaiah, e.g. 'his holy arm' (Isa. 52:10; cf. Ps. 98:1), 'in the sight of the heathen' (Isa. 52:10; cf. Ps. 98:2), 'clap the hands' (Isa. 55:12; cf. Ps. 98:8), 'from of old' (Isa. 44:8; 45:21; 48:3, 5, 7f;

cf. Ps. 93:2), etc. (see Snaith, 1934, pp. 66–9). We also find an actual quotation in Isa. 42:10 from Psalms 96 and 98. Both Pss. 96:1 and 98:1 begin 'O sing to the Lord a new song', and these words are taken up *verbatim* in Isa. 42:10. Moreover, both Pss. 96:11 and 98:7 declare, 'Let the sea roar and all that fills it', and it is widely accepted that Isa. 42:10 should be restored thus, i.e. *yir'am hayyām ûmĕlōʾô*; as it stands MT reads *yôrĕdê hayyām ûmĕlōʾô* 'Those who go down to the sea and all that fills it', which is clearly corrupt and appears contaminated from Ps. 107:23 (cf. Allen, 1971, pp. 146f).

## 5 PROPHETS QUOTING PROPHETS

For the pre-exilic and exilic periods attempts have been made to show that Isaiah was dependent on Amos (Fey, 1963), Jeremiah on Hosea (Gross, 1930 and 1931), Ezekiel on Jeremiah (Miller, 1955), Deutero-Isaiah on Jeremiah (Paul, 1969), and Deutero-Isaiah on Ezekiel (Baltzer, 1971). The strongest case can probably be made for Jeremiah's dependence on Hosea, and Lindars has written a fine article in support of this (1979).

However, it is my intention here to concentrate on the post-exilic period, for it is then that we find a really marked tendency of prophets to cite earlier prophets. The reinterpretation of earlier prophecies clearly became one of the most characteristic features of prophecy in that period, especially in those works sometimes dubbed 'proto-apocalyptic'. For instance, Trito-Isaiah cites Deutero-Isaiah on a number of occasions (e.g. Isa. 58:8b = 52:15b; 62:11 = 40:10; 60:4a = 49:18a), and Zimmerli (1963b) has written a thorough study of this subject.

Zechariah 9–14 shows evidence of dependence on a number of earlier prophets. Earlier studies by Stade (1881) and Delcor (1952) have offered comprehensive surveys of this topic. Deutero-Isaiah has obviously been used, e.g. Zech. 12:1, 'Thus says the Lord, who stretched out the heavens and founded the earth and formed the spirit of man within him', which echoes Isa. 42:5 (cf. 48:13). Also, Zech. 9:12, 'today I declare that I will restore to you double', sounds like a reversal of Isa. 40:2, where Israel is said to have received double punishment for her sins. On the other hand, Lamarche's attempt (1961) to trace the influence of the servant songs on Zechariah 9–14 does not seem convincing, with the exception of the fourth song, which possibly influenced Zech. 12:10–13:1. There are also echoes of other prophets, such as Amos, Jeremiah and Ezekiel. For example, in Zech. 13:5, we read of a coming time when the prophet will say, 'I am no prophet, I am a tiller of the soil', and it is difficult not to find here an echo of Amos 7:14. In the light of this allusion it is tempting to suppose that Amos may also be the source behind Zech. 14:5, where reference is made to the earthquake in the time of Uzziah king of Judah, attested elsewhere in the OT only in Amos

1:1. The influence of Jeremiah and Ezekiel may also be detected on Zechariah 9–14. Mason (1976) believes that Zechariah 9–14 was influenced by Zechariah 1–8, but I do not find the alleged parallels sufficiently striking as to warrant dependence (none of them is verbal).

We turn next to Joel. The presence of quotations from earlier prophetic works is here clearly marked. They are, in fact, one of several pointers to the relatively late date of the prophecy. Unlike a modern author, who would state when he is citing an earlier author, the OT prophets almost never admit explicitly that they are quoting. One exception to this is in the book of Joel, for in Joel 3:5 (ET 2:32) we read, 'for in Mount Zion and in Jerusalem there shall be those who escape, *as the Lord has said...*' When had the Lord said this? The answer is in Obad. 17, where we read, 'But in Mount Zion there shall be those that escape...'. Fishbane (1985, p. 479, n. 54) curiously thinks that Joel is here quoting Isa. 4:2, but this stands much less close in wording to Joel than Obad. 17, which he fails to mention.

In our Bibles Joel stands next to the book of Amos, presumably reflecting the belief that he was a contemporary of Amos. There are, in fact, a couple of clear citations from Amos in Joel, which may have contributed to this understanding. One is taken up from very near the beginning of Amos, Amos 1:2, 'The Lord roars from Zion and utters his voice from Jerusalem', which is cited in Joel 4:16 (ET 3:16), whilst the other is taken from very near the end of Amos, Amos 9:13, 'the mountains shall drip sweet wine', which is quoted in Joel 4:18 (ET 3:18).

In his depiction of the coming Day of the Lord Joel has been influenced by earlier prophecies, e.g. in Joel 1:15, where the words 'for the day of the Lord is near; as destruction from the Almighty it will come!' are a quotation from Isa. 13:6. Words applied to Babylon in Isaiah 13 are now applied to the Jews. This is in keeping with his tendency to reverse earlier prophecies. For example, in place of the famous prophecy of Isa. 2:4 (= Mic. 4:3) about men beating their swords into ploughshares and spears into pruning hooks, we read in Joel 4:10 (ET 3:10), 'Beat your ploughshares into swords, and your pruning hooks into spears'.

There are two striking parallels between Joel and Jonah, namely Joel 2:13 and Jonah 4:2 and Joel 2:14 and Jonah 3:9. In Jonah 4:2 the prophet declares, 'for I knew that thou art a gracious God and merciful, slow to anger, and abounding in steadfast love, and repentest of evil'. Of course, part of this quotation is attested a number of other times in the OT (Exod. 34:6; Neh. 9:17; Ps. 86:15; 103:8; 145:8). However, only in the Joel and Jonah passages do we find this citation with the concluding words about Yahweh repenting of evil. This indicates that there is a clear literary relationship between Joel and Jonah, something which is supported by the fact that there is a further parallel between Jonah 3:9 and Joel 2:14. In Jonah 3:9 the king of Nineveh declares,

'Who knows, God may yet repent...', and similarly in Joel 2:14 the prophet states, 'Who knows whether he will not turn and repent...?' Is Joel dependent on Jonah or is it the other way round? In this instance, unlike other cases I have mentioned, priority seems to lie with Joel. The classic citation about Yahweh's mercy found in Joel 2:13 and Jonah 4:2 is applied to Israel in the former and Nineveh in the latter. In the other allusions to this quotation referred to above, it is characteristically used, as in Joel, of Yahweh's mercy towards Israel. It is the use of this citation in connexion with Yahweh's attitude to the foreign city of Nineveh that is striking, and it is natural to suppose that this is a secondary derivation. It is attractive to suppose that the book of Jonah, with its universalistic message, has taken up this passage about Yahweh's mercy towards Israel from Joel and applied it instead to Nineveh. It is arguable that what we find in Jonah is a critique of the kind of proto-apocalyptic outlook attested in Joel. Whereas Joel looks forward to God's judgment coming on the heathen, the book of Jonah makes the point that foreigners can repent, with the result that Yahweh suspends his judgment. If so, this would tend to support the thesis of Payne (1979) that the book of Jonah was directed against the growing proto-apocalyptic movement with its longing for God's judgment to come on the heathen.

Another work commonly dubbed proto-apocalyptic is Isaiah 24-7. In an earlier article (1980b) I drew attention to a series of eight parallels between Isa. 26:13-27:11 and Hos. 13:4-14:10 (ET 9), all of them in the same order, with one partial exception, thus strongly suggesting the dependence of the Isaiah passage on Hosea.

   (i)   Israel knows no lords/gods but Yahweh
       Hos. 13:4. Cf. Isa. 26:13 (LXX)
  (ii)   Imagery of birthpangs with child refusing to be born
       Hos. 13:13. Cf. Isa. 26:17f
 (iii)   Deliverance from Sheol
       Hos. 13:14 (LXX, etc.). Cf. Isa. 26:19
  (iv)   Imagery of destructive east wind symbolic of exile
       Hos. 13:15. Cf. Isa. 27:8
   (v)   Imagery of life-giving dew
       Hos. 14:6 (ET 5). Cf. Isa. 26:19
  (vi)   Israel blossoming and like a vineyard
       Hos. 14:6-8 (ET 5-7). Cf. Isa. 27:2-6
 (vii)   Condemnation of idolatry, including the Asherim
       Hos. 14:9 (ET 8). Cf. Isa. 27:9
(viii)   The importance of discernment; judgment for the wicked
       Hos. 14:10 (ET 9). Cf. Isa. 27:11

The cumulative effect of these parallels, admittedly thematic rather than verbal for the most part, seems too much to be attributable to chance. A number of the themes are only rarely encountered elsewhere in the OT, and the fact that we find references to the birthpangs with child refusing to be born and deliverance from Sheol, occurring in successive verses in both cases, is particularly striking. The effect of all this is to question the view of those who find evidence of many redactions in Isaiah 24–7, since the fact that many of the verses in Isaiah 26–7 have their background in verses coming in the same order in Hosea 13–14, indicates that they belong together and therefore come from a single hand. However, for a detailed presentation of the case I refer the reader to my article.

## 6  RELECTURES

So far we have been considering instances where the prophets were indebted to other parts of the OT or at any rate to traditions which were later to be embodied in our OT. It is probable, however, that on occasions the prophetic oracles are themselves reworkings of earlier versions of those oracles. It is widely accepted, for example, that the deuteronomic prose sermons in Jeremiah were not simply created *ex nihilo* but often reflect a reworking of authentic Jeremianic logia (Nicholson, 1970), and Zimmerli's views on the redactional development of the Ezekiel tradition (1969) have gained some measure of support. The postulation of *relectures* is, however, something to be undertaken very warily, since some of the suggestions that have been put forward seem to reflect a high degree of subjectivity or are not sufficiently rigorously argued. Vermeylen (1977–8), for example, has written a large two-volume work giving a highly detailed redactional history of Isaiah 1–35, in which he claims to be able to plot with great accuracy when each verse or half verse was added, but the reasons are often very speculative and I do not believe such confidence is justified.

Recently, Macintosh (1980) has made a thoroughgoing attempt to apply the principle of *relecture* to a particular chapter, namely Isaiah 21. He claims that we have here an eighth-century BC text that has been 'overwritten' in the sixth century BC, 'overwritten' in such a way that the original recension can still be perceived, so that it constitutes a kind of palimpsest. Although this is highly ingenious, I do not find the grounds for postulating an original eighth-century BC recension convincing. Macintosh tells us that the reference to Elam in Isa. 21:2 cannot originally have referred to Cyrus (even though it did in the sixth-century BC revision), since Cyrus is nowhere else called an Elamite. This, however, is incorrect, since he is called an Elamite in the Babylonian Dynastic Prophecy (see Grayson, 1975, pp. 25, 33). Again, we are told that the prophet's trembling in Isa. 21:3f at the prospect of the fall of Babylon would be inexplicable in the sixth century BC, but this overlooks the fact that Habakkuk similarly trembles at the imminent overthrow of a power oppressing Israel, probably Babylon (Hab. 3:13), even though this will mean deliverance for Israel. Or again, we are told that the lack of anti-Edomite sentiment in the Dumah oracle (Isa. 21:11f) indicates an original pre-exilic date, but this is not so, since Dumah was not Edom but a place in North Arabia (Gen. 25:14; cf. 1 Chron. 1:30). It is clear that Macintosh's thesis is to be rejected (cf. Day, 1983). The positing of *relectures* is something that should only be done with great caution.

It is a pleasure to contribute this essay in honour of Professor Barnabas Lindars, a scholar who, unusually in our age of specialisation, has spanned both Old and New Testaments in his publications.

## BIBLIOGRAPHY

P. R. Ackroyd 'Hosea and Jacob', *VT* 13 (1963), 245–59.

L. C. Allen 'Cuckoos in the Textual Nest at 2 Kings xx. 13; Isa. xlii. 10; xlix. 24; Ps. xxii. 17; 2 Chron. v. 9', *JTS* n.s. 22 (1971), 143–50.

B. W. Anderson 'Exodus Typology in Second Isaiah', in B. W. Anderson and W. Harrelson (eds.), *Israel's Prophetic Heritage* (London, 1962), pp. 177–95.

'Exodus and Covenant in Second Isaiah and Prophetic Tradition', in F. M. Cross, W. E. Lemke and P. D. Miller (eds.), *Magnalia Dei, The Mighty Acts of God. Essays on the Bible and Archaeology in Memory of G. Ernest Wright* (Garden City, 1976), pp. 339–60.

R. Bach 'Gottesrecht und weltliches Recht in der Verkündigung des Propheten Amos', in W. Schneemelcher (ed.), *Festschrift Günther Dehn* (Neukirchen, 1957), pp. 23–34.

D. S. Bailey *Homosexuality and the Western Christian Tradition* (London, 1955).

D. Baltzer *Ezechiel und Deuterojesaja*, BZAW 121 (Berlin, 1971).

A. Bentzen 'The weeping of Jacob, Hos xii 5a', *VT* 1 (1951), 58f.

R. V. Bergren *The Prophets and the Law* (Cincinnati, 1974).

W. Beyerlin *Die Kulttraditionen Israels in der Verkündigung des Propheten Micha* (Göttingen, 1959).

F. F. Bruce 'The earliest Old Testament Interpretation', *OTS* 17 (1972), 37–52.

U. (M. D.) Cassuto 'The Prophet Hosea and the Books of the Pentateuch', in *Abhandlungen zur Erinnerung an Hirsch Perez Chajes* (Vienna, 1933), pp. 262–78 (in Hebrew). ET in U. (M. D.) Cassuto *Biblical and Oriental Studies* 1 (Jerusalem, 1973), pp. 79–100.

R. E. Clements *Prophecy and Covenant* (London, 1965).
*Prophecy and Tradition* (Oxford, 1975).
*Isaiah and the Deliverance of Jerusalem*, JSOTSS 13 (Sheffield, 1980).
*Isaiah 1–39*, New Century Bible (London, 1980).

G. H. Davies 'The Yahwistic Tradition in the Eighth Century Prophets', in H. H. Rowley (ed.), *Studies in Old Testament Prophecy* (Edinburgh and London, 1950), pp. 37–51.

J. Day 'The Daniel of Ugarit and Ezekiel and the Hero of the Book of Daniel', *VT* 30 (1980), 174–84 (= 1980a).

'A Case of Inner Scriptural Interpretation: the dependence of Isaiah xxvi. 13–xxvii. 11 on Hosea xiii. 4–xiv. 10 (Eng. 9) and its relevance to some theories of the redaction of the "Isaiah apocalypse"', *JTS* n.s. 31 (1980), 309–19 (= 1980b).

Review of A. A. Macintosh *Isaiah XXI. A Palimpsest*, in *JTS* n.s. 34 (1983), 212–15.

*God's Conflict with the Dragon and the Sea. Echoes of a Canaanite Myth in the Old Testament*, University of Cambridge Oriental Publications 35 (Cambridge, 1985).

'Pre-Deuteronomic allusions to the Covenant in Hosea and Psalm lxxviii', *VT* 36 (1986), 1–12.

M. Delcor 'Les sources du deutéro-Zacharie et ses procédés d'emprunt', *RB* 59 (1952), 385–411.

J. H. Eaton *Festal Drama in Deutero-Isaiah* (London, 1979).

O. Eissfeldt 'The Promises of Grace to David in Isaiah 55:1–5', in B. W. Anderson and W. Harrelson (eds.), *Israel's Prophetic Heritage* (London, 1962), pp. 196–207.

A. Feuillet 'Les Sources du Livre de Jonas', *RB* 54 (1947), 161–86.

A. Fey *Amos und Jesaja*, WMANT 12 (Neukirchen, 1963).

J. Fischer 'Das Problem des neuen Exodus in Isaias c. 40–55', *Theologische Quartalschrift* 110 (1929), 111–30.

M. Fishbane *Biblical Interpretation in Ancient Israel* (Oxford, 1985).

G. Fohrer 'Remarks on Modern Interpretation of the Prophets', *JBL* 80 (1961), 309–19.

A. Gelston 'Kingship in the Book of Hosea', *OTS* 19 (1974), 71–85.

H. L. Ginsberg 'Hosea's Ephraim, More Fool than Knave. A New Interpretation of Hosea 12:1–14', *JBL* 80 (1961), 339–47.

E. M. Good 'Hosea and the Jacob Tradition', *VT* 16 (1966), 137–51.

G. B. Gray 'The Parallel Passages in Joel and Their Bearing on the Question of Date', *Expositor* 8 (1893), 208–25.

A. K. Grayson *Babylonian Historical-Literary Texts* (Toronto and Buffalo, 1975).

K. Gross *Die literarische Verwandeschaft Jeremias mit Hosea* (Borne and Leipzig, 1930).

'Hoseas Einfluss auf Jeremias Anschauungen', *NKZ* 42 (1931), 241–56, 327–43.

D. M. Gunn 'Deutero-Isaiah and the Flood', *JBL* 94 (1975), 493–508.

T. R. Hobbs 'Jeremiah 3, 1–5 and Deuteronomy 24, 1–4', *ZAW* 86 (1974), 23–9.

W. L. Holladay 'Chiasmus, the key to Hosea XII 3–6', *VT* 16 (1966), 53–64.

A. Hurvitz *A Linguistic Study of the Relationship between the Priestly Source and the Book of Ezekiel*, Cahiers de la Revue Biblique 20 (Paris, 1982).

C. Jeremias 'Die Erzväter in der Verkündigung der Propheten', in H. Donner, R. Hanhart and R. Smend (eds.), *Beiträge zur Alttestamentlichen Theologie. Festschrift für Walther Zimmerli zum 70. Geburtstag* (Göttingen, 1977), pp. 206–22.

A. A. Johnson *Sacral Kingship in Ancient Israel* (2nd ed., Cardiff, 1967).

D. Jones 'The Traditio of the Oracles of Isaiah of Jerusalem', *ZAW* 67 (1955), 226–46.

K. Kiesow *Exodustexte im Jesajabuch*, Orbis Biblicus et Orientalis 24 (Göttingen, 1979).

P. Lamarche *Zacharie IX–XIV* (Paris, 1961).

B. Lindars '"Rachel weeping for her children" – Jeremiah 31:15–22', *JSOT* 12 (1979), 47–62.

A. A. Macintosh *Isaiah XXI. A Palimpsest* (Cambridge, 1980).

J. L. McKenzie 'Mythological allusions in Ezek 28:12–18', *JBL* 75 (1956), 322–7.

R. A. Mason 'The relation of Zech 9–14 to Proto-Zechariah', *ZAW* 88 (1976), 227–39.

J. W. Miller *Das Verhältnis Jeremias und Hesekiels sprachlich und theologisch untersucht* (Assen, 1955).

W. Moran 'Gen. 49, 10 and its use in Ez. 21, 32', *Biblica* 39 (1958), 405–25.

S. Mowinckel *Psalmenstudien* (6 vols., Kristiania, 1921–4).

D. H. Müller 'Der Prophet Ezechiel entlehnt eine Stelle des Propheten Zephanja und glossiert sie', in *Komposition und Strophenbau* (Vienna, 1907), pp. 30–6.

E. W. Nicholson *Preaching to the Exiles* (Oxford, 1970).

S. Paul 'Literary and ideological echoes of Jeremiah in Deutero-Isaiah', *Proceedings of the IVth World Congress of Jewish Studies* 1 (Jerusalem, 1969), pp. 102–20.

D. F. Payne 'Jonah from the Perspective of its Audience', *JSOT* 13 (1979), 3–12.

# Prophecy

D. L. Petersen *Late Israelite Prophecy: Studies in Deutero-Prophetic Literature and in Chronicles*, SBLMS 23 (Missoula, 1977).

A. Phillips 'Prophecy and Law', in R. Coggins, A. Phillips and M. Knibb (eds.), *Israel's Prophetic Tradition. Essays in Honour of Peter R. Ackroyd* (Cambridge, 1982), pp. 217-32.

G. von Rad *Theologie des Alten Testaments* (2 vols., Munich, 1957-60) (= ET *Old Testament Theology* (2 vols., Edinburgh, 1962-5)).

N. H. Snaith *Studies in the Psalter* (London, 1934).

H. F. D. Sparks 'The witness of the Prophets to Hebrew Tradition', *JTS* 50 (1949), 129-41.

B. Stade 'Deuterozacharja. Eine kritische Studie', *ZAW* 1 (1881), 1-96.

R. Tournay Review of A. Deissler and M. Delcor, *Les Petits Prophètes 2*, *RB* 72 (1965), 427-9.

J. Vermeylen *Du Prophète Isaïe à l'Apocalyptique* (2 vols., Paris, 1977-8).

T. C. Vriezen 'La tradition de Jacob dans Osée XII', *OTS* 1 (1942), 64-78.

M. Weinfeld 'God the Creator in Gen. 1 and the Prophecy of Second Isaiah', *Tarbiz* 37 (1968), 105-32 (in Hebrew).

R. N. Whybray *The Heavenly Counsellor in Isaiah xl 13-14* (Cambridge, 1971).

H. W. Wolff *Dodekapropheton 1. Hosea*, BKAT XIV/1 (2nd ed., Neukirchen, 1965) (= ET *Hosea* (Philadelphia, 1974)).

*Dodekapropheton 2. Joel und Amos*, BKAT XIV/2 (2nd ed., Neukirchen, 1975) (= ET *Joel and Amos* (Philadelphia, 1977)).

W. Zimmerli 'Der "neue Exodus" in der Verkündigung der beiden grossen Exilspropheten', *Gottes Offenbarung* (Munich, 1963), pp. 192-204 (= 1963a).

'Zur Sprache Tritojesajas', *Gottes Offenbarung* (Munich, 1963), pp. 217-33 (= 1963b).

*Das Gesetz und die Propheten* (Göttingen, 1963) (= ET *The Law and the Prophets* (Oxford, 1965)) (= 1963c).

*Ezechiel*, BKAT XIII/1,2 (Neukirchen, 1969) (= ET, *Ezekiel* (2 vols., Philadelphia, 1979-83)).

'Prophetic Proclamation and Reinterpretation', in D. A. Knight (ed.), *Tradition and Theology in the Old Testament* (London, 1977), pp. 69-100.

# 4 · Psalms

## A. A. ANDERSON

THE general purpose of this chapter is to discuss the use of the Old Testament in the Psalms, but due to practical limitations our particular task will be confined to a brief survey of the psalmists' use of three more or less related types of material, namely, Israel's historical traditions, creation stories and oracular material. We shall not concern ourselves with oracles or divine promises in general (see Mowinckel, 1962, pp. 62–3), but only with the *re-use* of older prophetical material, such as in Psalms 89 and 132, in particular. The re-application of existing material is very obvious in Pss. 60: 6–8 (MT 8–10) and 108: 7–9 (MT 8–10), although in this case it is difficult to define the actual source of the common oracle.

Although the Israelites may have been aware of some difference between their historical narratives and creation accounts, yet both themes are found, at times, side by side in the Psalter as if on the same level of reality, as in Psalm 136. Haglund (1984, p. 8) has remarked that 'in Genesis there is no strict differentiation between primal and other history...In spite of this there is a difference between what is told about the time before Terah and Abraham and about what took place later'; consequently, he excludes motifs found in Genesis 1–11 from his analysis. However, it seems that this collocation of historical themes and primal history is hardly accidental and that in the OT setting, especially in the Psalter, both themes are inseparably related and essentially understood as illustrations or instances of the mighty works of Yahweh. Creation may well have been regarded as the first work of Yahweh in the history of the world (see Kraus, 1979, p. 75), followed by other acts of God. Moreover it could be claimed, with some justification, that to some extent the above oracular material also serves the same basic purpose. To be able to announce 'from of old the things to come' (Isa. 44:7) or to give *effective* eternal promises is an important aspect of God's demonstration of his incomparability which is manifested not only in creation and history but also in prophecy. The essential interrelatedness of these three types of material is to be found in the creative power of the divine word: God spoke, and the world was created (cf. Pss. 33:6,9; 148:5). Furthermore, this effectiveness of the divine word did not come to an end with the creation of the universe. Perhaps it could be said that 'creation is a continuous activity' (Ringgren, 1966, p. 109; cf. Ps. 104:27ff) and also that 'subsequent historical deeds are regarded as creative acts…' (Anderson, 1962, p. 727; cf. Isa. 55:11). Consequently, creation, history and the word of Yahweh are seen as different manifestations of God's sovereignty and his incomparable power.

All three themes appear together in somewhat uneasy tension in Psalm 89 because the unconditional dynastic promise is seen as of irrevocable validity, and its ongoing fulfilment must express itself in appropriate events. Thus what originally started out as an oracle or dynastic promise has eventually become also a testimony of Yahweh's ability to control the course of events. The psalmist's predicament in Psalm 89 is that the more or less contemporary experiences have introduced a perplexing note. In this psalm vv. 5–18 (MT 6–19) praise Yahweh as the conqueror of chaos and as the creator of the world while vv. 3–4 and 19–37 (MT 4–5 and 20–38) are presented as the words of Yahweh in the form of an eternal promise to David and to his house. At the same time the dynastic oracle also serves in part as an historical account of what Yahweh has already done for David and his house in the more distant past. Over against this is set a review of Yahweh's acts in *recent* history (vv. 38–45 (MT 39–46)), because these events appear to contradict the cited divine word of assurance. The psalmist does not doubt Yahweh's power or his ability to intervene in world affairs; his problem is his inability to understand the practical outworking of Yahweh's purposes in the contemporary situation. It is clear to him that Yahweh is unequalled in effective power, whether manifested in creation or in world events in general (see Ps. 89:6, 11 (MT 7, 12)). At the same time, Yahweh is also absolutely reliable and faithful to his word and to his people. Therefore there exists a temporary unresolved tension between what could be expected (in view of Yahweh's nature and promises) and what is actually happening to the people and to the house of David. However, the implicit assumption behind the psalm is that the time must come when there will be a reversal of fortunes and when all the expectations will become a present reality. Hence the author's essential question is 'How long, O LORD?' (Ps. 89:46 (MT 47)).

1 ORACULAR MATERIAL

Psalm 89 provides a very good illustration of the potential difficulties which may arise when we try to assess the extent and nature of the use of the OT in the Psalms. That there is such a dependence, literary or otherwise, is often fairly clear but it is far from obvious, in most cases, in which direction this dependence lies and what is the exact nature of this connexion. Thus few scholars doubt that in 2 Sam. 7:1–17 and in Ps. 89:19–37 (MT 20–38) we are dealing with the same dynastic oracle, but how are we to understand their interrelationship? Is 2 Samuel 7 dependent upon Psalm 89, as argued by Pfeiffer (1941, pp. 371ff) and Ahlström (1959, pp. 182ff), or is the psalm the more recent version, 'a re-working of the prophecy of Nathan in the spirit of the Dtr movement' (Mettinger, 1976, p. 256). Alternatively, do these versions of the oracle (including 1 Chr. 17:1–15) go back to a common source (McKenzie, 1947, p. 215)? Veijola (1982, pp. 60f) may be right in asserting the priority of 2 Samuel 7 on the basis of his thorough examination of the linguistic and thematic links between Psalm 89 and the manifestly late OT material (such as Lamentations, exilic psalms of lamentation, Deutero-Isaiah, etc.) when contrasted with 2 Samuel 7. On the other hand, the relationship between Psalm 89 and 2 Samuel 7 may be more complicated than at first appears. It is plausible that Nathan's oracle should have been handed down through two media, a literary and cultic one. The incorporation of the oracle in the so-called History of David's Rise (see Weiser, 1966, pp. 346ff; Mettinger, 1976, p. 45) is a real possibility, and this document (including Nathan's oracle) may have overlapped with the Succession Narrative. The starting point of the latter document would be determined by its specific interests, and not by the contents or extent of some other earlier document. Thus the shared material could be adapted to the needs of the particular documents. Eventually both narratives must have been used and further adapted by the author of the Deuteronomistic History which, in its turn, may have undergone more than one redaction (see Dietrich, 1972). Hence it is doubtful that the dynastic oracle could have survived in its original form (see also McCarter, 1984, pp. 209–31). It is likely that the same original oracle, in some form or other, was used in the Jerusalem cult, perhaps at the enthronement of the king (so Ahlström, 1959, p. 182) or on some other appropriate royal occasion or in connexion with the Ark Narrative (see Weiser, 1965, p. 166). Also in this process the contents may have undergone further reinterpretation and reformulation. New motifs were probably added and others (such as the reference to the temple) may have been omitted. It seems that Psalm 89 may be dependent upon a *cultic* version of Nathan's oracle since the psalmist had already made use of other existing material, namely, an older creation hymn in vv. 5–18 (MT 6–19). Moreover, the author of our present psalm may well have intended this lamentation for cultic use (e.g. at an exilic fast; see Veijola, 1982, pp. 209–10); in such a case it is more likely that the writer depends upon a cultic version of the dynastic oracle because it might have been better known to the worshippers, and thus it may have been one of the causes of the contemporary theological tension.

There is no compelling reason why both traditions could not ultimately go back to an original oracle given to David (see McKenzie, 1947, p. 196) or to its revised form from the Solomonic (or some slightly later) period. Furthermore, the traditions could hardly have existed in complete isolation, and this further complicates any investigation of their interdependence. Thus it seems that even a detailed examination of all relevant materials (such as undertaken by Veijola, 1982) can only tentatively point us in the right direction while certainty seems to be an unattainable goal.

For our present purposes we have disregarded the Chronicler's version of Nathan's oracle (1 Chr. 17:1–15) because it is most likely later than Psalm 89, and dependent upon 2 Samuel 7 (cf. Williamson, 1982, pp. 132f; Ishida, 1977, p. 82). However, we should make some mention of Ps. 132:11–12 which reflects certain themes found in 2 Sam. 7:12–16 and Ps. 89:28–37 (MT 29–38). The question of their interrelationship largely depends upon the dating of Psalm 132. We regard it in its present form as comparatively late, and this is indicated by its deuteronomistic affinities (so Mettinger, 1976, pp. 256f; similarly, Veijola, 1982, p. 73). Some scholars (e.g. Cross, 1973, p. 233, and Gese, 1964, p. 16) have argued for an early monarchic date, but this seems less likely unless the suggested deuteronomistic influence can be explained away. Moreover, Veijola (1982, p. 75) has suggested that Psalm 132 may reflect the *present* redactional sequence and structure of 2 Samuel 6–7. He has pointed out that in Psalm 132 David's oath to find a dwelling place (temple?) for Yahweh (vv. 2–5) is matched by a corresponding oath on Yahweh's part (vv. 11–12) to establish David's dynasty. Similarly, in the ark story (2 Samuel 6) we see how David brought the ark to Jerusalem and provided a dwelling for it; he even planned a more permanent building for it (2 Sam. 7:2). This course of action, too, was matched by Yahweh's promise to build a house (i.e. dynasty) for David (2 Sam. 7:11–16).

One may also note that whereas in 2 Sam. 7:15 and Ps. 89:33 (MT 34) the divine promise is unconditional, in Ps. 132:12 Yahweh's oath could well be regarded as conditional. If so, this may imply that Psalm 132 is later than the two previous passages, and that in the light of the contemporary situation its author had to allow for the possibility that the Davidic dynasty might not be restored after all. However, Psalm 132 presents a problem too complicated to be solved in a paragraph or two (cf. Allen, 1983, p. 209).

## 2 HISTORICAL TRADITIONS

When considering the psalmists' use of the historical material in the narrower sense (disregarding the theme of creation), it is useful to differentiate three main types of application. First, there are psalms (such as Psalms 78, 105, 106, 135 and 136) which give a reasonably chronological and extensive record of Israel's history, especially of the early part. Second, we find psalms which include more or less identifiable links with Israelite historical traditions (cf. Psalms 44, 68, 74, 80, 81, 83, 89, 95, 107, 132 and 137). Third, there are a number of psalms which contain allusions to certain historical events or broad generalisations but whose descriptions are usually too general or too ambiguous to be regarded as historical motifs in the strict sense of the word (cf. Psalms 47, 66 and 111).

The first group, especially Psalms 78, 105 and 106, are often called 'historical psalms', and these correspond to Gunkel's *Legenden* (1966, p. 324). However, these psalms do not form a separate genre (but see von Rad, 1965, pp. 3–13) even though they share in common a shorter or longer review of Israel's fortunes which forms the main section of the respective poems. The psalms which incorporate recognisable historical motifs belong to different genres, e.g. hymns (Psalms 68, 81, 95, 105, 107, 135, 136), laments (Psalms 44, 74, 80, 106, 137), and royal psalms (Psalms 89, 132). Moreover, some psalms could easily be ascribed to more than one literary type, depending upon the emphasis placed on their different component parts (e.g. in Psalms 78 and 106).

The basic historical sequence in the so-called 'historical psalms' is reminiscent of the credo (see von Rad, 1958, pp. 11ff) and its four main elements are: Israel in Egypt, exodus deliverance, desert wanderings and settlement in Canaan. However, in some psalms even this broad outline may be further abbreviated (cf. Psalms 44 and 74), or some of the themes may be lacking, or the author may concentrate on only one specific event, as in Psalm 95. Psalm 105 is the only one that begins its historical review with Abraham, Isaac and Jacob (vv. 9f). It is also of some interest that the historical summaries omit the Sinai traditions and that only infrequently do they go as far as David, the monarchical period (cf. Psalm 78) or the exile (Psalm 106). Kühlewein (1973, p. 142) has suggested that this latter fact may be due to the greater antiquity of the pentateuchal traditions and to the royal psalms which in a special sense carried on the Davidic traditions (cf. Psalms 89, 132, 144). Perhaps the early, idealised (?) traditions were more impressive witnesses to the saving power of Yahweh than the more perplexing later experiences.

On the whole, one gains the impression that the historical psalms were not intended to be epic poems or substitutes for a detailed rehearsal of the acts of God; rather they functioned as reminders of such recitals or traditions. Even the more extensive synopses of the sacred history would be sadly incomplete on their own, not to mention the more limited historical allusions. It seems that the choice of the historical themes was often determined by the present distress experienced by the community and its particular needs (cf. Psalm 106) as well as by the purpose or function of the specific psalms (cf. Psalm 89). It may be of some interest that all the 'historical psalms', with the possible exception of Psalm 78 (see Clifford, 1981, p. 138), are of exilic or early post-exilic origin. If indeed the extensive narrative corpus comprising the Deuteronomistic History and the Pentateuch in its final form was a reflection of Israel's response to the experiences and problems of the Babylonian exile and its sequel, then our 'historical psalms' may be seen as pointing to, and summing up, that same response. Thus they are not so much a re-presentation of Israel's history (cf. Westermann, 1981, pp. 214–49) as a presentation of Yahweh as the lord of history. It is primarily by their actions that God and Israel are known; the people have been continuously and destructively rebellious while Yahweh has been unceasingly constructive and faithful. In a sense, the recital of Israel's history looks back to the past, but its real significance is the future aspect: the present praise of Yahweh's past deeds inspires hope (cf. Ps. 78:7a). Obviously, the historical reviews and allusions may have had more than one function. Among other things, they could have had a didactic purpose as pointed out, for instance, by Holm-Nielsen (1978, p. 22; cf. also Mowinckel, 1962, vol. ii, p. 112). One could also mention Weiser's emphasis on the cultic significance of these psalms (cf. 1962, pp. 538, 673, 679f).

The authors of these psalms show familiarity with the pentateuchal traditions, perhaps even with their final form (see Lauha, 1945, pp. 39–50) as well as with the Deuteronomistic History. However, in order to say anything more specific, each psalm would need to be examined in detail. Even then the results might not convince everybody because the psalmists exercised considerable freedom in producing their historical summaries and formulations. One would also have to reckon with the possibility that the authors may have known the actual traditions which were eventually incorporated in some form or other in the Pentateuch (see Kraus, 1979, p. 73), or they may even have known some other traditions as is implied, for instance, by the different sequence of the desert tradition (see Fishbane, 1985, p. 327) and the rigours of Joseph's prison experience (Ps. 105:18). However, the last example may well be an instance of poetic exaggeration not uncommon in the historical psalms (cf. Ps. 78:27 with Exod. 16:13 and Num. 11:31). One may also assume that the psalmists were steeped in the cultic language and traditions of their times, and this too may have coloured their creative work. Thus Psalm 135 contains quite a number of possible allusions or adaptations from other parts of the OT (for details, see Allen, 1983, p. 224), but there is no imperative need to argue for a literary dependence (see also Weiser, 1962, p. 788). Direct citations are rare (cf. Ps. 135:14 with Deut. 32:36a) while various kinds of possible adaptations are far more frequent (cf. Ps. 105:9 with Gen. 26:3; Ps. 106:27 with Ezek. 20:23; Ps. 135:7 with Jer. 10:13 (= 51:16)). There are also examples of what Fishbane (1985, pp. 398f, 426) calls haggadic transformations or illustrations of haggadic exegesis, as in the case of Phinehas who becomes an *intercessor* like Moses (cf. Num. 25:7f with Ps. 106:23, 29f).

Perhaps we should make some mention of the historical notes in the psalm titles or headings, even though they are most likely later additions which reflect the interpretation of the relevant psalms by subsequent generations (cf. Psalms 3, 7, 18, 34, 51, 52, 54, 56, 57, 59, 60, 63, 142; see also Childs, 1971, pp. 137–50). Fishbane (1985, p. 404) comments that 'the titles provide an exegetical bridge between two textual units – a psalm and a narrative', yielding in the end a singular exegetical correlation. Our specific point of interest is that, with the possible exception of Psalm 7, all the historical notes refer to events or persons attested in the Deuteronomistic History. However, this is what we should expect because of the comparative lateness of the historical notes.

## 3  CREATION STORIES

Turning to the theme of creation, we note first how common it is in the Psalter. According to Vosberg's count (1975, p. 11) there are some sixty-two psalms which have been taken by Kraus as referring to God as creator. However, some of the references are more or less vague and therefore Vosberg himself has reduced the number of Yahweh-as-creator psalms to twenty-two, namely, Psalms 8, 24, 33, 65, 74, 75, 89, 95, 96, 100, 102, 104, 115, 119, 121, 124, 134, 135, 136, 146, 147 and 148. Due to various exegetical difficulties there may also be other variations; for instance, Curtis (1978, p. 255, n. 1) finds clear references to creation in only some nineteen psalms (Psalms 8, 19, 24, 33, 65, 74, 89, 93, 95, 102, 104, 115?, 119, 124, 134, 136, 146, 147? and 148).

There is some justification for differentiating three main types of creation in the OT (see also Westermann, 1984, p. 26): creation by word (cf. Genesis 1; Pss. 33:6, 9; 104:7?; 148:5), creation by act, such as fashioning or making (cf. Genesis 2; Pss. 8:3–5; 24:2; 65:6–7 (MT 7–8); 95:5–6; 102:25 (MT 26); 136:5–9) and perhaps creation as the result of a conflict with the chaos waters (cf. Pss. 65:5–7) (MT 6–8); 74:12–15; 89:9–11 (MT 10–12); 104:5–9). These creation concepts need not be mutually exclusive as illustrated, for instance, by Genesis 1 and Ps. 33:6–7. It could be argued that variations of this nature may imply that the emphasis was usually on the creator and his majestic power rather than on creation as such or its nature.

Not infrequently it has been argued that 'concepts of creation are relatively rare in the pre-exilic period' (Schmidt, 1983, p. 170) or even that most, if not all, psalms referring to creation are post 587 BC (so Vosberg, 1985, p. 11). This latter suggestion in particular has been challenged most recently by John Day (1985), who has added his support for the view that the creation motif was an important element of the autumnal festival. Consequently some creation psalms at least must have belonged to that *Sitz im Leben* and hence to the pre-exilic period, even though there are considerable problems in dating the relevant material. All this is bound to have a decisive bearing on the evaluation of the use of the OT in the Psalter. It seems that the concept of creation must have been well known in the pre-exilic period, even though comparatively little use was made of it by authors other than the psalmists (but see such passages as Gen. 2; 14:19, 22; Deut. 32:6; Amos 4:13; 9:26; Jer. 5:22; 10:12–16; 31:35). It may well be that all the OT types of creation owe their origin to, or have been influenced by, either Near Eastern myths, e.g. the Babylonian *Enuma Elish*, the Egyptian creation stories, and especially the Canaanite mythology (see Westermann, 1984, pp. 26–47). Nevertheless, whatever the Israelites adopted they also adapted to suit their own religious and cultural framework.

The problems of dependence are well illustrated by Psalm 104. Most scholars would agree that this nature poem has certain affinities with Akhenaten's hymn to Aten (see *ANET*, pp. 370–1; Allen, 1983, pp. 28–31), but the exact relationship is difficult to determine. Even more striking and relevant to our discussion are the correspondences between Psalm 104 and Genesis 1. Day (1985, p. 61) argues that the latter is dependent upon the former (similarly also Voort, 1951) and he regards the psalm as of pre-exilic origin since 'it seems to have been extensively used by the Priestly writer (probably 6th century B.C.) in the creation account of Gen. 1' (1985, p. 34). On the other hand, Gunkel (1968, p. 453), for instance, has contended for the priority of Genesis 1. There is at least one other possibility, namely that instead of a *direct* relationship both texts may have drawn upon earlier Israelite traditions. All in all, Psalm 104 appears to reflect a less advanced thought and therefore its dependence on Genesis 1 is questionable. There are indeed similarities but also differences (cf. Day, 1985, pp. 51ff), and in the Psalm there is little if any emphasis on creation by word but more dependence on mythology (cf. vv. 7, 26). In Day's view (1985, p. 30) Psalm 104 associates creation with the primordial conflict (vv. 5–9); if so, the relevant passage must refer to a *well established* conflict tradition of a primeval battle with chaos. Other psalms (e.g. Psalms 74 and 89) are more explicit in their use of the *Chaoskampf* motif but they, too, presuppose a more detailed conflict mythology without which the conflict references and allusions would be somewhat incomprehensible. Earlier scholars understandably argued for a Babylonian background to this myth, but the Ugaritic texts and their terminology quite convincingly point to its Canaanite origin. However, a number of scholars has rejected the claim that the extant Ugaritic conflict stories should be regarded as creation myths because, in their view, there is little or no clear evidence in the texts themselves to support this suggestion (cf. Westermann, 1984, p. 33). Nevertheless, the impression gained from the Psalter is that the subjugation of the waters was tantamount to creation of order if not of the universe. Whatever may have been the original relationship between creation and the subjugation of the chaos, both have become aspects of Yahweh's work since he has taken over most of the functions of El and Baal. Thus one and the same deity is both the 'creator of creatures' and the victor over the chaos waters. This may have facilitated the later historicisation of the divine conflict with the sea and its allies (see Day, 1985, pp. 88–140).

The conflict motif is also found outside the Psalter, and one could, for instance compare Isa. 51:9–10 with Pss. 74:13f and 89:9f (MT 10f); see also Ezek. 29:3; 32:2; Job 3:8; 9:8, 13; 26:11–13; 38:8–11. It is possible that Deutero-Isaiah as well as the author of Job and others were making use of earlier creation hymns, but it is difficult to argue convincingly for a literary dependence since the psalms themselves presuppose more elaborate creation traditions, both cultic and wisdom. In some other cases it may be the psalms which are indebted to earlier sources; thus the language and thought of Psalms 8 and 33 suggest that they are poetic reflections of the Priestly creation story (cf. also Ps. 136:5–9).

In conclusion it must be said that although the Psalter has many affinities with various parts of the OT, it is an almost impossible task to establish the precise nature of these interrelationships. Perhaps in many instances the explanation will be found in the shared common traditions.

## BIBLIOGRAPHY

G. W. Ahlström *Psalm 89: Eine Liturgie aus dem Ritual des leidenden Königs* (Lund, 1959).

L. C. Allen *Psalms 101–150*, Word Biblical Commentary 21 (Waco, Texas, 1983).

B. W. Anderson 'Creation', in *IDB* 1, pp. 725–32.

B. S. Childs 'Psalm Titles and Midrashic Exegesis', *JSS* 16 (1971), 137–50.

R. J. Clifford 'Psalm 89: A Lament over the Davidic Ruler's Continued Failure', *HTR* 73 (1980), 35–47.

'In Zion and David a New Beginning: An Interpretation of Psalm 78', in B. Halpern and Jon D. Levenson (eds.) *Traditions in Transformation* (Winona Lake, Indiana, 1981), pp. 121–41.

P. C. Craigie *Psalms 1–50*, Word Biblical Commentary 19 (Waco, Texas, 1983).

F. M. Cross *Canaanite Myth and Hebrew Epic. Essays in the History of the Religion of Israel* (Cambridge, Massachusetts, 1973).

A. H. W. Curtis 'The "Subjugation of the Waters" Motif in the Psalms: Imagery or Polemic?', *JSS* 22 (1978), 245–56.

J. Day *God's Conflict with the Dragon and the Sea* (Cambridge, 1985).

W. Dietrich *Prophetie und Geschichte. Eine redaktionsgeschichtliche Untersuchung zum deuteronomistischen Geschichtswerk* (Göttingen, 1972).

M. Fishbane *Biblical Interpretation in Ancient Israel* (Oxford, 1985).

# Psalms

T. E. Fretheim 'Psalm 132: A Form Critical Study', *JBL* 86 (1967), 289–300.

E. Gerstenberger 'Psalms', in J. H. Hayes (ed.) *Old Testament Form Criticism* (San Antonio, 1977), pp. 179–223.

H. Gunkel *Einleitung in die Psalmen* (Göttingen, 1933; reprinted 1966).
*Die Psalmen* (Göttingen, 1926; reprinted 1968).

E. Haglund *Historical Motifs in the Psalms*, ConB OT Series 23 (Uppsala, 1984).

S. Holm-Nielsen 'The Exodus Traditions in Psalm 105', *ASTI* 11 (1978), 22–30.

F. N. Jasper 'Early Israelite Traditions and the Psalter', *VT* 17 (1967), 50–9.

H.-J. Kraus *Psalmen*, BKAT 15 (Neukirchen, 1961).
*Theologie der Psalmen*, BKAT 15/3 (Neukirchen, 1979).

J. Kühlewein *Geschichte in den Psalmen* (Stuttgart, 1973).

A. Lauha *Die Geschichtsmotive in den alttestamentlichen Psalmen* (Helsinki, 1945).

P. K. McCarter, Jr. *2 Samuel*, AB 9 (Garden City, New York, 1984).

D. J. McCarthy '"Creation" Motifs in Ancient Hebrew Poetry', in B. W. Anderson (ed.) *Creation in the Old Testament* (Philadelphia and London, 1984), pp. 74–89.

F. R. McCurley *Ancient Myths and Biblical Faith. Scriptural Transformations* (Philadelphia, 1983).

J. L. McKenzie 'The Dynastic Oracle: II Samuel 7', *TS* 8 (1947), 187–218.

T. N. D. Mettinger *King and Messiah. The Civil and Sacral Legitimation of the Israelite Kings*, ConB. OT Series 8 (Lund, 1976).

S. Mowinckel *The Psalms in Israel's Worship* (Oxford, 1962).

R. H. Pfeiffer *Introduction to the Old Testament* (London, 1941).

G. von Rad *The Problem of the Hexateuch and Other Essays* (Edinburgh and London, 1966) (English translation of *Gesammelte Studien zum Alten Testament* (Munich, 1958)).

H. Ringgren *Israelite Religion* (London, 1966) (English translation of *Israelitische Religion* (Stuttgart, 1963)).

W. H. Schmidt *The Faith of the Old Testament* (Oxford, 1983) (English translation of *Alttestamentliche Glaube in seiner Geschichte*, Neukirchener Studienbücher 6 (Neukirchen-Vluyn, 1982)).

T. Veijola *Verheissung in der Krise: Studien zur Literatur und Theologie der Exilszeit anhand des 89. Psalms* (Helsingfors, 1982).

A. van der Voort 'Genèse I, 1 à II, 4a et le Psaume CIV', *RB* 58 (1951), 321–47.

A. A. ANDERSON

L. Vosberg *Studien zum Reden vom Schöpfer in den Psalmen*, BEvTh 69 (Munich, 1975).

A. Weiser *The Psalms*, Old Testament Library (London, 1962) (English translation of *Die Psalmen*, ATD 14/15 (5th ed., Göttingen, 1959)).

'Die Tempelbaukrise unter David', *ZAW* 77 (1965), 153–68.

'Die Legitimation des Königs David', *VT* 16 (1966), 325–54.

C. Westermann *Praise and Lament in the Psalms* (Edinburgh, 1981) (English translation of *Lob und Klage in der Psalmen* (Göttingen, 1977)).

*Genesis 1–11. A Commentary* (London, 1984) (English translation of *Genesis 1–11*, BKAT 1/1 (Neukirchen, 1974)).

H. G. M. Williamson *1 and 2 Chronicles*, New Century Bible (London, 1982).

# 5 · Wisdom

## R. E. CLEMENTS

THE acceptance of the emergent canonical tradition of the Old Testament among the teachers of wisdom in the immediate pre-christian period was to pose one of the most decisive features of the intellectual encounter between Judaism and Hellenism. How and why this should have been the case rests in part on the distinctive characteristic elements of wisdom itself, as this originated outside Israel in the ancient Near East, and in part on the specifically literary form of the OT. Since literacy was to prove one of the most desirable intellectual attainments which the wise came to foster and promote, and the emergent biblical tradition was essentially a literature, the need for the relationship between wisdom and the biblical tradition to be made clear came to be of paramount importance.

We may begin this examination of the earliest manifestations of an interest among the wise in the interpretation and character of Israel's traditions about the world and its own national destiny by looking at the character of wisdom itself. All attempts to define the nature of wisdom, either in terms of a circumscribed set of intellectual presuppositions (cf. Scott, 1971), or by reference to its probable functional and professional utility (cf. McKane, 1965), may be set aside as only partial descriptions of its character. Clearly wisdom did have certain intellectual presuppositions, being both pragmatic and empirical, and it also possessed certain functional and professional affiliations, being closely associated with the spheres of both governmental administration and the wider needs of the education of the young. However neither feature can be adduced as providing an exclusive and comprehensive explanation for the origin and pursuit of wisdom in Israel. This was undoubtedly a broadly based intellectual movement (cf. Whybray, 1974), originating outside Israel, but finding support within it among the intelligentsia of the self-styled wise. It was designed to promote the mastery of life and the attainment of success, with a special interest in political and social eminence. It was both deeply interested in social and religious (cultic) tradition, but felt itself wholly free to criticise and modify this wherever this was thought desirable. It possessed a very practical moralistic strain, but also a speculative and markedly aesthetic range of concern. Its willingness to transcend national boundaries, to promote the ideal of the wise person irrespective of religious and national boundaries, required of it a skill in sifting, harmonising and re-interpreting a variety of inherited teachings.

We may single out three main areas where, so far as we can discern, wisdom teaching developed a direct and positive interest in the emergent biblical tradition at a surprisingly early stage. These are the spheres of creation and its mythology, the concept of *tôrâ* and its relationship to the emergent canonical tradition, and the notion of Solomon as the founder and patron of the Israelite wisdom tradition.

In view of the particular complexities of the way in which wisdom developed in the OT, it is important to preface this examination with some remarks concerning the particular difficulties of chronology in such an exercise. Even until the relatively recent past questions of the date of origin of specific literary elements in the OT canon were given a very prominent position by scholars in critical debate. In the case of both Proverbs and Psalms such questions of date can only be surmised within very broad limits. The very nature of these writings as anthological collections inevitably implies that the date of individual elements within the collections may be greatly at variance with the date of the later editing. Furthermore within the formation of the collections some modifications and revisions certainly must have taken place. In consequence the retention of early elements in late literary contexts, which we frequently encounter, makes the task of determining relative chronological relationships a hazardous undertaking. Nevertheless an inquiry into such inter-connexions is essential to the pursuit of our task in this essay. By the time of Ben Sira (*ca.* 180 BC) the content of the OT canon was very much in the form in which we have it today. Even here however it is questionable whether Ben Sira himself would have viewed the relationship between the writings of the canon and other compositions such as his own work in the way that came to prevail little more than a century later.

## I CREATION AND ITS MYTHOLOGY

We can proceed to consider the strong interest that Israelite wisdom evinced in the understanding of creation and, by consequence, in older traditions about how this had taken place and what it implied about the working of the world. In the later OT period the written accounts which have been preserved for us in Genesis 1–3 were available in virtually their extant form to the writers of wisdom. So it is not surprising to find that in Prov. 8:22–31 and also in Ecclesiastes (Qoheleth) the Genesis text has plainly provided the interpreter with a starting point for deeper reflection and elaboration. This is probably also the case with the speech of God to Job (Job 38:1–40:2), although the position is not so clear in this. The reference to wisdom as 'a tree of life' in Prov. 3:18 almost certainly knew the tradition of Gen. 3:22, although since this tree plays little role in the biblical story of the fall, some wider currency of the idea in mythology may also have been present to the wisdom writer.

The doctrine of creation possessed a special fascination for the wise men of ancient Israel, and the combining of a monotheistic belief in Yahweh with a sense of a harmonious and self-consistent world made it particularly susceptible to the development of wisdom ideas. The desire to master life and to understand the secrets of happiness and prosperity, with the avoidance of the pitfalls of misfortune, involved a quest for understanding of the nature of the world. From an early prehistoric period mankind had sought to understand how the physical world functioned and how these natural perceptions related to the functioning of human society upon it. The two were felt to be directly interconnected, an assumption which also prevailed in the rituals of the cultic sphere. In their search to understand the order and effective working of the world the wise endeavoured to trace patterns and connexions between perceptibly similar phenomena. We can take it for granted therefore that the early type of catalogue wisdom which we find in the Egyptian *Onomastica* (cf. Gardiner, 1947) was a part of the questing for order (cf. 1 Kgs 4:33).

Teaching about creation was present in various strands of ancient Near Eastern mythology, and is well illustrated for posterity in the Babylonian text *Enuma Elish* (see conveniently Heidel, 1951). It therefore became essential that what the wise had to say about creation should engage with, and if necessary correct, what was expressed in this earlier mythology. Even in this it should be recognised that this mythology almost certainly lacked any very fully co-ordinated and coherent presentation of how the world functioned. This was a feature that the wise men could discern and elaborate upon in relation to inherited ideas and stories about creation. Already therefore the possibility of tension and conflict was present, and this was greatly heightened since much of the mythology about creation, as in *Enuma Elish* itself, contained a strong emphasis upon the conflict and disharmony from which creation sprang. Wisdom, on the other hand, was desirous of perceiving order and unity.

Without accepting the claim that myths arose as a kind of commentary upon ritual actions of the cultus, it is evident nonetheless that some important connexions existed between mythology and cultic actions. Almost as a natural part of the scheme of things myths introduced ideas and themes that were important in the realm of ritual. It was only to be expected therefore that the teachings of the wise men should have become concerned with ideas and practices that belonged to the sphere of cult (Perdue, 1977). Just as the rituals of worship in an agricultural setting were especially concerned with the productivity of the soil and the fending off of the dangers of drought and famine, so also was wisdom interested in promoting success in work and a prosperous life. For both wisdom and cultus the understanding of the created order of the world, of promoting its beneficent features and excluding its hostile and dangerous ones, was significant.

In this regard it is important to recognise that for both areas of thought the primary attention was to understand the nature and pattern of creation as a means towards co-operating with it in the present. Interest was much less in the past and in the nature of primordial time and much more in the present and in the current functioning of the world. For this reason, both in the teaching of the wise as well as in earlier mythology regarding creation, the sequences through which the world came into being were of interest as a way of interpreting priorities and inter-relationships of the present. Creation was looked upon largely in terms of a *creatio continua* where the actions of the past related inseparably to the providential order of the present. For this reason a feature regarding the role of wisdom in the creation of the world that is given paramount importance is that it was formed as the 'first' of the actions of God. Before the physical universe came into being God created wisdom (cf. Prov. 8:22–31) so that thereby the skills, proportions and qualities of wisdom might be affirmed as present throughout all things. There could be no part of the world where the insights and benefits of wisdom were not present. Starting from this vital point of insistence upon the priority of the fashioning of wisdom before the creation of the physical world, the ordering of its diverse parts is essentially seen to be the product and expression of its foundation through wisdom. Both in wisdom and the ideas of the cult, therefore, primal time and present time readily merged into one another.

Hermisson points to Psalm 104 as 'definitely composed in the handwriting of wisdom' (1984, p. 47). The life-giving breath (Heb. *rûaḥ*) of God (Ps. 104:30) by which all creatures maintain their existence is understood as a purposive manifestation of divine power which embraces physical, moral and spiritual qualities. It is thereby related to the fact that God has made all things through wisdom (v. 24). Whereas 'spirit' emphasises the aspect of divine power, 'wisdom' points to its purposive and intelligent nature. An interest in the natural world, with the extraordinary multiplicity of living forms with which it abounds all of which maintain their place in the harmonious functioning of the whole, is evidence of this wisdom which pervades the universe. It is not by chance, therefore, that it is in the wisdom literature that we find the greatest abundance of allusion to wildlife and flora in the Bible (cf. Wheeler Robinson, 1946, pp. 5f: 'It is the Wisdom writers who display the most marked interest in nature, ...').

All of this was, in another direction, brought together and given positive and mature reflection in the Priestly doctrine of creation set out in Gen. 1:1–2:4a. Two major passages in the wisdom literature present a basis of considered reflection by the wise upon this creation account, drawing from it certain fundamental conclusions about the relationship between God, man and wisdom.

## Proverbs 8

The first of these passages is to be found in Prov. 8:22–31 where, despite some uncertainty about the exact date of its composition, the literary dependence upon the written Priestly (P) account of Gen. 1:1–2:4a must be regarded as certain. This is most strikingly shown by the identification of wisdom with the term 'beginning' (Heb. rē'šît) of Gen. 1:1. Wisdom is the primal creation of God (Prov. 1:22) so that, although herself a creature and not a divine being, she is nevertheless before all other created forms of life and matter. Thereafter the varied forms of created things and beings, with their interlocking places in the universe, are all controlled and assigned through wisdom (Prov. 8:29f). The conscious reinterpretation of the term rē'šît combined with a fresh understanding of the preposition b to mean 'through, by means of', make this a most important and instructive instance of the adaptation and development of Israel's creation tradition. Later this came to acquire a christological interpretation in the early church, as Col. 1:15–17 shows. To this extent the many arguments concerning a possible extra-Israelite origin for this portrayal of wisdom, and in particular the possibility of a dependence upon knowledge of a Canaanite tradition about a goddess of wisdom (cf. Whybray, 1965, pp. 83f) can be regarded as of only marginal significance. In the Babylonian epic *Enuma Elish* (tablet vi) Marduk is assisted in his work of creating the world by the skill of Ea the wise. In the text of Proverbs 8 the primary concern of the author has been to establish a place and role for wisdom in the tradition about creation where originally no explicit mention of it was made.

The consequences of this intellectual development are important in two main ways. In the first place wisdom is accorded a place under Yahweh as a created power or being, since she has beauty and intelligence, but this is in no way allowed to detract from her priority and superiority to all other creatures. A second very striking feature is that the themes of tension and conflict between God and the monster of chaos are reduced to vanishing point since, once wisdom has been created, order and harmony are enabled to prevail.

How far this marks a consciously planned hypostatisation of wisdom which was itself thereafter destined to develop in further, very speculative, ways may be left aside. The author's primary intention has been to establish the place and authority of wisdom in the sphere of creation in such a manner as to claim for it eternal permanence and universality. It pervades the whole of creation, and is praised as the 'master workman' (Prov. 8:30; Heb. ʾāmôn; Wheeler Robinson, 1946, p. 260, n. 2, suggests the analogy of 'the clerk of the works').

## *Job 38–40*

A similar poetic expansion and elaboration of Israelite creation traditions as a manifestation of the range, skill and unfathomable grandeur of wisdom is found in the speech of God to Job (Job 38:1–40:2). The extent to which it is legitimate to find in this speech a knowledge of the Priestly account of creation is less clear than in the comparable case of Prov. 3:22–31. Yet some measure of dependence upon the central narrative account of creation is highly probable and in any case a familiarity with the long established traditions in Israel about creation must be regarded as certain. It is of the greatest importance that, in seeking to provide an answer to the questions and dilemmas of Job, the author of this speech has based his appeal upon the marvels of wisdom in the created order. In a sense the case rests on the contention that the range and intricacies of wisdom are of such greatness that a degree of mystery and human inability to comprehend its marvels must be accepted. Of particular interest in the speech of Yahweh are the appeal to the firm and immovable foundation of the earth (Job 38:4–6; cf. Gen. 1:6; Ps. 104:5–9); the separation of light from darkness (Job 38:16–21; cf. Gen. 1:3–5); and the determining of the positions of the stars and heavenly bodies (Job 38:31–3; cf. Gen. 1:14–19; Ps. 104:19). Clearly the author of the divine speech to Job has exercised a large degree of poetic elaboration and development, but his claims rest on already established features of Israel's creation tradition. The appeal to the orderliness, firmness and law-abiding character of the natural world are ascribed in the poem to wisdom. In consequence the author offers a quite new explanation for features which had earlier taken a central place in Israel's mythology concerning creation. Habel (1985, p. 528) interprets the well-established wisdom concept of 'counsel' (Heb. *ʿēṣâ*) as referring here to the world's 'design'. The orderliness and balanced working efficiency of the world are claimed by the poet to be evidence of the wisdom through which the universe has been planned and constructed. We may compare the fact that the Priestly creation narrative is itself highly distinctive when set against earlier Mesopotamian and Canaanite texts of a mythological nature for the extent to which it has expunged the theme of conflict (God versus Dragon-monster = Chaos). The wisdom tradition then carries this still further. Where the older mythology stresses the divine power to control the unruliness and threatening character of chaos, the wisdom tradition perceives the divine presence to be most in evidence in the skilful design which obviates any scope for chaos or disorder. There is a conscious shift from the notion of power manifested through kingly authority to one of skilful design which precludes any break-down of the orderly running of the universe. So we find that it is by wisdom that the earth's measurements were made; even the movements of the clouds in the sky display the orderliness of wisdom (Job 38:36f; contrast Ps. 18:12f). Similarly the certainty and smoothness of the motions of time are seen to be a manifestation of wisdom (Job 38:39–39:4). In a more negative fashion the apparently poor maternal conduct of the ostrich is taken to be evidence that this odd-looking and unfamiliar creature had forgotten the wisdom with which she had once been endowed (Job 39:17).

To a surprising degree the entire natural realm of creation is seen to testify to orderliness and a law-abiding regularity of time and movement, so that the harmony and intricate functioning of the overall design are claimed to rest on their being fashioned through wisdom. In a sense it is the absence of 'miracle', understood as an aberration from the normal working of nature, that provides the strongest evidence of the skill of the Grand Designer. God has made a world through wisdom which functions reliably, and in such a varied multiplicity of forms, that they far exceed the comprehension of human beings. Nor does the poet lack feeling for the aesthetic quality of the design of the world. To this extent wisdom herself is claimed as a figure of great beauty.

The details of the varied ways in which wisdom is perceived in creation are of lesser importance than the repeated affirmation that this wisdom both antedates the creation of the universe and yet is present through all its parts. That this is so reveals the foremost way in which the adoption of a tradition of wisdom into ancient Israel introduced a distinctive refashioning of the older mythology concerning creation in order to draw from it a number of wholly new lessons. The consequence was certainly to arrive at a way of looking at the world in which the evidence of its divine origin was more to be found in its unity and harmonious working than in its more irregular and threatening features. The fact that the world functioned as a place of order and regularity pushed many of its apparently irregular and mysterious features to the periphery of understanding. Because, therefore, the skill of the divine creator was manifest in this design, the concept of wisdom pressed towards a very original evaluation of the distinctions between the 'natural' and the 'supernatural'. Mystery remained, as the author of the divine speech to Job makes expressly clear, but it was a mystery of range and magnitude, not a mystery of lawlessness and unaccountable threat. It is certainly not going too far, therefore, to claim that the development of wisdom and its teachings about creation went a long way towards striving for the 'disenchantment' of the universe in which its numinous and unpredictable features were no longer left in the forefront of theological interest.

Such a view of the universe certainly displays many affinities with the feeling for rationality, beloved of the Greeks, and later to exercise an important role in assisting the blending of hellenistic and hebraic ideas about God and the world. Wisdom could readily be compared to the idea of the *logos* which pervaded all things according to Greek speculative thought. It would be wrong, however, to think of wisdom as a fully 'rational' principle in Israelite thought, since it lacked the truly abstract and ideological basis for this. Its presence in physical phenomena, its role in the harmonious functioning of the natural world, and its manifestation in purely external features of things, all fell short of making it a truly abstract rational principle.

It may certainly be argued that the developing interest in wisdom and its close links with the ordering of the created world as a sign of its divine origin led to a dualistic stream in jewish thought. Once ideas concerning the prophetic revelation of the divine will through prophecy fell into conflict with the teachings of wisdom the ground was prepared for a contrasting of the 'wisdom of this world' with the 'wisdom of the world to come'. From being a kind of natural knowledge witnessing to a natural revelation of the divine creator, wisdom gradually acquired features of prophetic origin in which a wholly non-natural set of rules about the divine purpose could be claimed as a special wisdom (cf. Rylaarsdam, 1946, pp. 63ff and 1 Cor. 1:19; 2:6–13).

### Ecclesiastes

Further reflections from Israel's wisdom tradition about the nature of creation and its meaning are to be found in the book of Ecclesiastes. The author of this work, which must have originated during the third century BC, builds firmly upon certain inherited features of the Israelite wisdom tradition (Zimmerli, 1963, pp. 311f). For the author the doctrine of creation was of great importance, since from it he expected to be able to deduce fundamental truths about the nature of human existence. Familiarity with the text of Genesis 1–3 can be confidently presumed and the author engages in certain critical reflections upon what the received tradition about the created world could offer by way of explanation for the tensions and frustrations of life (cf. Hengel, 1974, I, pp. 117f). That God, in creating the world, created time with all its cyclical movement is pressed to a distinctly extreme and negative position (Eccl. 3:2–9; cf. Gen. 1:14). The biblical account of the reason for the necessity for labour (Gen. 3:17–19) is elaborated in a negative fashion to show its ultimate unprofitability (Eccl. 2:11, 22; 3:9; 5:18). So also the account of how the first man was fashioned from the dust of the ground (Gen. 2:7; 3:19) is elaborated into a doctrine of human frailty and weakness which excludes the possibility of any further existence after the ending of this life at death (Eccl. 3:20f). Moreover the author's intense preoccupation with death (cf. Crenshaw, 1978, pp. 205ff) may be seen as a sharply questioning response to the wisdom doctrine that all things belong within the orderly arrangements of the creator's purpose. How then, he argues, does death fit smoothly into this 'grand design' of God? Nevertheless, throughout the work the appeal to the understanding of God as creator remains basic to the expectation of finding meaning and satisfaction in life through pondering the wisdom of the creator (Eccl. 12:1).

How the world functions, as wisdom has learnt to formulate this in its reflections, continues to be accepted. What is questioned is whether this functioning can point to any larger meaning or ultimate set of values. The author clearly shared fully the traditional assumptions about the manifestations of wisdom in creation. His crisis is less one of comprehension of the received tradition as one of finding in it any indication of the ultimate meaning of life. So the frequent labelling of things as 'vanity' (Heb. *hebel*) is not a denial of the truth of received perceptions, but of their value as offering any compensations for the frustrations and dissatisfactions of life.

## THE CONCEPT OF *TÔRÂ*

In appealing to the manifestations of wisdom in creation the wise of ancient Israel reveal a measure of expectancy and confidence that this can provide a sound basis for a critical and constructive view of life. Where the author of Ecclesiastes displays a negative response to this quest another strong feature of the engagement of wisdom with earlier tradition was much less critical. This concerned the relationship between wisdom and *tôrâ* (the conventional rendering of 'law' is inadequate to bring out the full range of the nature of the *tôrâ* tradition as the central body of the OT canon). It was the choice of the term *tôrâ* to describe the law-book of Yahweh's covenant with Israel (Deut. 4:44) that made it central as a description for the canonical biblical tradition (cf. Clements, 1978, pp. 104ff). Since the teaching contained in this deuteronomic book of *tôrâ* could also be described as Israel's 'wisdom' (*hokmâ*; Deut. 4:6), the potential for an assimilation of wisdom to *tôrâ*, and through this with the emergent canonical tradition as a whole, was established. Furthermore it would appear that such a basis of connexion between wisdom and law arose at a relatively early stage within the rise of the canonical tradition.

The extent to which a scribal tradition of wisdom, itself nurtured and built up within the administrative circles of Jerusalem, exercised a formative role on the compositions of the deuteronomic school is not wholly clear (as advocated by Weinfeld, 1972, pp. 244ff). Certainly some degree of influence is evident, although it can easily be stressed to the detriment of other features which are also undoubtedly discernible. Some of the more characteristic features of the wisdom tradition are only peripherally present, or are even absent altogether, in the deuteronomic writings. We may nevertheless accept the basic contention of E. Würthwein (1958, p. 269) that during the post-exilic period there was a progressive and continuing tendency to assimilate the content and general notion of the revealed *tôrâ* of God to the concept of wisdom. The consequence was a tendency to adapt the prescriptions of *tôrâ*, which originally had a more distinct and clear-cut legal frame of reference to a wider ideological perspective. Legislative rulings became adapted to become principles, so that just as wisdom was held to be timeless and universal so also did the understanding of *tôrâ* take on a comparable timelessness and universality. *Tôrâ* came to combine within itself the not properly reconcilable functions of being a uniquely revealed law of God and at the same time a natural law, evident in the make-up of the natural world and applicable to a wide human experience.

Already at the close of the book of Ecclesiastes we find the admonition of a pious glossator (cf. Barton, 1908, p. 199) to the effect that the whole duty of humankind is to 'Fear God, and keep his commandments; for this is the whole duty of man' (Eccl. 12:13). There is a comparable reference to *tôrâ* in Prov. 28:4 where it appears to refer to the central tradition of the canonical OT. To forsake this *tôrâ* is to lend support to wickedness. There are a number of further occurrences of *tôrâ* in the book of Proverbs where it appears that some degree of assimilation has occurred between the simple idea of it as 'the teaching of the wise' and the teachings contained in the canonical tradition of the OT (Prov. 28:7, 9; 29:18). Comparable understandings of *tôrâ* as the central body of teaching of the OT, but now closely assimilated to the notion of wisdom, are to be found in the two didactic (wisdom) psalms 1 and 119 (cf. Ps. 1:2; 119:1 etc.). It is not at all difficult to see how it became natural, and eventually necessary, for the traditions of wisdom and of a scriptural *tôrâ* to be brought in ever closer agreement with each other. This has then fully occurred in the writing of Ben Sira (Ecclus 24:8ff) in the early second century BC. There was undoubtedly an apologetic motive present by this time in which the conformability of Israelite-Jewish teaching with that acceptable to the hellenistic world was being sought after. Yet it appears that such assimilation of wisdom to *tôrâ* was already in the process of taking place before the pressures of hellenisation brought new incentives to Judaism. That it inevitably gave rise to tensions and incongruities was to be expected.

We should not leave out of account the implicit demand which probably had a fairly early origin in the growth of Israelite wisdom (cf. von Rad, 1972, pp. 53ff) that the fundamental prerequisite for the attainment of wisdom was the 'fear of Yahweh' (Prov. 1:7). Once the rise of the canonical tradition in post-exilic times came to define the content of 'the fear of Yahweh' in specific scriptural terms, then this demanded, as of necessity, a measure of assimilation of wisdom to the emergent biblical tradition. When there was added to this the desire, for social and political reasons, to bring jewish teaching into line with the best of the hellenistic tradition then the close connexions between wisdom and *tôrâ* became a subject of great importance.

It may be remarked at this point that wisdom appears not to have become a fully defined reality, but rather remained a concept which could be stretched and applied in different ways. That the Wisdom of Solomon should therefore emerge as a distinctly hellenistic jewish writing is not an occasion for surprise. Wisdom could be looked upon as an abstract rational principle, as a code of moral practice, and also as a body of mathematical and physical laws affecting the structure and appearance of things without a sense of incompatibility between these different ideas showing through.

In examining the distinctively Israelite features of the growth and development of wisdom in Israel it is noteworthy that the belief that the rewards and experiences of individuals, as well as of whole communities, was controlled by demonstrable principles of righteousness and justice was of great importance. The belief that retribution by which individuals and communities eventually received their deserts was automatically operative remained a deeply felt principle akin to a kind of natural justice, and even a natural law (cf. Prov. 26:27). The wise believed that they could see such a principle operative in daily life and such an understanding of the principle of retribution seems to have provided a desirable framework for the development of historical narrative out of short anecdotal stories. The belief that such retribution should occur has lent a kind of enhanced beauty and didactic force whenever it became possible to string together stories to show that it had occurred. So it was that the inevitable final homecoming of the wrongdoer's deserts has provided the art of the narrator with a conventional and acceptable plot.

It is by appeal to this principle of retribution that Whybray (1968, pp. 56ff) has discerned a strong influence of the wisdom tradition upon the composition of the Succession Narrative in the books of 1 and 2 Samuel. This is probably to go too far in the direction of stressing some aspects of the rise of Israel's narrative tradition to the neglect of others. Nevertheless it is in any case probable that the scribal school of the Jerusalem court, which must have provided a central deposit for the emergent historical tradition of Israel, was influenced by the ideas of wisdom. It would be wrong to regard the concept of retribution as a uniquely wisdom concern, but it is certainly clear that the wisdom teachers did explore the workings of retribution in ways peculiar to themselves. History-writing itself required a certain type of wisdom, so that to be able to discern underneath the surface flow of events the principles of intelligence and justice which controlled their consequences was an ambition which the wise men of Israel could not conceivably have resisted. To this degree history-writing in ancient Israel probably owes as much to the wise as it did to prophecy.

## 3 SOLOMON AND WISDOM

Of all the features relating Israel's nurturing of wisdom to its own national tradition the feature that came to be most popularly accepted and developed was that which accorded to the royal figure of Solomon the role of chief founder and patron of wisdom. The precise reasons for the origin of this tradition of Solomonic patronage of wisdom has never been explained with complete satisfaction. Alt (1951) was particularly interested to note the tradition in 1 Kgs 4:31–4 concerning the nature and content of Solomon's reputation for wisdom. This claims that 'he spoke of trees, from the cedar that is in Lebanon to the hyssop that grows out of the wall; he spoke also of beasts, and of birds, and of reptiles, and of fish' (1 Kgs 4:33). This type of wisdom cataloguing of plant and animal life is well attested in Egypt from the *Onomastica* which represent such lists of naturally occurring features. Strikingly it is not otherwise independently attested in Israel from the surviving OT tradition so that the weight of Alt's contention for a Solomonic interest in it rests almost exclusively upon the uniqueness and unexpectedness of this claim on Solomon's behalf. It is thought to rest on an authentic basis because it stands somewhat apart from the more central features that came later to be more directly associated with Solomon's reputation for wisdom. Yet the case here is far from being conclusive and it is likely enough that, once Solomon had acquired a reputation for wisdom on other grounds, he should thereafter have been credited with a special eminence in this semi-scientific kind of wisdom.

Scott (1955, pp. 262ff), working from the preservation in the OT of a rather different item of evidence, which similarly appears quite unexpectedly, found in Prov. 25:1 a pointer to how the tradition about Solomon's wisdom arose. Since the men of Hezekiah 'copied out', or 'carried forward (? interpreted)' sayings attributed to Solomon, it may well have been the age of Hezekiah which was basically responsible for the tradition regarding Solomon's wisdom. However this rather circumstantial item of evidence from the book of Proverbs is certainly capable of being understood in other ways and does little more than affirm that, by Hezekiah's time, the tradition regarding Solomon's wisdom had become well established.

Two much broader avenues of understanding the tradition have for some time been extensively explored by scholars. The first of these concerns Solomon's undoubted connexions with Egypt through his marriage to an Egyptian princess (1 Kgs 3:1–2). Since the publication of a translation of the Teaching of Amenemope demonstrated close links between Israelite and Egyptian wisdom, it has been attractive to link Solomon's connexions with Egypt to his patronage of a tradition of wisdom teaching which had grown up in the culture of that country. It has then appeared comparably attractive to combine with this the claim that wisdom was especially nurtured among the ranks of the administrative officers of the Israelite state. Heaton therefore (1974, *passim*) argued that a remarkable convergence of evidence which has survived within the OT shows that 'Solomon's New Men' were responsible for introducing into Israel a complex and sophisticated administrative organisation for the state and added to this a powerful cultural impetus towards the nurturing of wisdom. For both developments, although they came to take on a distinctively Israelite character, the prototypes of Egyptian origin were encouraged through Solomon's reign. However, although some features of this reconstruction remain of great value for an understanding of Israel's nurturing of wisdom, it appears unlikely to represent more than a partial picture. Recently Rüterswörden (1985) has challenged the assumptions of a strong Egyptian background to the organisation of the Israelite state and, in any case, it appears highly probable that the intellectual, commercial and political contacts between Israel and Egypt in antiquity were a continuing factor. An influence from Egypt upon the rise and nurturing of wisdom in Israel is so certain as not to be a matter of continuing scholarly debate. Yet Israel's wisdom did not receive influences from this area alone, and contacts with Mesopotamia, as well as with the traditions and territories of Arabia (cf. 1 Kgs 9:16, 24; 11:1), were certainly in evidence. Wisdom itself was decidedly international in many of its most characteristic features. Furthermore, although some links with the circle of court officials and government administrators appears likely, wisdom was certainly not exclusive to them.

Much of the force and interest of Alt's contention regarding Solomon's wisdom is that it affirms a reason for understanding why Solomon should have been personally credited with an especial skill and insight in the composition of wisdom sayings. The tradition affirms that he himself was blessed with great insight (1 Kgs 3:3–15, 16–28) which enabled him to rule his kingdom with great skill and with the effect of bringing great prosperity. The historian clearly attached great importance to this personal reputation for wisdom which Solomon acquired (cf. 1 Kgs 10:1–10). Israel's memory of this king came to be heavily coloured by the desire to enhance his reputation for wisdom. To this extent we may suggest that it is this personal aspect of the tradition which should not be overlooked since, it may be argued, it is this claim which matters more than the unresolvable historical issue whether it first arose in Solomon's lifetime or came to be ascribed to him later. It is not at all difficult to see that there were very good reasons why it was necessary that the narrative tradition regarding Solomon, whose heavy exactions imposed upon his people provoked rebellion within his lifetime and a subsequent division of the kingdom (1 Kgs 11:14ff; 12:1ff), should have sought to foster a better image of him. The deuteronomic historian's concern for the unity of Israel and the divine election of the Davidic dynasty made it essential to present Solomon in as favourable a light as was possible. No doubt there arose at some stage a tradition regarding Solomon's wisdom that was fostered from within the Jerusalem court circle (cf. Prov. 25:1) and which was designed to honour the memory of this king. Such anecdotal stories as came to be told about him appear very much to be of the kind that could have been narrated of almost any king, since their primary role is that of enhancing the reputation of the royal office. It is highly probable, therefore, that it was primarily a feature of the deuteronomic historian's concern to rehabilitate the tarnished and compromised image of Solomon which made the emphasis upon his unique expertise in wisdom an important element in the recorded memory of this king.

So far as the composition of the late jewish writing The Wisdom of Solomon is concerned, the ascription of this to Solomon must have arisen as a consequence of the particular circumstances of its origin. Its markedly hellenistic character made it attractive for the writer to present his thoughts and apologetic for his hellenistic ideas under the guise of a venerable and highly esteemed name from the past. It is in the book of Ecclesiastes that the claim to Solomonic authorship takes on an interesting and elaborate role as part of the author's reflections about life. In Ecc. 1:12–2:26 the tradition concerning the purported origin from Solomon focuses upon the ruler's established reputation for wisdom and success. Hence it is that the claim that he possessed unique insight (1 Kings 3) is used to reflect upon the utility of great wisdom (Eccl. 1:12–18); the report of his many wives (1 Kgs 11:3) provides a basis for a reflection on the value of sensual pleasure (Eccl. 2:1–11); the overall picture of Solomon's reign and its consequences leads to a contemplation of the nature of folly, success and failure (cf. Eccl. 2:18–26). All of these themes, as used by the author of Ecclesiastes, indicate a writer who found in the traditions concerning Solomon excellent material on which to build his own disquisitions concerning the meaning and value of life. The king's reputation for wisdom, his great wealth and worldly success, his many wives and concubines, and the ultimate effect of his reign, all combined to make him an object for further thought and evaluation.

Bearing these considerations in mind it is evident that, however the tradition may have arisen in the first place (and this is clearly still not certainly known) the reputation of Solomon for wisdom provided a useful basis for further intellectual reflection. The deuteronomic historian has undoubtedly used the tradition in one direction in order to present the king in as favourable a light as the historical tradition would allow. Later, both the authors of Ecclesiastes and The Wisdom of Solomon have found in it a basis for wholly different developments of some of the fundamental themes of the pursuit of wisdom. The claim to great wisdom ascribed to Solomon came therefore to be a strong and interesting feature of the manner in which the later jewish schools of wisdom fastened upon and enriched a central affirmation belonging to Israel's historical record of the past.

Wisdom emerged in Israel with an already established set of aims and conventions which had their origin outside the nation. It came readily and effectively to find a home within Israel and, in the process, came to influence and modify the manner in which the older traditions of Israel were remembered and applied. The mythology about creation, the meaning and nature of God's *tôrâ* given to Israel, and the tradition about one of the most celebrated of Israel's kings, all came to experience major refashioning at the hands of the scribes of wisdom.

## BIBLIOGRAPHY

A. Alt 'Die Weisheit Salomos', *ThLZ* 76 (1951), cols. 139–44 = *Kleine Schriften zur Geschichte des Volkes Israel* ii (Munich, 1953), pp. 90–9.

G. A. Barton *The Book of Ecclesiastes*, ICC (Edinburgh, 1908).

R. E. Clements *Old Testament Theology. A Fresh Approach* (London, 1978).

J. L. Crenshaw 'The Shadow of Death in Qoheleth', in J. G. Gammie, W. A. Brueggemann, W. Lee Humphreys and J. M. Ward (eds.), *Israelite Wisdom. Theological and Literary Essays in Honor of Samuel Terrien* (Missoula, 1978), pp. 205–16.

*Old Testament Wisdom. An Introduction* (London, 1982).

A. H. Gardiner *Ancient Egyptian Onomastica* (London, 1947).

H. Gese 'The Crisis of Wisdom in Koheleth', in J. L. Crenshaw (ed.), *Theodicy in the Old Testament* (London, 1983), pp. 141–53 (English translation of 'Die Krisis der Weisheit bei Kohelet', in *Les Sagesses du Proche-Orient ancien* (Paris, 1963), pp. 139–51).

N. C. Habel *The Book of Job* (London, 1985).

E. W. Heaton *Solomon's New Men* (London, 1974).

A. Heidel *The Babylonian Genesis. The Story of the Creation*, 2nd edition (Chicago, 1951).

M. Hengel *Judaism and Hellenism* (London, 1974) (English translation of *Judentum und Hellenismus*, WUNT 10, 2nd edition (Tübingen, 1973)).

H.-J. Hermisson 'Weisheit und Geschichte', in H. W. Wolff (ed.), *Probleme biblischer Theologie* (Munich, 1971), pp. 136–54.

'Observations on the Creation Theology in Wisdom', in B. W. Anderson (ed.), *Creation in the Old Testament* (London, 1984), pp. 118–34 (first published in J. G. Gammie, W. A. Brueggemann, W. L. Humphreys and J. M. Ward (eds.), *Israelite Wisdom: Theological and Literary Essays in Honor of Samuel Terrien* (Missoula, 1978), pp. 43–57.

W. McKane *Prophets and Wise Men*, SBT 44 (London, 1965).

L. G. Perdue *Wisdom and the Cult*, SBLDS 30 (Missoula, 1977).

G. von Rad 'Job xxxviii and Ancient Egyptian Wisdom', in *The Problem of the Hexateuch and Other Essays* (Edinburgh and London, 1966), pp. 281–91 (English translation of 'Hiob xxxviii und die altägyptische Weisheit', SVT 3 (1955), pp. 293–301).

*Wisdom in Israel* (London, 1972) (English translation of *Weisheit in Israel* (Neukirchen-Vluyn, 1970)).

J. J. M. Roberts 'Job and the Israelite Religious Tradition', *ZAW* 89 (1977), 107–14.

H. Wheeler Robinson *Inspiration and Revelation in the Old Testament* (London, 1946).

U. Rüterswörden *Die Beamten des israelitischen Königszeit*, BWANT 117 (Stuttgart, 1985).

J. C. Rylaarsdam *Revelation in Jewish Wisdom Literature* (Chicago, 1946).

H. H. Schmid 'Creation, Righteousness and Salvation. "Creation Theology" as the Broad Horizon of Biblical Theology', in B. W. Anderson (ed.), *Creation in the Old Testament* (London, 1984), pp. 102–17 (English translation of 'Schöpfung, Gerechtigkeit und Heil', *ZThK* 70 (1973), 1–19 = *Altorientalische Welt in der alttestamentlichen Theologie* (Zürich, 1974), pp. 9–30).

R. B. Y. Scott 'Solomon and the Beginnings of Wisdom in Israel', SVT 3 (1955), 262–79.

*The Way of Wisdom* (New York, 1971).

G. T. Sheppard *Wisdom as a Hermeneutical Construct*, BZAW 151 (Berlin and New York, 1980).

M. Weinfeld *Deuteronomy and the Deuteronomic School* (Oxford, 1972).

R. N. Whybray *Wisdom in Proverbs*, SBT 45 (London, 1965).

*The Succession Narrative*, SBT, 2nd series 9 (London, 1968).

*The Intellectual Tradition in the Old Testament*, BZAW 135 (Berlin and New York, 1974).

E. Würthwein 'Der Sinn des Gesetzes im Alten Testament', *ZThK* 55 (1958), 255–70 = *Wort und Existenz. Studien zum Alten Testament* (Göttingen, 1970), pp. 39–54.

W. Zimmerli 'Zur Struktur der alttestamentlichen Weisheit', *ZAW* 51 (1933), 177–204 = ET 'Concerning the Structure of Old Testament Wisdom', in J. L. Crenshaw (ed.), *Studies in Ancient Israelite Wisdom* (New York, 1976), pp. 175–207.

*Das Buch des Prediger Salomo*, ATD 16/1 (Göttingen, 1962).

'Ort und Grenze der Weisheit im Rahmen der alttestamentlichen Theologie', in *Les Sagesses du Proche-Orient ancien* (Paris, 1963), pp.

121–36 = *Gottes Offenbarung. Gesammelte Aufsätze zum Alten Testament* (Munich, 1963), pp. 300–15; an abridged ET appeared as 'The Place and Limit of the Wisdom in the Framework of the Old Testament Theology', *SJTh* 17 (1964), 146–58 = J. L. Crenshaw (ed.), *Studies in Ancient Israelite Wisdom* (New York, 1976), pp. 314–26.

# Between the Testaments

# 6 · Translating the Old Testament

## S. P. BROCK

As anyone who attempts to translate a literary text rapidly comes to realise, translation inevitably involves interpretation; significantly enough, many of the words for 'translate', both in Greek and Latin, and in Hebrew and Aramaic, also mean 'interpret, explain' (ἑρμηνεύειν, *interpretari, targem, paššeq*). The translator of any ancient text, in particular, constantly finds himself obliged to decide between two (or more) exegetical possibilities. Thus, at the beginning of God's words to Cain in Gen. 4:7 הלוא אם תיטיב שאת the last word can be taken in (at least) four entirely different ways, even though there is no ambiguity over the identity of the root:

(1) *nāśāʾ* = 'raise up', i.e. 'offer'. Thus LXX προσενέγκῃς, taking *śʾt* as part of the protasis, 'If you offer well...'.

(2) *nāśāʾ* = 'lift up', i.e. 'accept'. This is reflected in different ways by Aquila's *ἄρσις (MSS ἀρέσεις, but see Gen. 49:3), Theodotion's δεκτόν, and Peshitta's *qabblet* 'I will certainly receive' (or 'I would have accepted'). The Vulgate's *recipies* may be a development of this, 'you will receive sc. a reward'. As with the next two interpretations, this takes *śʾt* as the apodosis of the conditional sentence.

(3) *nāśāʾ* = 'lift up', i.e. 'forgive'. This is found in Symmachus, ἀφήσω and the targumim (both Palestinian and Babylonian traditions), *yištbeq lāk*, 'it will be forgiven you'. (The Vulgate's *recipies* may belong here, with 'forgiveness' as the implied object.)

(4) *nāśāʾ* = 'lift up', i.e. 'suspend (judgment?)'. Thus the Samaritan targum *ʾtly*, 'I will suspend'.

Each of these four choices can claim to offer a reasonably close translation, given the oblique character of the Hebrew, yet each serves as the starting point for a different understanding of the episode.

The translator will likewise be forced to make a choice – and so introduce an element of interpretation – whenever the Hebrew text before him is capable of two (or more) different analyses, both consonant with the context. Such a case concerns the folk etymology given to the name 'Israel' in Gen. 32:28(29) – כי שרית עם אלהים. In the ancient versions we find the verb identified in three different ways:

87

(1)  *šrr* = 'be strong'. So LXX Theodotion ἐνίσχυσας, Peshitta *d-ʾeštarrart*, Vulgate *fortis fuisti*, and three manuscripts (EBN in Tal's edition) of the Samaritan targum *šarrīr (at)*.

(2)  *šrr/šrh* (denominative of *šār*) = 'rule'. So Aquila ἤρξας, Palestinian targum (and Samaritan targum MS A) *itrabrabt*, and Onqelos *rab at*.

(3)  *šrh* in the Aramaic sense of 'begin'. So Symmachus ἤρξω, and possibly Samaritan targum MS J *šryt*.

These two examples suffice to show how interpretation was imposed upon the translators every time they encountered an ambiguity in the source text and a choice had to be made. This is a dilemma which faces all biblical translators, ancient and modern, including those who, in their striving for literal translation, may imagine that they are thus avoiding any interpretative element (an illusory ideal). The perception of what the available choices are, however, will of course frequently differ between the ancient translator and his modern counterpart.

It is in cases where the provision of an interpretational element is *optional*, rather than required, that we are best able to discern the individual interests and concerns of a particular translator. Thus, for example, when confronted with a geographical name the translator may reproduce the Hebrew (sometimes in hellenised form, as *Tyros* for Hebrew *Ṣôr*), or he may introduce an interpretative element by 'updating' the geography, as at Gen. 8:4, Ararat:

(1)  Hebrew kept. Thus LXX and Samaritan targum MS J.
(2)  Identification made. Thus we have:
(a)  Qardu (in N Iraq). Thus Peshitta, Onqelos and the Palestinian targumim.
(b)  Armenia. Thus Ps. Jonathan (as a doublet) and Vulgate.
(c)  Serendib (i.e. Sri Lanka!). Thus Samaritan targum MS A.

In other passages where Ararat occurs (2 Kgs 19:37 = Isa. 37:38; Jer. 51:27) we find these options taken as follows:

|      | LXX | Pesh. | Vg. | Tg. Jonathan | A′ | S′ | Th′ |
|------|-----|-------|-----|--------------|----|----|----|
| Kgs  | 1   | 1     | 2b  | 2a           |    | 2b |    |
| Isa. | 2b  | 2a    | 1   | 2a           | 1  | 1  | 1  |
| Jer. | 1   | 1     | 1   | 2a           | 1  | 1  | 1  |

The frequency of this type of interpretation is much higher in some translators than others: while Isaiah LXX is exceptional among the Greek translators in having a large number of instances, this feature is common in the targumim (both Palestinian and Babylonian traditions). What distinguishes Tg. Onqelos and Tg. Jonathan, both here and elsewhere, is the consistency observed over a range of different books.

Another type of 'optional' interpretation, not infrequent in all the ancient versions, is to be found in passages where the translator chooses a particular rendering in order to point the reader to a specific understanding of the passage as a whole. Thus at Gen. 22:12 the Peshitta translated 'Now *I have made known* (ʾawdʿet; MT yādaʿtî 'I know') that you are a fearer of God...', implying a scenario for the aqedah similar to that provided by Job 1. Such a scenario is indeed explicitly found in Jub. 17:15–18:19, while in later midrashic tradition it reappears in modified form: it is to the angels or to the peoples of the world that God *makes known* Abraham's faith. Pointers to midrashic traditions have likewise been identified in several places in the LXX (e.g. Prijs, 1948; Gooding, 1969; Tov, 1978).

Numerous other levels of interpretation of this 'optional' variety can readily be identified, showing a whole range of different concerns on the part of the various translators. At one end of the scale we have minor clarifications of one sort or another, small glosses, removal of ambiguities, euphemisms, avoidance of phraseology considered inappropriate (e.g. varying sensitivities to anthropomorphisms), specialisation of vocabulary, identification of cultural equivalents etc. The majority of these are in fact features which were continuously affecting the Hebrew text itself as a result of scribal activity (e.g. Seeligmann, 1961; Barthélemy, 1982; pp. *78–*95; Tov, 1985). At the other end of the scale we have the deliberate imposition of novel and (to our eyes) forced interpretations, the rewriting of passages thought unsuitable, the introduction of matter which we would consider as belonging to commentary rather than translation, the alteration and updating of legal matters, the subtle and consistent imposing on to the biblical text of a particular *Weltanschauung*.

Interpretative renderings at the lower end of this scale occur to some degree in all the ancient biblical translations, including those which opt for a very literal style of translation technique (thus Aquila opts for a cultural equivalent when he renders ʾôb by μάγος). The *sustained* presence of interpretative renderings belonging to the top end of the scale, however, is characteristic only of the jewish targumim; this applies not only to the Palestinian targumim, but also to the Babylonian tradition, namely Onqelos and Jonathan, whose ideology has been largely shaped by R. Aqiba and his disciples (Aberbach and Grossfeld, 1982, p. 10; Smolar and Aberbach, 1983, p. 64). A concern for interpretation at this level is not typical of any of the translators whose work goes to make up the LXX and Peshitta, although examples of some of these types of interpretation can sporadically be found (e.g. Bickermann, 1956), and the seeds for some of the developments characteristic of the jewish targumim are certainly present in the earlier translations (Vermes, 1970; Le Déaut,

1971). It is true that in the past scholars have attributed to the translators of the LXX various major alterations of an editorial nature in order to explain the differences between LXX and MT, but a greater awareness of the translators' aims and methods (e.g. Rabin, 1968), and the new evidence from Qumran for the existence of a plurality of Hebrew text types prior to the standardisation of the consonantal text in the late first century AD, suggest that it is most unlikely that any of the LXX translators acted in a high-handed way with the texts they were rendering into Greek (Tov, 1981).

In order to help account for this radical difference between the LXX, Peshitta and Vulgate, on the one hand, and the Babylonian and Palestinian targum traditions on the other, in the type and level of interpretative translation employed, we need to try to ascertain something of the aims and self-awareness of these different translators (cf. Kelly, 1979, pp. 219–20). For this purpose it is necessary to look at biblical translation in antiquity from a wider perspective.

Whereas the earliest Greek translators were hampered by the lack of any precedent in their undertaking of a large-scale translation of an oriental religious text, by the end of the second century BC there had emerged an awareness that the original Greek translations of 'the law, prophets and other writings' did not represent the Hebrew originals sufficiently accurately (translator's preface to Sirach; for its significance see Barr, 1979, p. 317). It was this dissatisfaction which gave rise to the series of 'corrections' of the LXX, bringing it into closer line with the Hebrew, which culminated in the highly sophisticated literalism of Aquila in the early second century AD. Literal translation, working *verbum e verbo*, had come to be seen as the ideal for the 'faithful' biblical translator. This literalist ideal for biblical translation, which was to be taken over by the christian church (eventually to become the norm for virtually all translation until the end of the middle ages), happened to be diametrically opposed to the principles for translation of literary texts laid down by Cicero and Horace: their practice, as reformulated by Jerome in his important Letter 57, was to work *sensus de sensu*, in contrast to the despised *interpretes indiserti* who proceeded *verbum e verbo* in their renderings of official documents and such like (Brock, 1979).

The difference between these two approaches happens to be very clearly brought out in the preface to the ninth-century translation from Greek into Latin, made by John Scotus, of the Corpus attributed to Dionysius the Areopagite (Schwarz, 1944):

If someone should consider the translation opaque and obscure, he should realize that I am (just) the translator (*interpres*) of this work, and not its *expositor*.

In other words, the *interpres*, or literalist translator, does not regard it as his role to remove or elucidate the obscurities of the text he is translating, whereas the *expositor* will both translate and elucidate. Put differently, the *interpres* will be content (indeed, feel it his duty) to pass on to his readers a difficulty of the source text in the form of a nonsense translation, whereas such a procedure will be anathema to the *expositor*.

Underlying this contrast between the translator who acts as an *expositor* (the classical ideal for literary translation) and the one who works as an *interpres* (the emerging jewish and christian ideal for biblical translation) is an important difference of attitude: the interpretative *expositor* aims to bring the source text to his readers, whereas the literalist *interpres* seeks to bring the reader to the source text. The *interpres* deliberately renounces taking on the added interpretative role of the *expositor* (even though, as we have seen, literalist translation inevitably involves a certain level of interpretation).

Whether the *interpres* or the *expositor* is the more 'faithful' translator is not our concern here; it suffices to observe that virtually all biblical translators since the sixteenth century have reverted to the classical ideal of the translator as *expositor*, in sharp contrast to the practice of biblical translators in antiquity, who saw their role solely as that of the *interpres* – with one notable exception, namely the targumim, for reasons which will emerge below.

The earliest Greek translators of the Hebrew Bible of course did not have the benefit of a century or more's reflection on the proper role of the biblical translator, and this was why their work was considered in some circles to be in need of revision. The dilemma posed for diaspora Judaism by this new awareness of the differences between the LXX and its Hebrew original in fact gave rise to two courses of action: alongside those who set out to 'correct' the LXX texts, bringing them into closer line with an authoritative text form of the Hebrew, there were others who cut the Gordian knot by claiming an authority for the LXX Pentateuch equal to that of the Hebrew original. The first witness to this approach is provided by the so-called 'Letter' of Aristeas to Philocrates, probably dating from the later second century BC. The author cleverly undercuts the position of the would-be revisers by making a number of significant points. At the outset he acknowledges that copies of the Hebrew Pentateuch at Alexandria were not very accurate; it was an awareness of this state of affairs that led to the embassy to Jerusalem where the High Priest provided, not only an authoritative Hebrew manuscript from which to work, but also the translators – representing every tribe – to do the work. As a crowning point, it is asserted that, so accurate was their translation, that any subsequent revision (διασκευή) was totally unnecessary. The accompanying curse laid on those who dare to make any such changes was clearly aimed at those who were beginning to undertake the work of 'correcting' the LXX (cf. Brock, 1972; Barthélemy, 1974; Orlinsky, 1975).

This line of approach was taken a stage further by Philo who claims that those who know the two languages 'speak of the authors not as translators (ἑρμηνέας, corresponding in sense to the Latin *interpretes*), but as prophets and priests of the mysteries, whose sincerity and singleness of thought has enabled them to go hand in hand with the purest of spirits, the spirit of Moses' (*Life of Moses* ii, 40; tr. Colson).

By describing the translators as 'prophets' Philo was claiming that the Greek translation has an authority equal to that of the original: both original and translation are to be held in 'awe and reverence *as sisters*' (*ibid.*). On such a view (inherited by the early christian church) any observable differences between the Greek and the Hebrew were no longer a matter of concern, requiring correction on the ground that the translators had failed in what later generations saw as their proper role as merely *interpretes*, word for word translators: since they were in fact 'prophets', rather than *interpretes*, the translators could be regarded as having been in a position to act as authoritative expositors as well. In passing, it is worth noticing that this attitude to the LXX on the part of diaspora Judaism takes on a new significance (*mutatis mutandis*) in the context of modern discussion of 'scriptural authenticity', as opposed to 'literary authenticity', as a criterion for selecting a base text for modern translations (Barthélemy, 1982, Introduction, esp. pp. \*111–12).

Whereas the original translators of the LXX could (from our own perspective) be said to have acted unintentionally and in a haphazard way as *expositores* as well as *interpretes*, the translators who produced the Aramaic targumim seem to have been conscious of their role as *expositores*, rather than as mere *interpretes*, thus going against the ideal that had grown up in antiquity that the biblical translator should merely act as *interpres*, and not take on this added role of *expositor* as well. This can be said to apply to the 'literal' Babylonian targumim (Onqelos and Jonathan) just as much as to the expansive Palestinian tradition.

The reason for this surprising and anomalous state of affairs lies in the fact that the targumim were regularly read in the context of the Hebrew original: Hebrew and Aramaic texts were read in conjunction with the Hebrew, one verse at a time for the Pentateuch, three for the prophets/haftarah (*m. Meg.* 4:4; compare York, 1979; Alexander, 1985). This liturgical practice (which evidently did not obtain for any other ancient biblical translation) served to highlight the role of the Aramaic targum as an exposition or interpretation of the Hebrew, and not just as a translation. But in order to prevent the targum, *qua* interpretation, being accorded equal status with the Hebrew original, the use in synagogue of a written text of the targum was expressly forbidden (*b. Meg.* 32a; *y. Meg.* 4:1). Likewise the very layout of the written form of the targumim, as they come down to us, points to the consciously expositional character of these biblical versions: at the beginning of each verse the opening words of the Hebrew original are cited (a feature rarely reproduced in printed

# Translating the Old Testament

editions). Indeed one could speak of the targumim as constituting a unique species of commentary: the Hebrew lemma represents the text being commented upon, while the Aramaic translation (whether or not it is expanded) constitutes the commentary (cf. Vermes, 1970, p. 199 for the Palestinian targumim, and the title of a recent book by Rappel, 1985, on Onqelos). This 'commentary' may consist of two quite separate elements:

(1)   In so far as the targum represents a translation (whether literal or not), this translation will correspond in function to the translations given by modern editors of Greek papyri, whose purpose is essentially to serve as a commentary, in succinct form, on how the editor understands his (often fragmentary and obscure) text.

(2)   Where, however, the targum provides an expansion (as is most notably and frequently the case in the Palestinian targumim), this expansion could be said to correspond to modern commentaries, which are likewise selective in their choice of passages upon which they comment at greater length.

Looked at from this point of view, although on the one hand the targumist shares with the modern translator a concern for an expositional type of translation, on the other hand he differs from his modern counterpart in that the latter will not include the targumist's second element, for the simple reason that supplementary 'commentary' of this sort has, in the intervening period, developed into an independent genre, and so become inappropriate to the work of the translator.

Two examples will suffice to illustrate the element of commentary incorporated into the targum tradition (Babylonian, as well as Palestinian). At the end of Gen. 6:3 God states והיו ימיו מאה ועשרים שנה, 'and his days shall be 120 years'. Although the earlier part of the verse poses well-known problems (variously solved in the ancient versions), this last element does not provide the translator with any difficulty, and the LXX, Peshitta and Vulgate all translate the Hebrew word for word. The only obscurity lies in the identity of the persons referred to in 'his days' (the suffix refers back to ʾādām earlier in the verse): is it humanity in general, or just the generation that preceded the flood? The Peshitta does not resolve this ambiguity of the Hebrew, and by translating yādôn with 'dwell', it opens up the way for a drastic exegesis found in some later Syriac liturgical texts: God henceforth removed his Spirit from humanity, only to return it at Pentecost (Siman, 1971, pp. 44–6). The LXX, on the other hand, by adding τούτοις to ἐν τοῖς ἀνθρώποις, limits the reference to the immediate context of the pre-flood generation. The targumim, however, not only go a stage further by identifying ʾādām as 'this generation', but they also provide a commentary to explain the purpose of the 120 years; this is found in two related forms:

93

(1) Onqelos: 'a span is granted them of 120 years, if (= in case) they repent'.

(2) Palestinian targumim: 'behold, I have granted them a span of 120 years in case they might perform repentance, but they failed to do so'.

For the commentary form of this particular exegesis (found in many sources, both jewish and christian: Ginzberg, 1968, V p. 174) one can compare Ephrem (d. 373), *Comm. Gen.* vi. 4:

'let his days be 120 years', for if they have repented during these then they will have been delivered from the wrath which is about to come upon them; and if they do not repent, they will invite it upon themselves. For Grace gave to them 120 years – to a generation which would not have been held worthy of repentance by Justice.

For a second example Isa. 53:5 will serve (compare Koch, 1972, pp. 135–6). Although Tg. Jonathan identifies the 'servant' as the messiah at 52:14, by a remarkable tour de force of exegesis any idea of a suffering messiah in chap. 53 is rigorously avoided, by allocating the suffering to Israel. At 53:5 the Hebrew reads:

והוא מחלל מפשעינו מדכא מעונתינו

מוסר שלומנו עליו ובחברתו נרפא לנו

Both LXX and Peshitta render the Hebrew reasonably closely, but if we turn to the targum we find that a radical transformation is effected by means of small additions (in brackets) and the alteration of some suffixes (italics):

And he (will rebuild the sanctuary which) was profaned by our sins, handed over by our wickedness, and at (his) teaching *his* peace (will abound) upon *us*; and when *we* incline (to his words, our sins) will be forgiven us.

As far as the translation proper is concerned Tg. Jonathan has deliberately taken certain exegetical options which go against the understanding of the Hebrew which has otherwise become traditional, in particular: *mḥll* is derived from *ḥll* III 'profane' (so too Aquila), rather than *ḥll* I 'pierce, wound'; *wbḥbrtw* is taken as a derivative of *ḥābēr* 'associate' (i.e. 'in association with him'), rather than as *ḥabbûrâ* 'stripe'.

It is significant that the sophisticated literalism of Aquila and the expositional approach of the targumim both, in their different ways, are constantly pointing their readers/hearers back to the Hebrew original – Aquila by his deferential attitude to the Hebrew (δουλεύων τῇ Ἑβραικῇ λέξει, as Origen, *Ep. Afric.* 4, put it), and the targumim by their symbiotic role with the Hebrew original, expressed both in the way in which they were used in synagogue and by their format in writing.

It is of importance to note at this point that none of the Aramaic biblical translations from Qumran (4QTgLev; 4QTgJob; 11QTgJob) yet exhibit the format of the later targum tradition as it comes down to us, giving the Hebrew *incipit* for each verse. Indeed, to judge by the character of the translation in 11QTgJob (the only extensive set of fragments), the translator evidently saw himself solely as *interpres*, and not yet as *expositor* as well. Until recently the earliest textual evidence for the combining of the Aramaic translation with its Hebrew original came from the Geniza fragments, of which the oldest (Kahle's MS A) is dated to the seventh or eighth century. Considerably earlier evidence now happens to be available from an unexpected source: a unique magic bowl, found during excavations at Nippur, contains a collection of biblical quotations in Hebrew from Ezek. 21:21–3 and Jer. 2:1–3, two verses of which are followed by the Aramaic translation (basically identical with Tg. Jonathan). The bowl has been provisionally dated to *ca.* 350–500 AD (Kaufman, 1973).

The evidence of the Qumran fragments of Aramaic translations of the Bible thus suggests that the double phenomenon that we find in the Babylonian and Palestinian targum traditions, of the symbiosis of the Aramaic translation with its Hebrew original, and of the resulting new role of the translation as exposition, is a development subsequent to the period of the Qumran texts. If this was indeed the case, it would then seem likely that this important development is to be associated with the process of standardising the Hebrew biblical text and the reshaping of Judaism in the aftermath of the destruction of the second temple in 70 AD. This is not to deny that the common roots of the extant Palestinian and Babylonian targum traditions may not go back earlier, but if they do (as indeed seems likely), and if these Aramaic translations originally circulated *independently* of the Hebrew (as did 11QTgJob at Qumran), then, with the perspective offered here, our expectations will be that the translators will have seen their role solely as *interpretes*, and not yet as *expositores*. It would, incidentally, be from these same roots that the Peshitta Pentateuch is likely to have emerged. A development such as the one just outlined here would in fact fit well into the picture emerging from recent studies of the interrelationship and prehistory of the extant targum traditions (cf. Le Déaut, 1966, p. 122 [schema]; Schäfer, 1980).

Having emphasised the basic difference of approach between the translator who sees himself solely as *interpres* and the translator who consciously takes on the role of *expositor* as well, we also need to remember that in actual practice, between the two extremes of the work of the most conscientious and self-effacing *interpres* and the most self-confident expositional translator there is going to be a continuum in the amount of interpretation that can be observed in the various translation styles, just as there is a continuum between the poles of 'literal' and 'free' translation (Barr, 1979). What distinguishes the two approaches is that, in the case of the *interpres*, the interpretational element is either necessarily imposed upon him by the ambiguity of the original Hebrew, or, when the introduction of this element is optional, it features only sporadically and in a limited way, perhaps often occurring at a subconscious level; whereas in the case of the *expositor* the interpretational element is deliberately and usually consistently introduced. With *both* approaches we can readily acknowledge the truth of the observation that 'the ancient versions of the Bible are themselves also part of exegetical literature' (Vermes, 1970, p. 203).

The abundance and richness of exegetical traditions embedded in the ancient versions still remain to be fully explored. Many fruitful beginnings have been made, but a systematic study, in the form of a compendium, along the lines of Ginzberg's *The Legends of the Jews*, remains a task for the future. Such a compendium might be expected to provide a summary listing, verse by verse for each book, of the different interpretational options followed by the ancient translators, together with references to support for these options to be found in other early exegetical sources, both jewish and christian. It goes without saying that such an undertaking can only take place if the ancient versions are regarded as worth studying in their own right, and not merely as appendages to the study of the Hebrew text.

The particular perspective on the ancient versions offered in this chapter could be set out schematically as follows:

| Period | Style of translation | Trends and texts |
|---|---|---|
| 3rd cent. BC | Inconsistent | Earliest translations into Greek. |
| 2nd cent. BC to 2nd cent. AD | Ideal of literal translation (translator as *interpres*) | GREEK: the new ideal results in *either* correction of LXX (thus Aquila and predecessors), *or* LXX seen as authoritative in its own right (thus Ps. Aristeas, Philo and church fathers, apart from Jerome). |
| | | ARAMAIC: *Earlier*: translator acts as *interpres* (thus 11QTgJob, Peshitta, Samaritan targum, and probably the hypothetical proto-Palestinian targum/proto-Onqelos); *Later*: the translation co-exists in a symbiotic relationship with the Hebrew original, by now in a standardised text form; the translation is seen as commentary (which may be extended in places) alongside, and on, the Hebrew. Thus the extant Palestinian and Babylonian targum traditions (with the commentary element much fuller in the former). |
| 2nd cent. AD to 7th cent. | Inconsistent beginnings followed by ideal of literal translation (Jerome). | SUBSEQUENT CHRISTIAN BIBLICAL TRANSLATION (from Greek into Latin, Syriac, Armenian, Coptic etc.): ideal of translator as *interpres* gradually emerges, leading to 'correction' of earliest versions, bringing them into ever closer line with the Greek. Process well exemplified in history of Syriac NT text (Brock, 1983): Old Syriac (3rd cent.?), Peshitta (*ca.* 400), Philoxenian (507/8), Harklean (615/6). |

Translating the Old Testament

In conclusion a final observation is not out of place. Given that an element of interpretation is inherent in all translation, this means that the qualifications for good biblical translation will not be confined to the appropriate linguistic and textual skills and knowledge (though this is obviously a *sine qua non*): the translator must also have insight into, and empathy with, the biblical texts he is translating – or, as Philo put it in the passage quoted above, the translator needs to have that 'sincerity and singleness of thought' which will enable him 'to go hand in hand with the purest of spirits, the spirit of Moses'. Although it can be claimed that modern translators are often better equipped in the former respect than their predecessors in antiquity, it would be arrogant to assume that they excel them in the latter respect as well. And this of course is another reason why the ancient versions still retain their interest today.

BIBLIOGRAPHY

M. Aberbach and B. Grossfeld *Targum Onkelos to Genesis* (New York, 1982).

P. S. Alexander 'The Targumim and the Rabbinic Rules', SVT 36 (1985), 14–28.

J. Barr *The Typology of Literalism in Ancient Biblical Translations* (Nachrichten der Akademie der Wissenschaften in Göttingen, phil.-hist. Kl. Nr. 11 = Mitteilungen des Septuaginta-Unternehmens (MSU) xv, 1979).

D. Barthélemy 'Pourquoi la Torah a-t-elle été traduite en grec?', in *On Language, Culture, and Religion: in Honor of Eugene E. Nida* (The Hague, 1974), pp. 23–41, = *Études d'histoire du texte de l'Ancien Testament*, Orbis Biblicus et Orientalis 21 (Freiburg and Göttingen, 1978), pp. 322–40.
*Critique textuelle de l'Ancien Testament* 1, Orbis Biblicus et Orientalis 50/1 (Freiburg and Göttingen, 1982).

E. J. Bickermann 'Two Legal Interpretations of the LXX', *Revue internationale des droits de l'antiquité* 3 (1956), 81–104.

S. P. Brock 'The Phenomenon of the Septuagint', *OTS* 17 (1972), 11–36.
'Aspects of Translation Technique in Antiquity', *Greek Roman and Byzantine Studies* 20 (1979), 69–87 = *Syriac Perspectives on Late Antiquity* (London, 1984), chap. 3.
'Towards a History of Syriac Translation Technique', in R. Lavenant (ed.), *IIIe Symposium Syriacum*, Orientalia Christiana Analecta 221 (Rome, 1983), pp. 1–14.

L. Ginzberg *The Legends of the Jews* (Philadelphia, 1968).

D. W. Gooding 'Problems of Text and Midrash in the Third Book of Reigns', *Textus* 7 (1969), 1–29.

S. A. Kaufman 'A Unique Magic Bowl from Nippur', *JNES* 32 (1973), 170–4.

L. G. Kelly *The True Interpreter* (Oxford, 1979).

K. Koch 'Messias und Sündenvergebung in Jesaja 53-Targum', *JSJ* 3 (1972), 117–48.

R. Le Déaut *Introduction à la littérature targumique* 1 (Rome, 1966). 'Un phénomène spontané de l'herméneutique juive ancienne, le targumisme', *Biblica* 52 (1971), 505–25.

H. M. Orlinsky 'The Septaugint as Holy Writ and the Philosophy of the Translators', *HUCA* 46 (1975), 89–114.

L. Prijs *Jüdische Tradition in der Septuaginta* (Leiden, 1948).

Ch. Rabin 'The Translation Process and the Character of the Septuagint', *Textus* 6 (1968), 1–26.

D. Rappel *Targûm ʾOnqělôs kě-pêrûš la-Tôrâ* (Tel Aviv, 1985).

P. Schäfer 'Targumim', *TRE* 6 (1980), pp. 216–28.

W. Schwarz 'The Meaning of *fidus interpres* in Medieval Translation', *JTS* 45 (1944), 73–8.

I. L. Seeligmann 'Indications of Editorial Alteration and Adaptation in the MT and the LXX', *VT* 11 (1961), 201–21.

E.-P. Siman *L'expérience de l'Esprit par l'Église d'après la tradition syrienne d'Antioche* (Paris, 1971).

L. Smolar and M. Aberbach *Studies in Targum Jonathan to the Prophets* (New York, 1983).

E. Tov 'Midrash-type Exegesis in the LXX of Joshua', *RB* 85 (1978), 50–61. *The Text-Critical Use of the Septuagint in Biblical Research* (Jerusalem, 1981). 'The Nature and Background of Harmonizations in Biblical Manuscripts', *JSOT* 31 (1985), 3–29.

G. Vermes 'Bible and Midrash: Early Old Testament Exegesis', in P. R. Ackroyd and C. F. Evans (eds.), *The Cambridge History of the Bible* 1, *From the Beginnings to Jerome* (Cambridge, 1970), pp. 199–231.

A. D. York 'The Targum in the Synagogue and in the School', *JSJ* 10 (1979), 74–86.

# 7 · Retelling the Old Testament

## PHILIP S. ALEXANDER

### I    THE 'REWRITTEN BIBLE': THE PROBLEM

W ITHIN the corpus of post-biblical jewish literature are a number of texts devoted to retelling in their own words the story of the Bible. These texts are often treated as constituting a literary genre, for which the titles 'rewritten Bible' (Vermes, 1973, pp. 67–126) and 'texte continué' (Perrot and Bogaert, 1976, pp. 22–8) have been proposed. This type of composition has been briefly defined as 'a narrative that follows Scripture but includes a substantial amount of supplements and interpretative developments' (Vermes in Schürer, 1986, p. 326). Much has been written about the content of these texts – its relationship to Scripture and to the midrashic tradition as a whole. Little, however, has been said about their formal literary characteristics. The supposed genre as such remains ill-defined. No one has yet established the differentia of the genre, or compared and contrasted it with the other genres attested in early jewish literature. This lack of clarity becomes obvious once we raise the question of which texts belong to the genre. There is little agreement. Vermes (in Schürer, 1986, pp. 308–41) includes the following: Jubilees; Genesis Apocryphon; Pseudo-Philo's *Liber Antiquitatum Biblicarum*; the Book of Noah (1Q19,19bis = 1QNoah); the Testament of Kohath (4QTQahat); the Testament of Amram (4QAmram[a-e]); the Samuel Apocryphon (4Q160 = 4QVisSamuel); the Martyrdom of Isaiah; and Josephus' *Jewish Antiquities* (cf. p. 326). Nickelsburg (1984), however, produces a rather different list: 1 Enoch 6–11; 1 Enoch 12–16; 1 Enoch 65–67 and 83–84; 1 Enoch 106–107; the Book of Giants (4QHenGiants[a-f]); Jubilees, Genesis Apocryphon; Pseudo-Philo's *Liber Antiquitatum Biblicarum*; Apocalypse of Moses; Vita Adae et Evae; Philo the Epic Poet; Theodotus the Epic Poet; Ezekiel the Tragedian; 1 Esdras 3–4 (the story of Darius's bodyguards); the Additions to Esther; the catalogue of David's compositions in 11QPs[a] 27:2–11; 1 Baruch; the Epistle of Jeremiah; the Prayer of Azariah and the Song of the Three Young Men.

The aim of the present chapter is to study the use of the OT in, and thus to advance the definition of, the rewritten Bible type of text – to establish criteria for admission to, or exclusion from the genre. Our method of proceeding will be simple. We shall focus attention on four works normally included in the genre (Jubilees, Genesis Apocryphon, the *Liber Antiquitatum*

*Biblicarum*, and Josephus' *Jewish Antiquities*), and analyse these with respect to their form, their attitude towards the authority of the Bible, their use of biblical and non-biblical material, and their exegetical methods. On the basis of this analysis we shall try to decide if these texts do constitute a meaningful literary genre, and, if they do, what the distinctive characteristics of that genre might be. (Chronicles, arguably the prototype of all the rewritten Bible texts, lies outside the scope of the present chapter, but cf. chap. 2 above.)

## 2 THE 'REWRITTEN BIBLE': FOUR CASE STUDIES

### (a) *Jubilees*

Jubilees, the oldest of our four rewritten Bible texts (dating from *ca.* 150 BC) contains an extensive reworking of Gen. 1:1–Exod. 16:1.[1] Unlike some of the other works belonging to this group (notably Pseudo-Philo), it attempts to define its relationship to Scripture. Jubilees lays claim to high status and authority. It states that the angel of the presence – acting on God's express orders (Jub. 2:1) – dictated its contents to Moses during the forty days he was on Sinai to receive the law (cf. Jub. 1:1–4 with Exod. 24:12–18). The reader is never allowed to forget that this is the setting of the text: the narrative is regularly punctuated by first-person interventions by the angel, and passages in the second-person addressed by the angel to Moses.

The import of such a claim is clear: Jubilees puts itself on a par with Scripture; it carries its own origins back to the same supreme moment of revelation that gave birth to the canonical Pentateuch. Jubilees did not, however, intend to supplant the Pentateuch, but rather to supplement and to explain it. This emerges from Jub. 6:2: 'I (the angel of the presence) have written in the book of the first law which I have written for you, that you should celebrate it (the Festival of Shavuot) at its proper time, on one day of the year, and I have explained to you the details of its sacrifices, so that the sons of Israel may remember it and celebrate it in every generation, on this month, on one day every year.' The canonical Pentateuch is 'the first law', Jubilees (by implication) the 'second law'. Both are divine in origin, both given to Moses on Sinai: the latter contains the authoritative interpretation of the former (cf. Jub. 1:1; 6:11; 30:12, 21; 50:6). Jubilees, then, does not present itself as a self-sufficient statement of the law. Throughout it presupposes and alludes to Scripture; it was meant to be read side by side with Scripture.

There are similarities here to the rabbinic doctrine of the two torahs. The rabbis too claimed that Moses received on Sinai more than the canonical Pentateuch. He too was given the authoritative interpretation of the law. The only difference is that the rabbis insisted that their 'second torah' was passed down through the centuries from Moses as an oral tradition, whereas for the author of Jubilees the 'second torah' took the form of a book, comparable to the Pentateuch itself, and like the Pentateuch written in Hebrew.

Up to this point Jubilees' doctrine of torah is reasonably clear. But now some obvious questions arise: How could an author writing in the second century BC seriously claim Mosaic authorship for his work? How did he suppose that the book which he was presenting to the public had been passed down from Moses' time to his own? To these questions Jubilees does not give straight answers, but it does throw out some suggestive hints. Jubilees appears to draw a distinction between a text written on Sinai by Moses himself (= Jubilees) and a text written by the angel of the presence (= the Pentateuch).[2] This distinction may allude to the fact that while Exod. 24:12 speaks of *God* writing on the tablets, in Exod. 34:27 it is *Moses* who is said to write. Following typically midrashic reasoning Jubilees sees in this discrepancy evidence that *two* torahs were given to Moses on Sinai. But how could the author of Jubilees claim that his work represented that other torah alluded to in the canonical Pentateuch? We should not jump too quickly to the conclusion that he was simply a charlatan who deliberately tried to pass off one of his own compositions as the work of Moses – not if there are other explanations available. Nor should we suppose that the author of Jubilees used pseudepigraphy purely as a literary device (which his audience were expected to see through), in order to present his material in a certain way. The claim to Mosaic origin seems much too serious for that. It is possible he believed himself an inspired interpreter of Scripture, like the Teacher of Righteousness at Qumran (1QpHab 7:4–5; cf. 4 Ezra 14:21–6). The likeliest explanation is, however, that he was the recipient of certain traditions which he honestly supposed went back to Moses himself. He alludes from time to time to extra-canonical books or teachings passed down from the patriarchs. Jub. 45:16 is especially noteworthy: 'He (Israel) gave all his books and his fathers' books to his son Levi to preserve them and keep them in repair (or: have fresh copies made of them; literally: renew them) for his children till today' (cf. 10:14). Behind Jubilees may lie ideas similar to those found in 4 Ezra 14:5–6: 'I (God) led him (Moses) up on Mount Sinai, where I kept him with me many days; and I told him many wondrous things, and showed him the secrets of the times, and declared to him the end of the times. Then I commanded him saying, "These you shall publish openly, and these you shall keep secret"' (cf. 4 Ezra 14:23–6, 42–8). The author of Jubilees may have felt that he was simply collecting and editing the esoteric traditions that had been faithfully passed down in priestly circles from the time of Moses to his own day. In view of the imminence of the end he was publishing the esoteric torah for the good of all Israel.

The manner in which Jubilees handles Scripture, and generates its material, may be illustrated from two passages: (1) Jub. 8:10–10:35 = Gen. 10:1–11:19; and (2) Jub. 33:1–20 = Gen. 35:22.

(i) *Jubilees 8:10–10:35 = Genesis 10:1–11:19*. Jubilees skilfully weaves into a coherent whole these two rather disparate chapters of the Bible, the first of which contains the genealogies of the sons of Noah (Genesis 10), the second the episode of the Tower of Babel (Genesis 11). According to Jubilees Genesis 10 refers to a formal division of the world among the sons of Noah which took place after the flood. This division is dated to the time of the birth of Peleg, whose name (derived from the root *pālag*, 'to divide') alludes to the event. (Cf. the use of the name Reu in Jub. 10:18 to date the Tower of Babel.) The sons of Noah did not, however, immediately occupy their territories. Instead they journeyed eastwards from Ararat to the land of Shinar, where they built the Tower of Babel. It was only after God had confounded their speech that they were compelled to scatter to their allotted territories.

Jubilees' interpretation of the table of the nations in Genesis 10 shows clear signs of hellenistic influence. Jubilees has tried to harmonise Genesis 10 with the Ionian world-map, the dominant type of world-map in the popular Greek geography of its day. The territories of the three sons of Noah have been correlated with the three continents of the Ionian geographers: Japhet = Europe; Shem = Asia; Ham = Africa. The correlation is proved by the fact that the boundaries between Shem, Ham and Japhet's allotments in Jubilees correspond to the boundaries between the continents as laid down by the Ionian geographers. Such a neat equation doubtless appealed to the author of Jubilees' penchant for schematisation, and to his love of symmetry. Here his material has been generated by the desire to contemporise Genesis 10, and to harmonise the Bible with science (see further Alexander, 1982).

The treatment of the table of the nations also betrays strong polemical overtones. The correlation of the sons of Noah with the Ionian continents created two anomalies: Madai the son of Japhet and Canaan the son of Ham both historically ended up residing within the patrimony of Shem. As to Madai, Jubilees states that he simply did not like his allotted territory in north-west Europe, so 'he begged a portion from Elam and Asshur and Arpachshad, his wife's brother, and he dwelt in the land of Media, near to his wife's brother until this day' (Jub. 10:35). In other words he took up his new domicile by peaceful agreement with his neighbours. Canaan, by way of contrast, refused to go into his allotted territory (located in the vicinity of Carthage in north Africa). Instead he usurped 'the land of Lebanon to the river of Egypt', thus bringing down upon his head the curse pronounced on those who violated the boundaries solemnly sworn to in the presence of Noah (Jub. 8:10–11; 9:14–15; 10:30–2). The powerful anti-Canaanite thrust of this section, coupled with the assertion of the rights of Shem's descendants to the 'land of Canaan', should surely be seen as propaganda for the territorial expansion of the Hasmonean state.[3]

Jubilees follows more or less faithfully the sequence of the biblical narrative, but in a selective fashion: some sections it expands, some it abbreviates, some it omits altogether. The most notable omission in the section under consideration is Gen. 10:8–12 on Nimrod. In rabbinic aggadah Nimrod plays a leading role in the building of the Tower of Babel (see Ginzberg, 1968, I, pp. 178–81, and V, pp. 201–4). He is totally missing from the Jubilees account. In this instance we have a minus in the text of Jubilees. In the case of Jub. 10:1–14, on Noah and the demons, by contrast, we have a plus: there is no way this material could have been generated from Scripture. It has long been recognised that Jubilees is here quoting from a lost Book of Noah (cf. Charles, 1902, p. 78, who also identifies Jub. 7:20–39 as a fragment of the Book of Noah, and Vermes in Schürer, 1986, pp. 332–3). Here, then, is a piece of evidence that Jubilees was in possession of extra-biblical sources. The way it integrates those sources into its retelling of the biblical story suggests it regarded them as on a par with Scripture. Where relevant it uses them to supplement, or throw light on, the biblical narrative. Its canon of sacred Scripture was wider than the Pentateuch, and apparently embraced works attributed to Noah, and possibly to Enoch as well.

(ii) *Jubilees 33:1–20 = Genesis 35:22.* Jub. 33:1–20 illustrates another type of expansion of the biblical text – the sermonic. Jubilees hangs on Gen. 35:22's reference to Reuben's incest with Bilhah a vehement sermon against incest in particular, and sexual immorality in general (Jub. 33:10–20). The sermon opens (Jub. 33:1–10) with a vivid retelling of the story which fleshes out, in an aggadic manner, all the dramatic details so patently absent from the brief, enigmatic biblical account: How did Reuben come to be attracted to Bilhah? How was the deed accomplished? Was Bilhah a willing partner? What was Jacob's reaction when he 'heard of it'? This opening serves as a *captatio benevolentiae* to gain the reader's interest. The sermon was doubtless aimed at the author of Jubilees' contemporaries, who, presumably in his view, needed its message. But it was also inspired by an exegetical problem. The punishment for incest, as Jubilees itself recognises, is death for both parties (Lev. 20:11). Though Jacob expresses displeasure at Reuben's behaviour (Jub. 33:8), neither Reuben nor Bilhah was put to death. Was, then, so fundamental a law inoperative at the time of the patriarchs? Might not this text be used to excuse incest? It is to these problems that Jub. 35:15–16 is addressed: 'Let no one say, Reuben was granted life and forgiveness after he had lain with his father's concubine, and so also was Bilhah, although she had a husband, and her husband Jacob (Reuben's father) was still alive. For at that time the ordinance and the decree and the law in its completeness, to cover every case, had not been revealed; but in your (Moses') days it has been revealed as a law for all times and seasons, and as an everlasting law for all generations for ever.'

### (b) Genesis Apocryphon

The fragmentary state of the Aramaic Genesis Apocryphon from Qumran makes analysis of its relationship to the Bible difficult. The decipherable portions seem to follow Genesis from the birth of Noah (Gen. 5:28) down to God's promise to Abraham of a son and heir (Gen. 15:4). It is far from clear how extensive the full text was. The title *Genesis* Apocryphon may be misleading in this regard since there is no proof that the original work covered the whole of Genesis, or, for that matter, confined itself to Genesis. As it stands Genesis Apocryphon falls into two parts: (a) from column 2 down to column 21:22 we seem to have a series of 'autobiographies' of the patriarchs in which they recount their experiences in the first person; (b) from 21:22 on, however, in the middle of the Abraham section, the narrative suddenly switches to the third person. In the second part Genesis Apocryphon follows the Bible much more closely than in the first. There are passages in the second part which are almost literal translation of the original, and close in form to the Aramaic targumim. The first part, however, contains considerable quantities of expansive aggadah which appears to have little or no basis in the text of Scripture, but belongs to the same sort of legendary material as is found in the quotation from the Book of Noah in Jub. 10:1–14.

Genesis Apocryphon probably dates from after the Book of Jubilees (see the discussion by Vermes in Schürer, 1986, pp. 318–25. The fullest discussion of its genre is in Fitzmyer, 1971, pp. 5–12). Like Jubilees it can be seen basically as an interpretative paraphrase of the Bible. Like Jubilees it presupposes the biblical text and is addressed to an audience which will have the biblical text in mind. Note, for example, how the extreme abbreviation at 1QGenAp. 21:5 implies a knowledge of the biblical story. Unlike Jubilees Genesis Apocryphon is in Aramaic. This gives it a greater distinctness from the biblical text, and avoids the risk of confusing it with Scripture. It is probable that Genesis Apocryphon, unlike Jubilees, made no exalted claims to divine inspiration.

Genesis Apocryphon's detailed handling of the text of Scripture may be illustrated from 1QGenAp. 20:33–22:26 (= Gen. 13:1–14:24) – a passage from the Abraham cycle which covers the 'join' between the first- and third-person narratives.

*1QGenAp. 20:33–22:26 = Genesis 13:1–14:24*. Genesis Apocryphon gives a well thought out and remarkably scholarly reading of this section of Genesis.

The care with which its author worked is exemplified by the attention he gave to geographical detail. He had a considerable knowledge of the geography of Syria-Palestine, and he used that knowledge to good effect.

God's command to Abram in Gen. 13:14 to survey the land which he will give to Abram's descendants allows Genesis Apocryphon to name some of the principal boundaries of the land and to block in some of its major regions. Abram says: 'I looked at the land...from the River of Egypt to Lebanon and Senir, and from the Great Sea to Hauran, and all the land of Gebal as far as Kadesh, and at all the Great Desert which is to the east of Hauran and Senir as far as the Euphrates' (1QGenAp. 21:10-12). Though the Bible does not say so, Genesis Apocryphon reasonably infers that such an overview implies that Abram is up a height. Since Gen. 13:3 locates Abram at this moment at Bethel, Genesis Apocryphon has him ascend the highest peak in the vicinity, Ramath Ḥazor = Baʿal Ḥazor (2 Sam. 13:23), some five miles north-east of Bethel.

Genesis Apocryphon's response to the divine command to Abram to 'walk through the land' (Gen. 13:17) is to send Abram on a circuit round the borders of his patrimony – perhaps in a symbolic act of claiming the territory as his own. He starts out from the River Gihon (= the Nile), moves north along the coast of the Mediterranean till he reaches the Mount of the Bull (ṭūr ṭōrāʾ), i.e. the Taurus range which according to the ancient geographers extended across the centre of Asia in an east–west direction. He turns eastwards along the Mount of the Bull till he reaches the Euphrates, follows the Euphrates down to the 'Red Sea' (yammāʾ śimmōqāʾ), the Erythraean Sea of the Greeks, i.e. the Persian Gulf and the Indian Ocean. He then moves westwards till he reaches the tongue of the 'Reed Sea' (yam sūph) 'which goes out from the Red Sea' (either the present-day Red Sea, or the Gulf of Aqaba), and from there returns to the River Gihon (1QGenAp. 21:15-19). This is a clearly visualised and coherent geographical image which in its use of the terms ṭūr ṭōrāʾ and yammāʾ śimmōqāʾ probably betrays a knowledge of Greek geography.

Genesis Apocryphon's account of the war of the four kings against the five (Genesis 14) shows particular interest in the geography of the campaigns. 'Chedorlaomer, king of Elam' is left as in the biblical text, probably because the location of Elam was self-evident to the author of Genesis Apocryphon. However, Chedorlaomer is moved to the head of the list because the subsequent biblical account makes it clear that he was the leader of the northern confederacy. 'Amraphel, king of Shinar' becomes 'Amraphel, king of Babylon'. The equation of Shinar with Babylon can be made on the basis of Gen. 10:10 and 11:2-9. 'Arioch, king of Ellasar' becomes 'Arioch, king of Cappadocia'. The identification of Ellasar with Cappadocia was probably dictated by the fact that in Genesis Apocryphon's geography the next region moving westwards from the territories of the other three kings was Cappadocia.

For 'Tidal, king of Goiim', Genesis Apocryphon has 'Tidal, king of Goiim, which is between the two rivers'. This does not give a contemporary equivalent for Goiim (which it clearly treats as a proper name), but firmly locates it in northern Mesopotamia (1QGenAp. 21:23–4). Thus the territories of the four lie along the northern border of the land promised to Abram, as it was defined earlier in Genesis Apocryphon. From east to west they run: Elam, Babylonia, northern Mesopotamia and Cappadocia.

Genesis Apocryphon makes it clear that there were *two* campaigns by the northern confederacy against the southern confederacy led by the king of Sodom. In the first the northern kings defeated the southern and placed them under tribute. Then, thirteen years later, when the southern kings rebelled, the northern confederacy marched south to subdue them. Genesis Apocryphon is careful to point out that the first campaign took place *before* Abram settled at Hebron (note 1QGenAp. 21:23, '*Before* those days...'). In fact, if it took place thirteen years before the second campaign, it must have occurred while Abram was still in Haran (cf. 1QGenAp. 22:27–9). All this may well be implied by the biblical text, but it takes careful analysis and a scholarly turn of mind to tease it out.

Genesis Apocryphon gives a clear indication of the route south taken by the four kings. It does not identify all the geographical names mentioned in the Bible, but it gives sufficient equivalents to chart their progress southwards through Transjordan to the Gulf of Aqaba, and then north to Sodom. Genesis Apocryphon then plots them a route home, after their defeat of the five kings, via the 'Great Valley' (1QGenAp. 22:4) = the Jordan Valley. The reason for this route is that the Bible locates the four kings at Dan (Gen. 14:14) when Abram attacks them. The rout of the four kings extended, so Genesis Apocryphon informs us, 'as far as Ḥelbon, which is situated to the north of Damascus' (1QGenAp. 22:10). 'Ḥelbon' for the Biblical Ḥobah (Gen. 14:15) is probably not a *varia lectio* but an identification based on Ezek. 27:18, and on similarity of sound. Ḥelbon is the modern *Ḥalbun*, about fifteen miles north-west of Damascus (cf. Fitzmyer, 1971, p. 152).

Genesis Apocryphon also sorts out neatly the geography of Abram's triumphant return. The king of Sodom, who (on the basis of Gen. 14:21; contrast Gen. 14:10) is assumed to have escaped with his life, comes up from Sodom to Salem ('that is Jerusalem', 1QGenAp. 22:13), and he and Melchizedek, king of Salem, go out to meet Abram who is encamped in the 'Vale of Shaveh, that is the King's Vale' (Gen. 14:17), identified by Genesis Apocryphon as 'the Valley of Beth Hakkerem' (1QGenAp. 22:14). From other biblical references Beth Hakkerem can be located in the vicinity of Jerusalem (cf. Jer. 6:1; Josh. 15:59).

There are a number of noteworthy aggadot in the section of Genesis Apocryphon under consideration, some of them with no obvious basis in the

Bible. 1QGenAp. 20:34 states that Lot's wife was Egyptian. According to 1QGenAp. 21:6, before Lot parted from Abram to go towards Sodom, Abram 'added greatly' to Lot's flocks. This anticipates a detail introduced later, to the effect that the 'one who escaped' and told Abram about Lot's capture (Gen. 14:13) was 'one of the herdsmen of the flock which Abram had given to Lot' (1QGenAp. 22:1–2). This is typical of the holistic approach to the biblical text found in Genesis Apocryphon: the author thinks ahead, and does not (as often happens in rabbinic midrash) treat the Bible atomistically as a series of discrete statements. The holistic approach also comes out in the way in which Genesis Apocryphon integrates Abram's three Amorite friends, Mamre, Arnem and Eshcol (cf. Gen. 14:13, 24) more fully into the story. It anticipates their introduction into Abram's campaign against the four kings by having them dine with Abram when he returns from making the circuit of the promised land (1QGenAp. 21:21–2; cf. 1QGenAp. 22:6–7; 22:23–4). 1QGenAp. 22:3–5 fills out the bald statement of the Bible that 'there came one that had escaped, and told Abram the Hebrew', by giving a resumé of what the messenger said. Thus it fills in a lacuna in the biblical narrative. This is precisely the sort of expansion which results naturally from an imaginative retelling of the biblical story. None of the aggadic supplements in this section of Genesis Apocryphon is very substantial, and most are closely linked to the biblical text. In the earlier columns the aggadah was clearly much more extensive, and of a kind which points to the use of non-biblical sources. It seems that, like Jubilees, Genesis Apocryphon integrated into a smooth narrative material drawn both from the Bible and from extra-biblical tradition.

Genesis Apocryphon shows great skill in bringing other parts of Scripture to bear on the interpretation of the passage directly under consideration. As we have already noted, it uses geographical information culled from elsewhere in Scripture to identify places mentioned in Genesis 14 (Ḥobah = Ḥelbon; Shinar = Babylon; note also 'the Zumzammim who were in Ammon', 1QGenAp. 21:29, derived from Deut. 2:20). The places mentioned in the descriptions of the promised land in 1QGenAp. 21:11–12, 15–19 were not plucked out of the air: all are derived from the various definitions of the borders of the land of Israel scattered throughout Scripture (for evidence, cf. Alexander, 1974, pp. 247–9).

This is all rather impressive. The author of Genesis Apocryphon was a scholar who studied the text of the Bible in a close and disciplined manner, and who had a distinct interest in 'archaeological' matters. However, he wears his learning very easily; he introduces it unobtrusively into an attractive and readable retelling of the biblical text. His touch is light and lacks the heavy theological, moralising emphasis of Jubilees.

## (c) *Pseudo-Philo*, Liber Antiquitatum Biblicarum

The date of LAB is rather uncertain. The common view is that it was written in the first century AD; whether before or after AD 70 is disputed.[4] The work was almost certainly composed in Hebrew, but survives now only in a fourth-century AD Latin translation, made from an intermediate Greek version. LAB retells the biblical history from the creation of the world (Genesis 1) to the death of Saul (2 Samuel 1). As it stands, the text ends abruptly, and is possibly incomplete. How much further it may have continued is a matter of conjecture. The expansions of the Bible are unevenly distributed. Post-Mosaic times are on the whole covered in greater detail. Particularly noteworthy is the treatment of the period of the Judges. In view of the sparse coverage of Judges elsewhere in the aggadah LAB's originality here is remarkable. Unlike Jubilees LAB does not attempt formally to define its attitude to the Bible. Despite having been written in Hebrew it is unlikely the author made any claim to divine inspiration, or intended his text in any way to replace the Bible. His text is not totally free-standing: it presupposes the Bible at a number of points, and was evidently meant to be read by an audience who knew the Bible well. Note, for example, how at three separate points (18:5; 32:1–4; 40:2) LAB refers to the aqedah, yet this story is passed over at the proper chronological point in the retelling of Genesis (LAB 22:1–4 [= Jud. 5:1] looks like a belated attempt to repair the earlier omission).

LAB's account of Jephthah and his daughter (Jud. 10:17–12:7) will serve to illustrate how it handles the biblical text.

*LAB 39:1–40:9 = Judges 10:17–12:7.* The author of LAB displays a strong artistic sensibility. The changes which he introduces into the story of Jephthah and his daughter can be seen as motivated, at least in part, by literary and aesthetic considerations. He has turned the story into a tautly constructed drama. His retelling is, however, well-disciplined: most of his expansions and changes take as their starting-point an objective feature or problem within the biblical text. To this extent LAB may be classified as midrashic. It also aims to produce a theological reading of the biblical story, to impose on a barbarous tale from the heroic age the values of its own times. It must be said, however, that the values which it reads in (apostasy leads to punishment, repentance to forgiveness) are rather trite and predictable. This aspect of LAB's recasting of the Bible is much less memorable than the powerful sense of tragedy it has created, and the lively interplay between the two principal characters.

LAB's literary concerns are to be seen in the way it reshapes the biblical dialogue. This is particularly evident in Jephthah's reply to the elders who come to persuade him to be their champion (LAB 39:3–5 = Jud. 11:4–10). Only Jud. 11:7 is left more or less intact. The arguments and counter-arguments in LAB become more weighty and theological. Jephthah is exhorted to imitate God who forgets the wrongs done to him and delivers his people, or to follow the example of the dove, who, 'though her young be taken away from her, yet departs she not out of her place, but spurns away her wrong and forgets it as it were in the bottom of the deep' (LAB 39:5).

LAB omits any reference to Jephthah's dubious parentage (Jud. 11:1) – perhaps because it rather detracts from his nobility, and so lessens the subsequent tragedy (see LAB 39:2).[5]

LAB 39:6 dramatises the people's choice of Jephthah as king, and also gives a reason why the Israelites were being oppressed by the Ammonites: they had apostasised and followed the gods of Ammon. When Jephthah taxes the people with their sins they repent and pray to God who forgives them. Jephthah's speech and the people's intercessions have been suggested by the pregnant brevity of the original: 'Then Jephthah went with the elders of Gilead, and the people made him head and chief over them; and Jephthah spoke all these words before the Lord in Mizpah' (Jud. 11:11). In typical midrashic fashion LAB takes 'all these words' as pointing to a 'lacuna' in the biblical narrative, which it fills out with a suitable speech.

LAB 39:8–9 severely curtails Jephthah's exchange with the king of Ammon (Jud. 11:12–28), by omitting the long historical defence of Israel against the charge of usurping another's land. LAB (unlike Genesis Apocryphon) is not interested in purely archaeological matters.[6] Jud. 11:23 caused some unease: 'Will you not possess that which Chemosh your God gives you to possess? So whomsoever the Lord our God has dispossessed from before us, them will we possess.' LAB tries to correct any misapprehension: 'You have not been commanded by the God of Israel to destroy them that dwell in the land' (LAB 39:8). 'They are not, as you say, gods which have given you the inheritance which you possess' (LAB 39:9).

LAB 39:11 clearly establishes the *hamartia* which precipitates the tragedy. Jephthah's rash vow provokes God's anger. God decides to requite Jephthah for his rashness by having his vow 'backfire' on his daughter. God himself is dramatically introduced to comment on the action: 'The Lord was very angry and said: Behold Jephthan has vowed that he will offer unto me that which meets him first. Now, therefore, if a dog meet with Jephthan first shall a dog be offered unto me? Now let the vow of Jephthan be upon his firstborn, even upon the fruit of his body, and his prayer upon his only begotten daughter. Nevertheless, I will verily deliver my people at this time, not for his sake, but for the prayer which Israel has prayed.' The final sentence repudiates the idea that Jephthah's improper vow might have influenced God: what moved God was Israel's repentance.

LAB gives greater precision to the narrative by introducing names: the king of the Ammonites is Getal (LAB 39:8), Seila the daughter of Jephthah (LAB

49:1), Stelac the mountain where she goes to bewail her virginity (LAB 40:5). In LAB Seila becomes a major actor in the drama, the protagonist of Jephthah. From Jud. 11:36 LAB concludes that Seila was a willing victim. She compares her sacrifice with the sacrifice of Isaac (LAB 40:2).[7] Divine approval of her sacrifice is registered by a direct comment from God: 'And after this she went into the mount Stelac, and by night the Lord thought upon her, and said: Lo, now I have shut up the tongue of the wise among my people before this generation, that they could not answer the word of the daughter of Jephthan, that my word might be fulfilled, and my counsel not destroyed which I had devised: and I have seen that she is more wise than her father, and a maiden of understanding more than all the wise that are here. And now let her life be given her at her request, and her death will be precious in my sight at all times' (LAB 40:4). This second divine comment on the action, registering approval, counterbalances the earlier comment disapproving of Jephthah's vow. The reference to the 'tongue of the wise' being 'shut up' picks up an earlier statement to the effect that 'Seila the daughter of Jephthan went forth, she and the virgins that were her fellows, and came and told it to the wise men of the people. And no man could answer her words' (LAB 40:4). The sense of this is obscure. There is a rabbinic tradition that the sages were ignorant in Jepthah's day and so did not realise that since his vow was invalid the sacrifice of his daughter need not have taken place (Gen. Rab. 60:3; Lev. Rab. 37:4. See further Ginzberg, 1968; VI, p. 203, n. 109). A similar idea presumably lies behind LAB. What we have here is an example of allusive aggadah. Note, however, the striking fact that in LAB the sages' ignorance is apparently brought about by divine providence. It seems God prefers Seila dead, rather than alive! One feels that the sacrifice of Seila had a deep significance for the author of LAB: it has become the feminine counterpart of the *aqedat yizḥaq* (on feminism in LAB, cf. Perrot, 1976, pp. 52–3). But what the relevance of the story was to him in his time and place is now unclear.

The most striking of all LAB's literary elaborations of the biblical text is Seila's lament (LAB 40:5–7). Jud. 11:37–8 simply states that Seila and her companions 'bewailed her virginity upon the mountains', but draws a veil over what she said. LAB fills the lacuna in the biblical narrative by supplying an appropriate lament. This powerful poetic composition marks the climax of the story, and effectively shifts the focus away from Jephthah to Seila (cf. Alexiou and Dronke, 1971; Bogaert, 1972; Philonenko, 1973). In contrast the actual sacrifice, when Seila returns, is treated in a very summary fashion. For LAB interest in the story is at an end. It omits totally the war between Ephraim and Gilead recounted in Jud. 12:1–6. Perhaps it regarded such internecine strife as unedifying. Like the other rewritten Bible texts LAB is selective in its approach to the Bible.

So then, analysis shows that many of the changes introduced by LAB to the biblical story are motivated, at least in part, by literary considerations. LAB is a highly learned text, aimed at a sophisticated, educated readership. It is a serious misjudgement to see it as a popular work.[8] It is perhaps not too fanciful to suppose that LAB's purpose was to create a national epic. His use of biblical material is reminiscent of the way Vergil uses legend in the *Aeneid*, or Euripides in the *Iphigeneia in Tauris*.

### (d) *Josephus*, Jewish Antiquities

Josephus' *Jewish Antiquities*, written in Greek and published in Rome *ca.* AD 94,[9] stands out from the other rewritten Bible texts in one obvious way: it has a preface in which Josephus addresses his readers and explains why he has written. Of the four works under consideration the *Antiquities* is by far the most articulate and explicit as to its aims, and its relationship to the Bible.

Josephus' basic purpose, he tells us, was to acquaint the Greek-speaking world with the entire ancient history (*archaiologia*) and political constitution (*politeuma*) of the Jews (*Ant.* i, 5). His belief that the Greeks would find this a subject worthy of their attention was fostered by the interest in jewish history shown by his patron Epaphroditus. Josephus also recalls the example of Ptolemy II (Philadelphus) who commissioned the translation of the jewish law into Greek, though he is careful to note (in oblique contrast to his own work), that the king did not receive 'all our records' (*Ant.* i, 12). Thus, Josephus makes it quite clear that he is addressing a Greek-speaking, gentile audience, that he wishes to mediate jewish culture to the Greeks. Throughout the *Antiquities* Josephus kept his audience constantly in mind: there are numerous points where he hellenises jewish history, i.e. presents it in terms of categories understandable in the Greek-speaking world (for details, see, for instance, Feldman, 1968*a* and *b* and 1970).

Josephus also makes it clear that he is writing *history*: i.e. he aims to produce a consecutive, chronological narrative of what happened (*Ant.* i, 26). He is not writing a theological treatise. He reserves his discussion of the jewish creed for a separate work which he plans to write after completing the *Antiquities* (*Ant.* i, 25). What this means, in effect, is that Josephus ignores large parts of the Hebrew Bible – the prophetical books, the wisdom literature, the Psalms and other poetry. He does, however, cover in reasonable detail the content of the law of Moses (*Ant.* iv, 196ff), since part of his declared aim was to describe the constitution of the Jews.

Though Josephus' main concern was to produce a narrative of events, like most ancient historians he held that history teaches lessons, and that historiography should serve moral ends. The lessons he draws are hardly profound; they are commonplaces of Greek and Hebrew historiography. He writes: 'The main lesson to be learnt from this history by any who care to peruse it, is that men who conform to the will of God, and do not venture to transgress laws that have been excellently laid down, prosper in all things beyond belief, and for their reward are offered by God felicity; whereas, in proportion as they depart from the strict observance of these laws, things (else) practicable become impracticable, and whatever imaginary good thing they strive to do ends in irretrievable disasters' (*Ant.* i, 14). Throughout the *Antiquities* Josephus adopts a moralising tone.

Josephus' preface further suggests that he has certain apologetic aims. He delivers an encomium on the wisdom of 'Moses our lawgiver', contrasting Moses' pure and exalted views of God with the disgraceful fables accepted by other legislators (*Ant.* i, 18ff; cf. i, 15). And he emphasises the great antiquity of the Mosaic legislation: 'He (Moses) was born two thousand years ago, to which ancient date the poets never ventured to refer even the birth of their gods, much less the actions or the laws of mortals' (*Ant.* i, 16). Antiquity conveyed great prestige in the ancient world: it was a positive cultural value. Josephus' aim was to show to the Greeks that the Jews were a law-abiding, pious people – heirs of an ancient civilisation and an exemplary constitution.

Though written with the benefit of hindsight, the introduction to the *Contra Apionem* further serves to define the apologetic aims of the *Antiquities*. Josephus writes: 'In my history of our antiquities, most excellent Epaphroditus, I have, I think, made sufficiently clear to any who may peruse that work the exceptional antiquity of our jewish race, the purity of the original stock, and the manner in which it established itself in the country which we occupy today' (*CAp.* i, 1). It becomes clear that in asserting the great antiquity of jewish civilisation Josephus is polemicising against the hellenists: 'My first thought is one of intense astonishment at the current opinion that, in the study of primeval history, the Greeks alone deserve serious attention' (*CAp.* i, 6). Josephus allies the Jews with the old 'oriental' cultures of Egypt, Babylonia and Phoenicia to resist the cultural imperialism of the Greeks by pouring scorn on the 'modernity' of Greek civilization (*CAp.* i, 7ff). His interest in chronology in the *Antiquities* is more than a matter of antiquarian scholarship: the chronology played an important polemical role.

Josephus states that the *Antiquities* is based on 'the sacred writings' (*Ant.* i, 5, 13, 17). He defines his canon of sacred Scripture in *CAp.* i, 38–41. Though it comprises twenty-two books, as against the standard twenty-four of the synagogue, it was probably identical to the synagogue canon. The numerical discrepancy was caused by Josephus counting Ruth in with Judges, and Lamentations with Jeremiah. Josephus was clearly aware of extra-canonical literature, but he did not regard it as Scripture: 'From Artaxerxes to our own time the complete history has been written, but has not been deemed worthy of equal credit with the earlier records, because of the failure of the exact succession of the prophets' (*CAp.* i, 41). Josephus claims to have based his account on the *Hebrew* text of the sacred writings (*Ant.* i, 5). This claim appears to hold good for the Hexateuch. In the later books of the Bible, however, he has clearly consulted the Septuagint.

In the *Antiquities*, says Josephus, 'the precise details of our Scripture records will be set forth, each in its own place, as my narrative proceeds, that being the procedure that I have promised to follow throughout this work, neither adding nor omitting anything' (*Ant.* i, 17). Such fidelity to his sources emerges naturally from Josephus' doctrine of Scripture as set out in *CAp.* i, 22ff. There he stresses the divine inspiration of the Scriptures, the care with which they have been transmitted, the veneration in which they are held by Jews ('Although such long ages have now passed, no one has ventured either to add, or to remove, or to alter a syllable'; cf. Deut. 4:2). Josephus' claims, however, do not entirely square with his actual practice: he does regularly add and omit, and as an interpreter frequently exercises a heavy hand. This discrepancy between theory and practice has troubled many scholars. Some have argued that the claim to fidelity is purely conventional: it is made in one form or another by most ancient historians and is not to be taken too seriously. Others have suggested that Josephus did not base himself directly on the Hebrew Bible but on a paraphrase which already contained many of his changes to the biblical text. He was faithful enough to his source, but that source was not the Hebrew Bible *simpliciter*. Yet others have proposed that Josephus' sacred canon was more extensive than the present Hebrew Bible and contained aggadic works on which he freely drew. This suggestion, like the previous one, is thought to go some way towards defending Josephus' integrity (cf. Feldman, 1984, pp. 122–5 for bibliography). However, none of these solutions is really necessary. Josephus clearly had access to the Hebrew Bible, so there is no good reason to dispute his claim that he consulted the original text. It is equally clear from *CAp.* i, 38–41 that he had a restricted canon of Scripture which corresponded to the present Hebrew Bible (though he unquestionably consulted other works as well). It does not necessarily follow that because a claim is conventional it need not be regarded as true. Despite all his changes, expansions and omissions, Josephus doubtless sincerely believed that he was being faithful to the original records. We must be careful not to impose unduly literalistic standards of fidelity upon him. His fidelity can only be measured by his actual practice.

What, then, were the sources of Josephus' expansions and alterations of the biblical narrative? Some changes must have arisen quite naturally from the process of retelling the story in his own words in an interesting and instructive way for a gentile, Greek-speaking audience. Others were generated by exegesis of the biblical text. The *Antiquities* everywhere presupposes a close reading of the Bible – an attention to the obscurities, contradictions and lacunae in the narrative. Josephus often resolves the problems in typical midrashic fashion.

His interpretations can hardly be all his own invention. As an educated Jew of priestly descent he must have been well acquainted with the tradition of Bible interpretation current in his day. From time to time he incorporates extra-biblical aggadah into his narrative, some of which probably came to him orally, some from written sources (on the problem of Josephus' use of written sources, cf. Rajak, 1978).

As to its form the *Antiquities* is Greek: it belongs to the 'archaeological' tradition of historiography represented by Manetho, Berossus, Philo of Byblos, and Dionysius of Halicarnassus, which was well established in the Greek-speaking world. It has long been suspected that Josephus consciously modelled his work on that of Dionysius. As to its content, the *Antiquities* is in all essential respects similar to the rewritten Bible texts which we considered earlier – texts which belong to the corpus of jewish literature, and which have an early forerunner in the books of Chronicles. There is surprisingly little tension between the Greek form of the *Antiquities* and its jewish content. The fact is that the way Josephus handles his sources, the midrashic methods of exegesis which he employs, would have been thoroughly at home in the Greek world: they were part and parcel of the scholarship of his time (cf. Daube, 1953; Lieberman, 1962, pp. 47–82). If we could control the process in detail we should probably find that Dionysius and the other 'archaeologists' treated their sources in much the same manner as Josephus treated his. The *Antiquities* lives easily in two worlds – as a work of hellenistic historiography, and as an example of jewish Bible exegesis – because it occupies a position where the jewish and hellenistic worlds coincide.

To illustrate Josephus' detailed treatment of the Bible we shall consider his retelling in *Ant*. i, 222–37 of the story of the binding of Isaac (Gen. 22:1–19).

*Ant. i, 222–237 = Genesis 22:1–19.* Josephus adopts a typically moralising tone in his retelling of the aqedah. Taking his cue from Gen. 22:12 ('Now I know that you are a god-fearing man...'), he presents the story as an illustration of the piety (*thrēskeia*) of Abraham (*Ant*. i, 223, 224, 234) – piety being defined as obedience to God (*Ant*. i, 225, 232, 233). More significantly the story is presented as an illustration of the piety of Isaac, seen in his obedience to his father and to God (*Ant*. i, 222, 232). Isaac is portrayed as a willing victim, twenty-five years old at the time of the incident (*Ant*. i, 227, 232). It is perhaps to avoid complicating this picture that Josephus omits any reference to the 'binding' of the victim (Gen. 22:9): he was concerned lest the binding be construed as evidence of Isaac's reluctance.

Josephus dramatically sets the scene by stressing Abraham's love for Isaac. This is clearly an explanation of the Biblical 'your only son whom you love' (Gen. 22:2). He adds, however, a comment on Isaac's reciprocal devotion to his parents: 'On his side, the child called out the affection of his parents and endeared himself to them yet more by the practice of every virtue, showing a devoted filial obedience and zeal for the worship of God' (*Ant*. i, 222). The vague 'after these things' in Gen. 22:1 is clarified thus: 'After God had enumerated all the benefits he had bestowed on Abraham – how he had made him stronger than his enemies, and how it was his benevolence to which Abraham owed his present felicity and his son Isaac' (*Ant*. i, 223–4). Thus in typical midrashic fashion Josephus fills out a lacuna in the biblical narrative and at the same time provides a motive for the testing.

It is characteristic of Josephus' narrative style that he reduces the *oratio recta* of the original to *oratio obliqua*, but then marks the climax of the drama by adding a long speech in *oratio recta* in which Abraham, just before the sacrifice, justifies his actions to Isaac (*Ant*. i, 228–31). He also reports at some length on Isaac's reactions to Abraham's speech (*Ant*. i, 232), and has God clarify his motives for imposing the test (*Ant*. i, 233). Such changes come about quite naturally when a narrator attempts to recast a story in his own words. The vivid little detail that Abraham and Isaac embraced each other after Isaac's deliverance (*Ant*. i, 236) is another example of a natural aggadic addition.

Josephus commits a number of 'unforced errors' in his retelling of the story. He has Isaac ask where is the victim 'while constructing the altar' (*Ant*. i, 227). Gen. 22:7–8 makes it clear that this question was raised *on the journey*. Josephus coalesces the two interventions of the angel of the Lord (Gen. 22:11, 15), with the result that, contrary to the original, the divine promises are made *before* the ram is sacrificed (*Ant*. i, 232–6). Such lapses (for which no deep reason is apparent) tend to occur when a story is being summarised. They may indicate that in writing up his version, Josephus did not have the Bible open beside him.

Josephus' attention to the details of the biblical story, and his broadly midrashic approach to expounding it, are illustrated by the following:

(a) Gen. 22:2 sites the aqedah on 'one of the mountains' of the 'land of Moriah'. Josephus speaks of the Morian Mount (*Ant*. i, 224, *to Mōrion oros*), which he later identifies as 'that mount whereon king David afterwards erected the temple' (*Ant*. i, 226). The equation of Mount Moriah with the temple mount in Jerusalem may be as old as 2 Chron. 3:1. In fact it could be deduced midrashically from Gen. 22:14: 'Abraham called the name of that place Adonai-jireh: as it is said to this day, "In the mount of the Lord it shall be seen"'.

(b) Gen. 22:3: 'Abraham rose early in the morning and saddled his ass...and he cleaved the wood for the burnt offering'. *Ant*. i, 225: 'Abraham...concealed from his wife God's commandment and his own resolve concerning the immolation of the child; nay revealing it not even to any of his household, lest haply he should have been hindered from doing God's service...having laden his ass etc.' This was Josephus' solution to the problem of why Abraham 'rose early' and himself performed such menial tasks as saddling the ass and chopping the wood.

(c) Josephus gives two noteworthy interpretations of the divine promises to Abraham. Gen. 22:17: 'Your seed shall possess the gate of his enemies' = *Ant.* i, 235: 'They will subdue Canaan by arms'. Gen. 22:18: 'In your seed shall all the nations of the earth be blessed' = *Ant.* i, 235: 'They shall be envied of all men'.

Like the other rewritten Bible texts Josephus has a selective approach to the Bible, stressing and expanding some elements, ignoring or glossing over others. He omits the passage about Abraham and Abimelech which precedes the aqedah (Gen. 21:22–33). He also omits the genealogical section following the aqedah (Gen. 22:20–4). Presumably he regarded both these passages as tangential to the main line of the narrative. By omitting the first he was able to sharpen up the contrast between Ishmael and Isaac.[10]

## 3   THE 'REWRITTEN BIBLE': TOWARDS THE DEFINITION OF THE GENRE

Does our analysis of these four texts justify the conclusion that they represent a definite literary genre? The answer to this question must be an emphatic, Yes. The differences between the texts as to language, audience, style and individual emphasis, are much less important than their similarities. The principal characteristics of the 'rewritten Bible' genre which emerge from the analysis are as follows:[11]

(a) Rewritten Bible texts are narratives, which follow a sequential, chronological order. Their framework is an account of events, and so they may be described broadly as histories. They are not theological treatises, though an account of events may incidentally serve theological ends.

(b) They are, on the face of it, free-standing compositions which replicate the form of the biblical books on which they are based. Though they make constant use of the words of Scripture, they integrate these into a smooth, seamless retelling of the biblical story. Unlike rabbinic midrash, the actual words of Scripture do not remain highlighted within the body of the text, either in the form of lemmata, or by the use of citation-formulae (such as šenneʾĕmar).

(c) Despite the superficial independence of form, these texts are not intended to replace, or to supersede the Bible. Of the four examples we studied Josephus' *Jewish Antiquities* is perhaps the most self-sufficient. Since his account was aimed at a Greek-speaking, gentile audience, it presumably demanded no prior knowledge. Yet Josephus explicitly acknowledges the existence and authority of Scripture; he defines his role as that of the interpreter/translator (*Ant*. i, 5). Jubilees also explicitly acknowledges the existence and continuing authority of Scripture, and Genesis Apocryphon and the LAB appear to presuppose a knowledge of Scripture from time to time. Jubilees, Genesis Apocryphon and the LAB were addressed to an audience who knew the originals well, and who were expected to call the originals to mind as they read these works.

(d) Rewritten Bible texts cover a substantial portion of the Bible. The most extensive is Josephus' *Antiquities*, which spans the whole of biblical history. The least extensive is Genesis Apocryphon, which now runs from Noah to Abraham, but which was once longer. It is doubtful if the legendary expansions of the Bible such as the Book of Noah or the Book of Giants should be regarded as belonging to the genre. These expansions take as their starting-point a single episode of the Bible, or a very short passage, and expand it almost beyond recognition. They are basically centrifugal. Rewritten Bible texts are centripetal: they come back to the Bible again and again. The rewritten Bible texts make use of the legendary material, but by placing that material within an extended biblical narrative (in association with passages of more or less literal retelling of the Bible), they clamp the legends firmly to the biblical framework, and reintegrate them into the biblical history. The single legendary expansions constitute a separate genre.

(e) Rewritten Bible texts follow the Bible serially, in proper order, but they are highly selective in what they represent. Some passages are reproduced more or less literally, some are omitted altogether, some abbreviated, some expanded. There are few omissions which would create a serious chronological hiatus, and in the end all the texts contain a reasonably balanced proportion of straightforward retelling and expansion. A proper balance between the 'literal' and the 'non-literal' sections is probably of fundamental importance to the genre.

(f) The intention of the texts is to produce an interpretative reading of Scripture. They offer 'a fuller, smoother and doctrinally more advanced form of the sacred narrative' (Vermes in Schürer, 1986, p. 305). They constitute a kind of commentary. The commentary is, however, indirect, and its full significance can only be grasped if the original is borne constantly in mind. They carry on an intense, if silent, dialectic with the original.

(g) The narrative form of the texts means, in effect, that they can impose only a single interpretation on the original. The original can be treated only as monovalent. By way of contrast, the commentary form adopted by the rabbis and by Philo allows them to offer multiple interpretations of the same passage of Scripture, and to treat the underlying text as polyvalent.

(h) The limitations of the narrative form also preclude making clear the exegetical reasoning. The rewritten Bible texts read the Bible with close attention, noting obscurities, inconsistencies and narrative lacunae. The methods by which they solve the problems of the original are essentially midrashic, i.e. similar to those found in the rabbinic midrashim. But unlike the midrashim (or Philo) they cannot make explicit their midrashic working.

(i) Rewritten Bible texts make use of non-biblical tradition and draw on non-biblical sources, whether oral or written. As already noted, they use legendary material which, though concerned with biblical figures (Noah, Moses, Cenez), or taking its starting-point from biblical episodes, bears little relationship to the biblical text, and certainly cannot be derived from it exegetically. In certain cases we can be sure the legendary material pre-existed its incorporation into the texts. By fusing this material with the biblical narrative the rewritten Bible texts appear to be aiming at a synthesis of the whole tradition (both biblical and extra-biblical) within a biblical framework: they seek to unify the tradition on a biblical base. Though they accord the Bible priority in the synthesis they have a high regard for non-biblical tradition. As in the case of Jubilees they may even regard it as inspired. So their intention may be seen as both exegetical and eisegetical: they seek to draw out the sense of Scripture and to solve its problems, and at the same time to read non-biblical material into Scripture, thereby validating it and preventing the fragmentation of the tradition.

## NOTES

1 Jubilees is now fully extant only in Ethiopic. That the original language was Hebrew has been put beyond reasonable doubt by the discovery of Hebrew fragments at Qumran. Surprisingly little has been written about Jubilees' relationship to the Bible. For a general introduction see Vermes in Schürer (1986), pp. 308–18, and Wintermute (1985). The most thorough discussion of the date of Jubilees is VanderKam (1977).

2 It must be admitted that the text is far from clear. The confusion is in part caused by the fact that God and his agent, the angel of the presence, appear to be interchangeable. Thus in Jub. 1:1 God writes, but in 1:27 it is the angel who writes; in 1:26 God dictates, whereas in 2:1 the angel performs this role.

3 The author of Jubilees may also have had in mind the accusation, well attested at a later date, that the Jews were 'brigands' (*lēstai*) who had stolen the land of others: see, for instance, Procopius' *De Bello Vandalico* II (= *De Bellis* IV), 10, 13–22. Further Bacher (1891); Lewy (1933); and Hirschberg (1974), pp. 45–8.

4 For a general introduction to LAB and a discussion of its date, see Vermes in Schürer (1986), pp. 325–31. Further, Harrington (1985); Feldman (1971); Wadsworth (1975). A useful summary of the exegetical methods of LAB is given in Bauckham (1983).

5 The text of LAB is awkward at this point. It reads: *Cum zelaret fratres suos qui eiecerant eum de terra sua*. James translates: 'Because he was jealous of his brothers, they had cast him out of his land'. This ignores *qui*. Cazeaux's rendering ignores the *cum*: 'Il gardait de la rancoeur contre ses frères qui l'avaient chassé de son pays' (Harrington and Cazeaux, 1976, p. 273). Harrington, however, correctly notes that the sense required is:

'His brothers who had thrust him forth from his own land envied him' (Harrington, 1985, pp. 352–3).

6 LAB's interest in genealogy (see, for instance, 1:1–2:10; 4:1–5:8) is not evidence to the contrary. Many of its non-biblical names are pure invention, and seem to have been introduced simply for artistic effect.

7 In comparing Seila with Isaac the author of LAB may have been impressed by the fact that both are described as 'only-begotten': in Gen. 22:1 Isaac is called *yāḥîd* (Vulgate *unigenitus*); in Jud. 11:34 Seila is called *yĕḥîdāh* (LAB 40:1 *unigenita*). According to the rabbinic principal of *gezerah shavah* the use of the same significant term in two passages allows one passage to be interpreted in the light of the other.

8 Perrot (1976), p. 23, describes LAB as a 'collection de narrations populaires, issues pour une bonne part de la tradition orale', and contrasts it with Josephus' *Antiquities* – 'l'oeuvre beaucoup plus savante d'un homme qui se veut averti en matière historique'.

9 Feldman's magisterial survey (1984) offers the best introduction to Josephus. Note especially chapter 10: 'Josephus' Paraphrase of the Bible'. See further Rajak (1974 and 1983); Attridge (1976 and 1984); Franxman (1979); Cohen (1979), pp. 35–43; and Downing (1980).

10 It is certain that Josephus based his retelling of the *aqedah* directly on the Hebrew text. Note the following: (1) Gen. 22:2 MT *yāḥîd*; LXX *agapētos*; Josephus (*Ant.* i, 222) *monogenēs*. (2) Gen. 22:2 MT *'el 'ereṣ hammōrîyyāh*; LXX *eis tēn gēn tēn hypsēlēn*; Josephus (*Ant.* i, 224) *eis to Mōrion oros*. (3) Gen. 22:2: MT *wĕhaʿălēhû...lĕʿōlāh*; LXX *anenenkon auton...eis holokarpōsin*; Josephus (*Ant.* i, 224) *holokautōsai*. (4) Gen. 22:3: MT *šĕnê nĕʿārâw*; LXX *duo paides*; Josephus (*Ant.* i, 225) *duo oiketai*. (5) Gen. 22:9: MT *wayyiben...'et hammizbēaḥ*; LXX *kai ōkodomēsen...thysiastērion*; Josephus (*Ant.* i, 227) *ton bōmon kataskeuazontos*.

11 In literary criticism 'genre' is a controversial term, in need of definition. For a useful introduction to the problem see Shuler (1982), pp. 24–57. In this chapter I have used 'genre' simply as a type of literary composition distinguished from other types of composition by certain characteristics of subject-matter and form. The characteristics do not differentiate the genre singly, but only as a collection. Any text admitted to the genre must display *all* the characteristics.

## BIBLIOGRAPHY

P. S. Alexander *The Toponymy of the Targumim* (Oxford D.Phil. thesis, 1974).

'Notes on the "Imago Mundi" of the Book of Jubilees', in G. Vermes and J. Neusner (eds.), *Essays in Honour of Yigael Yadin = JJS* 33 (1982), 197–213.

M. Alexiou and P. Dronke 'The Lament of Jephtha's Daughter: Themes, Traditions, Originality', *Studi Medievali* 3rd series 12 (1971), 819–63.

H. W. Attridge *The Interpretation of Biblical History in the Antiquitates Judaicae of Flavius Josephus*, Harvard Dissertations in Religion 7 (Missoula, 1976).

'Josephus and His Works', in M. E. Stone (ed.), *Jewish Writings of the*

*Second Temple Period*, Compendia Rerum Iudaicarum ad Novum Testamentum, Section II (Assen, 1984), pp. 185–232.

W. Bacher 'The Supposed Inscription upon "Joshua the Robber"', *JQR* 3 (1891), 354–57.

R. J. Bauckham 'The Liber Antiquitatum Biblicarum of Pseudo-Philo and the Gospels as "Midrash"', in R. T. France and D. Wenham (eds.), *Gospel Perspectives*, vol. III (Sheffield, 1983), pp. 33–76.

P.-M. Bogaert 'Les Antiquités Bibliques du Pseudo-Philon. Quelques observations sur les chapitres 39 et 40 à l'occasion d'une réimpression', *Revue Théologique de Louvain* 3 (1972), 334–44.

J. Cazeaux *see* D. J. Harrington.

R. H. Charles *The Book of Jubilees* (London, 1902).

S. J. D. Cohen *Josephus in Galilee and Rome: His Vita and Development as a Historian* (Leiden, 1979).

D. Daube 'Alexandrian Methods of Interpretation and the Rabbis', in *Festschrift Hans Lewald* (Basel, 1953), pp. 27–44.

F. G. Downing 'Redaction Criticism: Josephus' Antiquities and the Synoptic Gospels', *JSNT* 8 (1980), 46–65.

L. H. Feldman 'Abraham the Greek Philosopher in Josephus', *Transactions of the American Philological Association* 99 (1968), 143–56 (= 1968*a*).

'Hellenizations in Josephus' Portrayal of Man's Decline', in J. Neusner (ed.), *Religions in Antiquity: Essays in Memory of E. R. Goodenough* (Leiden, 1968), pp. 336–53 (= 1968*b*).

'Hellenizations in Josephus' Version of Esther (Ant.Jud. 11.185–295)', *Transactions of the American Philological Association* 101 (1970), 143–70.

'Prolegomenon' to the reprint of M. R. James, *The Biblical Antiquities of Philo* (New York, 1971), pp. ix–clxix.

*Josephus and Modern Scholarship 1937–1980* (Berlin, 1984).

J. A. Fitzmyer *The Genesis Apocryphon of Qumran Cave 1* (Rome, 1966; 2nd edition, 1971).

T. W. Franxman *Genesis and the 'Jewish Antiquities' of Flavius Josephus* (Rome, 1979).

L. Ginzberg *The Legends of the Jews* (reprint, Philadelphia, 1968).

D. J. Harrington 'Pseudo-Philo', in J. H. Charlesworth (ed.), *The Old Testament Pseudepigrapha*, vol. 2 (Garden City and London, 1985), pp. 297–377.

D. J. Harrington and J. Cazeaux *Pseudo-Philon, Les Antiquités Bibliques*, vol. 1, Sources Chrétiennes 229 (Paris, 1976).

H. Z. Hirschberg *A History of the Jews in North Africa*, vol. 1 (Leiden, 1974).

M. R. James *The Biblical Antiquities of Philo* (London, 1917).

H. Lewy 'Ein Rechtsstreit um Boden Palästinas im Altertum', *MGWJ* 77 (1933), 84–99, 172–80.

S. Lieberman *Hellenism in Jewish Palestine* (2nd edition, New York, 1962).

G. W. E. Nickelsburg 'The Bible Rewritten and Expanded', in M. E. Stone (ed.), *Jewish Writings of the Second Temple Period*, Compendia Rerum Iudaicarum ad Novum Testamentum, Section II (Assen, 1984), pp. 89–156.

C. Perrot and P.-M. Bogaert *Pseudo-Philon, Les Antiquités Bibliques*, vol. 2, Sources Chrétiennes 230 (Paris, 1976).

M. Philonenko 'Iphigénie et Sheila', in *Les syncrétismes dans les religions grecque et romaine*, Bibliothèque des centres d'études supérieures spécialisés: Travaux du centre d'études supérieures spécialisé d'histoire des réligions de Strasbourg (Paris, 1973), pp. 165–77.

T. Rajak *Flavius Josephus: Jewish History and the Greek World* (Oxford D.Phil. thesis, 1974).

'Moses in Ethiopia: Legend and Literature', *JJS* 29 (1978), 111–22.

*Josephus: the Historian and his Society* (London, 1983).

E. Schürer *History of the Jewish People in the Age of Jesus Christ*, vol. III.1, revised by G. Vermes, F. Millar and M. Goodman (Edinburgh, 1986).

P. L. Shuler *A Genre for the Gospels* (Philadelphia, 1982).

J. C. VanderKam *Textual and Historical Studies in the Book of Jubilees*, HSM 14 (Missoula, 1977).

G. Vermes *Scripture and Tradition in Judaism* (Leiden, 1961; 2nd ed., 1973).

M. P. Wadsworth *The "Liber Antiquitatum Biblicarum" of Pseudo-Philo: Doctrine and Scriptural Exegesis in a Jewish Midrash of the First Century A.D.* (Oxford D.Phil. thesis, 1975).

O. S. Wintermute 'Jubilees', in J. H. Charlesworth (ed.), *The Old Testament Pseudepigrapha*, vol. 2 (Garden City and London, 1985), pp. 35–142.

# 8 · Commenting on the Old Testament (with particular reference to the pesharim, Philo, and the Mekilta)

## B. D. CHILTON

### I  THE PESHARIM

O F the documents or fragments of documents which have been discovered at Qumran, perhaps the most distinctive are the pesharim. Formally, they are continuous interpretations of the biblical passages to which they relate, Habakkuk (1QpHab), Micah (1QpMic), Zephaniah (1QpZeph and 4QpZeph), Psalms (1QpPs and 4QpPs [a, b]), Isaiah (4QpIsa [a–e]), Hosea (4QpHos [a, b]) and Nahum (4QpNah). Other fragmentary material might also have belonged within pesharim (cf. Horgan, 1979, p. 1; Horgan's edition of the Hebrew texts is to be found in an appendix, here cited with 'I' before the arabic numeral of the page number), so that the task of identification must continue. The most complete of the pesharim is that of Habakkuk, which has been subjected to diligent investigation since the publication of Elliger's magisterial treatment (1953). By reason of its relative completeness and the close attention it has attracted, 1QpHab is a suitable point of departure for understanding the pesharim generally.

1QpHab is commonly cited by column and line of text, as here, but it proceeds systematically in the order of Habakkuk, until Hab. 2:20 is cited in the thirteenth column. The pesher therefore ends on the openly eschatological climax of what is called the 'burden' of Habakkuk in 1:1, and does not take up the 'prayer' of Habakkuk, from 3:1. On both external and internal grounds, the ending of the document should be seen as the result of a deliberate decision; blank space follows the four lines of the thirteenth column, and the chief concern of the pesher appears to be unequivocally eschatological (cf. Brownlee, 1979, pp. 218f for an unrepresentative attempt to explain the ending as accidental). What will perennially surprise readers of other eschatologically oriented documents is the superficially punctilious procedure of the pesher, in which Habakkuk is cited, and then related to subsequent events.

After Hab. 1:1–2a is cited in 1QpHab 1.1–2, for example, we are informed, 'The *pešer* of the passage concerns everything Habakkuk prophesied regarding the beginning of the generation of the visitation in the latter days, everything that happens to them' (cf. Horgan, 1979, I.2, 3; 12, 21, 22 and Vermes, 1965, p. 235). Although this reading is largely the result of textual restoration, the restoration is plausible, especially as far as the word *pešer* is concerned, which typically follows biblical citations in 1QpHab. The wording might be 'the *pešer* of the passage', 'the *pešer* of the passage concerns', 'the *pešer* of the passage, which is that', 'the *pešer* of the passage for the latter days', 'its *pešer*', or some other variant (cf. Horgan, 1979, pp. 239–43), but the point is that its absence in such a context, not its presence, is remarkable.

Although no certainty attaches to the judgment that the various pesharim within 1QpHab concern the 'beginning' of the last generation, the orientation of the document as a whole emerges as such. Column 2 clearly represents the state of affairs. The pesher of Hab. 1:5, we are told, concerns 'the traitors, with the lying man, because they did not believe the righteous teacher when he spoke from the mouth of God' (2.1–3, here restored in a manner different from Horgan's, 1979, I.1; 24, cf. 2.6, 7, and Brownlee, 1979, p. 53). But the text goes on:

And it concerns the traitors against the new covenant, because they did not believe in God's convenant, and they profaned his holy name. So also, the *pešer* of the passage concerns the traitors in the latter days; they are the violators of the covenant who will not believe when they hear... (2.3–7)

The interpretation here involves three stages of pesher, involving the fomulae *pšr hdbr ᶜl, wᶜl*, and *wkn pšr hdbr ᶜl*. The temporal aspects of the stages appear to correspond loosely to the use of tenses, the perfect of 'believe' in 2.2 (as restored by Horgan, 1979, I.1, 2; 13, 24; Vermes, 1965, p. 236 presupposes a different stem, but also in the perfect tense), the participle 'traitors' in 2.3 (followed by the perfect of 'believe'), and the imperfect of 'believe' in 2.6.

Column 2 has been cited at some length, because it is commonly agreed that it cogently expresses the interpretative stance of 1QpHab. The final rebellion of traitors is given a precise occasion in lines 7–10a:

when they hear all that is coming upon the last generation from the mouth of the priest in whose heart God placed the understanding to interpret all the words of his servants, the prophets, by whose hand God related everything that is coming upon his people...'
(cf. Horgan, 1979, I.2; 13, 25, 26; Vermes, 1965, p. 236; Brownlee, 1979, p. 53; Dupont-Sommer, 1980, pp. 271, 272)

It is precisely this perspective which gives the pesharim their distinctive character. The Scriptures are held to refer to the last days, and only those committed to the teacher of the past and the priest of the future can claim access to prophetic truth (cf. Dupont-Sommer, 1980, p. 267; Vermes, 1975, pp. 44, 45). Because the end is viewed as imminent, the divinely related Scripture, together with the divinely bestowed interpretation, are portrayed as the most crucial realities (cf. Bruce, 1961, p. 77).

## The interpretative procedure of 1QpHab

The question obviously emerges: how is one to get from the prophetic writings, imbued with secret oracles, to an open statement of (a) what has recently gone on, (b) what is happening, and (c) what will be? In an influential summary of the procedure employed with the biblical text, Bruce lists four principal devices: (1) the simple change of temporal focus, (2) the atomisation of statements, (3) the use of variant readings, and (4) allegorisation (1961, p. 77; see also 1959, pp. 7–17, and 1971). The phenomena to which Bruce refers can be instanced within column 2.

The alteration of temporal focus is entirely evident here; indeed, it must be stated that column 2 is unusual in combining all three stages of the end in its explication of a single verse. Ordinarily within 1QpHab, a biblical passage is applied to one of the three temporal stages (that is: the recent past [a], the present [b], and the future [c]); often the treatment of a particular sequence within a stage extends over a substantial body of cited text and interpretation. Following 2.10a, there is a long section on the 'Kittim', 2.10b–4.12, and perhaps through line 16a. The state of the scroll does not permit of certainty regarding the extent of the passage, but the Kittim – who are probably to be identified with the Romans – are a favourite preoccupation in 1QpHab, and crop up again in column 6, and less substantively in 9.7. Column 5 deals with God's eschatological judgment (lines 1–8a), and then complains against 'the house of Absalom', which failed to support the righteous teacher against the lying man (lines 8b–12a). Column 7 adds significantly to our knowledge of the hermeneutical perspective of the Habakkuk pesher. God is said expressly to have told the prophet to write down what was to come, but not to have made known 'the completion of the end' (7.1, 2). Rather, 'all the secrets' of the prophets' words were made known to the righteous teacher (7.4, 5). On the basis of implicit continuity with this teacher, 1QpHab announces from 7.7 the glorious end, on behalf of those who perform the law (7.11), according to divine decree (7.13). Column 8 pursues the theme, via Hab. 2:4 (cited at the end of column 7), of those who perform the law in the house of Judah, namely those who are faithful to the righteous teacher (8.1–3a). The sobering message of Hab. 2:5f is pressed into service against 'the wicked priest' (8.8; 9.9), 'the priest who rebelled' (8.16; 9.16[?]), and 'the last priests of Jerusalem' (9.4, 5). The same figure or figures is/are at issue in 11.4, 12; 12.2, 8. The references from column 10, however, insist on the condemnatory judgment of God (10.3bf, cf. column 13) against such enemies of the teacher (whether historically, or in the present), including the 'lying spouter' (10.9, cf. 10.17–11.1).

The resumé of contents offered above highlights the significance of what has been said in respect of column 2; it is a unique amalgam of typical elements in 1QpHab. At the same time, Bruce's characterisation of the first phenomenon of interpretation in this pesher, the alteration of temporal focus, is vindicated. That atomisation is another such phenomenon ought by now to be evident. Within column 2, our paradigmatic passage, the very word 'traitors' in 1QpHab 1.16 (*bwgdym*) in respect of Hab. 1:5 triggers the interpretation, which is worked out at the stages of the teacher, the new covenant, and the end of days. Similarly, the description from Hab. 1:6a is applied to the Kittim; the statement that they are a 'hasty' (*hnmr*) nation leads to their characterisation as 'swift' (*qlym*) in battle (1QpHab 2.11–13). In both instances, little more than verbal play seems evident.

The term 'traitors' in 1QpHab 1.16 (for 'among the nations' in the MT of Hab. 1:5) is a restored reading, but the restoration is most probably correct (see Bruce, 1959, p. 12; Horgan, 1979, pp. 12, 23, I.1). It may be that *bwgdym*, rather than *bgym* was the reading underlying 1QpHab, the LXX and Acts 13:41 (cf. Bruce, 1959, pp. 12, 71). The degree to which a deliberate invocation of a variant reading is evidenced here, however, must remain a matter of doubt. Nonetheless, it is notable, as Horgan has observed (1979, p. 26), that the description of the Kittim as strong (*gbwrym*) in 1QpHab 2.12 might reflect knowledge of the textual tradition behind *tous makhētas* in some Greek witnesses of Hab. 1:6. The extent to which we may properly speak of textual variants in the period of 1QpHab (as distinct from creative accommodation), however, is problematic (cf. Rabin, 1955, pp. 152–60). Vermes has shown that in certain instances, for example in the use of the figure of 'Lebanon' for the temple (see 12.3), 1QpHab is in line with the *exegetical* tradition represented later in rabbinic midrashim (1975, pp. 46, 47, and 1973, pp. 26–39).

Bruce's characterisation of an exegetical phenomenon of allegorisation is the only unhelpful item on his list. Within this category, Bruce classes the interpretation of 'Lebanon' in 1QpHab 12.3, 4. As has already been observed, the identity between 'Lebanon' and 'the council of the community' seems to be cut from similar cloth as the rabbinic equation between 'Lebanon' and the temple. Vermes goes so far as to claim that the interpretation in 1QpHab consciously replies to a more generally prevalent understanding (1975, p. 47 and 1973, pp. 26–39). Horgan (1979, p. 52) demonstrates that other interpretative understandings of 'Lebanon' within the pesharim must be taken into account, but Vermes's study has enduring value insofar as it documents the similarity between figurative identifications of biblical imagery in the pesharim and the midrashim, although to argue the former depends on the latter is anachronistic. The phrase 'figurative identification' is Horgan's (1979, p. 52), and more precisely describes the phenomenon in question than does 'allegorisation', which (as we shall consider below) implies a distinctive understanding of the function of Scripture.

Horgan herself drops the phrase 'figurative identification' as a category by which Scripture is interpreted in the pesharim, and instead refers to 'metaphorical identification of figures or things named in the lemma' (1979, p. 245). But in the cases she discusses, the text serves as an occasion to identify figures, not metaphors, so that her earlier designation, made within a comment on 1QpHab 12.1 in particular, seems preferable. Horgan also distinguishes interpretations which adhere more (or less) closely to the content of the lemma, those which refer to the wording of the lemma, and those 'in which the pesher seems to be only loosely related to the lemma' (1979, pp. 244, 245). It is, of course, useful for the modern interpreter to appreciate the range of relatedness to the biblical text in the pesharim; a more nuanced classification is developed by Fitzmyer (1974, pp. 16–58), who distinguishes among (1) 'literal or historical', (2) 'modernized', (3) 'accommodated', and (4) 'eschatological' types of interpretation in quotations in sources from Qumran other than the pesharim. Similar categories may also be applied to 1QpHab, but only on the understanding that they are our own (so, rightly, Fitzmyer, 1974, pp. 57, 58).

Within the most general of terms, we might say that the interpretation of 1QpHab is literal, that is, predicated on the wording of Scripture. That wording, however, is taken to be the ciphered counsel of God, which it is the business of *pešer* to decode. What the text is held to manifest, in other words, is neither a historical complex of events, nor a sequence of ideas allegorically intimated, but the contemporary unfolding of God's final victory. For that reason, the ethos of *pešer* more nearly approaches typology than allegory, although – as Fitzmyer points out (1974, p. 55) – the language of types is, of course, absent. The more substantive difference between *pešer* and typology, however, is that the latter (in the christian sources in which it appears) portrays the reference of Scripture as belonging to the past, while 1QpHab is concerned with the immediate past, the present, and the immediate future (cf. Braun, 1966, pp. 306, 307).

## The ideology of the pesharim

Bruce (1959, p. 8) expresses the consensus when he links the pesharim of Qumran to Daniel (see 4:6, for example), where the *pešar* sought by Nebuchadnezzar is the interpretation of a 'mystery' (*rāz*, cf. 1QpHab 7.5, 8, 14). Horgan masterfully fills out the discussion, bringing it up to date, but she does not come to a different conclusion (1979, pp. 230–37); the similarity between the pesharim and writings styled apocalyptic continues to excite interest (1979, pp. 249–59). Horgan also provides an account of the usual approach to the pesharim, according to which the history of the sect of Qumran can be seen reflected in them (1979, pp. 5–9; cf. Bruce, 1959, p. 15;

Vermes, 1975, p. 47). Those who remark on the evidently historical allusions within 1QpHab and other pesharim do not, of course, presuppose that the identities of figures can be known precisely today given the present state of our knowledge; that state of affairs may be taken to support the argument for a certain kinship with apocalyptic literature. There may also be a case to be made for the argument that certain figures in the pesharim may be more fruitfully approached as representative of ideals, fears, and aspirations within the sect, rather than as ciphers precisely to be decoded (cf. Violette, 1983, pp. 64, 65; and van der Woude, 1982). On the other hand, the historical aspect of pesharim such as 4QpNah, however qualified, has long been recognised (cf. Amussin, 1968, pp. 10, 11; Horgan, 1979, pp. 158–62).

It is therefore curious to find the old argument resurfacing that the pesharim can be discounted for historical purposes (cf. Davies, 1983, p. 2), especially in a monograph which asserts that the *Damascus Document alone* 'contains explicit *(sic)* historiographical statements'. Ironically, one of these 'historiographical statements' involves a *pešer* of Isa. 24:17 (CD 4.14): the attempt to polarise the usage of Scripture within the corpus of Qumran does not appear fruitful. As recognised long ago by Betz (1960, pp. 40–45, 74, 75), there is an interpretative continuity within the material which unites its halakic stance and its peculiarly eschatological understanding of history (cf. also Schiffman, 1975; Brooke, 1981 and 1985; Friebel, 1981). Indeed, that is the reason for which no document in the corpus can be read simply as a historical chronicle. That has clearly been established by nearly a generation of research, so that the status of the pesharim as tokens of the sect's ideology, including its view of history, is to be granted.

## 2 PHILO

The conviction which is betrayed in the pesharim, that Scripture refers to esoteric realities, may be taken to be basic within that sort of interpretation which is called allegorical. As has already been observed, Bruce actually characterises the sectarians of Qumran as allegorical in their approach. Although we have criticised such an understanding, it must be admitted that scholars have referred to 'allegory' in respect of any perspective under which a text says something 'other' *(allē)* than its strict sense (cf. Ginzberg, 1916). In practice, however, the noun is generally used of the attempt to relate sacred texts, especially myths, to philosophical ideas (cf. Büchsel, 1978, pp. 260, 261), as became common in late antiquity. It appears that the establishment of the practice in Alexandria influenced the first Jewish representatives of the perspective, Aristobulus and the author(s) of *Aristeas* (Büchsel, 1978, pp. 260, 261). The pre-eminent practitioner for both Judaism and Christianity, however, is Philo of Alexandria.

As measured by his impact on successors, Philo is of greater importance to Christianity than to Judaism; classical attempts at midrash were not congenial to the systematic development of philosophical speculation by means of Scripture. For both movements, however, Philo is of great historical interest, as a most erudite spokesman of Greek-speaking Judaism. The astonishing range of his literary output has defied the agreement of a consensus concerning the classification of his writings. Nonetheless, the bulk of his work, on any reading, is more or less closely related to Scripture.

*Quaestiones et solutiones in Genesim* and *Quaestiones et solutiones in Exodum* are preserved in Armenian, although 'preserved' may be an overstatement, since it has been argued that the work is incomplete (cf. Sandmel, 1979, p. 79). They proceed in a relatively straightforward manner, however, with passages cited, interpreted literally, and then (at greater length) philosophically. Whether the reason for this comparative simplicity of the *Quaestiones* is that they represent preliminary notes (so Sandmel), or approximate to homilies as might have been given in a synagogue (so Nikiprowetzky, 1977, pp. 179, 180), they confirm the impression that, whatever else Philo was, he was a self-conscious commentator on Scripture.

A more discursive and explanatory element characterises the works collectively known as 'exposition' (cf. Sandmel, 1979, p. 30; Amir, 1971, pp. 410, 411), which deal with the most basic of matters, such as biblical characters and the meaning and purpose of laws (cf. Sandmel, 1979, pp. 47–76). *De Abrahamo*, *De Josepho*, *De Decalogo*, *De Specialibus Legibus* (i–iv), and *De Virtutibus* are typically assigned to the class. As Sandmel observes, however, there are works which are only notionally assigned to the group, and which may belong to another genre. Classification in such cases is often for want of more precise categories. Moreover, Sandmel cites references within the corpus to the succession of Philo's treatises (for example, *De Abrahamo* after *De Opificio Mundi*, cf. Sandmel, 1979, p. 55), but quite rightly points out that the usual arrangement does violence to that apparently obvious order (cf. the placement of *De Opificio Mundi* prior to the treatises styled 'allegory' (Sandmel, 1979, p. 178)). If the usual order is followed, the genre of *De Opificio Mundi* is not expository, but allegorical, and Philo's reference to the treatise in *De Abrahamo* becomes an aporia, rather than a useful index of genre. This state of affairs might be held to be consistent with the occasional nature of Philo's work, with a complicated textual history (cf. Sandmel, 1979, pp. 29, 30), or both. Such matters might be more confidently settled if Philo's purpose in his expository works were better known.

Sandmel (1979, p. 47) is rather dismissive of Goodenough's suggestion (1933), in respect of *De Vita Moses* i, ii, that Philo's aim in the 'exposition' was apologetic. Rather than explaining Philo's elementary style as an effort at conversion, Sandmel takes it as evidence of an address of 'uninformed Jews on the threshold of apostasy'; the thought of Gentiles wading avidly through Philonic exposition does not commend itself to his imagination (p. 47). The substance of Goodenough's argument, however, namely his reference to the attitudes towards Roman rule and jurisprudence, and towards proselytes, and his observations on the balance of allegory and explanation (1933, pp. 116–19), is not accounted for by Sandmel's refutation. If Goodenough (who consciously built on Schürer's observations, cf. 1933, p. 113) is correct, then the 'exposition' would be of immediate interest to the entire question of converts in hellenistic Judaism (1933, p. 125); if Sandmel is correct, we are informed rather of the diversity and divisions within Judaism itself. On either reading, the treatises which have been assigned to the class of exposition are of especial interest to the study of early Judaism.

Commencing with Genesis 2, the treatises classed as 'allegory' begin with three works entitled *Legum Allegoriae*. The treatises start with a scriptural passage, after which they are named; the titles therefore appear as *De Cherubim*, *De Sacrificiis Abelis et Caini*, and so forth. As a result, short pericopae from the first thirty-seven chapters of Genesis are used. After their initial citation, the treatises proceed through their quintessentially Philonic interpretation. Indeed, the treatment is so characteristic of Philo as to appear idiosyncratic. His comment on Gen. 3:14, 'You shall eat earth all the days of your life', is representative (*Leg. Alleg.* iii, 161–81; cf. Colson and Whitaker, 1929). Having cited the passage, Philo observes that earthly food is appropriate to the body, while the soul requires the divine food of understanding (161). That the food of the soul is heavenly is, to Philo's satisfaction, attested by the 'sacred word' of Scripture in the episode of the manna in Exodus 16 (162–4). This apparent digression leads to an exhortation to the soul to seek its appropriate portion of understanding, according to the moderating principle of how the lamb should be eaten at Passover, as stated in Exod. 12:4 (165, 166). The worthy aim of seeking the manna during the day in Exod. 16:4 is an instance of the soul's willingness to walk in the divine law, which is its proper purpose (166–8). The soul's food, then, is God's word, whose delicacy Philo described by way of comparison to the manna (169–171). The divine word attracts the soul much as the manna attracted the Israelites, prompting the question, 'What is it?' (Exod. 16:15; 172, 173). At the same time, the reference to the manna in Deut. 8:3 shows that deprivation can also lead the soul to the knowledge of its true sustenance (174–6). But if God's word sustains the soul, how can Jacob say he is fed by God himself, rather than by God's word, in Gen. 48:15, 16? Jacob here speaks in a truly scientific manner (*phusikōtata*): God himself bestows food, while the removal of ills is accomplished by 'angels and words' (177, 178). Jacob therefore gets the better of Joseph, who claimed for himself the ability to feed his father (Gen. 45:9, 11). Philo closes with remarks directed to the edification of Joseph, and to his mother Rachel, since in Philo's judgment she made a similar category mistake (179–81).

## Philo's scriptural programme: De Opificio Mundi

Philo's treatment of Scripture is sufficiently unusual to have evoked some remarkably negative comments from even the most sympathetic of his readers. Sandmel regretted that there is seldom a 'discernible (sic) clear thread of exposition' (1979, p. 78), while Colson and Whitaker remarked that 'Philo, entirely devoid of creative genius, could never get away from the rôle of interpreter' (1949, p. xvi). Such opinions are reviewed by Nikiprowetzky (1977, pp. 1, 2) in the course of a stimulating monograph which characterises Philo's work generally as commentary. Philo's task, according to Nikiprowetzky, is to explain what Scripture refers to (p. 161), not to develop a philosophical system (pp. 181, 182), and the main lines of his argument were accepted by Sandmel (1979, pp. 80, 123).

The portrait of Philo as a commentator becomes more defensible when it is observed that what Sandmel called his '"stream of consciousness" manner' (1979, p. 78) is far from sui generis. The transitions involved in the passage from Legum Allegoriae iii cited above can be enumerated simply. The notion of eating earth in Gen. 3:14 brings on the idea of the soul being fed by knowledge (161). That is the trigger for coping with the episode of the manna in Exodus 16 (162–73) and Deuteronomy 8 (174–6); the subsidiary motif of Exodus 12 is explained by the theme of Passover, the context of the episode of the manna. The shift to Jacob in Gen. 48:15, 16 is occasioned by the mention of God feeding the patriarch directly, rather than by means of his word (177–81). Such movement from passage to passage falls well within the conventional, rabbinic understanding of what degree of analogy in wording or substance might justify the association of passages (cf. Finkel, 1964, pp. 123–6). In another article, the present writer has treated rabbinic interpretations of Isa. 24:23 (Chilton, 1983). It was there shown that in Leviticus Rabbah 11.8, the citation of Lev. 9:1 leads to an extensive listing of passages which mention 'glory', as does the biblical verse initially cited, and culminates in a particular discussion of the passage from Isaiah, but in its own terms (Chilton, 1983, pp. 14–16). Another discussion of the passages, presented in b. Pesaḥim 68a, attempts to resolve the apparent discrepancy between Isa. 24:23 and Isa. 30:26 concerning what is to become of the sun in the age to come (Chilton, 1983, pp. 17, 18). The movement of Philo from passage to analogous passage (Genesis 3; Exodus 16; Exodus 12; Deuteronomy 8), and then to an apparently discrepant passage (Gen. 48:15, 16) falls within the range of the midrashic repertoire which the rabbis were later to represent.

Even Nikiprowetzky acknowledges that Philo treats Scripture as a means to an end, the instrument by which access to divine reality becomes possible

(1977, pp. 181, 182, 188–91). Of course, immediately that is said, the question emerges: what, for Philo, is the end of the quest? Should it be explained in hellenistic or jewish terms, or in some hybrid language? Sandmel voices an old consensus in new garb when he concludes, 'the intuitions, assumptions, and loyalties in Philo are Jewish, but the basic intent of Philo's thought is Grecian' (1979, p. 28). In other words, all of Sandmel's agreement with Nikiprowetzky is in respect of Philo's method, not his purpose. In the end, allegory for Sandmel is the bridge between Philo's instincts and his reason.

Sandmel rejects Goodenough's attempt at a less dichotomous formulation. Goodenough insistently maintained that the unity of Philo's enterprise was to be discovered in a mystical tendency, in which hellenistic aspects were taken up in a contemplation of the supreme God by means of the torah (1963, pp. 13–19, 134–60). For that reason, Goodenough attacked, as beside the point, the distinction between Philo as 'a hellenized Jew' and Philo as 'a judaized Hellenist' (p. 26). Goodenough's perspective allowed of the philosophical development which Wolfson attempted to trace, without requiring an argument to the effect that Philo was a systematic thinker (Goodenough, 1963, pp. 16–19; Wolfson, 1947). The strength of Goodenough's thesis is that it accommodates both the philosophical and exegetical aspects of Philo, rather than exacerbating the divide. Indeed, the sort of governing impulse suggested by Goodenough would serve to explain the exegetical instrumentality of Philo's work, as described by Nikiprowetzky. Sandmel surely expresses the consensus when he doubts the Jungian aspects of Goodenough's characterisation of hellenistic Judaism (1979, p. 147), but he seems too eager to resist the possibility that Philo might represent a significant feature of that Judaism. Burton Mack's thesis, however, presents Philo's distinctive understanding of the *logos* as the development of a more general theology of wisdom in sources of hellenistic Judaism (1973, pp. 148, 149). Precisely that connexion, were it substantiated, would unravel a mystery which has plagued investigators since the time of Colson: 'why did he (*sc.* Philo) confine his scriptural labours to the Pentateuch?' (Colson, 1940, p. 240). For Philo, it may have been axiomatic that torah and wisdom were to be identified (cf. Ecclesiasticus 24 and Nikiprowetzky, 1977, pp. 154, 155; Bentrich, 1910, pp. 143–49).

The Philonic programme, however, obviously included the allegorical technique which was an inheritance from Hellenism (cf. Colson, 1917, pp. 153, 154), and the equally pronounced speculative interest which is evidenced by those discursive writings which cannot be fitted into the category of biblical interpretation, no matter how wide the category is stretched. This class of material, called 'Miscellaneous Writings' by Sandmel (1979, p. 30), includes the *Hypothetica*, *Quod omnis probus liber sit*, *De vita contemplativa*, *in Flaccum*, and *Legatio ad Caium*. These treatises present a mixture of philosophical speculation, historical description, and apologetic appeal. Given that understanding, and familiarity with the convention of hellenistic literature, according to which genre followed purpose, the assignment of these writings to the overall category of discourse should not mislead us.

An instance of the intersection between discourse and interpretation is provided by *De Opificio Mundi*. As has already been mentioned, the work's classification is problematic, but that is an advantage from the point of view of considering the fluidity of Philo's treatment of Scripture. Gen. 1:1 is cited in the LXX, the usual version of Philo (cf. Katz, 1950), but not until *De Opificio* 26, after an extensive exordium. The long introduction is most apposite, since Philo thinks of Moses' account of what happened *en archē* as an *archē*, preface (*De Opificio* 3; cf. Müller, 1841, p. 119). In other words, Philo treats Moses within the terms of reference of hellenistic rhetoric, not merely hellenistic philosophy (cf. Mack, 1984). He waxes enthusiastic in respect of Moses' decision to speak of the *kosmopoiia*, which implies that the *nomos* of which he speaks is in harmony with the world, and *vice versa* (*De Opificio* 3–6; cf. Müller, 1841, pp. 113, 114). He insists, however, that God stands in relation to the world as father and maker (cf. Müller, 1841, pp. 133, 134); what can be seen is not eternal, since it is subject to 'genesis' and change (7–12).

Such matters occupy Philo's attention because, in his understanding, they explicate the very topic Moses addresses (cf. Soulier, 1876, pp. 30–4). The next major section is devoted to a related task (13–25, cf. van Winden, 1983, p. 209): Philo embarks on a comment regarding the six days of creation in *De Opificio* 13. The choice of subject may seem odd, but it is significant to Philo that the 'perfect number', six (*De Opificio* 14; cf. Müller, 1841, pp. 140–5), should be at issue, since what God first made was, not the visible world, but the divine pattern thereof (*De Opificio* 16). That notion triggers the idea, borrowed from Plato's *Timaeus* (cf. Goodenough, 1963, pp. 35–8 and Müller, 1841, pp. 145f), that God functioned as an architect, who forms a plan before he builds (*De Opificio* 17–23). The world of ideas, framed by God, can be found only in the divine reason (*theios logos*, *De Opificio* 20; Müller, 1841, p. 149). The intelligible (as distinct from the visible) world is none other than God's *logos*, or reason, as it creates the world (*De Opificio* 24).

According to Philo, his teaching must be accepted as a Mosaic doctrine, not merely his own. After all, if the genesis of man is according to God's image, how much more the whole world (*De Opificio* 25). Although Philo's reading is complicated, it follows logically from his apprehension of the wording, form and function of Genesis 1 (cf. van Winden, 1983, p. 215).

Even in this erudite discussion, there are tantalising similarities to rabbinic interpretation. The targumic 'memra' is certainly not recognisably cognate with the *Timaeus*, and yet its involvement with creation, albeit as a subsidiary motif, is notable (cf. Chilton, 1982, pp. 56–69). When Philo says man is made as an *eikōn eikonos* (*De Opificio* 25), it is for philosophical reasons, to portray visible man as the imprint of a divine image. When man is said to be made *bdmwtyh bdmw* in Neophyti I (Gen. 1:27; cf. Stein, 1931, pp. 2, 3), it is for reasons of exegetical convention, to avoid speaking of God coming into direct contact with people. Nonetheless, the echo is as loud as when God is compared to an architect in Genesis Rabbah 1.1 (cf. Nikiprowetzky, 1977, p. 155). Even after one allows for coincidence, and for the theoretical possibility of rabbinic borrowing from Philo, the impression remains that we meet in the Alexandrian teacher an erudite spokesman for Judaism, and not simply a learned dabbler in traditions to which he was only partially committed.

## 3 THE MEKILTA

The Mekilta, or 'standard', is a midrash on a substantial portion of the book of Exodus. Jacob Lauterbach, the editor and translator of the edition which is most widely cited, estimated that nearly the whole of the book's legal matter, and much of its important narrative, is dealt with (1949, pp. xviii, xix). The absence of a reference to the midrash in the Talmud led Lauterbach to the conclusion that the Mekilta was subsumed within Sifre by the amoraic period (1949, p. xxiv, but cf. Wacholder, 1968, pp. 122, 123). The work is widely regarded as a tannaitic midrash (second century), although that consensus has been challenged by Ben Zion Wacholder (1968), who placed the work in the eighth century. The only positive indication he supplies in favour of a late dating, however, is that the Mekilta uses a greater variety of phrases to cite Scripture than do the Tannaim, at least as cited elsewhere (1968, pp. 135, 136). His underlying assumption is that such variety is a baroque refinement, rather than an early feature, and in that presumption he may or may not be correct.

These widely varying estimates represent divergent attempts to do justice to the striking exegetical profile of the Mekilta, and the silence of the Talmud concerning it. What sort of work would be motivated by the concern to explain the removal of leaven at Passover, as in Mekilta Pisḥa 8? As Lightstone remarks, the 'halakic aspects of the pericope seem innocuous at best' (1983, p. 35). That finding leads him to the conclusion that 'the editor's purpose is other than halakic instruction' (p. 35). The strangely tangential relationship of the Mekilta to halakic discussion among the rabbis can be taken to support either an early or a late dating.

The preponderance of Ishmael's teaching in the Mekilta led to its attribution to that tanna, in order to distinguish our midrash from the Mekilta de R. Simeon ben Yoḥai. (The title is apparently attested in the tenth century; cf. Wacholder, 1968, p. 120.) Lauterbach credits the attribution to Ishmael, but he does so with caution, and allows of the contribution of later redactors (1949, pp. xxiv–xxviii). The possibility that the attribution to tannaim is pseudepigraphic is stressed by Wacholder (1968, pp. 126–34); a less extreme, but sceptical, approach is represented by Gary Porton (1982, pp. 167–73). In view of the late attestation of explicit interest in the work, it is quite possible to conceive of this layered process of transmission and interpretation extending to the period posited by Wachholder, but the substance of the work appears to be tannaitic (cf. Stemberger, 1976, pp. 238–40). A recent study by Niditch lends support to that finding, in that it establishes that the opening of the Mekilta in Pisha 1 conveys an emphasis on the efficacy of martyrdom (1982). Such an orientation is also expressed by the midrash that, when God sees the blood on the lintels in Exodus 12, he 'sees the blood of the Aqedah of Isaac' (Pisha 7.78, 79; 11.93). The notion that Isaac actually shed his blood on Moriah is not attested before the tannaitic period. On the other hand, the more elaborate references of a later period, to Isaac's being burned, are absent from the passage (cf. Chilton, 1980, and Lauterbach, 1949, pp. 57, 58 n. 7).

### The sense of Scripture in Ten Songs

The precise purpose of the midrash, however, remains a mystery. The work proceeds in sectional divisions which deal with the biblical text sequentially (from Exod. 12:1 in Pisha, from 13:17 in Beshallah, from 15:1 in Shirata, from 15:22 in Vayassaᶜ, from 17:8 in Amalek, from 19:1 in Bahodesh, from 21:1 in Nezekin, from 22:24 in Kaspa, from 31:12 in Shabbata; cf. Lauterbach, 1949, for the names of the designations, whose relation to the text of Exodus will be obvious). Unlike the pesharim, there is no attempt in the Mekilta to relate Scripture consistently to the specific events or expectations of a subsequent period; neither is there the programmatic attempt of a Philo to discover explicit, philosophical themes in Exodus. There is, however, if not a programme, then a consistent tendency, to portray the coherence of Exodus with God's revelation in Scripture generally.

So, for example, the song of Exod. 15:1 becomes an occasion to meditate on various celebrations of divine victory: 'Is there only one song, are there not ten?'. Shirata 1 goes on to speak of the ten songs (from line 15), understood as a song prior to Passover (Isa. 30:29), the song of Exodus 15 itself, the song in thanksgiving for water in the wilderness (Num. 21:17), the song which followed the conclusion of Moses' writing the torah (Deut. 31:24–30), the 'song' of Joshua (Josh. 10:12), the song of Deborah (Judg. 5:1), the songs of David (2 Sam. 22:1) and of Solomon (Ps. 30:1), the song of Jehoshaphat (2 Chron. 20:21), and the song which will be sung at the end of the world (Isa. 42:10). As Sibley Towner discovers in his classic study (1973, pp. 165, 166), 'a basic criterion of selection', according to which the list was compiled, was the presence of some form of the stem *šyr* in the lemma. But as Towner also – and importantly – points out, lexicography is only *one* criterion of selection. In the case of Josh. 10:12, the criterion is only met if *yāšār* in v. 13 is associated with the stem *šyr* (Towner, 1973, p. 165). In any case, the midrash is by no means a mere catalogue of passages which included the criterial root. Rather, the passages are selected, and shaped into a chronological enumeration, framed by passages from Isaiah, in which the victory of Passover, as reflected in various other songs of victory, 'instil(s) faith in future salvation and the world to come' (Towner, 1973, p. 166).

The functional integrity of the list of ten songs is demonstrated by the very similar list in Tanḥuma Beshallaḥ 10, which appears in connexion with the narrative of the ten plagues (cf. Towner, 1973, pp. 166, 167). Indeed, the prominence given to Isaian texts in both lists, on the understanding that 30:29 is sung on the eve of Passover (cf. Lauterbach II, 1949, p. 2, n. 1, with *b*. *Pesaḥim* 95b and Genesis Rabbah 6.2), undermines the apparent dominance of the text from Exodus. That is hardly surprising, since it is a characteristic feature of midrash that Scripture is cited expressly in respect of Scripture, in order to illuminate the understanding of God and Israel which the texts corporately convey (cf. Chilton, 1983, and Basser, 1984). Because the corporately scriptural attestation of the divine hope for Israel is axiomatic within the Mekilta, its exposition can sit loosely in respect of the text of Exodus, the putative point of departure.

The looseness of its relation to Exod. 15:1 becomes all the more apparent when digressions within Shirata 1 are considered. The eighth song, ascribed to Solomon, gives pause for thought, since David is referred to in the heading of Psalm 30 (Shirata 1.25, 26). The midrash takes *ldwd* in respect of the temple, rather than the psalm, which makes the defence of Solomonic authorship possible (Shirata 1.26, 27). The exposition is then given that David devoted his very life to the temple, and so it is called by his name (Shirata 1.27–34). This leads to the gnomic remark, 'Everything a man devotes his life to is named after him' (Shirata 1.34, 35). For that reason, the torah, Israel and judges could all be named after Moses (Shirata 1.35–63).

By this point, the digression from the putative text of the midrash may seem to be of Philonic proportions, but it should be kept in mind that Exod. 15:1 is only formally commented upon; the 'song' to which it relates, as one of the ten principal instances of the history and promise of Israel, is the actual burden of the midrash. The defence of Psalm 30 as Solomonic becomes crucial within that context. The list of three items named after Moses, on the other hand, corresponds to a type of scriptural enumeration which Towner calls 'syntactical analogy' (1973, pp. 181–4). The independence of this subsidiary list is demonstrated by its presence, in modified form, in Exodus Rabbah (30.4, cf. Towner, 1973, pp. 183, 184). Logically, however, the syntactical list serves to buttress what is said about Solomon, which in turn supports his placement in the lexical list of songs. In other words, the fact that the Mekilta has a complex history of tradition does not obviate the discernment of its integrity as a collection.

Viewed as lateral, rather than as linear, logic, the reference back to Moses in Shirata 1 is especially effective, since Moses is the principal in the song which triggers the midrash. Functional usefulness is characteristic of apparent digressions in Shirata 1. The song of Jehoshaphat in 2 Chron. 20:21 omits the words 'for he is good' from the usual pattern, 'Give thanks to the LORD, for he is good, for his mercy endures forever'. The Mekilta explains that the reason for the omission is that God does not rejoice in the sort of destruction of the wicked in which Jehoshaphat was involved (Shirata 1.63–71). By the well-known rule of *qal wāḥōmer*, that applies all the more to the righteous (1.71–2). The mention of the righteous leads into the citation of Isa. 42:10 as the climactic, eschatological song (1.73–81), since such a hymn of celebration was associated with the righteous (cf. Tg Is 24:16 and Chilton, 1982, pp. 81–6). The midrash closes with the thought that the tenth song is definitive, since the 'song' of Isa. 42:10 is masculine, rather than feminine, and is therefore not to be followed by any subjugation (1.75–81). That observation is used to underline the importance of the last song, although other songs in the list are also referred to by means of the masculine noun.

The midrash of the ten songs in Shirata 1 is striking for several reasons. Unlike the situation in the citation of many other phrases in the Mekilta, it is the only interpretation of 'this song' which is conveyed. That fact, along with the length of the midrash, serves to emphasise its claim to pursue the significance of Moses' song. The emphasis makes it all the more apparent that, in the narrow sense of the term, the interpretation cannot be described as halakic: it does not issue in explicitly prescriptive teaching. There are sections of the Mekilta which do function in a more precisely halakic way; the discussion of matters attendant on circumcision in Pisḥa 15.25–45 might be cited by way of example. The fact remains, however, as Lauterbach pointed out (1949, I, p. xix), that the bulk of the material in the document could better be described as haggadic than as halakic.

## The purpose of the Mekilta

At this point, the designation of the Mekilta as halakic midrash, along with Sifra and Sifre, begins to appear problematic. Strictly speaking, that characterisation is no more accurate than 'tannaitic midrash', which – for chronological reasons that have already been discussed – is also problematic (cf. Stemberger, 1976, pp. 233–6). The point of the midrash of the ten songs is not that the songs must be sung, but that these songs – which have been, are, and will be sung – are warranted in Scripture. The principle of selection is not merely lexical; Scripture speaks of many more songs. The function of the midrash is to work out Israel's identity in terms of Scripture. In that regard, the Mekilta approximates to the Mishnah, where the selection of scriptural texts also proves crucial (cf. Neusner, 1981, pp. 217–29, 329–51). The radical claim of the Mishnah, itself to constitute torah, is of course not that of the Mekilta. Precisely that is Neusner's starting point (p. 218), and it is what makes his analysis penetrating and apposite. He contrasts the Mishnah formally with Sifra, where the programme is to relate the Scripture to stated positions which approximate to those of the Mishnah (pp. 219, 220). The continuity and contrast between the Mishnah (whose framers are here described) on the one hand and Sifra (and the Talmud) on the other is described as follows:

Their program itself constituted a statement *upon* the meaning of Scripture. They and their apologists of one sort hastened to add, their program consisted of a statement *of* and upon the meaning of Scripture (1981, p. 223).

The Mekilta can be located within such an apologetic tendency, but its programme appears less explicit than that of Sifra. In the Mekilta, as Lightstone (1983) has suggested, the form of the argument conveys meaning more than any discursive statement of theme. Wacholder must be credited with making an early statement that 'the basic purpose of the Mekilta may well have been to vindicate rabbinic tradition', although his contention that it does so against the Karaites may be doubted (1968, pp. 143, 144). Within the Mekilta, the texts of Exodus which are halakically redolent and narratively constitutive of Israel relate logically and demonstrably to rabbinic discussion. The document may usefully be described as halakic in the sense that its programme is to demonstrate the congruity between Scripture and mishnaic reason. The prominence of the format of lists, as principles of discourse, within both the Mishnah and the Mekilta, serves to underline and illustrate their relationship.

## 4   CONCLUSION

This chapter has described the place of Scripture in three superficially disparate interpretative works: the Habakkuk Pesher, Philo, and the Mekilta. In each, of course, explicit recourse to Scripture, in the form of a comment, is the structural point of departure for the document, or group of documents, concerned. Moreover, in each case there is a positive correlation between what Neusner has called the principles of exegesis, the purposes of exegesis, and the programme of collecting and arranging exegeses (1986, pp. 183, 184). All these types of interpretation might be styled 'midrash', if by that is meant conscious reflection on the torah (Neusner, 1986, pp. 176–8). But Neusner is at pains to point out, and he demonstrates beyond a reasonable doubt, that documents,

# B. D. CHILTON

not individual exegeses, are the appropriate starting point of analysis. For that reason, *pešer*, Philonic allegory, and midrash might profitably be viewed as genres within the species of biblical interpretation generally.

In each genre, Scripture is taken to be a pre-eminent disclosure of God, the revelation which makes sense of, and gives sense to, the interpretative task. And Scripture is assumed to be coherent and reasonable in its statements: ordinarily logical procedures, such as the development of implication, verbal syllogism, and analogy, are held to apply. The difference among the genres is less a matter of precise method of approach than of what Scripture is essentially taken to be. Scripture *is* the ciphered account of the end in the pesharim; it *is* the soul's map toward union with God for Philo; it *is* Israel's covenant of survival in the Mekilta. Such visions are more than a matter of procedure or of method. They are part of a people's understanding of themselves, of their world, and of their God.

## BIBLIOGRAPHY

Y. Amir 'Philo Judaeus', *Encyclopedia Judaica* 13 (New York, 1971), pp. 409–15.

J. D. Amussin 'Bemerkungen zu den Qumran-Kommentaren', in S. Wagner (ed.), *Bibel und Qumran. Beiträge zur Erforschung der Beziehung zwischen Bibel- und Qumranwissenschaft. Hans Bardtke zum 22.9.1966* (Berlin, 1968), pp. 9–19.

B. J. Bamberger 'Philo and the Aggadah', *HUCA* 48 (1977), 153–85.

H. W. Basser *Midrashic Interpretations of the Song of Moses*, American University Studies – Theology and Religion 2 (New York, 1984).

N. Bentrich *Philo-Judaeus of Alexandria* (Philadelphia, 1910).

O. Betz *Offenbarung und Schriftforschung in der Qumransekte*, WUNT 6 (Tübingen, 1960).

H. Braun *Qumran und das Neue Testament* II (Tübingen, 1966).

G. J. Brooke 'Qumran Pesher: Toward the Redefinition of a Genre', *RQ* 40 (1981), 483–503.

    *Exegesis at Qumran. 4QFlorilegium in its Jewish Context*, JSOTSS 29 (Sheffield, 1985).

W. H. Brownlee *The Midrash Pesher of Habakkuk*, SBLMS 24 (Missoula, 1979).

F. F. Bruce *Biblical Exegesis in the Qumran Texts* (Grand Rapids, 1959).

    *Second Thoughts on the Dead Sea Scrolls* (Grand Rapids, 1961).

    'Pesher', *Encyclopedia Judaica* 13 (New York, 1971), pp. 331–3.

P. Büchsel '*allēgoreō*', *TDNT* 1, pp. 260–3.

B. D. Chilton 'Isaac and the Second Night', *Biblica* 61 (1980), 78–88.

    *The Glory of Israel. The Theology and Provenience of the Isaiah Targum*, JSOTSS 23 (Sheffield, 1982).

Commenting on the Old Testament

'Varieties and Tendencies of Midrash: Rabbinic Interpretations of Isaiah 24.23', in R. T. France and D. Wenham (eds.), *Gospel Perspectives* III (Sheffield, 1983), pp. 9–32.

F. H. Colson 'Philo on Education', *JQR* 18 (1917), 151–62.

'Philo's Quotations from the Old Testament', *JTS* 41 (1940), 237–51.

F. H. Colson and G. H. Whitaker *Philo* I, Loeb Classical Library (New York, 1929).

P. R. Davies *The Damascus Covenant. An Interpretation of the 'Damascus Document'*, JSOTSS 25 (Sheffield, 1983).

A. Dupont-Sommer *Les écrits esséniens découverts près de la Mer Morte*, Bibliothèque Historique (Paris, 1980).

K. Elliger *Studien zum Habakkuk-Kommentar vom Toten Meer*, Beiträge zur historischen Theologie 15 (Tübingen, 1953).

K. G. Friebel 'Biblical Interpretation in the *Pesharim* of the Qumran Community', *Hebrew Studies* 22 (1981), 13–24.

A. Finkel *The Pharisees and the Teacher of Nazareth. A Study of their Background, their Halachic and Midrashic Teachings, the Similarities and Differences*, AGSU 4 (Leiden, 1964).

J. A. Fitzmyer *Essays on the Semitic Background of the New Testament*, Sources for Biblical Study 5 (Missoula, 1974).

*The Dead Sea Scrolls. Major Publications and Tools for Study*, Sources for Biblical Study 8 (Missoula, 1977).

L. Ginzberg 'Allegorical Interpretation', *Jewish Encyclopedia* I (New York, 1916), pp. 403–11.

E. R. Goodenough 'Philo's Exposition of the Law and His De Vita Mosis', *HTR* 26 (1933), 109–25.

*An Introduction to Philo Judaeus* (New York, 1963).

M. P. Horgan *Pesharim: Qumran Interpretations of Biblical Books*, CBQMS 8 (Washington, 1979).

P. Katz *Philo's Bible. The Aberrant Text of Bible Quotations in some Philonic Writings* (Cambridge, 1950).

W. L. Knox 'A Note on Philo's Use of the Old Testament', *JTS* 41 (1940), 30–4 (cf. Colson, 1940).

J. Z. Lauterbach *Mekilta de-Rabbi Ishmael* (Philadelphia, 1949).

J. N. Lightstone 'Form as Meaning in Halakic *Midrash*: A Programmatic Statement', *Semeia* 27 (1983), 23–35.

B. L. Mack *Logos und Sophia. Untersuchungen zur Weisheitstheologie im hellenistischen Judentum*, SUNT 10 (Göttingen, 1973).

'Decoding the Scripture: Philo and the Rules of Rhetoric', in F. E. Greenspahn, E. Hilgert and B. L. Mack (eds.), *Nourished with Peace. Studies in Hellenistic Judaism in Memory of Samuel Sandmel* (Chico, 1984), pp. 81–115.

J. G. Müller *Des Juden Philo Buch von der Weltschöpfung* (Berlin, 1841).

139

J. Neusner *Judaism. The Evidence of the Mishnah* (Chicago and London, 1981).

*Midrash in Context. Exegesis in Formative Judaism* (Philadelphia, 1983).

*Comparative Midrash. The Plan and Program of Genesis and Leviticus Rabbah*, Brown Judaic Studies 111 (Atlanta, 1986).

S. Niditch 'Merits, Martyrs, and "Your Life as Booty:" an Exegesis of Mekilta, Pisha i', *JSJ* 13 (1982), 160–71.

V. Nikiprowetzky *Le Commmentaire de l'Ecriture chez Philon d'Alexandrie*, Arbeiten zur Literatur und Geschichte des hellenistischen Judentums 11 (Leiden, 1977).

G. G. Porton *The Traditions of Rabbi Ishmael* iv, SJLA 19 (Leiden, 1982).

C. Rabin 'Notes on the Habakkuk Scroll and the Zadokite Documents', *VT* 5 (1955), 148–62.

S. Sandmel *Philo of Alexandria. An Introduction* (New York and Oxford, 1979).

L. H. Schiffman *The Halakhah at Qumran*, SJLA 16 (Leiden, 1975).

L. H. Silberman 'Toward a Rhetoric of Midrash: A Preliminary Account', in R. Polzin and E. Rothman (eds.), *Biblical Mosaic: Changing Perspectives* (Philadelphia, 1982), pp. 15–26.

H. Soulier *La doctrine du Logos chez Philon d'Alexandrie* (Turin, 1876).

E. Stein *Philo und der Midrasch. Philos Schilderung der Gestalten des Pentateuch verglichen mit der des Midrasch*, BZAW 57 (Giessen, 1931).

G. Stemberger (after H. L. Strack) *Einleitung in Talmud und Midrasch* (Munich, 1976).

W. S. Towner *The Rabbinic 'Enumeration of Scriptural Example.' A Study of a Rabbinic Pattern of Discourse with Special Reference to Mekhilta d'R. Ishmael*, SPB (Leiden, 1973).

A. S. van der Woude 'Wicked Priest or Wicked Priests? Reflections on the Identification of the Wicked Priest in the Habakkuk Commentary', *JJS* 33 (1982), 349–59.

J. C. M. van Winden 'The World of Ideas in Philo of Alexandria: An Interpretation of *De opificio mundi* 24–25', *VC* 37 (1983), 209–17.

G. Vermes *The Dead Sea Scrolls in English* (Harmondsworth, 1965).

*Scripture and Tradition in Judaism*, SPB 4 (Leiden, 1973).

*Post-Biblical Jewish Studies*, SJLA 8 (Leiden, 1975).

J.-C. Violette *Le Esséniens de Quomrân* (Paris, 1983).

B. Z. Wacholder 'The Date of the Mekilta de-Rabbi Ishmael', *HUCA* 39 (1968), 117–44.

H. A. Wolfson *Philo: Foundations of Religious Philosophy in Judaism, Christianity and Islam* (Cambridge, 1947).

# 9 · Citing the Old Testament

ANDREW CHESTER

I T is important at the outset to indicate the scope and limitations of this chapter. The main aspects that will be dealt with are scriptural citations, along with allusions to Scripture and developments of biblical themes, in a number of intertestamental texts. These texts, as distinct from those discussed in the other chapters in this section, are not translations or commentaries, based on the biblical text itself, nor do they represent a single genre of literature; correspondingly, the usage of Scripture that they exhibit is not homogeneous. Clearly, therefore, the discussion can only touch on a few texts, and a few points of interest within them; the aim is to provide a survey which is merely illustrative, not comprehensive. The texts which will be discussed and drawn upon are: several of the main Qumran texts (excluding the targumim, Genesis Apocryphon and pesharim, dealt with in the preceding three chapters), specifically: the Damascus Document (CD), the Community Rule (1QS), the War Scroll (1QM), the Hymns Scroll (1QH), and the Temple Scroll (11Q Temple); and several of the so-called apocryphal or deuterocanonical writings: 1 and 2 Maccabees, Tobit, Judith, Ben Sira and Wisdom of Solomon.

In all these texts, specific scriptural citations are relatively infrequent, still more so where they are identified as such by means of an introductory or related formula. Much more common, and in many cases much more interesting, are the allusions of various kinds made to Scripture and the development or reinterpretation of important biblical themes. It is these allusions and developments that are for the most part more indicative than the citations proper of the significance that Scripture has for the writer and his audience.

## 1   THE QUMRAN TEXTS

The whole of the Qumran literature is saturated with Scripture. From the texts thus far published, it is evident that the biblical writings were of fundamental importance to the whole existence and way of life of the community (see for example Dimant, 1985; Gabrion, 1979; Roberts, 1968). Clearly there was constant engagement in copying, translating, commenting on and drawing upon these sacred sources. The several different kinds of texts found at Qumran all have a considerable amount in common, not least in their use and interpretation of the Bible. Thus even in the copies made of biblical books, there is evidence of preferred readings being introduced, implying a particular interpretation of the text. So also in the case of the texts which the community itself produced, there is no absolute distinction between the pesharim and other writings in their interpretation of Scripture. Hence it is important to realise that the few texts considered here should be seen not in isolation but within the context of the whole collection of the Qumran library.

## (a)  CD, 1QS, 1QM

These three 'rules' of Qumran all differ considerably from each other; but, along with other features which they share in common, they are all impregnated with scriptural reference and usage (for details and further discussion, see Carmignac, 1956, 1958; Rabin, 1958; Wernberg-Møller, 1955, 1957; Jongeling, 1962; Gabrion, 1979). Explicit citations with introductory formulae (for example 'as it was written' or 'as it said') are proportionately infrequent compared with the use of Scripture overall. The use of such citations is in fact characteristic only of CD (*ca.* 26 times), and is quite rare in 1QS (3 times) and 1QM (5 times). A full list, along with discussion, is usefully provided by Fitzmyer (1971). A few, all from CD and mainly comprising biblical precepts, are taken over with more or less the same sense that they have in the original biblical context; thus, for example, CD 10:16–17 cites Deut. 5:12, 'Observe the sabbath day, to keep it holy', at the start of its series of injunctions concerning the keeping of the sabbath in the community. Even here, however, the sense of the scriptural verse is modified by the detailed regulations for sabbath observance, and much more characteristic overall is the use of scriptural citations related directly to the community and its setting in the last days. So, for instance, CD 1:13–14 reads, 'This is the time of which it was written, "Like a stubborn heifer, so Israel is stubborn"' (citing Hos. 4:16); so Hosea's prophecy against Israel finds its fulfilment by being applied to the people from whom the community has had to withdraw into the wilderness.

This way of applying scriptural texts directly to the community's situation is very close to the characteristic usage of the pesharim, and in this respect there are notable similarities between CD and the pesharim overall. Indeed, in one passage (4:12–19), CD uses the term *pešer* instead of its usual identification formula ('This is ...' or equivalent), in interpreting Isa. 24:17 of the three nets of Belial or three kinds of unrighteousness presently afflicting Israel, and connecting this with Isa. 24:18. Here again the principle of interpretation, as throughout the pesharim and also CD, is that the words of the prophet are finally fulfilled in the contemporary situation of the community, and that they can be understood only in relation to this context.

CD and the pesharim share not only these perspectives, but also the main exegetical methods that they use to arrive at their interpretation. In the case of the pesharim, it has been clearly demonstrated (thus, for example, by Brownlee, 1951, 1979; Finkel, 1963–4; Slomovic, 1969–71; Brooke, 1985) that a variety of exegetical techniques is used, many of them closely related to techniques used in rabbinic literature. It can also be shown that the same techniques are used in CD and other Qumran texts (see, for instance, de Waard, 1965; Slomovic, 1969–71; Brooke, 1985). An illuminating example is provided by CD 7:9–8:2; this A text differs considerably from the B text (CD 19:5–13), and almost certainly represents a redactionary revision (see Davies, 1983; Brooke, 1985), but in any case shows how exegetical techniques allow scriptural texts to yield a particular interpretation. The passage is part of a warning issued against those who despise the marriage laws (as interpreted by the community), and invokes Isa. 7:17, applying it to them as the final divine judgment upon them. This verse is interpreted by Amos 5:26f, which in turn is interpreted by Amos 9:11 and Num. 24:17. The introduction of these latter two verses represents a clear instance of the exegetical technique of verbal analogy (what is known in rabbinic terminology as *gezera šawa*): thus the 'booth' (*sukkat*) of Amos 9:11 and the 'star' of Num. 24:17 provide links respectively with the '*Sikkut*' and 'star' of Amos 5:26f. In fact it is probably the same technique that prompts the use of Amos 5:26f itself to interpret Isa. 7:17; there is no connexion in the verses as they are cited, but the immediate context in Isaiah 7 is concerned with the 'king(s)' of Assyria; this use of the extended verse or context (attested otherwise in Qumran literature, and still more so in rabbinic writings) would thus provide the basis for the interpretation by means of the Amos verse.

There is also, in this CD passage, striking use of the technique of paranomasia, or play on words (so Bruce, 1959, pp. 37f): thus the 'departed' (*sār*) of Isa. 7:17 is interpreted by 'ruler' (*śar*). Similarly, the proper-names of Amos 5:26, *Sikkut* and *Kiyyun*, are interpreted by *sukkat* ('booth', itself taken up, as we have seen, by the 'booth of David' of Amos 9:11) and *kiyyun* ('pedestal'). Further techniques are also used, as Brooke (1985, pp. 305–7) shows; thus, for example, *notariqon*, the device of dividing a word and using the parts of a word as abbreviations of other words, is probably involved in the use of the Amos 5:26f citation, where the אתכם of v. 27 is not cited, but employed in the divided form את כם to introduce phrases from the previous verse (את כיון צלמיכם and את סכות מלככם). Similarly, the interpretation of 'booth' as 'the books of the law' and 'pedestal' as 'the books of the prophets' is probably achieved by taking the final letters of סוכת and כיון, respectively as the first letters of תורה and נביאים. Again, the מהלאה, 'beyond (Damascus)' of Amos 5:27 is probably read deliberately (the rabbinic technique of *al tiqre*) as מאהלי ('from the tents [of Damascus]'/'from my tent [to Damascus]').

Along with these detailed considerations of exegetical method, stress must also be laid on the overriding hermeneutical perspective that governs the use of Scripture in this passage. Above all, it involves taking over and combining biblical prophecies, understood as relating to the last days or the messianic age, and applying these directly to the situation of the community, especially as a warning against those who reject the sect's distinctive law and teaching. Thus it is in this situation, in the present experience and controversies of the community, that these prophecies find their fulfilment. It is also in this context that the messianic beliefs of the community are developed; it is probable (so Brooke, 1985) that the introduction apparently of two messianic figures in the A text, using Numbers 24, represents a deliberate change from the B text, with one messianic figure based on Zech. 13:7. Certainly the precise identity and function of the star and sceptre in this interpretation are difficult, but the point again is that the prophecy of Num. 24:17 is to be realised within the community.

There are, as we have noted, more scriptural citations in CD than in the other Qumran texts considered here, and closer affinity to the pesharim; hence it would be misleading to generalise from this CD passage for the Qumran texts as a whole. Nevertheless, the same basic methods and perspectives can be found quite widely within our texts. Thus for example in 1QS 8:14, Isa. 40:3 is cited, in a section dealing with the founding and organisation of the community, and given the following interpretation (8:15–16): 'this is the study of the law, which he commanded by the hand of Moses, to do according to all that has been revealed from age to age, and as the prophets have revealed by his holy spirit.' Again, as in CD 7, the interpretation employs the simple identification formula, and again specific exegetical methods are used as well. So, for example, making the 'way' or 'path' mean 'the study of the law' probably involves the use of the *al tiqre* technique, either by reading מדרש for ישרו (so de Waard, 1965, pp. 48–53), or else דרש for דרך (so Betz, 1960, p. 157). It may be possible to see as well an extended use of paranomasia, based on an Aramaic rendering (de Waard, 1965, refers specifically to the Targum) of Isa. 40:3; thus כבישו could mean both 'make level' and also 'make plain', מישרא both 'plain' and 'camp', and כבשן, both 'paths' and 'secret'. Hence the latter half of the verse could not only be given a relatively literal rendering but could also take on the more developed sense 'make plain in the camp the secrets before the people of our God'. This latter sense would fit well with the way that Isa. 40:3 is further alluded to, although not specifically cited, in 1QS 9:19, 'This is the time to prepare the way into the wilderness', in context of the master concealing the teaching of the law from the men of falsehood, but imparting true knowledge and mysteries to the men of the community. At any rate, it seems clear in 1QS 8:12–16, where the citation of Isa. 40:3 is prefaced by a reference to the need for the community to leave the habitation of ungodly men and go into the wilderness, and followed by the interpretation discussed above, that this verse is invoked to provide specific scriptural support for the community's decision to move out into self-imposed exile in the wilderness of Qumran, and also for their constant preoccupation with Scripture and their claim that its secrets have been revealed to them (cf. Betz, 1960). Thus Isa. 40:3, understood in an eschatological sense (as it is also in the NT), is again interpreted as a prophecy that is fulfilled only within the Qumran community.

It has also been cogently argued (Brooke, 1985, pp. 295–301) that the technique of providing scriptural support for a particular interpretation (given the designation *asmakta* in rabbinic writings) has been used in the developed interpretation of the Aaronic benediction (Num. 6:24–6) in 1QS 2:2–4. The passage reads: 'May He bless you *with all good* and keep you *from all evil*. May he enlighten *your heart with life-giving wisdom* and grant you *eternal knowledge*. May he raise his *merciful* face towards you for *everlasting peace*'. Brooke suggests that of the changes and additions (italicised here), the first three derive respectively from Deut. 26:11; Ps. 121:7; and Prov. 16:22a, the 'eternal knowledge' results from interpreting Prov. 16:22 by means of Jer. 31:31–4, while the underlying formula of the final clause, 'for his mercy is for ever', is found in a number of Psalms, for example 105, 106. What is striking about these biblical passages is that they all belong to covenant ceremonies or concepts. Further, it has been shown that the whole section to which this passage belongs, 1QS 1:18–2:18, represents a covenant liturgy for the community (cf. esp. Baltzer, 1971, pp. 168–9; 189–91; Dimant, 1985, pp. 500ff), while the effect of the expansions in 2:2–4 is to emphasise the blessings that apply to the community in contrast to the curses that are set against those outside. Thus these scriptural passages that are used to expand and interpret Num. 6:24–6 also serve to validate the community's taking over the priestly blessing for their own covenant ceremony. At the same time, the distinctively developed concept of the covenant is now appropriated exclusively for the community itself.

Especially characteristic of these Qumran texts is what is often referred to as the 'anthological' style (see Gabrion, 1979, 791ff), where a whole series of scriptural citations and allusions follow closely on one another. These 'anthological' passages may superficially give the impression of being an arbitrary assortment of texts strung together for cumulative effect, but this is misleading. There are clearly exegetical techniques involved, in some cases *asmakta* (cf. Betz, 1960, p. 176), but especially that of verbal analogy (*gezera šawa*). This is clearly the case in the striking 'anthological' passage 1QM 10:1–8 (so Brooke, 1985, pp. 292–5). The opening citation is typically composite, formed from Deut. 7:21 and, probably, Deut. 6:19 or 23:15, this link itself being achieved by verbal analogy. It is then followed by a citation of Deut. 20:2–4, which is linked to the opening passage not only by the common use of 'enemy' but also by its בקרבכם 'when you draw near', the same root as in בקרבנו, 'in our midst', of Deut. 7:21. There then ensues an allusion to Deut. 20:5, 8, with the further use of 'battle' already found at Deut. 20:2–4, and a citation of Num. 10:9, which in turn is linked to the preceding citations by both 'enemy' and 'battle'. This process of tracing the verbal links between citations and allusions could be continued for the following lines, and could be undertaken for many other passages in 1QM as well. The effect of bringing all these biblical passages together in close connexion in 1QM 10:1ff is to emphasise that God will be with his people and will fight for them in the final, eschatological battle, in fulfilment of his promises in Scripture and of his activity for his people in the past.

### (b)  1QH

The 'anthological' style is above all characteristic of 1QH, which draws on Scripture even more extensively than any other of the Qumran texts considered here, but also does so even more allusively. Thus, for example, at 1QH 8:4ff, in the hymn beginning 'I (thank you, Lord, for) you have set me beside a fountain of streams in a dry land, and by a spring of waters in a parched land, and by a watered garden (...)...', there is probably allusion to Isa. 44:3; 49:10; 41:18f, passages that are all linked together by the word 'water' (and there may also be allusion to Isa. 32:6; 58:11; 51:3). Then in the following lines, allusion is probably made to Isa. 60:13, connected to Isa. 41:18f by the word 'tree'; Gen. 2:9, 3:8, again linked by 'tree', and Ps. 1:3; Ezek. 31:3ff; Psalm 80, all again connected by 'tree' and 'water'. This brief analysis could also be extended to the rest of the hymn, showing a succession of verses where the verbal analogies of 'water', 'tree' or 'garden' especially would hold. Again, all these allusions are made to apply directly to the community and take on a sense that goes beyond that of the scriptural verses themselves. Here the point is to emphasise the importance of the Teacher of Righteousness and the absolute, predetermined dualism of the elect community in contrast to those outside (see especially Gabrion, 1979, pp. 791ff).

Certainly the use of Scripture in 1QH differs from that in CD, 1QS, 1QM; there are no introductory formulae, and no real citations as such, while it is often difficult to be sure whether there is a deliberate scriptural citation or whether the hymn merely reflects more general biblical usage. Indeed, the hymns achieve their impressive effect at least partly by the way in which they imitate and develop the poetic style and phraseology of the biblical psalms; they use Scripture not to validate a particular interpretation or practice, but to set themselves firmly in the developed tradition of biblical psalmody. At the same time, it is frequently apparent that allusion to a scriptural verse is conscious and intentional; the books that are drawn on most frequently are the Psalms (particularly the individual laments and thanksgiving psalms) and Isaiah, along with other prophetic books to a lesser extent (cf. Holm-Nielsen, 1960; Carmignac, 1960). Yet while the mode, range and intention of scriptural reference differ markedly from CD and 1QS especially, throughout 1QH it is again implicit that Scripture finds its fulfilment in the community. The use of Scripture serves to express the relationship between God and the community, and the favourite terms drawn from the Psalms – especially 'poor' and 'dejected' – indicate how the community understands and identifies itself (so Holm-Nielsen, 1960).

### (c)   11Q Temple

The Temple Scroll is a remarkable document in many respects. It is the longest of the scrolls thus far discovered at Qumran, and the main body of it is made up of biblical material, primarily but not exclusively from the Pentateuch. The most striking feature is that the biblical text thus taken over is presented almost entirely in the first person singular, without any introductory formula, as the direct address of God (see Yadin, 1983, 1, p. 71; Dimant, 1985, p. 526). That is, the great mass of pentateuchal material is set out in the scroll deliberately as though it were torah spoken directly by God to Moses at Sinai. Wherever the biblical text is taken over, but it is not explicitly stated that it is God who is speaking, the text is changed from the third person to the first, to make it clear that it is God himself who is involved.

Not only does the scroll consistently put the scriptural text into the first person singular, it also expands and develops many of the laws and injunctions that it takes over, and even more strikingly it adds large sections of new laws. Here again, in these expansions and additions, the text is set in the first person, as of God speaking directly, and for the most part also the scroll imitates the style and phraseology of the biblical laws, especially those of Deuteronomy. It also takes up often veiled references to codes of laws mentioned in the biblical text, pentateuchal or other, and makes good the gaps that exist, especially concerning the details and scope of festivals (3–30), the plans for the building of the temple (30–45), and the laws concerning the king (56–60). In thus setting these additional laws alongside the biblical laws that it takes over, the scroll clearly claims for itself unique authoritative status, on a par with the biblical text of the Pentateuch itself. Indeed, in using the first person singular throughout, both for the biblical material and also for its own additions without distinction, it goes beyond what the Pentateuch itself purports to present, and certainly beyond the interpretations of torah offered in the Mishnah and other rabbinic writings.

So also the scroll, in taking up much of the pentateuchal legislation, skilfully weaves together related material in different chapters or books to produce a single, coherent injunction, and successfully harmonises apparently contradictory pieces of legislation, again into a single whole. Yet although in the course of this it ranges over the whole of Exodus, Leviticus, Numbers and Deuteronomy, it nevertheless contrives to arrange the sequence of the main themes that it treats according to the order of the pentateuchal books (see Yadin, 1983, I, p. 74). Again, therefore, it clearly sets out to be fully torah itself.

It is impossible to discuss here all these different aspects of the Temple Scroll in detail, and all that can be attempted is brief illustration of some of the main points. Thus the long section (30–45) dealing with the construction of the temple sets out to remedy a surprising defect in the Pentateuch itself and provide a clear command on how the temple is to be built. To achieve this, the author draws on the account in 1 Chronicles 28, which speaks of such a divine instruction, and also the details of the building of the Solomonic temple in 1 Kings 6 and 2 Chronicles 3, along with some of the material relating to the future temple in Ezekiel 40–8, and perhaps parts of Ezra; but the description the author provides goes far beyond anything that can be found in any of these sources. Similarly, the detailed provision for the major Feast of the Wood Offering (23–5) has as its basis brief references in Neh. 10:34; 13:31, but goes far beyond this. So also in the rest of the long section dealing with the feasts and sacrifices (13–30), as well as taking over, combining and developing the instructions for the main feasts that are found in the Pentateuch, the scroll also provides detailed regulations for feasts and sacrifices that are hardly more than hinted at in the biblical sources. Again, the law concerning the king (56–60) is based mainly on the short section Deut. 17:14–20, but is extended considerably, partly by bringing in and expanding other biblical material.

The section of the law of the king also contains a good example (cf. Yadin, I, pp. 76, 359–61) of the way in which the scroll brings together and harmonises contradictory texts, in treating of the division of booty at 58:11–15. The main source for this passage is Num. 31:27f which lays down the detailed division of spoil after battle, but the author combines with this the contrary command of 1 Sam. 30:24f, that all should have equal shares, and also introduces the further theme (probably deriving from 1 Sam. 8:15–17, or possibly Gen. 14:20) that a tenth should be given for the king.

Even where there is no inherent contradiction between different passages, the author still shows great skill in producing a single coherent command from the different material found in two or more texts (cf. further Yadin, I, pp. 73–75; also pp. 46–70, and II, *passim*). Thus at 49:7–10 the basic injunction derives from Lev. 11:33f, but the author combines with it that concerning open vessels in Num. 19:15. In many instances, the author adds his own further interpretation of or supplement to the law; in some cases the developed version of the law is set out extensively, and clearly polemically, often as a more rigorous interpretation, certainly compared to what is found in the Mishnah. Again, however, it has to be stressed that the extraordinary aspect of all this is that the pentateuchal laws are incorporated into the text, combined, interpreted, added to, and large sections of original material included, but all alike set as the direct speech of God at Sinai without distinction, that is, as revealed torah.

In the Temple Scroll, a number of important biblical themes are distinctively developed; most obviously, of course, the temple itself and its central importance for the life of the people. The overriding theme and concern, however, both in the temple section and throughout the scroll is that of holiness and purity (cf. Maier, 1985, p. 6), which above all is taken up from the pentateuchal basis and further intensified. Yet although this use and development of central biblical themes is particularly clear in the case of the Temple Scroll, where so much of the Pentateuch is taken over, it is also a feature of the other scrolls that we have considered here. Thus, for example, the important theme of the covenant is central to CD, where indeed the whole work is set in covenantal form (cf. Dimant, 1985; Davies, 1982), providing its own distinctive developments both of particular biblical covenantal formulae and also of the understanding of the theme more generally. The concept of the covenant is also important for 1QS, for example 1:16–2:25, but again it takes on distinctive modifications, not least in the way it is already predetermined who belongs and does not belong to the covenant community (cf. Dimant, 1985, p. 500). Again, the theme of the messiah is distinctively developed in several of the texts, particularly in the idea of two messiahs, as we have seen for example at CD 7:9–8:2; the prophecy of Num. 24:17, cited there, is clearly important for the developed community understanding (cf. 1QM 11:4–6).

It is hazardous to come to general conclusions about the use of Scripture at Qumran on the basis of this brief survey of a few texts, especially since doubts have been raised about whether the Damascus Document and the Temple Scroll are original compositions of the Qumran community or whether they were simply inherited by them. Nevertheless, on the basis of these texts, it is worth stressing again the sheer importance of Scripture and of studying and interpreting it, for the Qumran community as a whole. The close connexions with the pesharim should also be emphasised.

There is also frequent use of exegetical techniques clearly held in common with much of the rest of Judaism. The skilful application of these techniques should not greatly surprise us, but the controlling hermeneutical perspective for their whole interpretation of Scripture, that is the eschatological setting of the community, is especially striking. It is precisely because the community sees itself as living in the last days, and itself as the only true remnant of Israel and inheritor of the covenant, that it can interpret Scripture, and above all the prophetic utterances of Scripture, as being fulfilled in this very community, and as applying directly to it and to the age in which it finds itself living. It is this perspective also that allows it to hold that the true meaning and hidden secrets of Scripture are now finally and uniquely made known to it through direct revelation and inspired interpretation. Given that this is the overriding perspective for the community's understanding of itself and of Scripture, it is perhaps not so surprising that the community can produce (or at any rate preserve) so remarkable a document as the Temple Scroll, purporting to be the direct revealed words of God himself.

## 2 APOCRYPHAL/DEUTEROCANONICAL WRITINGS

### (a) 1 Maccabees

1 Maccabees is replete with allusions to biblical phrases and usage, although it contains only one explicit citation (with an introductory formula), at 7:16f. This in fact turns out to be not a verbatim quotation but a paraphrase, or probably better a deliberate summary, of Ps. 79:2–3. The main point of citing it is clearly to show that the words of the psalmist are fulfilled in the action of Alcimus against the Hasidim. The importance and relevance of Psalm 79 for the author of 1 Maccabees are further demonstrated by the allusion to vv. 1–3 at 1:37. Here the point is to show that the terror and sacrilege depicted in the Psalm are fulfilled in the period immediately preceding the Maccabean uprising; but thus also that the revolt itself is therefore justified.

Both these themes, the fulfilment of prophecy, and the justification of the revolt and the Hasmonean dynasty, are important to the author, and to an understanding of how he uses Scripture. A pivotal passage for the author's purpose and for his use of Scripture (cf. Goldstein, 1976, pp. 7–9) is 2:50–61, a main section of Mattathias' farewell speech.

Here we are presented with a wide-ranging review, in short scope, of important figures and events in Israel's history. In all these cases, faithfulness to God and decisive action in obedience to him are rewarded in significant ways. Thus in this short section there is a wealth of brief allusion and reference to particular scriptural verses and passages, but so also to much more extensive biblical narrative and other material. Hence these biblical figures and the extensive traditions attaching to them are implicitly called to mind and presented in paradigmatic fashion. The point is that the example of their faithfulness, zeal and action has been fulfilled in the Maccabean family; and so also, therefore, the promised rewards belong to them as well. These themes are developed further in the allusions in this section, and in the rest of the book.

Thus the purpose is explicitly set out in vv. 50–1; zeal for the law and martyrdom for this cause, as evidenced in the case of the Maccabees, alone inherit the covenant with the fathers and bestow an everlasting name. The phrase 'the covenant of our fathers', along with its biblical resonance, also serves to identify the Maccabees with this tradition and appropriate it for them (as does the specific identification of Phineas as 'our father' in v. 54). Above all, it is clear that the decisive zeal for the law is anticipated by Mattathias and taken over by his sons in succession. So also in v. 52 the example of Abraham, the supreme patriarchal figure and father of Israel, is invoked; there is a partial citation here, since the latter half of the verse represents Gen. 15:6b. The first half of the verse, however, involves a striking development, since Abraham is not simply spoken of as faithful, but his faithfulness is defined by reference to his action in Genesis 22. As Abraham was obedient to God and prepared to sacrifice his son, so also Mattathias was obedient, and put his own and his sons' lives at risk, and so also (as the narrative goes on to show) his sons remained faithful throughout their time of testing. Again in v. 53 allusion is made to Gen. 39:8–10 and 41:40, and the causal connexion between Joseph's keeping the commandment and becoming lord of Egypt is explicitly spelled out! There is probably further allusion to the Joseph saga in 2:14, 17–22, where there is particular emphasis on Mattathias and his family keeping the law, and on Mattathias himself being recognised as a lord, while in chapters 10–11 there is clear recognition of Jonathan as such a lord as well.

The reference in v. 54 to Phineas's zeal (Num. 25:7–13) is especially important for the author. Thus Phineas is explicitly cited at 2:26 as the model for Mattathias's zeal for the law, but allusions to the whole story and context of Phineas are probably implicit throughout 1:64–2:27. This role is then taken over by Judas, as is made clear by the description of his actions at 3:8, especially the phrase 'turned away wrath from Israel', alluding to Num. 25:11. Thus the author deliberately interprets Phineas's zeal as 'zeal for the law'; it is this exemplary zeal and activity that now again finds its full expression in Mattathias and his sons.

The reference to Joshua and Caleb in vv. 55–6 alludes to the narrative of Num. 14:6–10, 24 (and Josh. 1:1–9). The idea that Joshua became a judge is deliberately added here, to fit the roles that Judas (7:49–50) and Jonathan (9:23–31) subsequently take on. So also the Joshua narrative is drawn on more widely throughout the book; thus at 2:20 Mattathias's affirmation of allegiance to the covenant alludes to that of Joshua (Josh. 24:15), while the accounts of the conquests carried out by Judas and Jonathan (5:9–54; 9:44–50; 11:71–74) contain a number of allusions to parts of Joshua and the early parts of Judges, and these sections as a whole are probably intended to bring these biblical narratives to mind. The figure of David, referred to in v. 57 (alluding to 1 Sam. 24:6; 26:9; 2 Sam. 7:16), is also important for the author. Thus the account in 2:27–48 of Mattathias fleeing to the mountains is perhaps deliberately made parallel to what is recounted of David in 1 Samuel 22–3, 30 (Goldstein, 1976, p. 7). Further allusions to David are made in chapter 4 (especially vv. 24, 30, and later in the chapter) and the narrative of 1 and 2 Samuel is drawn on more widely (cf. 3:18; 4:30; 9:21).

In v. 58, the reference to Elijah (1 Kgs 19:10, 14) is again specifically interpreted as zeal for the law, and thus again made a paradigm for Mattathias's action. The Elijah tradition is further invoked at 13:4–5, where Simon's appeal to the people is made to allude to Elijah's prayer (1 Kgs 19:4). The examples of deliverance in vv. 59–60 represent the same deliverance that God effects for the sons of Mattathias and point to the conclusion in v. 61. Other themes and instances of deliverance are worked into the rest of the book: for example, at 4:8–11 Judas explicitly appeals to the precedent of the biblical account of the deliverance at the Red Sea; so also 3:25–6 alludes to Deut. 2:25. Again, 7:41–2 alludes to the account of the deliverance from the siege of Sennacherib (2 Kgs 19:35 = Isa. 37:36), while 10:67–89 deliberately echoes the deliverance of Ahab from the king of Syria (1 Kings 20).

Thus the biblical prototypes of zeal and faithfulness are paralleled and the paradigms of promise and deliverance fulfilled, in the way that 1 Maccabees depicts the deeds of Mattathias and his seven sons. Along with this, the book also alludes to the fulfilment of particular biblical prophecies in the context and times of the Maccabees. Thus for example the first part of 14:9 probably alludes to Zech. 8:4–5, and there are several allusions to Zechariah 9 within the sections 11:60–74; 12:1–38; 13:6–11. So also 1:26 may allude to Amos 8:13, and the lament of 1:25–8 as a whole may be intended to reflect the fulfilment of Joel 2:10–17 and similar prophecies of woe. Conversely, 14:12, as part of the portrayal of peace and prosperity under Simon, draws on Mic. 4:4 to show that what the Maccabees have achieved is the fulfilment of that prophecy; this verse also reflects the language of 1 Kgs 4:25, depicting the idyllic conditions in Solomon's empire, and again the implication is that life under Simon and the Hasmonean dynasty is completely comparable to this. Overall, then, it is implied that the time of crisis, oppression and despair that gave rise to the Maccabean revolt is to be seen as the fulfilment of prophetic oracles, as is the deliverance that God has brought about through the zealous action of Mattathias and his sons. The rule of the Hasmonean kingdom is represented as recreating the golden age of the monarchy, fulfilling prophetic expectation.

Finally 1 Maccabees uses biblical formulae and phraseology, especially in alluding to summary statements from the historical works. Thus for example 2:49 draws on what is said of David at 1 Kgs 2:1 (cf. also Gen. 47:29), while 9:22 and the longer formulation at 16:23–4, reflect the usage at 2 Chr. 27:7 (cf. 2 Kgs 15:36). The use of these formulae is consonant with the way that biblical phrases and language are deliberately echoed throughout the book; the point here specifically may be to set the account of the Maccabees consciously in the same line of tradition as the biblical historical books. Overall, however, the main point corresponds to that which we have already noted: the author uses Scripture primarily to support and legitimate the conduct of Mattathias and his sons, and the continuing claim by the Hasmonean dynasty to both kingship and priesthood.

### (b)   2 Maccabees

2 Maccabees contains very few scriptural citations, and a striking paucity of allusions to Scripture otherwise. There are four passages altogether where it appears that the writer uses a formula to point to the fact that Scripture is being cited: 1:29, apparently referring to Exod. 15:17; 2:11 (Lev. 10:16–20); 7:6 (Deut. 32:36); and 10:26 (Exod. 23:22). In none of these cases, however, is the supposed citation exact; 1:29 is a very free paraphrase, while 2:11 can at best be considered as a rather general allusion. At the most, the citations of Scripture in the book are both limited and very free.

The most interesting section of the book as far as the use of Scripture is concerned is the famous account in chapter 7 of the martyrdom of the mother and her seven sons. The citation of Deut. 32:36 at 7:6 has already been noted; it is further probable that 7:37–8 alludes to Deut. 32:39, 41, and it can be plausibly argued that a considerable part of Deuteronomy 32, especially vv. 35–43, underlies much of what is said in chapter 7 as a whole (cf. Goldstein, 1983, pp. 294–5; 303–4), especially in the theme of divine vengeance on Israel's enemies and the restoration and resurrection of the martyrs. The developed themes of resurrection and immortality are particularly important, and the language used to depict them at v. 9, especially, and v. 14, is clearly intended as an allusion to Dan. 12:2 (and, at least indirectly, to Isa. 26:19). There are several other scriptural allusions here, but it is also worth pursuing the possibility of a biblical basis for the chapter as a whole. The striking feature of a mother and her seven sons being martyred is itself probably a deliberate allusion to Jer. 15:9 and 1 Sam. 2:5, which both speak of a woman with seven children languishing. Given this fundamental point of contact, it is easy enough to suppose that the account here draws more extensively on the larger context of Jer. 14:19–15:11 and 1 Sam. 2:2–10, with their portrayals of suffering and slaughter, and God strengthening and restoring the afflicted and taking vengeance on Israel's enemies.

Apart from chapter 7, there are other probable instances of allusion to Scripture, both in detail and also more generally. Thus, for example, 'the blood that cries out' at 8:3 clearly alludes to the incident of Cain and Abel (Gen. 4:10); the section dealing with the affliction of the widow and orphan, at Exod. 22:22–4, may underlie the whole of 8:3–4 (and perhaps indeed chapter 7 as well). The plea to God 'to send a good angel' (11:6; 15:23) probably alludes to God's provision of an angel to protect Israel at Exod. 23:20. There may also be an allusion to the deliverance at the Red Sea at 15:23–4 (cf. Exod. 15:16) and 15:8 (cf. Exod. 14:13; cf. Doran, 1981, pp. 71–72). More generally, the author may deliberately take over important themes of the deuteronomic school, such as the schema of sin-punishment-repentance-salvation (chapters 4 onwards), the theological reflections on and interpretations of history (4:16–17; 5:17–20; 6:12–17), and the constant stress on the fact that God guarantees to protect his people and temple only if they are obedient to him (Doran, 1981), but there are few precise parallels. 2 Maccabees also alludes to biblical prophecies being fulfilled, not as 1 Maccabees in heroic victories, but rather in acts of piety, prayer and repentance, and consequent divine forgiveness (Goldstein, 1983, p. 386); examples of this would be 10:24–38 (alluding to Isa. 30:15–36; Zech. 9:9–16; Joel 2:11–3:21), 11:13–38 (alluding to Zech. 9:16–17), 14:37–46 (alluding to Isa. 24:16–25:11), and 15:1–36 (alluding to Zech. 9:8–10:8). Again, however, the parallels are at most quite general. According to Goldstein (1976, pp. 42–54; 1983, pp. 55–71, and *passim*), the author not only (at 7:9, 14) explicitly confirms the belief in resurrection and immortality of Dan. 12:2, but is also at pains throughout to show, at least implicitly, that the prophecies of Daniel 7–11 hold true, over against 1 Maccabees, which constantly implies that they are false. This is to a large extent an argument from silence, although it is certainly clear that 2 Maccabees sees Daniel as an inspired and authoritative work, and takes up important themes from it. Overall, then, 2 Maccabees uses Scripture to support important themes and emphases in its account, but this use is not extensive nor for the most part direct or very clear; rather, it is allusive, general and remote.

## (c) Tobit

The tale of Tobit is rich in biblical themes and allusions. It cites Scripture specifically only twice: 2:6, where notably it changes the first person active of Amos 8:10 (ascribing negative action to God) to the third passive, and 8:6 c (citing Gen. 2:18). Yet it is not in individual citations and allusions that the full force of Tobit's use of Scripture is felt. Much more significant is the way in which it draws on scriptural material more widely for the overall construction of its narrative, in conjunction with the other sources that it employs (especially the story of Ahikar and the Legend of the Grateful Dead). Hence scriptural passages are drawn upon at least partly in order to help adapt and accommodate these non-biblical sources to the specific purposes of the book and the distinctively jewish themes that the story is concerned with.

Thus Deselaers (1982) argues cogently that it is the use of Genesis 24 that is above all determinative for fashioning the basic structure of the work, and that at the same time allows the adaption of the non-biblical sources. For example, Tobit like Abraham is a father who appears to be nearing death (3:6; 4:2; cf. Gen. 24:1), while Tobias, as Isaac, is an only son who has to undertake a journey in order to find a wife. It is constantly stressed that the wife must come from the same family (1:9; 4:12–13; 6:10–12, 15; 7:10, 12; 8:7; cf. Gen. 24:3, 4, 7, 38, 40). The son has a companion, who takes on the responsibility for finding the wife (5:3–16; 6:10; cf. Gen. 24:2ff). The chosen woman comes out to meet the strangers and effects their entry as guests into the family house (7:1–8; cf. Gen. 24:15–32), but they will eat nothing until they have accomplished their task (7:11; cf. Gen. 24:33). Those in the house pledge the daughter with a solemn promise and blessing (7:12; cf. Gen. 24:51, 60); the bride leaves her family and returns with her new husband to his (7:13; 10:7–12; cf. Gen. 24:58–9), where the father comes out to meet his daughter-in-law (11:16; cf. Gen. 24:63–5). There are many other close links and parallels and striking similarities in vocabulary. Deselaers (1982, pp. 206–9) also sees 12:6–22 as being constructed largely on the basis of Genesis 17 (for example, 12:15; cf. Gen. 17:1; 12:16; cf. Gen. 17:3) and incorporating themes (for instance, the appearance of an angel, and falling down in fear) from Judges 6 and 13; but the similarities both in structure and in detail are much less marked than is the case with Genesis 24 and Tobit as a whole.

According to Ruppert (1972, 1976), the influence of Genesis 24 on Tobit was much more limited, and instead it was the Joseph narrative that was instrumental in adapting the non-biblical sources to the writer's purpose. Certainly this narrative has been drawn on extensively in Tobit, but it is more plausible (Deselaers, 1982, pp. 441–8) that it was used only secondarily, mediated by means of the Ahikar story. Thus both Tobit and Joseph have been taken from their homeland (1:2–3; cf. Gen. 37:28; 39:1); they both hold high office at a royal court (1:13, 22; cf. Gen. 41:42–3), are attacked or accused and brought close to death (1:19–20; cf. Gen 37:18–28; 39:7–20), but are delivered and restored to prosperity (1:21–2; cf. Gen. 39:1–2, 21–3), and show concern for those in need (1:17; 4:16; cf. Gen. 45:11; 47:12). Yet all these and other traits common to both Tobit and Joseph are shared by Ahikar as well. Indeed, it is important for the construction of the narrative, and the integration of the Joseph material, that Ahikar is introduced into it, as a true Israelite and member of Tobit's family who helps him and shares in the fortunes of his family, as well as also holding office in the royal court and being delivered from dire straits (1:21–2; 2:10; 11:18; 14:10). This allows the story of Tobit to take over many themes from the Joseph narrative. So, in addition to the parallels already cited, the father has to send his only or favourite son into a foreign country (4:20; 5:16; cf. Gen. 42:36–8; 43:11–14) in order to obtain provisions or money, and gives him a trusted companion (5:10–16; cf. Gen. 43:9–13). There are, however, also obvious differences;

thus the Joseph narrative has nothing of going to seek a wife, while the parallels have to assume some fusion of the Genesis characters. Hence the importance of at least a developed version of the Joseph narrative for the book of Tobit is not to be doubted, but it scarcely serves as the basis on which the whole is built.

It has also been suggested (Pfeiffer, 1949, pp. 267–8) that the writer drew on Job for his portrayal of Tobit: in both cases, an innocent man loses his possessions and becomes ill; he is rebuked by his wife, but this serves only to enhance his faith, and finally he enjoys restoration of his health and wealth. Again, Di Lella (1979) claims that Deuteronomy has exercised considerable influence on the farewell discourse of 14:3–11, but also on much of the rest of the book as well. He sees, for example, the final exhortation of 14:9–11 as being based on Deut. 30:10–20, the formulae 'fear', 'love', 'bless' and 'praise', all with 'God' as object (14:6–7, 9, and elsewhere) and the themes of joy, rest, long life, the good land, and mercy (14:4–7, and elsewhere in Tobit) as all being characteristic of Deuteronomy, as also the theme of the centralisation of the cult in Jerusalem (14:5, 7; cf. Deut. 12:1–14; 16:6). Some of the similarities are striking, and the claim that Deuteronomy was important for the writer and his community quite plausible.

Apart from Genesis and Deuteronomy, the rest of the Pentateuch is important for Tobit as well (see Simpson, 1913, p. 192, for a list of passages), not least to show that actions should be properly carried out according to the law. Thus for example the marriage laws of Num. 27:1–11; 36:1–13 underlie the narrative of 6:9–15, while 4:14 reflects the law laid down at Lev. 19:3. The use at 2:6 of Amos 8:6, already noted, could be taken as indicating the fulfilment of prophecy; certainly that is explicitly claimed for the prophecies referred to at 14:4, 8 (Jonah 3:4) and 14:5 (Jer. 50:4–5), and there are many other implicit hints at prophecies that will be fulfilled.

All these claimed parallels and points of reference for Tobit may seem mutually contradictory. Certainly some of the supposed points of contact are general at most. Nevertheless, the use of Scripture in Tobit is multi-layered and multi-faceted, and variously serves the author's purpose. Writing for a diaspora community, probably in the early second century BC, he can use Genesis 24 to emphasise the importance of preserving the identity of the jewish people, and not losing this by mixing with other nations. Hence the importance of family solidarity and kinship marriage are stressed; in a critical situation, where the promise of a great nation (cf. Genesis 17) or the very continuance of the people of God is at risk, all depends on a single individual and family, and the proper observance of the law. So also the Joseph narrative is centred on a jewish individual and family set in the diaspora, and also enjoins proper respect for jewish burial custom (Abrahams, 1893). The deuteronomic themes can offer encouragement and consolation to the jewish people under foreign domination in the diaspora, with emphasis especially on the positive aspects of their religious and social experience, and the assurance that God's mercy and aid still belong to them. Similarly, it is implied that what the prophets have foretold will be fulfilled for the jewish people. Along with all this, then, there is constant stress on the need to observe torah, and to live fully as the distinctive people of God.

### (d) Judith

The whole of Judith is full of biblical phrases and allusions, although there is only one specific citation (9:2, consisting of a few words from Gen. 34:7). Yet the real significance of the use of Scripture in Judith attaches above all to the way in which important biblical events, narratives and themes, especially of deliverance, are taken up, developed and interwoven (Haag, 1963; Dubarle, 1966; Zenger, 1981). The most prominent and distinctive theme is that the deliverance is effected, at least on a human level, by a woman. For the portrayal of the central character, Judith, the writer draws especially on the figures of Jael and Deborah, and the narrative of Judges 4–5 as a whole. In the accounts in both Judith and Judges the decisive action is taken by a woman; she devises a trap for the enemy military leader, and kills him while he is asleep. Judith 9:10, 13:15 and 16:5 all stress that the defeat of the enemy has been brought about by the 'hand of a woman', the same phrase that is used at Judg. 4:9. Again, Judith's speech of exhortation to the people of Bethulia (8:11–27) takes up the main theme of Deborah's address to Barak (4:6–9), that the God of Israel is able to give them victory, while the blessing invoked on Judith (13:18; 14:7) takes up that used of Jael in the song of Deborah (Judg. 5:24).

The theme of the decisive role played by a woman probably draws on other sources both within Judges (as 9:53, relating briefly how a woman killed Abimelech) and otherwise from accounts involving a skilful device or trick. Thus the story of Abigail's device for averting David's anger (1 Sam. 25:1–35) portrays her as wise and beautiful, bringing food to him, and bowing before him, all traits found in Judith (8:7, 29; 10:5; 14:23). Similarly, some aspects of the account in Genesis 38 of the trick Tamar plays on Judah are taken up; thus she puts on the clothes of her widowhood to beguile Judah, who in turn fears that he may be humiliated (38:14, 23; cf. Jdt. 10:3–4; 12:12). The story of Ruth and her mode of dealing with Boaz may also serve as a source. Further, the theme of a device or trick draws on other Judges material, especially Ehud deceiving Eglon, king of Moab (Judg. 3:12–31). So for example Judith, like Ehud, is portrayed as bringing a special divine revelation (11:16–19; cf. Judg. 3:20); she kills the enemy leader and leaves his body on the ground (13:6–9; cf. Judg. 3:21–2, 25), shuts the windows and doors so that the discovery of the body will be delayed (14:13–15; cf. Judg. 3:23–4), and tells all the people to pursue the enemy (14:4; 15:3–7; cf. Judg. 3:28–9), all again on the pattern of Ehud. So also the victory comes after the people cry to God for help, and it brings with it a long period of peace (7:19; 16:25; cf. Judg. 3:15, 30). There are also some points of contact, although more general, with the account of Gideon's device for defeating Midian (Judges 6–8). Other accounts of a device or stratagem are also taken up; the whole of 9:2–4 represents a developed interpretation of the account in Genesis 34, emphasising the zeal of the Israelites and the vengeance and destruction brought upon their enemy.

A further biblical tradition important for Judith is that of David, especially the account of his victory over Goliath (1 Samuel 17). In both cases it is the weak who overcomes the mighty (16:6; cf. 1 Sam. 17:33, 51), and cuts off his head (13:6; cf. 1 Sam. 17:51); in both, Israel is terrified of the enemy and taunted by them (4:1; 5:21; cf. 1 Sam. 17:10–11). Again, both emphasise that the mighty God of Israel is able to bring victory over a powerful enemy who relies on its military strength (9:7–14; cf. 1 Sam. 17:45–7), and the theme that 'God is with' them is common to both (13:11; cf. 1 Sam. 17:37). The climax in both accounts comes with the enemy, now terrified, fleeing, pursued by the Israelites, who take the spoils of battle (15:1–11; cf. 1 Sam. 17:51–4), and the women lead a victory dance, procession and song (15:12–16:17; cf. 1 Sam. 18:6–7). Other parts of the David tradition are probably also taken up, as for example Jonathan's exploit against the Philistines (1 Sam. 14:1–23; see especially 9:11; cf. 1 Sam. 14:6; 10:5–6; 15:1–7; cf. 1 Sam. 14:1, 21:2).

Military victories in the history of the monarchy are drawn on otherwise, especially the account of Jehoshaphat's victory in 2 Chron. 20:1–30. In both accounts, the Israelites are terrified at the approach of the enemy (4:1–4; cf. 2 Chron. 20:3), and all, including women and children, come fasting or mourning in penitence to pray at the temple (4:9–15; cf. 2 Chron. 20:3–13). Achior reviews at length the way that God has defended his people and given them victory in the past, as Jehoshaphat does (5:5–21; cf. 2 Chron. 20:6–12; there are further striking similarities: 16:12; cf. 2 Chron. 20:15; 14:11–15:7, 11; cf. 2 Chron. 20:20–5; 15:12–14; cf. 2 Chron. 20:26–8; 16:15; cf. 2 Chron. 20:30). The developed tradition of Hezekiah's victory over Sennacherib (2 Kings 18–19/2 Chron. 32:1–23/Isaiah 36–7) has also influenced Judith at least in general terms.

Twice in Judith (9:8; 16:3) there occurs the striking LXX rendering at Exod. 15:3, 'God who shatters battles', and there are further links between 9:2–13 and 16:1–17 and the song of Miriam at the Red Sea (Exod. 15:1–21), and more widely in Judith otherwise with the Exodus tradition of the deliverance from Egypt. The main theme in both passages in Judith, as in Exod. 15:1–21, is that the mighty God of Israel defeats the powerful enemy and delivers his people, and these accounts clearly draw on other themes and phrases in Exodus (for example, 16:13; cf. Exod. 5:11; 14:31; cf. Exod. 15:20; 9:7; cf. Exod. 15:1, 21; 9:12; cf. Exod. 15:2; 9:9, 13; cf. Exod. 15:7 9, 17). Both Nebuchadnezzar and Holofernes take on traits of Pharaoh, and a decisive part of the deliverance takes place at night (13:1–8; cf. Exodus 12).

At 8:25–7 the writer refers specifically to the example of the testing of Abraham (Gen. 22:1–14) as also that of Isaac and Jacob, as part of the exhortation to the people; there is also implicit reference to God leading Abraham in Achior's speech (5:6–9). The writer probably makes further use of the Abraham tradition by drawing on the account of his campaign against the kings of the east in Genesis 14. Again the decisive action takes place at night (Gen. 14:15), and Abraham pursues the enemy (Gen. 14:15), while the blessing invoked upon Judith by the high priest (15:8–9; cf. 13:18) takes up the theme and language of that which Abraham receives from Melchizedek (Gen. 14:18–20).

Much more might be said both in detail and in general about the use of Scripture in Judith. It should already be clear, however, that the writer has constructed the story skilfully, employing biblical traditions and allusions in a multi-layered and interwoven way. It thus invokes and evokes a succession of familiar scriptural events and characters, to portray God as able to deliver his people even in the face of overwhelming oppression and apparently invincible domination, punishing his people and putting them to the test but constantly intervening for them in their history, and (again in spite of appearances) as God over all nations. The fact that the very limited biblical tradition of a woman playing the leading role is made central to the book is remarkable. Partly Judith may be intended as representative of the jewish people as weak, yet able to throw off foreign domination if they obey God and act zealously for him, but the positive use of a woman as the central character surely implies more about the perspective of the writer and community from which the work derives.

### (e) Ben Sira

There are no scriptural citations, formally introduced as such, in Ben Sira, although occasionally part of a biblical verse is used in a form quite close to the original (as, for example, 1:14, using Prov. 9:10/Ps. 111:10; or 27:26a using Prov. 26:27a/Qoh. 10:8a). Much more characteristic, however, are allusions that draw on Scripture in a free and paraphrastic way (thus, for instance, 2:18, drawing on 2 Sam. 24:14; 17:27; cf. Ps. 6:6; and 45:23–4; cf. Num. 25:11–13). It is indeed the case that there is constant allusion to Scripture throughout the book, in the use variously of biblical phrases, style and themes (for a detailed list of possible verbal allusions see Eberharter, 1911, pp. 6–54; see also Schechter and Taylor, 1899, pp. 13–25; Snaith, 1967), although it has to be recognised that a considerable proportion of these may simply reflect common usage, without intending any conscious biblical reference (while the divergent Hebrew and Greek texts also present problems in this respect).

It is worth noting the way in which Ben Sira himself speaks (especially at 38:24–39:3; cf. also 32:15–16; 33:3) of the scribe as occupied with the constant study and interpretation of Scripture. The emphasis in 39:1–3 is particularly on wisdom, and this is reflected in the rest of the book, where the influence of large parts of the wisdom literature is evident. It is clear that Ben Sira makes use of Proverbs especially; its style, phraseology and thought permeate the whole of the book (see for example Middendorp, 1973, pp. 78–85), and there are frequent parallels with Psalms and Job as well (see Middendorp, 1973, pp. 72–8). Ben Sira does not, however, make merely passive use of the wisdom tradition but develops it significantly as well. This is clear, for example, in chap. 24 (see especially Marböck, 1971, pp. 34–96), where the self-presentation of wisdom in vv. 1–22 is based especially on Prov. 8:22–31 (thus 24:9, 'He created me from the beginning before the world...'; cf. Prov. 8:22–3), but also a heightened wisdom tradition more widely (as Proverbs 1–9; Job 28). Along with this, however, it develops (in vv. 5–6) a much more universal and cosmic conception of wisdom, probably drawn from Isis aretalogies; yet at the same time, it specifically limits wisdom's dwelling to Israel (vv. 7–8, in contrast to Prov. 8:31), and in 24:23 goes even further and equates wisdom with the law given to Moses. Here it draws directly on Deut. 33:4; similarly in v. 12 it takes up Deut. 32:9, and more generally in vv. 8, 12–20 it appropriates for wisdom (thus limited to Israel and torah) the central deuteronomic emphases on the inheritance of the land, the election of Israel, and the rest and fruitful prosperity that will be enjoyed. The same basic position emerges also from chap. 1, especially the hymn in vv. 1–10; both here and throughout the chapter as a whole Ben Sira again draws on Prov. 8:22–31 especially, but also other parts of Proverbs 1–9 and the wisdom literature more generally (see Marböck, 1971, pp. 17–34). Yet in addition to 1:14, it is emphatically asserted (1:16, 26), against the threat of hellenistic philosophy, that *all* human wisdom in fact derives from the God of Israel, and that it is bound up with observing the law of Moses. Thus, again in contrast to Proverbs, *tôrâ* is no longer used in the general sense of 'instruction' but instead specifically of the Mosaic law; thus once again it is evident that Ben Sira, for apologetic and polemical reasons, ties wisdom almost exclusively to the law, in a deliberate development and change from the wisdom tradition, especially Proverbs, that underlies not only chapters 1 and 24 but also the whole work.

The same main apologetic and polemical themes are also fundamental to the remarkable section 44:1–49:16, the 'praise of the fathers', where scriptural sections and themes are drawn upon and developed more than anywhere else in the book. The overall purpose of this superbly constructed list of Israel's great heroes and God's great deeds for his people is, as the introduction in 44:1–15 makes clear, to show Israel's tradition, history and wisdom to be superior to all others, especially Hellenism. Thus Ben Sira develops and interprets the tradition of Abraham (a figure of universal significance; cf. 44:19) by emphasising his circumcision and faithfulness in testing (44:20c, d; thus implying a link between Genesis 17 and Gen. 22/15:6), his covenant with God, and also the fact that he 'kept the law' (44:20, 21). The theme of obedience to the law is important throughout this section (cf. 45:4–5, 'the law of life and knowledge'; 45:17; 46:10, 14; 49:4; cf. also Siebeneck, 1959), while the continuity of the covenant can be seen as the main theme of the whole *laus patrum* (Stadelmann, 1980, pp. 154–5; cf., for example, 44:11, 18, 22, 23; 45:5, 15, 24, 25; 50:24). A further aspect of this is the emphasis on the inheritance of the land, and the safeguarding of Israel's tradition and heritage, throughout chapters 44–5 and above all 46–9 (so Stadelmann, 1980, pp. 155–216), as also the theme of the remnant (see Siebeneck, 1959). The figures Ben Sira gives prominence to in these chapters are characterised especially by their mighty deeds for God and the true religion of Israel, as in the developed interpretation of Num. 25:11–13, and the theme of Phinehas's zeal (45:23–4; cf. also Elijah's 'zeal for the law', 48:2). The remarkable emphasis given to the prophets in chapters 46–9 is again especially on their great deeds for God. At the same time, the themes of divine retribution and the need for repentance are also stressed in this section (as with Elijah; 48:6–10), and these recur constantly (e.g. chap. 36(33); see Koole, 1965), while other themes from the prophetic tradition, such as fulfilment of the divine promise (36(33):15–16) are also used. The importance of the priesthood and cult is stressed constantly, drawing on the pentateuchal material (see Stadelmann, 1980), and the eternal priesthood of Phinehas (and Aaron; 45:23–4) is brought to fulfilment at 49:11–13 and in the eulogy of Simon in chap. 50. The implications of the use of all these developed themes, within the *laus patrum* and throughout the book, for Ben Sira's situation, in context of the threat of Hellenism, are clear.

From these few examples, then, something of the distinctive nature of Ben Sira's use of Scripture emerges. Thus he stands firmly in the tradition of biblical wisdom literature, but not only skilfully adapts and develops the style and structure of this, but also interprets the central theme of wisdom specifically in terms of the law. The whole section comprising chapters 44–9 exhibits an extraordinarily impressive ability to draw on a vast range of scriptural tradition, alluding briefly and apparently effortlessly to a great deal of biblical material, which is thus called to mind for the reader, but again developing and interpreting this to support the main themes it wants to emphasise. So also throughout the work he alludes easily and skilfully to Scripture, using it for the particular point he wants to make; thus he clearly feels the need to anchor in Scripture controversial or polemical arguments that he is adducing, as with his concern to show that rational behaviour effects atonement (as at 45:23–4; cf. Stadelmann, 1980, pp. 125–8). Again, at 38:1–15 he uses biblical material not only in support of medical practice but also to argue further for his theme of reward and retribution; 3:1–16 provides a fully religious interpretation of what it means to 'honour your father and mother' (3:1; cf. Exod. 20:12; cf. Stadelmann, 1980, pp. 132–6), while 35(32):1–7 give a spiritualising interpretation of the sense of 'you shall not appear empty before the Lord' (35:4; cf. Deut. 16:16; cf. Stadelmann, 1980, pp. 98–9). Thus Ben Sira shows how, already at this stage in the scribal tradition, Scripture can be used, by means of skilful techniques of allusion and interpretation, to apply to the contemporary situation and to emphasise particular themes.

### (f) The Wisdom of Solomon

This whole work is notable for the way it combines scriptural usage with hellenistic philosophical tradition (especially Philo and the Stoics; see Winston, 1979). Thus for example it develops, and attempts to make integral for the jewish faith as a whole, distinctively hellenistic themes, such as the pre-existence and immortality of the soul, freewill and determinism, and the quasi-independent figure of wisdom; yet for all these it draws for support on its biblical heritage, to effect a synthesis between jewish faith and hellenistic culture and philosophy.

As with Ben Sira, there are no specific citations with introductory formulae, but there is constant allusion to Scripture throughout, even though it is often difficult to be certain which passage the writer has in mind. The book, as the title suggests, deliberately sets itself again in the tradition of the biblical wisdom literature, and it is not surprising therefore to find that not only the style, but also the themes and phrases, of this appear most prominently. Again as with Ben Sira, it is Proverbs particularly that is drawn upon, above all in chapters 1–9 (see Skehan, 1971, pp. 173–91), although Psalms and Job, for example, are also used (Skehan, 1971, pp. 149–62; 191–213). Yet this material is not taken over passively, but is given distinctive development and interpretation. This is clear, for example, in 6:22–9:18. The underlying basis for this whole section is Prov. 8:22–31 (although other biblical passages, for example Proverbs 3 and Job 28, are also drawn upon). Here, however, the personified figure of wisdom is given a much more heightened interpretation than anything hitherto, going far beyond the Proverbs material in what is attributed to wisdom, especially in using central themes of Stoic philosophy to interpret it (as for example in 7:22–8:1).

In chapters 1–5 especially the influence of much of Proverbs (in particular) is evident, and the didactic style is taken over, but again the material is selected and interpreted to illustrate the main themes already indicated, above all that of immortality. It has frequently been argued that 2:1–9 has been deliberately composed as an attack upon the pessimistic, cynical development of the wisdom tradition represented by Qoheleth (so, for example, 2:1; cf. Qoh. 8:8; 2:6; Qoh. 2:24; 11:9; 2:9; cf. Qoh 3:22; for more detailed argument, see, for example, Goodrick, 1913, pp. 23–31), but on closer examination the parallels turn out not to be very precise, and it may be better to see the author as opposing more generally some aspects of Epicurean philosophy rather than drawing on Qoheleth directly (so, for example, Skehan, 1971, pp. 213–36).

In chapters 1–9 as a whole, it is in any case not the wisdom literature alone that is drawn on. So for example Suggs (1957) argues that 2:10–5:23 is intended as an exposition of Isa. 52:13–53:12. The section as a whole is a theodicy, dealing with the problem of the righteous (wise man) suffering at the hands of the unrighteous, and the experiences of the servant (*pais*) of Isaiah are made to be the experience of the child (*pais/huios*) of wisdom (thus for instance 2:13; cf. Isa. 52:13; 2:14–16; cf. Isa. 53:2–3; 2:19–20; cf. Isa. 53:7–9; 5:3–4; cf. Isa. 53:3, 10); the middle section, 3:15–4:13, which lacks obvious reference to Isaiah, is to be seen as a commentary on the Isaianic themes of the righteous barren woman and eunuch, by means of hymns in praise of them. What is especially striking, Suggs argues, is the method the author uses, taking over main themes and much of the detail from the Isaiah passage, but using very little of the precise wording; the same technique can be observed at 13:11–19, drawing on Isa. 44:13–20. Not all of the parallels are equally convincing; but there can be no doubt of the influence of Isaiah in this section and on the book as a whole (so Skehan, 1971, pp. 163–71).

It is also clear that chapters 7–9 draw on the Solomon tradition, and Gilbert (1984) argues that the author uses the Kings and Chronicles material directly, but selectively, 7–9 being built on the Gibeon episode, and above all Solomon's prayer for wisdom, as recorded in 1 Kings 3/2 Chronicles 1. Thus 7:7–12 is best understood as being based on 1 Kgs 3:9–14; there are points of contact throughout chap. 8 (e.g. 8:2; cf. 1 Kgs 3:7, 9; 8:11; cf. 1 Kgs 3:28; 8:19; cf. 1 Kgs 3:7; 8:21; cf. 1 Kgs 3:9), as well as the obvious links provided by the prayer itself in chap. 9 (e.g. 9:3; cf. 1 Kgs 3:6; 9:10, 12; cf. 1 Kgs 3:9; 9:13; cf. 1 Kgs 3:8). Yet the author has omitted much of the detail and several of the themes of 1 Kings 3 (as with the lack of reference to the 'dream'). At the same time he interprets and develops the basic tradition, both by drawing on a wide variety of other biblical material and also by introducing further themes, such as the personification of wisdom and Solomon seeking wisdom as a bride. Thus he deliberately combines different biblical passages (especially 1 Kings 3 and Proverbs 8), themes and motifs, and fuses these together with themes and terminology from hellenistic philosophy. His purpose in doing so is to make important themes relating to Solomon (his wisdom, kingship, prayer, building of the temple, encyclopaedic knowledge) as universal and accessible as possible, but at the same time rooting them firmly in the biblical tradition and jewish heritage.

Chapters 10–19, the final main section of the book portraying wisdom as intervening throughout history in Israel's favour, show strong dependence on and use of biblical (especially pentateuchal) traditions, drawing above all on the exodus narrative. Thus chapters 10–12 are mainly concerned to interpret the wilderness and conquest traditions in relation to wisdom, and therefore draw not only on material from Exodus, but also from Genesis, Numbers and Deuteronomy as well. The following section, consisting of an attack on idolatry, draws mainly on Second Isaiah and Jeremiah; the use of the parable of the woodcutter (Isa. 44:13–20) at 13:11–19 has already been noted, but to this could be added the theme of the potter (Isa. 45:9; Jer. 18:1–6) at 15:7ff, and many other instances. In chapters 16–19, the author returns to the pentateuchal material, drawing above all on the plague tradition of Exodus, and using this in developed form. Again throughout the author does not take over scriptural traditions as the basis of his work in a passive way, but fuses this material together integrally with the main philosophical themes that we have already noted. In addition, in these chapters especially, he shows acquaintance with the deliberate use of developed jewish interpretation of Scripture, particularly some of the traditions reflected within some of the pentateuchal targumim (so Clarke, 1973; thus, for example, the reference to Adam as created 'alone' at 10:1 reflects the tradition of Adam as 'unique', found in Neofiti and other targumim of Gen. 3:22).

Overall, therefore, there is a very widespread and diverse use of biblical texts and traditions in Wisdom, which overlap in a multilayered way and with several levels of significance. The conscious drawing on biblical material, then, informs the character and purpose of the work as a whole; but it also involves a deliberately developed and distinctive use of scriptural traditions (as with the Exodus themes in chapters 16–19, and Proverbs 8 in chapters 7–9). Both Wisdom of Solomon and Ben Sira represent a notable interaction of jewish biblical and hellenistic philosophical traditions. They use the biblical wisdom tradition (especially Proverbs), but also Scripture more generally, to show jewish faith and tradition to be intellectually sophisticated, and intellectually and morally superior to hellenistic culture. The process, however, is two-way; in using the biblical tradition to show that it represents true wisdom and God's way for man, they thus modify the scriptural tradition itself, and make it inextricably part of hellenistic acculturation. Thus the use of Scripture, in Wisdom of Solomon especially, is double-edged.

## 3 Conclusion

Clearly the use of Scripture is important and central for all the disparate texts considered in this chapter. This is most obvious in the case of the Qumran texts, least of all so in 2 Maccabees, but overall a wide range of biblical books is drawn on throughout. It is also clear that Scripture is used not in a passive way but is moulded creatively for the author's purpose, and frequently to support a particular position. There are obvious differences of hermeneutical perspective; the dominant eschatological framework of the Qumran texts, where Scripture finds its fulfilment in the community and its situation, stands in marked contrast, for example, to Tobit and Ben Sira (and to an extent 1 Maccabees). Particular exegetical methods and techniques (belonging to the common stock of jewish interpretation of Scripture) have been noted, especially in the case of the Qumran texts. Also notable are the ways in which familiar biblical narratives or sections are used as the basis for a whole book (Tobit, Judith), but creatively developed with a multi-faceted use of other scriptural passages. The compressed, sustained rehearsal of important figures and events in Israel's history (Ben Sira 44–49; 1 Macc. 2:51–60) is also impressive, in alluding and calling attention to a great wealth of biblical material, thus providing a paradigm for the present situation or legitimation for a particular course of action. Important biblical themes (covenant, detailed prescriptions of torah, exodus and deliverance, temple and cult, zeal for the Lord, wisdom) are variously developed and reinterpreted. Throughout these texts, of course, there are striking differences in the use of the biblical tradition. Equally, however, Scripture is manifestly a basic resource in several ways, providing simple phraseology, fundamental themes, and authority and support for contentious positions, often by means of different interpretations of the same biblical passages.

## Bibliography

F.-M. Abel *Les Livres des Maccabées* (Paris, 1949).
I. Abrahams 'Tobit and Genesis', *JQR* 5 (1893), 348–50.
K. Baltzer *The Covenant Formulary* (Philadelphia, 1971) (English Translation of *Das Bundesformular*, WMANT 4 (Göttingen, 1960)).
E. G. Bauckmann 'Die Proverbien und die Sprüche des Jesus Sirach', *ZAW* 72 (1960), 33–63.
O. Betz *Offenbarung und Schriftforschung in der Qumransekte*, WUNT 6 (Tübingen, 1960).
G. J. Brooke 'Qumran Pesher: Towards the Redefinition of a Genre', *RQ* 14 (1980), 483–503.

*Exegesis at Qumran. 4Q Florilegium in its Jewish Context*, JSOTSS 29 (Sheffield, 1985).

W. H. Brownlee 'Biblical Interpretation Among the Sectaries of the Dead Sea Scrolls', *BA* 14 (1951), 54–76.

*The Meaning of the Qumran Scrolls for the Bible* (New York, 1964).

F. F. Bruce *Biblical Exegesis in the Qumran Texts* (Grand Rapids, 1959).

E. Burrows 'Wisdom X.10' *Biblica* 20 (1939), 403–7.

J. Carmignac 'Les citations de l'Ancien Testament dans la "Guerre des fils de lumière contre les fils de ténèbres"', *RB* 63 (1956), 234–60, 375–90.

*La Règle de la Guerre des Fils de Lumière contre les Fils de Ténèbres* (Paris, 1958).

'Les citations de l'Ancien Testament, et spécialement des Poèmes du Serviteur, dans les "Hymnes" de Qumrân', *RQ* 2 (1959–60), 357–94.

R. H. Charles *The Apocrypha and Pseudepigrapha of the Old Testament. I. Apocrypha* (Oxford, 1913).

E. G. Clarke *The Wisdom of Solomon* (Cambridge, 1973).

P. R. Davies *1QM, the War Scroll from Qumran. Its Structure and History*, Biblica et Orientalia 32 (Rome, 1977).

*The Damascus Covenant. An Interpretation of the "Damascus Document"*, JSOTSS 25 (Sheffield, 1983).

P. Deselaers *Das Buch Tobit. Studien zu seiner Entstehung, Komposition und Theologie*, Orbis Biblicus et Orientalis 43 (Freiburg and Göttingen, 1982).

A. A. Di Lella 'The Deuteronomic Background of the Farewell Discourse in Tob 14, 3–11', *CBQ* 41 (1979), 380–9.

D. Dimant 'Qumran Sectarian Literature', in M. E. Stone (ed.), *Jewish Writings of the Second Temple Period*, Compendia Rerum Iudaicarum ad Novum Testamentum II.2 (Assen, 1985).

R. Doran *Temple Propaganda: the Purpose and Character of 2 Maccabees*, CBQMS 21 (Washington, DC, 1981).

A. M. Dubarle *Judith. Formes et Sens des Diverses Traditions. I: Études*, Analecta Biblica 24 (Rome, 1966).

A. Dupont-Sommer *The Essene Writings from Qumran* (Oxford, 1961) (English translation of *Les écrits esséniens découverts près de la Mer Morte* (Paris, 1960)).

A. Eberharter *Der Kanon des Alten Testaments zur Zeit des Ben Sira*, Alttestamentliche Abhandlungen 3.3 (Münster, 1911).

A. Finkel 'The Pesher of Dreams and Scriptures', *RQ* 4 (1963–4), 357–70.

J. A. Fitzmyer 'The Use of Explicit Old Testament Quotations in Qumran Literature and in the New Testament', in *Essays on the Semitic*

*Background of the New Testament* (London, 1971), pp. 3–58 (reprinted from *NTS* 7 (1960–61), 297–333).

H. Gabrion 'L'interprétation de l'Écriture dans la littérature de Qumrân', in W. Haase (ed.), *Aufstieg und Niedergang der Römischen Welt*, II, 19.1 (Berlin and New York, 1979), pp. 779–848.

J. Gamberoni 'Das "Gesetz des Mose" im Buche Tobias', in G. Braulik (ed.), *Studien zum Pentateuch. Festschrift für W. Kornfeld* (Vienna, 1977), pp. 227–42.

J. K. Gasser *Das althebräische Spruchbuch und die Sprüche Jesu Ben Sira* (Gütersloh, 1903).

M. Gilbert 'L'éloge de la Sagesse (Siracide 24)', *Revue théologique de Louvain* 5 (1974), 326–48.

'La figure de Salomon en Sg 7–9', in R. Kuntzmann and J. Schlosser (eds.), *Études sur le Judaïsme hellénistique* (Paris, 1984), pp. 225–49.

T. F. Glasson 'The Main Source of Tobit', *ZAW* 71 (1959), 275–7.

J. A. Goldstein *I Maccabees*. AB 41 (New York, 1976).

*II Maccabees*. AB 41A (New York, 1983).

E. Haag *Studien zum Buche Judith. Seine theologische Bedeutung und literarische Eigenart*, TTS 16 (Trier 1963).

C. Habicht *2. Makkabäerbuch*, JSHRZ I.3 (Gütersloh, 1976).

M. Hengel *Judaism and Hellenism. Studies in their Encounter in Palestine during the Early Hellenistic Period* (2 vols. London, 1974) (English translation of *Judentum und Hellenismus. Studien zu ihrer Begegnung unter besonderer Berücksichtigung Palästinas bis zur Mitte des 2 Jh.s v. Chr.*, WUNT 10 2nd ed. (Tübingen, 1973)).

S. Holm-Nielsen *Hodayot. Psalms from Qumran* (Aarhus, 1960).

B. Jongeling *Le Rouleau de la Guerre des Manuscrits de Qumrân* (Assen, 1962).

J. L. Koole 'Die Bibel des Ben-Sira, *OTS* 14 (1965), 374–96.

C. Larcher *Le Livre de la Sagesse ou La Sagesse de Salomon* (2 vols. Paris, 1983–4).

S. Lowy 'Some Aspects of Normative and Sectarian Interpretation of the Scriptures', *ALUOS* 6 (1969), 98–163.

J. Maier *The Temple Scroll. An Introduction, Translation and Commentary*, JSOTSS 34 (Sheffield, 1985) (English translation of *Die Tempelrolle vom Toten Meer* (Munich, 1978)).

M. Mansoor *The Thanksgiving Hymns* (Leiden, 1961).

J. Marböck *Weisheit. Untersuchungen zur Weisheitstheologie bei Ben Sira*, BBB 37 (Bonn, 1971).

T. Middendorp *Die Stellung Jesu Ben Siras zwischen Judentum und Hellenismus* (Leiden, 1973).

D. Patte *Early Jewish Hermeneutic in Palestine*, SBLMS 22 (Missoula, 1975).

R. H. Pfeiffer *History of New Testament Times with an Introduction to the Apocrypha* (London, 1949).

J. Reider *The Book of Wisdom* (New York, 1957).

B. J. Roberts 'Bible Exegesis and Fulfilment in Qumran', in P. R. Ackroyd and B. Lindars (eds.), *Words and Meanings. Essays Presented to David Winton Thomas* (Cambridge, 1968), pp. 195–207.

L. Rost *Judaism Outside the Hebrew Canon. An Introduction to the Documents* (Nashville, 1976) (English translation of *Einleitung in die alttestamentlichen Apokryphen und Pseudepigraphen einschliesslich der grossen Qumran-Handschriften* (Heidelberg, 1971)).

L. Ruppert 'Das Buch Tobias – Ein Modellfall nachgestaltender Erzählung', in J. Schreiner (ed.), *Wort, Lied und Gottesspruch I, Festschrift für Joseph Ziegler* (Würzburg, 1972), pp. 109–19.

'Zur Funktion der Achikar-Notizen im Buch Tobias', *BZ* NF 20 (1976), 232–7.

J. T. Sanders *Ben Sira and Demotic Wisdom* (Chico, 1983).

G. Sauer *Jesus Sirach* (*Ben Sira*), JSHRZ III.5 (Gütersloh, 1981).

S. Schechter and C. Taylor *The Wisdom of Ben Sira. Portions of the Book Ecclesiasticus from Hebrew Manuscripts in the Cairo Geniza Collection presented to the University of Cambridge by the editors* (Cambridge, 1899).

K.-D. Schunck *1. Makkabäerbuch*, JSHRZ I.4 (Gütersloh, 1980).

R. T. Siebeneck 'May their Bones Return to Life! – Sirach's Praise of the Fathers', *CBQ* 21 (1959), 411–28.

D. C. Simpson 'The Book of Tobit', in R. H. Charles (ed.), *The Apocrypha and Pseudepigrapha of the Old Testament, I. Apocrypha* (Oxford, 1913) pp. 174–241.

P. Skehan *Studies in Israelite Poetry and Wisdom* (Washington, DC, 1971).

E. Slomovic 'Toward an Understanding of the Exegesis in the Dead Sea Scrolls', *RQ* 7 (1969–71), 3–15.

J. G. Snaith 'Biblical Quotations in the Hebrew of Ecclesiasticus', *JTS* n.s. 18 (1967), 1–12.

H. Stadelmann *Ben Sira als Schriftgelehrter. Eine Untersuchung zum Berufsbild des vor-makkabäischen Sōfēr unter Berücksichtigung seines Verhältnisses zu Priester-, Propheten- und Weisheitslehrertum*, WUNT 2.6 (Tübingen, 1980).

M. J. Suggs 'Wisdom of Solomon 2:10–5:23: A Homily Based on the Fourth Servant Song', *JBL* 76 (1957), 26–33.

S. Talmon 'The "Desert Motif" in the Bible and in Qumran Literature', in A. Altmann (ed.), *Biblical Motifs* (Cambridge, Mass., 1966), pp. 31–63.

G. Vermes *Scripture and Tradition in Judaism* (Leiden, 1961).

'The Qumran Interpretation of Scripture in its Historical Setting', in *Post-Biblical Jewish Studies* (see below), pp. 37–49 (reprinted from *ALUOS* 6 (1969), 84–97).

*Post-Biblical Jewish Studies* (Leiden, 1975).

*The Dead Sea Scrolls. Qumran in Perspective* (London, 1977).

J. de Waard *A Comparative Study of the Old Testament in the Dead Sea Scrolls and in the New Testament* (Leiden, 1965).

P. Wernberg-Møller 'Some Reflections on the Biblical Material in the Manual of Discipline', *ST* 9 (1955), 40–66.

*The Manual of Discipline* (Leiden, 1957).

D. Winston *The Wisdom of Solomon* (New York, 1979).

Y. Yadin *The Scroll of the War of the Sons of Light Against the Sons of Darkness* (Oxford, 1962).

*The Temple Scroll* (3 vols., Jerusalem, 1983).

F. Zimmermann *The Book of Tobit* (New York, 1958).

E. Zenger *Das Buch Judit*, JSHRZ 1.6 (Gütersloh, 1981).

J. K. Zink *The Use of the Old Testament in the Apocrypha* (Ph.D. Dissertation, Duke University, 1963).

# 10 · Apocalyptic literature

## CHRISTOPHER ROWLAND

THE fact that Scripture is quoted explicitly so infrequently in the apocalypses should not lead us to suppose that the whole process of scriptural interpretation was a matter of little or no concern to the writers of the apocalypses and the unknown visionaries concealed behind them. Those who have studied the book of Revelation will know that, while it may be true to say that Scripture is not formally cited by the author, allusion to the Bible is to be found in virtually every verse. The extant jewish apocalypses do not set out to make obvious connexions with particular biblical passages (Stone, 1984, p. 390). However, the absence of such clearcut connexions should not lead us to suppose that the material has only tenuous links with the Scriptures, for the apocalypses do not set out to be in the first instance biblical commentaries. The links that there are will frequently be allusive and indirect. Thus an analysis of the way in which Scripture is used needs to follow a more subtle approach, allowing full weight to the often allusive character of reference to Scripture and the complexity of the relationship.

But first it is necessary to specify which works will be considered as examples of apocalypses. There has been much discussion recently about the genre of the apocalypse (see Collins, 1979, and Rowland, 1982), from which there has emerged a surprising amount of agreement on which works should be included within the corpus of apocalyptic literature. There has been debate about the status of the Sibylline Oracles and the book of Jubilees. The latter will be considered here because, in formal terms at least, it claims to belong to the category of revelatory literature. The works which will be given particular consideration are as follows: 1 Enoch, 2 Enoch, 4 Ezra, Syriac Baruch, the Apocalypse of Abraham, the Testament of Abraham, Jubilees, the Testament of Levi, Daniel, and Greek Baruch.

All of them were written in the period *ca.* 300 BC to AD 100, though the places of origin are probably diverse (2 Enoch and the Testament of Abraham probably being products of Egyptian Judaism; see Collins 1983).

The first two sections of this study will deal with explicit quotations of Scripture, concentrating on those passages from Ezekiel and Daniel which give some indication of the character of the interpretative process which was going on. The third section will focus more particularly on what one may term the distinctive use of Scripture in the apocalypses, a feature which sets the apocalypses apart from the other extant literature of the second temple period.

Analysis of the use of Scripture in the works mentioned here would be too large a task to cover in the space available in this chapter. The aim is a much more modest one: to confirm that we *are* dealing with works where the use of Scripture (by whatever means) is an essential ingredient of their character; and to analyse some of the key passages of Scripture which have contributed to the outlook of the apocalypses. It is most important that we recognise that in considering the use of Scripture in the apocalypses we do not expect the kind of *explicit* midrashic activity which is to be found, say, in a rabbinic commentary or a retelling of the biblical narrative such as we find in the Biblical Antiquities of Pseudo-Philo (Stone, 1984, p. 391).

Detailed examination of the apocalypses has indicated how much these are indebted to parts of the prophetic books of the Bible (Hartman, 1969). The emergence of a hope for the future in the period of the second temple is a subject which demands more detailed consideration than is possible here, taking fuller account of the varied circumstances in which the different works emerged. While we must always recognise the variety of eschatological belief, there does appear to have emerged a certain degree of uniformity in the expectation of a restored Israel as the centre of a new world order of peace and righteousness following a period of disaster and cataclysm which would affect the whole of humankind. In the emergence of these ideas certain key passages seem to have played their part. Thus we find that the extended description of the messianic age in Isaiah 11 has contributed to the future hope in passages like 1 Enoch 62:2; 4 Ezra 13:10; cf. Ps. Sol. 17:27. Also, the doctrine of the so-called messianic woes which has its origins in the prophetic predictions of disaster for Israel and Judah (e.g. Isa. 13:10; 34:4; Jer. 14:12; 21:7; Ezek. 13:11) emerges in passages like Dan. 12:1, and Syriac Baruch 25ff, where it finds its most systematic presentation outside the book of Revelation (chapters 6, 8–9 and 16). Similarly, while it may not be easy to pinpoint with exactitude which scriptural passages have contributed to specific messianic doctrines in these works, the general contours of the belief are to be derived from the central importance of 2 Sam. 7:14 and Deut. 18:15 as an impetus for future hope in later periods (e.g. Psalms 89 and 132, Ps. Sol. 17).

This underlying indebtedness to Scripture needs to be stressed because a superficial glance at the eschatological material in the apocalypses would give an impression of having little contact with Scripture. Such an impression would, in all likelihood, be the result of the particular forms in which such future hopes are couched. Thus, the visions of the cedar and the vine and the black and bright waters in Syriac Baruch, the man rising from the sea and the eagle in 4 Ezra, the vision of the ram and the he-goat in Daniel 8 and the Animal Apocalypse and the Apocalypse of Weeks in 1 Enoch couch their eschatological hope in the distinctive imagery which characterises the dream visions of the apocalypses. This imagery in itself is in essential continuity with some of the more exotic prophetic texts like Ezekiel, where prophetic symbolism is evident, and the early chapters of Zechariah (1–8), where scholars have recognised antecedents to apocalyptic symbolism. But behind the particular forms of the symbolism, which is highly idiosyncratic and may only with difficulty be related to specific scriptural archetypes, there lies an outline of a common doctrine of the future hope which concentrates on the twin items of disaster followed by a this-worldly age of peace and righteousness. The particular form (and extent) of messianic doctrine differs between the various documents. Thus, for example, the participation of gentiles is not universally mentioned. There is, however, sufficient uniformity of eschatology and connexion with Scripture to find here a logical extension of the biblical archetypes in a different age, and an outlook which the apocalypses share with other jewish texts mediating the biblical tradition in the hellenistic and Roman periods.

In this chapter I shall seek to explore some of the distinctive patterns of biblical interpretation which are to be found in the jewish apocalypses of the second temple period and the years immediately following the destruction of the temple. No attempt will be made to offer a complete survey of all the references and allusions to Scripture found in these texts. The goal is a much more modest one. It consists of laying bare the character of the scriptural usage by focusing on the influence of certain key passages and on the peculiar relationship which this revelatory literature has with the paradigmatic revelation of God to Moses on Sinai.

I

First of all, I want briefly to go over ground which I have covered elsewhere (Rowland, 1979; Gruenwald, 1978), namely, the way in which the first chapter of Ezekiel has contributed to the way in which the immediate environs of God are described in those apocalypses which speak of a heavenly ascent to the throne of God. It is now widely recognised that these descriptions of the divine throne owe their inspiration principally to the first chapter of Ezekiel, though it is apparent that Isaiah 6 has also been incorporated (e.g. 1 Enoch 14; Daniel 7, 9; Apocalypse of Abraham 17; the Testament of Abraham 11; Revelation 4; 4Q Siroth Sabbat ha-ᶜolam; Slavonic Enoch 22). These passages are widely regarded as important pieces of evidence for the character of the jewish mystical tradition in the second temple period and are in all probability the starting point for that tradition which developed via the hekaloth texts of the early centuries of the christian era to the medieval Kabbalah (Gruenwald 1978; Scholem 1954).

There has been much debate recently about the character of that tradition, with the earliest rabbinic texts related to the first chapters of Ezekiel and Genesis being subjected to detailed scrutiny. On the one hand there are those who consider that the evidence indicates that the study of Ezekiel involved a seeing again of Ezekiel's vision by the apocalyptists and rabbinic mystics (Scholem, 1954 and 1965; Gruenwald, 1978; and Rowland, 1982). On the other hand there are those who argue that the material (particularly the rabbinic sources) will not bear the weight of such an interpretation and prefer to see the references as indicating a midrashic activity connected with these chapters which did not differ substantially in the earliest period from that connected with other parts of Scripture (Halperin, 1980). No doubt the debate about the precise setting in which Ezekiel was used and interpreted in these texts will continue to be a subject for debate and elucidation. Nevertheless there can be little doubt that what we have in this use of Ezekiel 1 is clear evidence of variant expansions of the chapter, in which various elements are either expanded or ignored, and where the very variety of usage indicates the versatility of the interpretative process even if the ultimate inspiration of the texts is not in doubt. Particularly worthy of note is the fact that in the apocalyptic texts the vision of the *merkabah* is preceded by an ascent to heaven. This is a notable development as compared with the biblical exemplars. Although Isaiah believes that he can be part of the heavenly court during the course of his call-vision in the temple (Isaiah 6; cf. 1 Kgs 22:16), there is no suggestion that this involves an ascent to the heavenly world. We probably have no way of knowing whether the descriptions of God's throne in the apocalypses with their amalgam of various biblical passages are the product of conventional exegetical activity carried on in the confines of scribal activity. But the possibility should not be ignored that in the study of Scripture creative imagination could have been a potent means of encouraging the belief that the biblical passages were not merely written records of past events but vehicles of contemporary manifestations of the divine. That, of course, is precisely what the writer of the NT Apocalypse asserts in speaking about being 'in the spirit' (4:2; cf. 1:9). Such indications, when taken together with the obvious absence of the kind of orderly exegetical activity which we find in contemporary biblical commentaries, should make us wary of ruling out the possibility of the biblical text being in the imaginations of the apocalyptic visionaries a door of perception in which the text could become a living reality as its details merged with parallel passages to form the distinctive visions of heaven now found in some of the apocalypses.

A related creative use of the prophecy of Ezekiel can also be discerned in the way in which certain aspects of its theophany have been taken up in the book of Daniel and have contributed to an emerging angelomorphic tradition in Judaism. While one needs to recognise that the stock of biblical angelomorphic categories which could be used by the apocalyptic visionaries was strictly limited and that the common features in various angelophanies could in part be explained in this way, there seems to be sufficient evidence to suppose that various texts do owe their inspiration to an often complex tradition whose origin is ultimately Ezekiel 1 and 8 but to which passages like Dan. 7 and 10:5 have contributed (Rowland, 1985; Fossum, 1985).

The impact of Scripture is also apparent in another area of the apocalypses: those stories of biblical heroes which so often provide a framework (usually at the start of apocalypses) for the revelations of divine secrets which follow. In the earliest apocalyptic material in 1 Enoch the story of the sin of the sons of God is linked with the emerging Enoch saga to provide an extended account of the sin of the angels, their rejection by God, their pleas for repentance and Enoch's intercession and their final condemnation (VanderKam, 1984; Hanson, 1977; Nickelsburg, 1977). Elsewhere the sacrifice of Abraham in Genesis 15 offers the basis of an account of Abraham's ascent to heaven in which the sacrificial victims provide the means of ascent for the patriarch and the angel Jaoel. The closely related 4 Ezra and Syriac Baruch, which were written in the aftermath of the fall of Jerusalem (Harnisch, 1969), have been placed in a similar environment in Israel's previous history. Syriac Baruch is set in the period immediately preceding and following the destruction of the city and 4 Ezra, somewhat awkwardly connected with the period of Ezra the scribe, reflects the situation after the destruction. There has been much discussion about the precise literary genre of the book of Jubilees (Rowland, 1982, p. 51). It is frequently (and with some justification) linked with the retelling of Israel's history as is to be found in Pseudo-Philo and the Genesis Apocryphon. But the revelatory framework is not in doubt: the work is said to be a revelation by an angel to Moses. It is placed on a similar level to the Torah itself as divine revelation and in this respect resembles the Temple Scroll (11Q Temp.). Other apocalyptic works like Slavonic Enoch and the Testament of Levi utilise the testament form (von Nordheim, 1980) and incorporate the visionary material into death-bed pronouncements by the patriarch.

Much of the material we find in the apocalypses seems to have only a tenuous relationship to specific OT passages with indirect connexions emerging via common use of scriptural material from the common stock of belief and practice as it had emerged over the centuries. But when specific passages are subjected to minute examination, as has been carried out, for example by Hartman (1969 and 1979) and Knibb (1982 b), the contribution of various scriptural passages becomes apparent. Knibb has investigated the way in which the books of Job and Genesis and Daniel (treated briefly below) have influenced 4 Ezra. Thus he notes the way in which Job 38 (as well as other aspects of the wisdom tradition) underlie 4 Ezra 4:7f, and the common dialogue form in both works. Elsewhere he notes that 4 Ezra 3:4ff and 6:38ff are dependent on the early chapters of Genesis, and 7:132ff may be a midrash on Exod. 34:6f. While the vision of the eagle and the lion and the man from the sea in chapters 12 and 123 take their inspiration from Daniel 7, other OT passages have in Knibb's view played their part, e.g. Ps. 46:6; 97:5; Mic. 1:4 in 13:4; Isa. 11:4; Ps. 18:8 and 13 in 13:10; and Isa. 66:20 in 13:13. Knibb reminds us that

the wide range of this material serves as a...warning against the attempt to tie the apocalyptic writings, or at least this particular apocalypse, down to a single stream of tradition within the Old Testament...As a kind of interpretative writing 4 Ezra takes its place alongside other forms of interpretative literature.

These comments about 4 Ezra are a timely reminder that we are not dealing in the apocalypses with a phenomenon fundamentally opposed to the outlook of the torah. Those who find in the apocalypses a religious stream which is somehow opposed to the torah have to ignore the indebtedness which commentators like Knibb have noted. To make the apocalypses a vehicle of salvation history among those circles opposed to the legal concerns of the scribes and proto-rabbis is to play down the importance of the apocalyptic tradition for rabbinic Judaism and to relegate the importance of the torah in the apocalypses (see Nissen, 1967; cf. Rössler, 1960).

## II

Recent study has indicated that the apocalyptic texts themselves are in part the exposition of Scripture. Nowhere is this process better exemplified than in the case of the book of Daniel, and, in particular, its seventh chapter, which has had a significant impact on a variety of later writings both christian and jewish (Casey, 1980; Beale, 1984; Hartman, 1969 and 1979; and Kearns, 1980). But it has also contributed both explicitly and implicitly to several of the apocalypses, notably 1 Enoch and 4 Ezra, in the latter case involving an explicit attempt to reinterpret the meaning of the text by reference to angelic revelation (4 Ezra 12).

There is every likelihood that Daniel 7 itself forms part of a longer tradition of interpretation in which biblical and possibly much older semitic sources have contributed to the stock of images now contained in it. With regard to the latter there have been those who have found clear affinities with the Ugaritic material (most recently Day, 1985, and earlier Colpe, 1972). But there are biblical passages which have also been pointed out as possible resources for the distinctive imagery contained in this chapter (Niditch, 1977). There have been those who have wanted to find a resurgence of messianism stemming from Psalm 2 and its picture of the victory of the Lord's anointed over his enemies. But much closer to hand are the affinities with the *merkabah* tradition already alluded to earlier in this chapter. The connexions with Ezek. 1:26f have often been noted with the throne, fire, and human figure in 7:9 and 7:13. But we cannot ignore the superficial contacts which are to be found in the major preoccupation of both chapters with the four beasts/creatures, which in Ezekiel have four faces (man, lion, ox and eagle), whereas in Daniel the four beasts are identified as a lion with eagle's wings to which the mind of a man was given, a bear, a leopard and the terrible strong beast with horns. Whether in the visionary imagination the creatures of Ezekiel might have been the raw material for the vision of Dan. 7:1–8 we cannot be certain, but the similarity deserves to be noted.

Because of its importance for early christology, Daniel 7 has been the subject of detailed examination over the recent decades, and it is superfluous to go over the ground in detail once again. Nevertheless there is some point in indicating how the exegetical possibilities which have dominated and polarised study of this chapter among contemporary exegetes are in no small part the result of the ambiguities of the chapter itself, not least in the place which the Son of Man figure has within the structure of the chapter as a whole. The contrast between the two major positions is well put by Moule (1982):

The apocalyptic use of the phrase Son of Man, exemplified by the Similitudes, 1 Enoch 37–71, is not necessarily a reliable guide to that of the Synoptic Gospels, for which, rather, Dan. 7 is the proximate antecedent... The human figure of Dan. 7 need not have been understood by Jesus... as an essentially supernatural figure. In Dan. 7 itself, it simply represents or symbolises the persecuted loyalists, no doubt of Maccabean days, in their ultimate vindication in the court of heaven.

The other side in this debate (of which the present writer is a member) argues that we have in Daniel 7 a description of the 'coronation' of a heavenly being, one who is, in Moule's words, a permanent supernatural member of the heavenly court, probably the archangel Michael (Collins, 1977, and Day, 1985). As I have indicated, the significant fact about this chapter (and one which makes it important for the study of exegesis) is that the rival interpretations offered by modern commentators illustrate an ambiguity which is already picked up by ancient users of the chapter.

But first let me outline the common ground which exists between the two approaches.

(i)   In Daniel 7 we have an apocalyptic visionary form which, in outline at least, is familiar to us from other sources (Collins, 1979). In it the vision is followed by an interpretation given by an angelic interpreter. In one respect the form of the vision seems to differ from those of a similar type (e.g. Daniel 8 and Revelation 17 and the vision of the black and bright waters in Syriac Baruch). In the latter there is no question of any part of the vision being a glimpse of supernatural realities in the world above; the symbols have no real existence outside the context of the vision. As we shall see in due course, it could be argued that we have in Daniel 7 a mixture of visionary types: the symbolic vision, in which the items merely symbolise earthly persons or events; and the heavenly vision in which the participants are actually believed to have an independent existence in the world above. This leads me to my second point.

(ii)    Part of the vision (Dan. 7:9f at least) concerns a scene in the heavenly world in which God is enthroned in the celestial court. As we have seen, the description of God's throne is derived from the *merkabah* tradition deriving from the first chapter of Ezekiel and evident in other apocalyptic texts.

(iii)    In the interpretation of the vision it is apparent that there is a close link between the human figure and the saints. Just as the human figure receives the kingdom in v. 14, so also the saints are said to receive the same according to the interpretation (vv. 18, 22, 27).

(iv)    It is plausible that some ancient interpreters could have regarded the Son of Man figure as a symbol of the vindication of the saints. Indeed, there is evidence in jewish tradition of a bifurcating tradition of interpretation. The Similitudes of Enoch offer evidence of a tradition of interpretation which views the son of man figure as an angelic being seated on God's throne. In another passage indebted to Daniel 7, 4 Ezra 13, the man in the vision seems to be merely a symbol of the messiah and is not a heavenly being. It is true that the evidence of 4 Ezra on the messiah is rather confusing (Stone, 1968). Thus 7:28 seems to describe the messiah as a mortal man, whereas in 14:9 he is pre-existent. In 4 Ezra 13 with its pattern of symbolic vision and interpretation it would appear from v. 26 that the man from the sea is merely a symbol of the messiah whom the Most High has been keeping for many ages. What takes place in the vision is not in this case a glimpse of heavenly realities but is a vivid visionary account of the eschatological events to take place on earth in the new age.

There is a possibility, therefore, that, whatever the original meaning of Daniel 7, the interpretation in the gospels could be that part of the interpretative tradition which regards the son of man figure merely as a symbol, 4 Ezra 13 being an example of the interpretative possibilities exploited by one apocalyptic writer. The interpretative contrast can be exemplified by two other texts: Revelation 5 and 1QM 17:5. Many commentators on Daniel 7 are prepared to accept that a heavenly scene is described in Dan. 7:9f; but whereas God, the Ancient of Days, is regarded as a permanent member of the heavenly world, the human figure is merely a symbol of God's righteous people. Thus the pattern in Daniel 7 of a heavenly throne scene juxtaposed with apocalyptic symbolic vision corresponds to Revelation 5. In this chapter we have the continuation of the heavenly throne vision of Revelation 4 with the account of the exaltation of a lamb. The lamb is manifestly a symbol of the crucified messiah. Such a juxtaposition of heavenly vision and symbolic vision has few parallels in the apocalypses. Not only is it a telling pointer to the distinctive theological message of the Apocalypse but it is also indicative of the way in which the heavenly throne scene similar to Daniel could have been used in a way strikingly different from the use in the Similitudes of Enoch, exploiting the possible juxtaposition of heavenly and symbolic visionary types.

The other text relevant to the ongoing interpretation of Daniel 7 is 1QM 17:7:

God will raise up the Kingdom of Michael in the midst of the gods, and the realm of Israel in the midst of all flesh.

Here Michael's triumph in the heavenly world is paralleled on earth by the triumph of Israel. Similarly Daniel 7 may have provided the means whereby an ancient commentator viewed Dan. 7:13f as a picture of the exaltation of a heavenly being and the triumph of the saints on earth. The reference to Michael in this passage from the War Scroll reminds us that Michael, leader of the heavenly host, is spoken of as the great prince who has charge of God's people in Dan. 12:1, suggesting that he is an obvious candidate when it comes to identifying the human figure in Dan. 7:13. The resemblance to a man coincides with the angelophanies elsewhere in Daniel (3:25; 8:15; 10:5f). The close link between Michael and the people of God (as well as the heavenly host) thus explains the parallelism between the receipt of the kingdom by the human figure and the receipt of the kingdom by the saints. The triumph of the human figure in the heavenly court is a guarantee of the ultimate vindication of the saints in the lower realms. Also the identification of the human figure with the archangel Michael maintains a consistency of visionary type in Dan. 7:9 and 7:13. In the heavenly court the supernatural figures, God and his angels and the angelic representative of the saints of the Most High, are described.

But as we have seen it is quite likely that consistency of visionary type was not necessarily noted by all the apocalyptic authors who made use of this chapter. An important question has to be asked about the beasts: do they merely symbolise earthly kings? If so, we can see reasons why there might have been confusion over the identity of the human figure (though in contrast with the beasts nothing is said explicitly in the interpretation of the vision about any identification between the saints of the Most High and the Son of Man). Some understood the human figure after the manner of the beasts; others viewed him as a permanent member of the heavenly world, if, that is, we are justified in supposing that the beasts are not to be regarded as heavenly (demonic) beings. It might be argued that, just as in other apocalypses where the lower parts of heaven are populated by demonic beings, so here too the beasts (whatever the raw material drawn on by the apocalyptist may have been) are heavenly beings in some sense opposed to God.

A few words need to be said about Dan. 7:21f. In the interpretation of the vision Daniel approaches a participant in the vision and is given a brief interpretation (v. 17). After that he expresses his desire to know the truth about the fourth beast. This leads to a return to the vision (v. 21), where the horn is seen to make war on the saints and to prevail over them until the Ancient of Days comes and judgment is given for the saints and the saints receive the kingdom. Then in v. 23 there is a return to the explanation, this time concerning the fourth beast and the horns, concluding in v. 25 with a reference to the king who will speak words against the Most High. But even his dominion will be short lived, for the significance of the judgment of the court is that the kingdom and dominion will be given to the people of the saints of the Most High.

Dan. 7:21f presents problems to all interpreters. In the text as it stands we must assume that the evil treatment of the saints, judgment against the beast and for the saints, the receipt of the kingdom by the human figure and the consequent receipt of the kingdom by the saints are all separate parts of the same vision. We might have expected reference to the human figure in a visionary context; but these verses concentrate on the fate of the saints and need not exclude the possibility that the saints receive the kingdom because of the triumph of their heavenly representative. The confusion between earth and heaven, particularly with regard to the identity of the saints (are they angels or human beings?) which these verses engender is well exemplified by the belief of the Qumran sect that it had communion with angels (1QH 3:20ff; 11:13f; 1QS 11:7f). Such a close relationship between angels and the holy people makes a confusion between angels and the righteous explicable. Whether or not such a link derives directly from Daniel 7 we cannot be certain, but it is clearly important to recognise that it is not wise to distinguish too clearly between the two either in Daniel 7 or elsewhere.

I hope that this focus on an important chapter has served to indicate how much room there is for legitimate disagreement in interpreting Daniel 7. Particular note should be taken of the visionary material itself as the basis for variant interpretations at an early stage, for the jewish imagination was capable of exploiting to the full the ambiguities of a text. This would have been particularly the case when/if visionary material came into being in the context of the full exercise of the apocalyptic visionary imagination. It is no surprise that in the twentieth century those who still puzzle over this remarkable chapter should find themselves split into interpretative traditions not too dissimilar to those found in the world of ancient jewish apocalyptic.

## III

One of the dangers of discussing the use of Scripture in the apocalypses is that the treatment of this body of literature can so easily be like that given to any other jewish literature from this period. But this would be to minimise the significance of the distinctive literary form of the apocalypses. The fact is that we are dealing here with revelatory literature, which has many affinities with certain similar passages in the prophetic corpus in the Bible, but is found in this distinctive literary form because of its production within the hellenistic age. With all revelatory literature the question may immediately be asked: what basis does the idea of revelation (which in theory could be novel in content) have to do with the tradition embedded in the Scriptures? The simple answer is that the process of innovation inherent in the apocalyptic genre is itself rooted in tradition. We have already had reason to question the view of those who find very little evidence of any extensive use and connexion with Scripture in the apocalypses. Such a view hardly recognises the intense indebtedness to scriptural inspiration and precedents in the concept of apocalypse itself. The idea of revelation may bring with it connotations of novelty and a radical break with tradition; but there is very little evidence that the actual *content* of the revelations in the apocalypses themselves gives much warrant for supposing that such a thing did go on, even if the potential for it was in fact there. It is important to recognise that the concept of revelation is itself firmly rooted in Scripture, which provides the impetus for its use in later generations. As is well known the biblical call visions with their descriptions of God and the heavenly court provided a potent resource for the later apocalyptic visions. Even if it is not entirely clear what the precise relationship was between the contents of the revelation and the details of particular parts of Scripture, the apparent lack of midrashic precision should not blind us to the clear scriptural archetype which undergirds the apocalyptic framework of the revelations. Revelation is after all at the heart of the jewish religion: the manifestation of God's will to Moses on Mount Sinai. Nothing could be more characteristic of the kernel of Scripture than to claim continuity with the *character* of that original revelation, albeit in different circumstances and with a different process of authorisation at a later stage in jewish history. To speak in this way is not to suggest that we are supposing anything distinctive in the way Scripture is being used. After all, in the rabbinic tradition itself the ascent of Moses up the holy mountain was understood (at least in later midrash) as an ascent to heaven, where the law-giver received the whole gamut of Scripture and tradition (see e.g. Bowker, 1969, p. 41 n. 3).

The fact that the book of Jubilees and the Temple Scroll can set their particular and often distinctive revelations in the context of the revelation to God on Sinai inevitably raises the question of the relationship of that original revelation of God and from God to the claims to revelation made by subsequent generations. This would have been a problem for the prophets in their day, and the evidence suggests that it continued to be so for those who maintained the banner of the prophetic tradition after the exile (Hanson, 1975; Plöger, 1968). Of course, the fact that all the jewish apocalypses are themselves pseudonymous is a significant pointer to the problem posed by the fact that the revelations of the past have become Scripture. While we cannot be certain of all the reasons which led to the employment of pseudonymity by the apocalyptists, not least because it was a widespread phenomenon in the hellenistic world (Hengel, 1972), we may conjecture that the attribution of apocalypses to heroes of Israel's past reflects the need to give authority to the revelations by linking them with a biblical hero. Indeed, the use of pre-Mosaic figures like Enoch and Abraham may in itself testify to the sensitivity of the apocalyptists to ground their revelation in an older (and superior?) revelation of God (Barker, 1987). The emergence of a classic period of revelation when God spoke to Moses and the prophets and which came to an end with Haggai, Zechariah and Malachi (Tosefta Sotah 13:2), threw the ongoing prophetic claims into sharp relief and effectively outlawed (or at best marginalised) those who asserted that God still spoke to his people in ways similar to the way in which he spoke in the past to Moses and the prophets.

The character of divine revelation gives the apocalypses their distinctive view of the communication of God's will. Unless we grasp the high view of authority inherent in these texts, we shall not fully appreciate the potentially exclusive view of the value and content of the revelations. After all, what the apocalypses purport to offer is not the mere opinion of the expositor but a divine revelation emanating either from the throne of God or from an angelic intermediary commissioned by God for that purpose. Such a conviction is not arbitrary, that is to say based entirely on innovation. The implications of all this for our understanding of the attitude to Scripture within the apocalypses is important. While it is clear that only rarely can it be said that they manifest a concern to contradict Scripture or tradition, that factor is occasionally present, and the potential for radical contradiction is readily apparent. Certainly the book of Jubilees and certain portions of 1 Enoch use the apocalyptic framework to justify and support a method of calendrical calculation which differs significantly from what we know to have been the dominant view on such matters in the second temple period.

The problem became particularly acute towards the end of the first century AD. Some primitive Christians, Paul in particular, justified particular attitudes towards and interpretations of the torah by the conviction, based on apocalyptic awareness, that the messiah had come (Davies, 1984, and Rowland, 1985). The problem is found in its most acute form in the gnostic apocalypses of the second century and later. Here the revelatory form is used to give authority to understandings of Scripture which completely subvert the character and obvious meaning of the text, by arguing for a theological dualism and a complete denigration of the God of Israel. It is easy to dismiss such developments as the rogue use of the biblical tradition in the service of a rampant anti-Judaism. Such an assessment hardly does justice to the obvious indebtedness to the Bible and the evidence of exegesis, hardly the preoccupations of those who totally despised the jewish heritage.

The fact is that the apocalyptic framework could offer the basis for radical steps in religion. Radical in *content* the apocalypses may not be; all the evidence indicates that they repeat in various forms the common assumptions of most Jews. But it is the framework within which such information is communicated which is most significant. Who was to gainsay the authoritative visionary, particularly when the revelations also had the imprimatur of some biblical hero, as was the case with all the jewish apocalypses of the hellenistic period? The ground here was laid for those who wished to claim ultimate authority for belief and practice which was entirely inconsistent with the 'plain' meaning of the text of Scripture. As the Bible itself indicates, the issue of false prophecy always remained a problem (Deuteronomy 13; Jeremiah 23; Zechariah 13). When claims were made which seemed to be authenticated by God himself, in which current belief and practice were challenged, the difficulties are readily apparent. There is a sense in which the solution to the theological problem offered by the gnostics in their apocalypses was the fulfilment of this. In addition, in the eyes of those Jews who were implacably opposed to them, the early christian use of Scripture with its justification of the rejection of certain key commandments on the basis of revelation must have had all the hallmarks of false prophecy and led to precisely that type of suspicion of charismatic authority with which the NT and early christian life (such as the problem posed by figures like Elchesai, Cerinthus, Montanus, and later, of course, Muhammed; Widengren, 1950) is replete.

While there are certainly features of apocalyptic which make a link with gnosticism likely (Layton, 1980; Gruenwald, 1982; Wintermute, 1982), there is an essential epistemological difference between the two. We should recognise that while both apocalyptic and gnosticism lay claim to revelation as in varying degrees salvific, in the gnostic apocalypses the content of the revelation is itself salvific, whereas in the jewish apocalypses to know the content of the revelation may be an important, even indispensable, means of achieving salvation. The jewish apocalypses always seek to affirm the basic thrust of the tradition (however subtly they may change its content and emphasis, as we find, say, in the interpretation of Jeremiah in Daniel 9), while the gnostic apocalypses use the revelation to demean or subvert the OT material (see further Pearson, 1984).

As we have already noted, one of the mistakes made in the discussion of the relationship between apocalyptic and tradition is the polarisation which many have attempted to make between the form and the content of the apocalypses and other samples of jewish literature. While it would be wrong to play down the distinctive form of the apocalypses, there is the real danger of making too much out of this and erecting divisions within the history of ideas which were probably nothing like so clearcut in reality. The fact is that the evidence of the apocalypses themselves indicates that indebtedness to tradition (albeit a highly selective reading of it) is to be found throughout this literature. The conclusion of 4 Ezra 14 leaves us in no doubt that the writer of this apocalypse is just as interested in the canon of Scripture as in his revelations, even if he considers that those revelations are of more significance than the books already published (14:46). The problem is that we have accepted that the rhetoric of innovation and radical newness characterises the prophetic and charismatic as compared with the scribal to such an extent that we can easily miss the essential contribution that the tradition has contributed to the innovations of doctrine or practice. The apocalypses are no exception to this rule. The utilisation of an apocalyptic outlook in the history of both Judaism and Christianity is ample testimony to the deep-rooted nature of this outlook within the tradition itself. What is more, the validation of particular interpretations of tradition by recourse to visionary experience is itself merely a radical attempt to vindicate the kind of innovatory activity which is endemic within any vital religious culture.

Scribal activity no less than the visions of the apocalyptists was embarking on that difficult exploration of the integration of text and social setting which is at the heart of any vital hermeneutical enterprise. The authors of the apocalypses may have been claiming more for their interpretations than some of their contemporaries were wont to do (at least in the literary guise in which we find them). Nevertheless such an activity is itself part of that one wrestling with the resources and variety of a religious tradition in a context where its meaning and value appear to be under severe threat. In the use made of Scripture in all the literature of the hellenistic age we find an exploitation of what Frank Kermode has called the 'excess' of the text. The full resources of syntax, words and phrases are exploited so as to draw out all the hidden meanings. In this respect there is little to choose between the method of the apocalyptist and the ingenuity of the rabbinic expositor. Indeed, we find their methods converging in the 'apocalyptic' character of the Habakkuk

Commentary (1QpHab) at Qumran (Horgan, 1979). But for the rabbis there was an infinite treasure of meaning within the text which exegetical ingenuity could exploit to the full. In contrast, the claim in the Habakkuk Commentary that the Teacher of Righteousness had been given the true meaning of the words of the prophets (1QpHab 7:1ff) actually has the effect of cutting short the infinite character of that resource of meaning by limiting it to the 'final' and authoritative exposition by the emissary of God. In a similar vein Ephraim Urbach has pointed out how apocalyptic functioned in a similar way to curtail exegetical debate in a passage from the Babylonian Talmud (*b. Sanhedrin* 97b). This passage deals with the issue of the dependence of the coming of the final redemption on Israel's repentance. In it R. Eliezer and R. Joshua maintain their positions by citing various passages from Scripture in their support. The discussion is brought to a dramatic conclusion when R. Joshua quoted Dan. 12:7, a revelation from an angelic intermediary. When Joshua sought support for his argument from an apocalyptic vision, Eliezer saw no further possibility for continuing the argument. The last word had been said on the subject by a divine emissary; the authoritative pronouncement had been made on the matter (Urbach, 1975). That is not to suggest that the use of Scripture in apocalyptic necessarily means the closure of the text of Scripture as a resource of meaning; indeed, the evidence of the apocalypses themselves indicates what a wide variety of usage of particular passages is to be found there. Rather, the quest for authoritative revelation, when it is specifically related to the meaning of a text, can have the effect of preventing further innovation once the true meaning has been offered, as we find, for example in the Habakkuk Commentary.

It may be tempting to suppose that the social context in which apocalyptic flourished in ancient Judaism was fairly uniform: a situation of despair characterised by political subjection of the jewish people and the social marginalisation of the writer and his group. It has become something of a commonplace in studies of apocalyptic at the beginning of the christian era to accept such views without qualification.

Some of us have severe reservations whether apocalyptic does actually function in this way, even if there are reasons to suppose that, on other grounds, the claim to direct revelation serves the purpose of validating traditional beliefs and practices when they come under question from the circumstances of history. But the evidence suggests that apocalypses were not merely written by the marginalised (a point noted by Hanson, 1975). The apocalyptic tradition is not tied to one particular social stratum. The claim to direct revelation is used just as much by those who control the levers of religious power as those who do not. Indeed, there are many indications which support the view that works like 4 Ezra and Syriac Baruch were written in circles not far removed from the group which gained hegemony in Judaism after the fall of the second temple (see also Knibb, 1982b). Certainly 1 Enoch (at least in part) may resemble the views of those who wrote the Dead Sea Scrolls, in that it exhibits a reliance on a calendar which deviates quite markedly from what was widely accepted (Stone, 1984, p. 403). It can, therefore, be argued that in such a work the pseudonymous attribution to Enoch and the revelatory framework give the contents of the disclosure an authority which the peripheral nature of the groups which produced them would hardly support (see Rowland, 1982). Nevertheless the somewhat different revelatory form in 4 Ezra serves a rather different purpose: to enable the apocalyptic seer and his group to wrestle with the profoundest problems of theodicy within a framework where a definitive (if unsatisfactory) answer is given to the severe human questioning of God's righteousness (Stone 1984, p. 412). Such an uncompromising response could only be supported by an apocalyptic framework, as it makes no concessions to the demands of human wisdom for rational argument in support of the position it asserts.

There has been a tendency to contrast apocalyptic with other streams in ancient Judaism, notably the interpretation of the torah familiar to us in the rabbinic literature. The latter, we are often told, breathes the spirit of pragmatism and offers those who follow its precepts a practicable programme which will enable the righteous to walk in the ways of God. In contrast, the concentration of the apocalypses either on the world above or the world to come engenders unrealisable expectations which are liable to lead both to profound disappointment at the lack of evidence of their fulfilment and an unstable social environment as the result of the juxtaposition of a radically different view of the world order. Despite its wide currency there are many reasons for supposing that this contrast actually distorts the role of apocalyptic within ancient Judaism, not least the function of an apocalyptic outlook with relation to Scripture itself. If the rabbinic tradition is anything to go by, a realistic acceptance of the constraints placed upon the implementation of the holy environment by no means excluded a passionate attachment not only to dreams of a cosmic holiness in a new age but also a recognition that the holy space on earth created by the people of God was an extension of that wider holiness of God in the world above, accessible to those whose lives were particularly pure. Thus apocalyptic could be said to undergird the commitment to a limited goal for the people of God in the present age, because it offered a cause for hope and a retreat in adversity, precisely through those gateways into heaven which Scripture offered, in its occasional and daring glimpses of the transcendent God. The pessimistic realism of Qoheleth could not sustain attachment to the tradition. Indeed, there is a sense in which apocalyptic is a response of a sufficiently radical kind to precisely the kind of pessimism we find in that book. By its appeal to revelation and its stress on the need to pierce behind appearances to the realities which explain the incoherent jumble of history, apocalyptic supports continued attachment to Scripture and tradition. No doubt there were pious souls who found that faith in the unseen world of God and unrealised world of promise was difficult to sustain indefinitely. What became of them the traditions allow us only a tantalising glimpse. But for most Jews in the ancient world apocalyptic provided an indispensable resource which enabled them to continue to find in the Scriptures a resource which deserved adherence even when such commitment stretched human reason to its very limits.

## BIBLIOGRAPHY

M. Barker *The Older Testament* (London, 1987).

G. Beale *The Use of Daniel in Jewish Apocalyptic Literature and in the Revelation of John* (New York, 1984).

O. Betz *Offenbarung und Schriftforschung in der Qumransekte*, WUNT 6 (Tübingen, 1960).

J. W. Bowker *The Targums and Rabbinic Literature* (Cambridge, 1969).

P. M. Casey *Son of Man: the Interpretation and Influence of Daniel 7* (London, 1980).

J. H. Charlesworth (ed.) *The Old Testament Pseudepigrapha* (2 vols. London, 1983 and 1985).

J. J. Collins *The Apocalyptic Vision of the Book of Daniel*, HSM 16 (Missoula, 1977).

*Between Athens and Jerusalem. Jewish Identity in the Hellenistic Diaspora* (New York, 1983).

*The Apocalyptic Imagination* (New York, 1984) (= 1984a).

*Daniel; with an Introduction to the Apocalyptic Literature* (Grand Rapids, 1984) (= 1984b).

J. J. Collins (ed.) *Apocalypse: Morphology of a Genre*, Semeia 14 (Missoula, 1979).

C. Colpe 'ho huios tou anthrōpou', in *TDNT* 8 (1972), pp. 408–20.

W. D. Davies *Jewish and Pauline Studies* (London, 1984).

J. Day *God's Conflict with the Dragon and the Sea: Echoes of a Canaanite Myth in the Old Testament* (Cambridge, 1985).

J. E. Fossum *The Name of God and the Angel of the Lord* (Tübingen, 1985).

I. Gruenwald *Apocalyptic and Merkavah Mysticism*, Arbeiten zur Geschichte des antiken Judentums und des Urchristentums 14 (Leiden, 1978).

'Knowledge and Vision', *Israel Oriental Studies* 3 (1973), 63–107.

'Jewish Merkavah Mysticism and Gnosticism', in J. Dan and F. Talmage (eds.), *Studies in Jewish Mysticism* (Cambridge, Mass., 1982), pp. 41–55.

D. Halperin *The Merkabah in Rabbinic Literature*, American Oriental Series 62 (New Haven, 1980).

P. D. Hanson *The Dawn of Apocalyptic* (Philadelphia, 1975).
'Rebellion in Heaven, Azazel and Euhemeristic Heroes in 1 Enoch 6–11', *JBL* 96 (1977), 195–233.

W. Harnisch *Verhängnis und Verheissung der Geschichte*, FRLANT 97 (Göttingen, 1969).

L. Hartman *Prophecy Interpreted. The formation of some Jewish Apocalyptic Texts and of the Eschatological Discourse, Mark 13 par.*, ConB, NT series 1 (Lund, 1966).
*Asking for Meaning. A Study of 1 Enoch 1–5*, ConB, NT series 12 (Lund, 1979).

D. Hellholm (ed.) *Apocalypticism in the Mediterranean World and the Near East*, Proceedings of the International Colloquium on Apocalypticism, Uppsala, August 12–17, 1979 (Tübingen, 1983).

M. Hengel 'Anonymität, Pseudepigraphie und "literarische Falschung" in der jüdisch-hellenistischen Literatur', in K. von Fritz (ed.), *Pseudepigrapha 1. Pseudopythagorica – Lettres de Plato – Littérature pseudépigraphique juive* (Geneva, 1972), pp. 231–308.
*Judaism and Hellenism. Studies in their Encounter in Palestine during the Early Hellenistic Period* (2 vols. London, 1974) (English translation of *Judentum und Hellenismus. Studien zu ihrer Begegnung unter besonderer Berücksichtigung Palästinas bis zur Mitte des 2Jh.s v. Chr.*, WUNT 10, 2nd ed. (Tübingen, 1973)).

M. P. Horgan *Pesharim: Qumran Interpretations of Biblical Books*, CBQMS 8 (Washington, 1979).

R. Kearns *Vorfragen zur Christologie 2: Überlieferungsgeschichte und rezeptionsgeschichtliche Studie zur Vorgeschichte eines christologischen Hoheitstitels* (Tübingen, 1980).

F. Kermode *The Bible: Story and Plot*, Ethel M. Wood Lecture (London, 1984).

M. A. Knibb *The Ethiopic Book of Enoch* (2 vols. Oxford, 1978).
'Prophecy and the Emergence of the Jewish Apocalypses', in R. Coggins, A. Phillips and M. Knibb (eds.), *Israel's Prophetic Tradition: Essays in Honour of Peter R. Ackroyd* (Cambridge, 1982), pp. 155–80 (= 1982a).
'Apocalyptic and Wisdom in 4 Ezra', *JSJ* 13 (1982), 56–74 (= 1982b).

B. Layton (ed.) *The Rediscovery of Gnosticism*, Studies in the History of Religions 41 (Leiden, 1980).

J. T. Milik *The Books of Enoch* (Oxford, 1976).

C. F. D. Moule *Essays in New Testament Interpretation* (Cambridge, 1982).

J. M. Myers *I and II Esdras*, AB 42 (Garden City, 1974).

G. W. E. Nickelsburg *Resurrection, Immortality, and Eternal Life in Inter-testamental Judaism*, Harvard Theological Studies 26 (Cambridge, Mass., 1972).

'Apocalyptic and Myth in 1 Enoch 6–11', *JBL* 96 (1977), 383–405.

G. W. E. Nickelsburg and J. J. Collins (eds.) *Ideal Figures in Ancient Judaism*: *Profiles and Paradigms*, Septuagint and Cognate Studies 12 (Chico, 1980).

S. Niditch *The Symbolic Vision Form in Biblical Tradition* (Harvard Diss., 1977).

A. Nissen 'Tora und Geschichte im Spätjudentum', *NovT* 9 (1967), 241–77.

E. von Nordheim *Die Lehre der Alten*, Arbeiten zur Literatur und Geschichte des hellenistischen Judentums 13 (Leiden, 1980).

D. Patte *Jewish Hermeneutic in Palestine*, SBLDS 22 (Missoula, 1975).

B. A. Pearson 'Jewish sources in Gnostic Literature', in M. Stone (ed.), *Jewish Writings of the Second Temple Period*, Compendia Rerum Iudaicarum ad Novum Testamentum II.2 (Assen, 1984), pp. 443–81.

O. Plöger *Theocracy and Eschatology* (Oxford, 1968) (English translation of *Theokratie und Eschatologie*, WMANT 2 (2nd ed. Neukirchen, 1962)).

D. Rössler *Gesetz und Geschichte. Untersuchungen zur Theologie der jüdischen Apokalyptik und der pharisäischen Orthodoxie*, WMANT 3 (Neukirchen, 1960).

C. C. Rowland 'The Visions of God in Apocalyptic Literature', *JSJ* 10 (1979), 137–54.

*The Open Heaven. A Study of Apocalyptic in Judaism and Early Christianity* (London, 1982).

*Christian Origins* (London, 1985).

'A Man Clothed in White Linen', *JSNT* 24 (1985), 99–110.

G. Scholem *Major Trends in Jewish Mysticism* (3rd ed. London, 1955).

*Jewish Gnosticism, Merkabah Mysticism and Talmudic Tradition* (2nd ed. New York, 1965).

'Kabbalah', in *Encyclopedia Judaica* 10 (1971), cols. 489–653.

E. Schürer *History of the Jewish People in the Age of Jesus Christ*, revised by F. Millar and G. Vermes (Edinburgh, 1975 and 1979).

M. Stone 'The Concept of the Messiah in IV Ezra', in J. Neusner (ed.), *Religions in Antiquity. Essays in Memory of Erwin Ramsdell Goodenough*, Studies in the History of Religions 14 (Leiden, 1968), pp. 295–312.

'Lists of Revealed Things in the Apocalyptic Literature', in F. M. Cross, W. E. Lemke and P. D. Miller (eds.), *Magnalia Dei: The Mighty Acts of God. Essays on the Bible and Archaeology in Memory of G. Ernest Wright* (Garden City, 1976), pp. 414–52.

*Scripture, Sects and Visions. A Profile of Judaism from Ezra to the Jewish Revolts* (Oxford, 1980).

Apocalyptic literature

'Apocalyptic Literature', in M. Stone (ed.), *Jewish Writings of the Second Temple Period*, Compendia Rerum Iudaicarum ad Novum Testamentum II.2 (Assen, 1984), pp. 383–441.

E. E. Urbach *The Sages. Their Concepts and Beliefs* (2 vols. Jerusalem, 1975).

J. VanderKam *Enoch and the Growth of an Apocalyptic Tradition*, CBQMS 16 (Washington, 1984).

P. Vielhauer 'Apocalypses and Related Subjects', in E. Hennecke and W. Schneemelcher (eds.), *New Testament Apocrypha*, vol. 2 (London, 1965), pp. 581–607 (English translation of *Neutestamentliche Apokryphen in deutscher Übersetzung* (3rd ed. Tübingen, 1959)).

G. Widengren *The Ascension of the Apostle and the Heavenly Book* (Uppsala, 1950).

O. Wintermute 'A Study of Gnostic Exegesis of the Old Testament', in J. M. Efird (ed.), *The Use of the Old Testament in the New and Other Essays* (Durham, NC, 1972), pp. 241–70.

# The Old Testament in the New Testament

# 11 · Text form

## MAX WILCOX

I T is especially fitting to honour our colleague and friend Barnabas Lindars
with an essay on the text form of the Old Testament in the New Testament,
a subject to which he has himself contributed so much. It is also a pleasure to
have this opportunity to wish him many more years of happy and fruitful
work.

Investigation of text form is basic to any study of the use and role of the OT
in the NT, beginning as it does with the task of isolating and identifying those
elements in the text of the NT which we may suspect of being derived from
the OT. In practice this means determining as precisely as the evidence will
allow (1) whether the OT is in fact being referred to or reflected in a given NT
passage, and if so (2) just how much of that passage is intended to be included
in such a reference, (3) which (if any) known textual tradition or traditions of
the OT are represented by the words in question, and (4) whether any
deviation from known OT textual traditions finds attestation elsewhere in
early jewish or christian literature or exegesis. The value of such information
is great, not only for understanding the NT material investigated but also for
our knowledge of the state of the OT text and methods of interpreting it in the
first century of our era.

In this essay we shall look in detail at some of the problems raised by the
examination of text form and aim to define more closely the criteria and
methods by which that inquiry should proceed. This will involve consideration
of a number of concrete examples.

## I

The problem of isolating and identifying OT material in the NT is
complicated by the fact that manuscripts of the NT do not use conventional
markers (like our 'inverted commas') to indicate quoted material. Nevertheless, for any OT reference to have done its work it must have been
recognisable as such to at least some of the original readers (or hearers), and
this suggests that there must have been some common block of OT material
already in Greek and available to the group or groups for whom the books in
question were intended. Whether such OT material was a more or less
complete 'Bible' or perhaps rather a collection of extracts from the Bible is not

certain, and this is one of the points on which study of the OT text form in the NT may throw some light. At the least it is probably fair to argue that quotations of, and allusions to, OT material were drawn from those parts of the Bible which appear to have been used in the exposition and defence of the christian message, as Dodd (1952) argued.

There are, of course, places in the NT where we find explicit OT quotations, introduced by one of several more or less set formulae, e.g., καθὼς γέγραπται, and perhaps not surprisingly it is these so-called 'formula quotations' which have been studied most. Even here, however, there are problems. First, the words quoted sometimes seem to be ascribed to the wrong OT book, as for example in John 10:34 a quotation from Ps. 81(82):6 is said to be from the law; in other places we meet what seems to be a composite quotation, the whole of which is referred to one book, as in Mark 1:2 where Isaiah is made responsible for a pair of quotations, from Mal. 3:1 (cf. Exod. 23:20) and Isa. 40:3. Next, even these explicit OT quotations at times do not wholly coincide with any one known text or version and some account must be given of the divergence. Again, within the work of the one NT writer some such quotations may lean to the LXX, others to the MT or some other authority. The gospel of Matthew is a striking example of this diversity, as has long been known (see Swete, 1900, pp. 393–8). Yet explicit quotations are those most obviously vulnerable in the course of transmission to assimilation to Bible texts familiar to the scribes involved. It is perhaps tempting to treat such apparent aberrations as due to slips of memory, 'loose' citation and the like, but to do so does not explain anything: it merely draws attention to the fact of the divergence. If we cannot at present identify the basis of any deviation, we should simply record an open verdict and await further evidence. Much the same applies to cases where it has been asserted that the NT writer has modified his OT text to suit his 'theological' purposes; the danger of arguing in a circle must be seen and avoided.

However, when we are dealing not with explicit quotations but with allusions and reminiscences – smaller elements of OT material woven into the text of a NT book without any formula or other sign to mark their presence – the problems of both identification and isolation are vastly more serious. The position is still more complex in passages where the argument merely turns on knowledge of a jewish exegetical tradition interpreting some word, phrase or larger element from the OT. Yet these are just the cases where the evidence is less likely to have been influenced by assimilation of the type mentioned above, or indeed by other NT passages where the same OT passage is used.

In investigating the text form of the OT in the NT we need to keep several principles of method in mind. (1) We have no right to assume that the one NT writer will have always used the same OT textual tradition in his work(s). In the case of Matthew and Luke this is clearly not so, as a look at Dittmar's study (Dittmar, 1903) will show. (2) Apparently minor deviations, such as the 'replacement' of one word or phrase by another in a text which otherwise looks verbally identical with a known OT textual tradition (e.g., the LXX), also occur (a) between extant Greek OT versions, and (b) between the targumim, and in fact from one targum MS to another. In the one case it may reflect accommodation or 'correction' of a Greek version to another or to the Hebrew; in the other – apart from dialectal changes – it is a characteristic of targum to replace a word or phrase which more or less literally renders the Hebrew by another (or even a longer passage) which gives the traditional interpretation of it. Thus, targum Pseudo-Jonathan at Deut. 6:5 reads 'and with all your wealth (*wbkl mmwnkwn*)' for MT 'and with all thy strength (*wbkl-m⁾dk*)', an interpretation found also in the Mishnah (*Berakoth* 9:5). (3) The present 'deviant' form of an OT quotation or allusion may be the result of an earlier piece of exegesis, or a 'mixed' quotation may in fact show such exegesis at work. That exegesis may have been based on a Hebrew text or a version: in either case it may be of value for understanding the question of text form. (4) Careful consideration of the manuscript data and of early rabbinic, patristic and Qumran use of any OT text traced behind a NT passage is essential.

We shall now proceed to look at some examples of actual quotations and allusions in the NT.

## II

An instance of apparent independence of text form occurs in Acts 4:11 (cf. Ps. 117[118]:22):

Οὗτός ἐστιν ὁ λίθος ὁ ἐξουθενηθεὶς ὑφ' ὑμῶν τῶν οἰκοδόμων, ὁ γενόμενος εἰς κεφαλὴν γωνίας.

The allusion to Ps. 117(118):22 is clear, yet in reading ὁ ἐξουθενηθείς and οἰκοδόμων, it differs not only from the LXX but also from the other NT examples of the quotation, namely, Matt. 21:42, Mark 12:10b, I Pet. 2:7 and – perhaps most intriguingly of all – Luke 20:17b, all of which coincide with the LXX reading:

Λίθον ὃν ἀπεδοκίμασαν οἱ οἰκοδομοῦντες, οὗτος ἐγενήθη εἰς κεφαλὴν γωνίας.

The deviation can hardly have been a mere slip of memory: it fits the argument of Peter's speech (Acts 4:8b–12) far too well for that. The interpretation may be of the pesher type: Jesus is 'the stone', his detractors 'the builders' (as the inclusion of the words ὑφ' ὑμῶν makes clear). But why did the writer (or his tradition) not use the term ἀποδοκιμασθείς ('rejected'), in line with the LXX (which here suits the Hebrew), instead of ἐξουθενηθείς ('set at nought', 'denigrated')? Various suggestions have been offered: (1) an independent Greek version of Ps.118:22 may lie behind our text (Clarke, 1922, p. 97); (2) influence of Mark 9:12 (which may reflect Isa. 53:3), ἵνα πολλὰ πάθῃ καὶ ἐξουδενηθῇ (Wilcox, 1965, p. 173); (3) an ancient element of tradition is found here, as shown by the language of the early christian kerygma in v. 10, and Luke has taken over the whole as a unit (Holtz, 1968, pp. 162–3; cf. Preuschen, 1912, p. 24, and Haenchen, 1956, p. 180); and (4) direct influence on the form of Ps. 117 (118):22 by Isa. 53:3 which, in the versions of Aquila and Symmachus, reads ἐξουδενώμενος (traceable also in Mark 9:12) (Dupont, 1953/1967, pp. 260–1; Lindars, 1961, p. 170).

Now we must not overlook the fact that our verse contains a second deviation from the LXX, the use of οἰκοδόμων for οἰκοδομοῦντες. Further, although in the LXX ἀποδοκιμάζω always represents Hebrew $m^{\jmath}s$ (if there is a known equivalent), the converse is not true; in some 16 cases $m^{\jmath}s$ is translated by ἐξουθενέω/ἐξουδενέω/ἐξουθενόω/ἐξουδενόω. Hence $m^{\jmath}sw$ in Ps. 118:22 could easily have been translated ἐξουθένησαν, as presupposed in Acts 4:22. Thus we must keep open the option that an alternative Greek version underlies our text. This need not surprise us as there are other signs of traditional material preserved elsewhere in speeches in Acts. Again, in Acts 4:11 the exposition of the words of Ps. 117(118):22 by Isa 53.3 would make better midrashic sense if there were a common linguistic link: a form akin to ἐξουθενέω occurring in both could provide that link. But in this case the exegetical work would have taken place in Greek rather than Hebrew. Further, it is plain that only parts of Acts 4:11 are actually meant as verbal references to the Psalm. The verse thus gives us a good example of the need (1) to determine just how much of any passage investigated is likely to have been intended as an allusion to the OT, and (2) to allow for the presence of genuinely variant text forms in such allusions.

The need to define the precise limits of an OT allusion may be illustrated also from Acts 2:25–31. Even if we were to omit vv. 25–8, containing the 'formula quotation' of Ps. 15(16):8–11, we would be compelled to infer its influence from vv. 30–1: David, being a prophet (and knowing that God had sworn to him that one of the seed of his loins would sit upon his throne) foresaw and spoke of the resurrection of the Messiah, that 'neither would he be left in Hades' nor would his flesh 'see corruption'. Now the formula quotation itself coincides precisely with the LXX(B) of Ps. 15(16):8–11, whereas the allusion to that Psalm in v. 31 does not. It is usual to take the whole of v.31b as an allusion: ὅτι οὔτε ἐνκατελείφθη εἰς Ἅιδην, οὔτε ἡ σάρξ αὐτοῦ εἶδεν διαφθοράν. Apart from the minor tidying up of οὐκ...οὐδέ (Ps. 15(16):10) to οὔτε...οὔτε, other differences appear:

(1) The aorist passive ἐνκατελείφθη, 'he was (not) left/forsaken', instead of οὐκ ἐνκατάλειψεις τὴν ψυχήν [μου], claims that what was once seen as in the

future and merely 'predicted' is now fact, yet it avoids naming the Deity as the agent and τὴν ψυχήν [μου/αὐτοῦ] is treated as a periphrasis for αὐτόν. Both are traits well attested in early jewish texts and also in material special to Luke.

(2) The presence of ἡ σάρξ αὐτοῦ ('his flesh'). This may have entered our text under the influence of Ps. 15(16):9c (cf. Acts 2:26b), and would have made a neat parallel to the 'omitted' τὴν ψυχὴν αὐτοῦ 'his soul/person'. As it stands it may be either a familiar periphrasis for 'he', or perhaps an explicative gloss to stress the bodily nature of the resurrection of Jesus. If the latter, it would not be part of the allusion to the Psalm, but rather an exegesis of it. That the phrase may be meant as a form for 'he' is supported by the almost stereotyped repetition of the words εἶδεν διαφθοράν ('he saw "corruption"') in Acts 13:36, 37: David, after serving God's will in his own generation, fell asleep and was added to his fathers, and 'saw corruption', whereas he whom God raised 'did not see corruption'. As it stands there is no obvious case for suspecting use here or in Acts 2:31b of any text form other than that of the LXX, but that may not be the end of the story.

The quotation of Ps. 15(16):10 in Acts 13:35b is one of two texts (the other a quotation from Isa. 55:3) brought into play to support the claim in v. 34 that as God raised Jesus from the dead, he (i.e., Jesus) is 'no more going to return to "corruption"' (μηκέτι μέλλοντα ὑποστρέφειν εἰς διαφθοράν). Several points should be noted here. (1) The phrase εἰς διαφθοράν occurs twice in the LXX, at Job 33:28 and Ps. 29(30):9, both of which refer to 'going (down) to the the pit (šḥt)'; indeed šḥt is the most usual Hebrew word behind διαφθορά in the LXX, and also is in Ps. 15(16):10 where, however, there is no mention of a 'descent'. (2) In the targum to Ps. 16:10, the manuscripts present three differing interpretations of the Hebrew for the phrase ἰδεῖν διαφθοράν (lrʾwt šḥt): (a) lmḥmy bšḥywt, 'to gaze into the pit' (Lagarde, Solg 6.20); (b) lmḥmy byt šḥyyt, 'to see the "house of destruction"' (gehenna or such like) (1, Ee 5.9, 7, 17, 114, Or 72, 110, 114); and (c) lmyḥty byt šḥwwt, 'to go down (to) the "house of destruction"' (Codex Villa-Amil 5). Indeed for this last the whole line would run: 'thou wilt not deliver thy righteous one to go down to the house of destruction'. There is no way in which we can argue that Acts 13:34 may have influenced this MS (and its Latin translation), but the same tradition of interpretation of Ps. 15(16):10 may be preserved in both. Indeed Acts 13:34 would then look rather like Rom. 6:9: 'Christ, raised from the dead, does not die again: "Death" no more holds sway over him'. The link is stronger when we recall that Paul cites this statement as something which his readers already know. (3) The repeated and all but stereotyped use of the words εἶδεν διαφθοράν in Acts 13:36b, 37 suggests that it is the last phrase of Ps. 15(16):10 which is crucial to the argument there, yet in 13:34 διαφθορά seems to carry the force of the Hebrew šḥt, 'the pit', 'the grave'. If we were to apply the same meaning in Acts 2:31, we should not only restore the parallel between 'Hades' and 'the pit', but bring the whole argument there together, for in 2:24, the apparently immediate instance for bringing in a reference to Ps. 15(16):8–11, we hear that 'it was not possible for him to be held' by 'death'.

If we now return to the text of Acts 2:31, we may see that only the phrases εἰς Ἅιδην and (εἶδεν) διαφθοράν are to be regarded as strictly indicative of the text form of the allusion, and we may re-style it as follows:

> 'neither was he forsaken "in Hades",
> nor did his flesh "see the pit"'.

One final question: does the use of ἐνκατελείφθη in Acts 2:31 recall the problem raised in Matthew and Mark by the words of Jesus on the cross, Ps. 21(22):1, where the Greek uses the same verb? Luke knows the connexion of Ps. 22 with the passion narrative, but does the absence of these words from his form of it suggest that for him, as Acts 2:31 and 13:34 indicate, Jesus was not forsaken (in Hades) by God, as the resurrection demonstrates?

In a number of cases in the NT we have evidence of the use of an independent textual tradition of rather greater extent than the two instances just treated. We shall now look at a few of these.

It has long been known that Eph. 4:8 cites Ps. 67(68):19 in a form which diverges from both the MT and the LXX but in that deviation agrees with the targum. The text runs:

Ἀναβὰς εἰς ὕψος ᾐχμαλώτευσεν αἰχμαλωσίαν ἔδωκεν δόματα τοῖς ἀνθρώποις.

Apart from the fact that in the MT and the LXX the verbs are in the second person singular ('thou didst ascend...'), the key differences are in the last line:

LXX: ἔλαβες δόματα ἐν ἀνθρώπῳ MT: lqḥt mtnwt b°dm.

The targum however has:

'O Prophet Moses, thou didst ascend to Reqia, thou didst lead a host of captives, thou didst teach Words of Torah, thou didst give them (as) gifts to the sons of men (yhbt lhwn [ythwn MSS 1 5] mtnn lbny nš°)'

The present MSS and editions of the targum introduce explanatory material into the text here, but where it echoes the biblical text itself, it clearly presupposes the same Hebrew text as does Eph. 4:8. The precise form of the last line as found in the Targum is however found also in the Peshitta, Tertullian, (*Adv. Marcionem* 5:8), and also, as Harris (1920, pp. 39, 40–2) pointed out, in Justin, (*Dialogue* 87). Tertullian's argument hangs on the words *filiis hominum*: 'id est uere hominum, apostolorum'. But that text is a literal equivalent of the targum *lbny nš°*, 'to the sons of men'. Eph. 4:8 has the more idiomatic form τοῖς ἀνθρώποις 'to men'. The quotation appears in Justin twice, but the first occasion (*Dialogue* 39) could possibly have come from Ephesians; the second, however, could not: it reads τοῖς υἱοῖς τῶν ἀνθρώπων (*Dialogue* 87). It is interesting that the Peshitta to Eph. 4:8 has the targumic form, although this may possibly be due to knowledge of the Peshitta to Ps. 68:19. Rubinkiewicz (1975, p. 223) noted that the London Polyglot Bible of 1657 has the 'extra' words of the targum in square brackets, and wondered if this might indicate knowledge of a shorter form of the targumic tradition (which agrees with Pesh Ps. 68:19). Be that as it may, it is clear that a common text form underlies all of these authorities, and as a matter of fact Eph. 4:8 is the earliest known attestation of it. From the evidence of Justin and Tertullian, that text form was probably in Aramaic.

With Eph. 4:8 it happens that we have extant external evidence to demonstrate that it is using a variant OT text, but we are not always in such a happy position. It is nevertheless clear that extreme caution should be shown in seeking explanations of deviations in the OT text form found in the NT.

The well known quotation of Zech. 9:9 in Matt. 21:5 (cf. also John 12:15) is particularly instructive if compared not only with the MT, LXX, targum(s) and Peshitta, but also with the full range of known hexaplaric variants. The opening words, ἰδοὺ ὁ βασιλεύς σου ἔρχεταί σοι, coincide precisely with the LXX (and also with John 12:15, apart from the absence of σοι), but they would be a natural enough translation of the Hebrew. The next line of Zech. 9:9 (LXX δίκαιος καί σῴζων αὐτός = MT, targ.) is absent from Matthew as also from John. The text resumes:

πραῢς καὶ ἐπιβεβηκὼς ἐπὶ ὄνον
καὶ ἐπι πῶλον υἱὸν ὑποζυγίου.

Cf. LXX: πραῢς καὶ ἐπιβεβηκὼς ἐπὶ ὑποζύγιον
καὶ πῶλον νεόν.

At first sight we might be struck by the obvious kinship of much of the vocabulary with that of the LXX here, but this is where detailed comparison with the other known Greek versions (including that in John 12:15) is needed. The Hebrew ᶜny ('poor') is interpreted as 'humble, oppressed poor' (ᶜnw) by the LXX, Aquila, Matthew, targum and Peshitta, as Gundry (1967, p. 120) notes. But (1) this meaning for ᶜny is also given by the LXX in other places, e.g., Sir. 3:18, 10:14, and (2) contrariwise, ᶜnw is translated by πτωχός in the LXX in Ps. 68 (69):32, Prov. 14:21, Isa. 29:19, 61:1, and is read by Symmachus and Origen's Quinta at Zech. 9:9. The Matthean καὶ ἐπιβεβηκὼς ἐπὶ ὄνον, perhaps superficially akin to the LXX, is no mere lapse of memory: it is precisely the reading of Symmachus, and is also very close to that of Aquila (ἐπὶ ὄνου), whereas the Quinta and Theodotion agree here with the LXX. In the last line of the quotation Matthew's text form is very faithful to the Hebrew, except that with the targum, Peshitta, Symmachus and Theodotion, it presupposes the singular *ᵓtwn* instead of the plural *ᵓtnwt* (MT). However, his is the only Greek text (apart perhaps from John's) to reflect the repeated (*w*)ᶜ*l* ('and upon') of the Hebrew. His use of ὑποζυγίου for *ᵓtwn* (*ᵓtnwt*) need not be due to the LXX – or to the text reflected by the Quinta: although both use it they have it for MT *ḥmwr* in the previous line, not in the present phrase. The term, strictly meaning 'a beast of burden', occurs in the papyri as 'she-ass' (Moulton-Milligan, 1930, p. 657), whereas in the LXX it usually represents Hebrew *ḥmwr*; the sole exception, Judg. 5:10(A), interestingly reads ἐπιβεβηκὼς ἐπὶ ὑποζυγίων, possibly reflecting the present passage. Matthew's rendering of *wᶜl ᶜyr bn ᵓtnwt* (*ᵓtwn*) is also rather like those of the four extant non-LXX Greek versions. These differ among themselves and from Matthew in their equivalents for *ᵓtnwt*, but like Matthew (1) all four give υἱόν (Aq. υἱοῦ) after πῶλον (Aq πώλου) to render the *bn* ('son') of the Hebrew, against the LXX's πῶλον νεόν, and (2) two of them (Symmachus and Theodotion) also presuppose the singular *ᵓtwn*.

That Matthew is quite serious in his use and understanding of this text form shows in his reference in 21:6–7 to the two terms τὴν ὄνον and τὸν πῶλον as indicating two distinct animals. The objection that he has failed to appreciate the parallelism of Hebrew poetry here is off the point: he has given the individual words independent weight as one might expect from a jewish exegete of his time; there are many examples of this in rabbinic texts. If it be claimed that this difficulty is no more than another example of Matthew's tendency to double things, we may reply that in this case such doubling seems to have been all but formally justified on the basis of the text of Zech. 9:9. It may complicate his story and cause cares for those who feel that he has spoilt Mark's account, but it does show that he regarded the text of Zech. 9:9 as he cited it as authoritative, and this is the important point.

Further support for the view that Matthew regarded his own form of Zechariah as authoritative may emerge from a consideration of the opening words of Matt. 21:5, which come not from Zech. 9:9 but from Isa. 62:11. Yet our text is no mere 'mixed citation': the two elements which comprise it are linked by a common set of words:

| | |
|---|---|
| Isa. 62:11. Say to the *Daughter of Zion, Behold* | Zech. 9:9. Rejoice greatly, O *Daughter of Zion*, Shout, O Daughter of Jerusalem, *Behold* |
| *thy* deliverer (*yšᶜk*) is *coming*... | *thy* king (*mlkk*) *is coming* to thee... |

Put together this way, the two texts interpret one another by their common elements; further, this mutual interpretation would allow the terms 'thy deliverer' and 'thy king' to be equated. The link would be even closer in the

Syriac, where (1) the verb 'is coming' is of the form ʾtʾ in both cases, and (2) 'thy deliverer' (Isa. 62:11) is given as prwqk(y), while in Zech. 9:9b we have 'righteous and a deliverer (prmqʾ)'. It looks as though a conscious piece of exegesis underlies out text here.

Overall, then, the text of Zech. 9:9 presented in Matt. 21:5 must be taken as a valuable addition to our knowledge of the text form of the Greek OT in the period before Jamnia (cf. Longenecker, 1975, p. 152).

One of the most interesting examples of the use of a set but independent text form in the NT is that of Zech. 12:10 (+ ? 12) in Matt. 24:30; John 19:37 and Rev. 1:7. It also appears to underlie Justin, 1 *Apol.* 52:12, *Dialogue* 14:8, 32:2; 64:7 and 118:1. Of the three NT examples only John 19:37 is an explicit quotation: Ὄψονται εἰς ὃν ἐξεκέντησαν, 'They shall look upon him whom they pierced'. It is clearly used in its present context to show that Jesus' manner of death conforms to Scripture. The LXX, however, reads ἐπιβλέψονται πρὸς μὲ ἀνθ' ὧν κατωρχήσαντο, and presupposes a Hebrew text with rqdw in place of the MT's dqrw. John's text reflects our Hebrew text either directly or perhaps through another Greek version, as many scholars have agreed.

Now precisely the same text form underlies Rev. 1:7, καὶ ὄψονται αὐτὸν πᾶς ὀφθαλμὸς καὶ οἵτινες αὐτὸν ἐξεκέντησαν... ('And every eye shall see him, even those who pierced him'). Here the one who is seen is defined at the beginning of the verse in terms of Dan. 7:13, ἰδοὺ ἔρχεται μετὰ τῶν νεφελῶν, that is, as the 'Son of Man'-like figure. Once again the form of this allusion is not that of the LXX, but rather leans towards that of Theodotion, although it is if anything closer to the Aramaic text of Daniel. But to return to Zech. 12:10, we see that in Rev. 1:7 there is an additional element of it: καὶ κόψονται ἐπ' αὐτὸν (πᾶσαι αἱ φυλαὶ τῆς γῆς). The problem here is that, although the words καὶ κόψονται ἐπ' αὐτόν appear in the LXX, the others do not. Those who 'look upon' and 'mourn' the one pierced are 'the house of David and those who inhabit Jerusalem'; in Rev. 1:7 they are 'all the tribes of the earth' – or perhaps better, 'of the land'. Zech. 12:11–14 shows that by 'the land/earth' the holy land is meant. The expression 'all the tribes of the land' thus looks like a neat shorthand for vv. 11–14.

At this point, however, we turn to Matt. 24:30 where a very closely similar text form of Zech. 12:10 occurs, also in a strongly apocalyptic setting: καὶ τότε φανήσεται τὸ σημεῖον τοῦ υἱοῦ τοῦ ἀνθρώπου ἐν οὐρανῷ καὶ τότε κόψονται πᾶσαι αἱ φυλαὶ τῆς γῆς, καὶ ὄψονται τὸν υἱὸν τοῦ ἀνθρώπου ἐρχόμενον ἐπὶ τῶν νεφελῶν τοῦ οὐρανοῦ κτλ. Once again, the subject of ὄψονται and κόψονται is the phrase 'all the tribes of the land'; but the object in Rev. 1:7 and Zech. 12:10 is 'him whom they pierced', whilst in Matt. 24:30 it is 'the Son of Man...'. The two allusions taken together thus identify the one pierced with the Son of Man (or Son-of-Man-like figure). But what is really striking is the presence in both of the phrase 'all the tribes of the land', in precisely the same Greek form. That phrase, however, recalls Gen. 12:3; 29:14 and Ps. 71 (72):17, where it refers to those who inherit the blessing of Abraham and his 'seed'. It looks as if we have here the use of a stereotyped phrase, almost a piece of symbolic language, to cue in the idea that it is precisely those 'who bless themselves (or are blessed) through Abraham and his "seed"' who 'shall look upon him whom they pierced' and 'mourn for him as for an only son...'

Study of the fine detail of the text here reveals not only something of the textual history of the material from Zech. 12:10 used but also points to a careful piece of exegesis which seems to form a coherent pattern behind all three NT passages examined. Wyatt (1983, p. 208) has noted that not only is Zech. 12:10 linked in b. *Sukka* 52a with the idea of the (suffering) Messiah ben Joseph, but that in a 'Targum Yerushalmi' fragment, found as a marginal gloss in Codex Reuchlinianus, the same haggadic exposition appears in much greater detail, even containing a reference to his making war on Gog and Gog's killing of him outside the gates of Jerusalem. The three NT passages taken together enable us to reconstruct the Hebrew text upon which they depend, and also see that it was understood within a haggadic development which seems to have its origins prior to all three. It looks as if the same tradition also underlies the references in Justin.

Our last example is Matt. 27:43, which cites Ps. 21(22):9 in a form other than that of the LXX (although it has some words in common with it). It is nearer to the MT and especially to the Peshitta, as Stendahl (1967, pp. 140–1) and others have noted. The text is as follows: πέποιθεν ἐπὶ τὸν θεόν, ῥυσάσθω νῦν εἰ θέλει αὐτόν. First, πέποιθεν ('he trusted') is closer to the Hebrew (*gl*) and the Syriac (?*ttkl*) than is the LXX ἤλπισεν ('he hoped'). The targum does not really help, as it treats *gl* as if from *gyl* ('to shout for joy'), and renders by *šbḥ*. One group of targum MSS (including Codex Villa-Amil 5) changes the perfect to an imperfect, meaning 'may he sing praise', whereas those which retain the perfect read it as a first person: 'I sang praise...'. It thus looks as if the verse has provoked some exegetical interest. Matthew's τὸν θεόν, replacing the Divine Name, is a singular reading, but that change is well known from the targums, and in the targum to Psalms is quite often found in at least some MSS.

The second part of the verse differs from the LXX in several ways. Like the LXX it has ῥυσάσθω, but without following αὐτόν but it has no equivalent to the next line σωσάτω αὐτόν (Heb.: *ysylhw*). The νῦν may be due to adaptation to the present context (and so not part of the actual allusion), but εἰ θέλει αὐτόν differs from most MSS of the LXX, which read ὅτι θέλει αὐτόν (with the MT, *ky ḥps bw*), 'for he delights in him'. The LXX MS U may perhaps read εἰ here, but has it been influenced by Matt 27:43? The Peshitta of Ps. 22:9b, however, agrees with Matthew: ?*n ṣb? bh*. Stendahl asserted that the NT text here had influenced the Peshitta, but gave no reasons. It is interesting that the Old Syriac (sin) and the Peshitta of Matt. 27:43 have precisely the same form here, although elsewhere in the verse they differ from the Peshitta of Ps. 22:9. This seems to weigh against Stendahl's view and to suggest that Matt. 27:43 and Pesh. Ps 22:9 coincide rather than are mutually dependent. In the light of what we have seen with regard to the text of Ps. 67(68):19 in Eph. 4:8, we may feel that here also a common alternative tradition may underlie both Matt. 27:43 and the Syriac.

# III

It remains now to sum up our results. We have seen the need for quite meticulous care in checking for possible agreements between the various known OT textual traditions and apparently deviant OT text forms in the NT. The view of affairs which emerges is of considerable flexibility in choice of text form, not surprising in the light of what we know from Qumran. Variations may be due to a number of factors: (a) a different OT text form, (b) interpretation in the light of an exegetical tradition attested in other sources, (c) use of set phrases from one OT verse to interpret another – a kind of exegetical or even symbolic language, (d) correction of a more 'standard' form in the light of the Hebrew text, and (e) the simple fact that not all of a given suspected allusion may in fact be such – part of it may be no more than connecting language to hold together the actual (precise) references. In all of this the need for as early and widespread attestation of any variant forms is paramount. The results of the work set out above make it ever more necessary to check every detail, and be prepared to leave a question of text form open, rather than to resort to explanations in terms of slips of memory or deliberate alteration (for which – by definition – we have no actual evidence). Our patience will, however, be rewarded, both in more detailed knowledge of the text form of the OT in the NT period, and of how our authors treated it.

## BIBLIOGRAPHY

W. K. L. Clarke 'The Use of the Septuagint in Acts', in F. J. Foakes Jackson and Kirsopp Lake (eds.), *The Beginnings of Christianity, Part I, The Acts of the Apostles*, vol. 2 (London, 1922), pp. 66–105.

W. Dittmar *Vetus Testamentum in Novo. Die alttestamentlichen Parallelen des Neuen Testaments im Wortlaut der Urtexte und der Septuaginta* (Göttingen, 1903).

C. H. Dodd *According to the Scriptures. The Substructure of New Testament Theology* (London, 1952).

J. Dupont 'L'utilisation apologétique de l'Ancien Testament dans les discours des Actes', *EThL* 29 (1953), 289–327; repr. 1967 (*infra*), from which references are drawn.

*Etudes sur les Actes des Apôtres*, LD 45 (Paris, 1967).

R. H. Gundry *The Use of the Old Testament in St Matthew's Gospel*, SNT 18 (Leiden, 1967).

E. Haenchen *Die Apostelgeschichte*, MeyerK Bd. 3 (Göttingen, 1956).

Rendel Harris (with the assistance of Vacher Burch) *Testimonies Part 2* (Cambridge, 1920).

T. Holtz *Untersuchungen über die alttestamentlichen Zitate bei Lukas*, TU 104 (Berlin, 1968).

Paulus de Lagarde (ed.) *Hagiographa Chaldaice* (repr. Osnabrück, 1967 [orig. 1873]).

B. Lindars *New Testament Apologetic. The Doctrinal Significance of the Old Testament Quotations* (London, 1961).

R. Longenecker *Biblical Exegesis in the Apostolic Period* (Grand Rapids, 1975).

J. H. Moulton and G. Milligan *The Vocabulary of the Greek Testament* (London, 1930).

E. Preuschen *Die Apostelgeschichte*, HNT 4/1 (Tübingen, 1912).

R. Rubinkiewicz 'PS LXVIII 19 (= EPH IV 8): Another Textual Tradition or Targum?' *NovT* 17 (1975), 219–24.

K. Stendahl *The School of St Matthew and its Use of the Old Testament*, ASNU 20, 2nd ed. (Lund, 1967).

H. B. Swete *An Introduction to the Old Testament in Greek* (Cambridge, 1900).

M. Wilcox *The Semitisms of Acts* (Oxford, 1965).

R. J. Wyatt 'Jewish Exegesis and the Gospel of John', unpublished Ph.D. dissertation (University of Wales, 1983).

The author wishes to thank Prof. Luis Díez Merino; the Bibliothèque Nationale, Paris; the Stadtbibliothek, Nürnberg; Jews College, London; Cambridge University Library; the Biblioteca Mediceana Laurenziana, Florence; the Biblioteca Angelica, Rome, and the Biblioteca Apostolica Vaticana, Rome, for access to, and photocopies of, manuscripts of the targum to Psalms.

# 12 · Matthew

GRAHAM STANTON

QUOTATIONS and allusions to Old Testament passages are even more prominent in Matthew than they are in the other three gospels. Matthew's gospel includes a set of quite distinctive 'formula' quotations which have long intrigued scholars. These quotations are all theological 'asides' or comments by the evangelist. They have dominated discussion of Matthew's use of the OT and have frequently been appealed to in attempts to elucidate the origin and purpose of the gospel. In addition, there is a further important aspect of the use of the OT in Matthew which has often been neglected: the evangelist's modifications of the quotations found in his sources and the additional references he includes without using his 'introductory formula'. The OT is woven into the warp and woof of this gospel: the evangelist uses Scripture to underline some of his most prominent and distinctive theological concerns.

Some of the unusual features of Matthew's use of the OT were observed in the early church. In his *Dialogue with Trypho* Justin is well aware that Matthew's interpretation of Isa. 7:14 in Matt. 1:13 is open to jewish objections that it is based on mistranslation of the Hebrew (see chaps 77–8 which quote Matthew 1 and 2 extensively; also 67; 71; 84). In their commentaries on Matt. 27:9 Origen and Jerome both try to explain why the evangelist attributes to Jeremiah a citation which is taken from Zech. 11:13. In two of his letters (XX and CXXL) Jerome notes that in the quotations of the OT in Matt. 2:15, 2:23 and 12:17–21, the evangelist prefers the Hebrew text to the LXX. This latter observation raises a question which has haunted all modern studies of Matthew: why do some of the evangelist's quotations of the OT seem to reflect use of the Hebrew text and some use of the LXX?

Massebieau (1885, p. 93f) seems to have been the first to point to a distinct group of passages in Matthew which show knowledge of the Hebrew text. He claimed that they are all 'citations apologétiques' which have been formulated according to the same principles in order to present the main events of the life of Jesus as fulfilment of OT prophecy. It soon became customary for scholars to distinguish between Matthew's formula quotations (known in German as *Reflexionszitate*) which seemed to come from a source, and his other references to the OT which are linked more firmly to their immediate context in the gospel (*Kontextzitate*) and seemed to come from the evangelist himself.

There are, however, sound reasons for calling in question these distinctions and for considering carefully the terminology used. As we shall see, some of the 'formula' quotations are linked very closely indeed to their immediate context. And it is by no means clear that they have all been taken either from a testimony book or source of any kind, or from pre-Matthean tradition; some of them, at least, seem to have been chosen by the evangelist himself.

Rothfuchs (1969) has suggested that since the most striking feature of the formula quotations is Matthew's emphasis on the 'fulfilment' of Scripture in the life of Jesus, the term *Erfüllungszitate* should be used in place of *Reflexionszitate*. (The latter term cannot easily be translated into English; 'formula quotation' has been widely used over the last 100 years.) This suggestion has been accepted by Luz (1985) in what is now the standard commentary in German; some scholars writing in English also use 'fulfilment quotations'. While there is much to be said for focusing attention on the 'fulfilment' theme, the term 'fulfilment quotation' is also appropriate for some quotations which imply that Scripture is being fulfilled but which are not introduced by Matthew's usual 'formula' (e.g. Matt. 3:3; 11.10), and for some which are not comments by the evangelist himself (e.g. 9:13; 12:7 and 15:8–9). It would be possible to overcome these difficulties by using 'fulfilment formula quotations', but this is an unacceptably clumsy term. Hence we shall use the term 'formula quotations', even though for Matthew the 'fulfilment' theme is more important than the 'formula' used to introduce the quotation.

With some additions made in individual cases to fit the immediate context, Matthew's introductory formulae all include the words ἵνα (ὅπως) πληρωθῇ τὸ ῥηθὲν διὰ τοῦ προφήτου λέγοντος. At this point it is worth noting that the first edition of the New English Bible (1961) overlooked the importance of this formula in Matthew's gospel: a variety of phrases was used, including (twice) 'to make good the prophecy of...'. In the second edition (1970) the translators made very few changes, but they were more consistent and used either 'fulfil' or 'fulfilment' for all Matthew's formula quotations.

There are ten quotations which can be considered together as a group: Matt. 1:22–3; 2:15; 2:17–18; 2:23; 4:14–16; 8:17; 12:17–21; 13:35; 21:4–5; 27:9. They share three characteristics: they are all introduced by the 'formula' just noted; their text form is mixed, but it is less close to the LXX than the other references to the OT in Matthew; they all function as 'asides' of the evangelist and are not placed on the lips of Jesus or of other participants in the evangelist's story.

Matt. 2:5–6 should probably be added to this list as a marginal case: a pre-Matthean quotation seems to have been partly assimilated by the evangelist to the other formula quotations (so, for example, Soares Prabhu, 1976, p. 40). Three other possible candidates are now generally excluded. Matt. 26:54 and 56 both include the passive of πληρόω which is found in all the introductory formulae, but neither verse introduces a quotation from the OT; the former verse is a rhetorical question on the lips of Jesus and not a comment by the evangelist. Matt. 27:35b is not part of the original text of Matthew: it is an interpolation in some later manuscripts from John 19:24.

On any reckoning the quotation of Isa. 6:9f in Matt. 13:14–15 is unique: its introductory formula ἀναπληροῦται αὐτοῖς ἡ προφητεία Ἡσαΐου ἡ λέγουσα is not found elsewhere in Matthew – and neither the verb nor the noun is used elsewhere in the gospels or Acts; the quotation is not an 'aside' of the evangelist but is placed on the lips of Jesus; it comes rather awkwardly immediately after an allusion to Isa. 6:9f in the preceding verse; its text form is almost identical to the LXX. For these reasons it is taken by most exegetes to be a later interpolation, perhaps on the basis of Acts 28:26–7 where a very similar version of Isa.6:9f is cited. Segbroeck (1972, pp. 126f) has, however, mounted a cautious defence of its authenticity, claiming that this citation is very appropriate at this point in Matthew 13.

Although the extent and the characteristics of this important group of formula quotations are now widely agreed, their origin and function are keenly contested. Do they stem from the evangelist himself? Or are they taken from a source, perhaps from an early christian collection of OT passages – a testimony book? What theological purposes do they serve? Answers to these questions have been used to support widely differing views of the origin and purpose of Matthew's gospel.

RECENT RESEARCH

In order to clarify the issues, it will be helpful to consider several of the more influential modern studies. On the basis of careful analysis of the form of the textual traditions, Stendahl (1954) confirmed the results of several earlier studies: whereas the formula quotations had a mixed text form, the other citations followed the LXX fairly closely. In other respects his own suggestions broke quite fresh ground. He claimed that in the formula quotations the biblical text is treated in somewhat the same manner as in the Habakkuk scroll discovered at Qumran. Matthew contains a number of examples of *pesher*, a special type of biblical interpretation which presupposes an advanced study of the Scriptures (in the 'school' of Matthew) and familiarity with the Hebrew text and the traditions of interpretation known to us from the versions.

Partly because Stendahl's monograph was one of the first books by a NT scholar to utilise the Dead Sea Scrolls, his work attracted a good deal of interest. Although his detailed study of the individual quotations in Matthew retains its value, his conclusions have not gone unchallenged. Gärtner (1954) denied that the Habakkuk scroll was produced by the artificial *ad hoc* exegesis which Stendahl had proposed for Matthew and claimed that the formula quotations did not originate as scholarly desk work but from the ordinary techniques of preaching. Gärtner also stressed that Matthew's quotations of the OT differ in an important respect from the methods of interpretation of Scripture found in the Qumran writings. Whereas *pesher* exegesis is an exposition of a continuous text, Matthew, on the other hand, relates a consecutive story and refers here and there to words of Scripture which will show to the reader that Jesus has fulfilled the messianic prophecies. Hence it is inaccurate to refer to Matthew's quotations as *pesher* exegesis. These important points were developed further by Rothfuchs (1969) who emphasised that Matthew does not intend to comment on OT passages, but rather to use them to comment on the life of Jesus.

In the preface to the second edition of his book Stendahl (1968) noted that research completed since he wrote his monograph has shown that both the Hebrew and the Greek textual traditions were very much more fluid in the first century than had been earlier supposed. He referred especially to Cross's work and stressed that the manuscript evidence now available pointed to a series of attempts to bring the Greek Bible into conformity with a changing Hebrew textual tradition. (The relevant essays have been brought together in F. M. Cross and S. Talmon, ed., *Qumran and the History of the Biblical Text* (Cambridge, MA, 1975).) Stendahl readily conceded that some of his own results were called in question by more recent advances in our knowledge of OT textual traditions.

New data are about to allow new and better founded hypotheses about text forms available in the first century A.D. Such a promising yet unfinished state of affairs both hinders and helps further progress in the study of the Matthean quotations. It makes more probable that readings found in Matthew could witness to text forms actually available in Greek, prior to Matthew. It makes the recourse to testimonies less compelling as an explanation of textual peculiarities. (1968, p. iv)

The importance of this continuing research on OT textual traditions for the student of Matthew's gospel can hardly be overestimated, but it has not yet been taken seriously in Matthean scholarship. One partial exception is Brown (1977, p. 103) who, in his study of the infancy narratives, referred briefly to the multiplicity and fluidity of Hebrew and Greek textual traditions in the first century, as well as of Aramaic targums. 'When we add to these the possibility of a free rendering by the evangelist himself, the avenue of deciding what citation is Matthean and what is pre-Matthean on the basis of wording becomes uncertain.' Surely this observation is correct: we shall return to it a little later.

While Stendahl emphasised, as have most modern scholars, that the 'mixed' text form of the formula quotations differs markedly from the other largely septuagintal citations of the OT in Matthew, he failed to account clearly for the differing form of these two groups of traditions. The formula quotations are said to be the result of the exegetical work of Matthew's school – to which the evangelist himself presumably belonged. But surely the evangelist was also responsible for the other quotations? Stendahl wrote just a few years before the emergence of redaction criticism, so perhaps it is hardly surprising that he failed to address this important question.

In one of the first major redaction critical studies of Matthean theology, Strecker (1962), unlike Stendahl, did differentiate sharply between the two groups of quotations. He argued that although the formula which introduces Matthew's formula citations contains the evangelist's own turns of phrase, the citations themselves could not be the work of the evangelist. They do not contain Matthean words or phrases and their wording has not been influenced by the context in which they are set in the gospel. The evangelist has taken them from a distinct source – a collection of prophecies which reached him in written form (p. 83). These quotations, Strecker insisted, do not shed light on the interests of the evangelist, for they have been taken rather pedantically from a source. In Strecker's view they are used to set the history of Jesus back in the past as a chronologically and geographically distant event. The evangelist himself was not a jewish Christian familiar with jewish exegetical techniques and Hebrew or Aramaic textual traditions: evidence which seems to point in that direction comes from earlier tradition which the evangelist has simply taken over. Strecker claims that Matthew was a Gentile who 'historicised' the life of Jesus as the central period in the history of salvation.

Although nearly all Strecker's conclusions have been challenged, his sharp distinction between the formula quotations which came from a source and the other references to the OT which bear the marks of Matthean redaction set the agenda which has been followed by most more recent scholarly work. Gundry's monograph (1967), is, however, a notable exception. Although his book was published several years after Strecker's major study, it made no reference to Strecker's work since it had largely been completed in 1961. Gundry attempted to refute the view that the text form of Matthew's formula quotations is distinctive, a view widely accepted since the work of Massebieau (1885). Gundry argued that the text forms of the formula quotations are mixed. That was no surprise, but his claim that this mixed text form is found in *all* parts of the synoptic gospels was a novel proposal. Gundry insisted that it is the close adherence to the LXX found in the Marcan quotations used by Matthew which is out of line with the rest of the synoptic material. He also claimed that if we set aside the strongly septuagintal Marcan quotations, the other references to the OT in the synoptic gospels (including Matthew's formula quotations) can all be traced back ultimately to the apostle Matthew who was his own targumist and drew on his knowledge of the Hebrew, Aramaic and Greek textual traditions of the OT. The evangelist used his own 'body of loose notes' made during the ministry of Jesus (p. 172). On this view, then, the formula quotations are no longer the most distinctive feature of the use of the OT in Matthew's gospel.

Gundry claimed that earlier scholars had mistakenly overlooked the *allusions* to the OT in the synoptic gospels: their text form is mixed and they should be set alongside the formula quotations in Matthew and all other non-Marcan quotations in the synoptic gospels. Gundry's careful presentation of the Hebrew, Aramaic and Greek textual traditions which are relevant for study of references to the OT in Matthew is still unrivalled. But his hypotheses concerning the authorship of Matthew's gospel and the origin of the gospel traditions raise more questions than they answer. His strong reliance on allusions to the OT turns out to be an Achilles' heel, for the text form of allusions which rarely consist of more than two or three words is necessarily elusive! Where a writer does not indicate explicitly that he is quoting Scripture, there must be at least a good possibility that he is drawing on his memory.

## WAS THE LXX MATTHEW'S BIBLE?

At this point we must return to the question which has dominated discussion of Matthew's use of the OT. Are there two quite distinct groups of OT quotations in Matthew's gospel? It has often been urged that one group shows no traces of the evangelist's own hand and has mixed text forms (the formula quotations); the other group of quotations (some of which are taken from Matthew's sources and some of which are added redactionally) confirms that the LXX was Matthew's Bible. If this analysis is correct, then we seem to have little option but to accept the view pressed vigorously by Strecker (but shared by other scholars) that the formula quotations have been taken over by the evangelist from an earlier source. This is the conclusion reached by Luz (1985) in his impressive commentary, although he rejects Strecker's claim that the evangelist was a Gentile, and he quite rightly questions whether the formula quotations could ever have belonged together in some kind of testimony book. Luz does, however, still insist that the formula quotations stem from pre-Matthean tradition.

But this conclusion can be challenged. It is by no means clear that the LXX was Matthew's Bible. Although Kilpatrick (1946, p. 56) accepted the view of several earlier writers and claimed that 'agreement with the LXX is regularly made more exact', Stendahl (1954, p. 148) was less dogmatic and referred to 'a slight but obvious tendency to greater fidelity to the LXX'. But the four passages Stendahl does list as closer to the LXX in Matthew than in Mark turn out, on closer inspection, to provide little or no support for this conclusion. (1) In Matt. 19:18f it is just possible that the citation of the decalogue has been assimilated to the LXX. In Mark 10:19 the prohibitions are expressed with μή plus the subjunctive; in Matthew οὐ plus the future indicative is used. But the decalogue is found in several different forms in both the OT and the NT. So the variation in Matthew is probably purely stylistic: the changes may have been made in order to balance more precisely the negative commandments with the positive commandment ἀγαπήσεις τὸν πλησίον σου ὡς σεαυτόν which the evangelist adds here, the wording of which corresponds exactly both with the MT and with the LXX of Lev. 19:18. (2) At Matt. 21:9 Jesus is addressed as 'Son of David'. This is an important Matthean christological addition, but it is unrelated to the LXX. (3) At Matt. 22:32 εἰμί is added to ἐγὼ ὁ θεός in Mark 12:26. This may perhaps be classed as a septuagintal addition, but it is more likely to be simply a Matthean stylistic improvement. (4) At Matt. 24:30 phrases from Zech. 12:10 and an additional phrase from Dan. 7:13, τοῦ οὐρανοῦ, are added to Mark 13:26. But in neither case is there clearly closer conformity to the LXX.

Although most recent studies of Matthew's use of the OT have concentrated on the formula quotations, the evangelist's redaction of the quotations in Mark and Q is particularly instructive. There is little doubt that it undermines confidence in the widely accepted view that the LXX is Matthew's Bible. In a dozen or more passages Matthew retains with little or no alteration Mark's strongly septuagintal quotations: this is not surprising since throughout his gospel he usually follows his sources closely. Matthew does make some modifications, but they can be shown to be closely in line with the redactional changes he makes to his sources elsewhere.

The two examples noted above are important. Matthew's additional reference to 'love of neighbour' in 19:19 is characteristic: in 7:12b and 22:40 'love of neighbour' is emphasised redactionally as the essence of the law and the prophets. And Matthew's reference to Jesus as 'Son of David' in 21:9 in a Marcan OT quotation underlines one of the evangelist's most distinctive christological themes; this title is used redactionally in six passages.

Further examples of Matthew's redaction of references to Scripture in his sources confirm that his modifications are all of a piece with the redactional changes he makes to his main sources.

(1) In Matt. 16:9 the citation of Jer. 5:21 against the disciples in Mark 8:18 ('Having eyes do you not see, and having ears, do you not hear?') is dropped completely, as are the preceding harsh words of Jesus, 'Do you not understand; are your hearts hardened?' These changes form part of a consistent pattern: the evangelist omits or 'softens' all the Marcan passages which refer to the disciples' lack of understanding.

(2) In Matt. 21:13, πᾶσιν τοῖς ἔθνεσιν, part of Mark's citation of Isa. 56:7 is omitted. Although several redactional passages in Matthew imply acceptance of the Gentiles, in this case reference to the Gentiles is left out as part of

Matthew's sharpening of polemic against the jewish leaders: they are not using the temple properly for prayer. In Mark the quotation is introduced by, 'Is it not written?'; in Matthew it becomes, 'it is written', a firm accusation against the jewish leaders.

(3) The enigmatic allusion to Dan. 12:11 and 11:31 in Mark 13:14, 'the desolating sacrilege', is clarified by Matthew in 24:15 and made into an explicit citation of Scripture by the addition of τὸ ῥηθὲν διὰ Δανιὴλ τοῦ προφήτου. τὸ ῥηθὲν διὰ τοῦ προφήτου is found in all the introductions to Matthew's ten formula quotations; only the element of 'fulfilment' is missing here. τὸ ῥηθέν is also found in two other Matthean redactional additions (3:3 and 22:31) but it does not occur elsewhere in the NT. So there can be little doubt that these additional words stem from the evangelist himself; they also suggest that he is responsible for the introductions to the formula quotations. This is made still more probable by our fourth example of Matthew's redaction of a Marcan quotation.

(4) In Matt. 26:47–56 the evangelist sets out a more carefully structured version of Mark's account at 14:43–52 of the arrest of Jesus. In Matt. 26:54 a reference to the 'fulfilment of the scriptures' is added by the evangelist. There is a second important modification. The words of Jesus in Mark 14:49c, ἀλλ' ἵνα πληρωθῶσιν αἱ γραφαί are an ellipse which is clarified at 26:56 by expanding it and turning it into a comment of the evangelist himself – a comment which closely resembles the introductions to two of Matthew's formula quotations.

Matt. 26:56   τοῦτο δὲ ὅλον γέγονεν ἵνα πληρωθῶσιν αἱ γραφαὶ τῶν προφητῶν.

Matt. 1:22   τοῦτο δὲ ὅλον γέγονεν ἵνα πληρωθῇ τὸ ῥηθὲν ὑπὸ κυρίου διὰ τοῦ προφήτου λέγοντος.

Matt. 21:4   τοῦτο δὲ γέγονεν ἵνα πληρωθῇ τὸ ῥηθὲν διὰ τοῦ προφήτου λέγοντος.

The words πληρωθῶσιν αἱ γραφαί are taken over from Mark. The phrase τῶν προφητῶν instead of the usual διὰ τοῦ προφήτου comes as no surprise since Matthew does not cite a particular passage at this point. His intention is clearly to stress that the events which have just been recounted are to be seen as fulfilment of the Scriptures as a whole. This redactional verse contains two of the three characteristics of Matthew's formula quotations noted above: there is a declaration that the prophets have been fulfilled in the life of Jesus; the verse is a comment of the evangelist – a theological 'aside' which informs the reader of the deeper significance of the preceding events.

In this pericope the evangelist is following his Marcan source closely. But the changes he makes in 26:54 and 56 confirm that the introductions to his ten formula quotations come from his own hand: as in numerous other passages in the gospel, Matthew has developed Marcan traditions in his own characteristic way.

(5) In 9:13 and 12:7 Matthew has introduced into two Marcan passages an identical reference to Hos. 6:6: ἔλεος θέλω καὶ οὐ θυσίαν. The quotation could have been taken either from the LXX or the MT. In both cases Jesus is in dispute with Pharisees. The quotations are introduced in similar ways: πορευθέντες δὲ μάθετε τί ἐστιν (9:13) and εἰ δὲ ἐγνώκειτε τί ἐστιν (12:7). Since πορεύομαι is a favourite Matthean word and is used with an imperative six times (four of which are redactional) the introduction almost certainly comes from the hand of the evangelist himself. The emphasis on ἔλεος is certainly Matthean and is linked to the prominence given to the love commandment by the evangelist. As in several of the formula quotations, Matthew makes an essentially christological comment: Jesus acts in accordance with Scripture – and with God's will.

(6) In Matt. 3:3 there is a further interesting example of Matthean redaction of an OT citation which he found in his sources. The evangelist has carefully avoided Mark's citation of Exod. 23:20 + Mal. 3:1 which is mistakenly said to be from Isaiah. Once again Matthew's introductory words are significant: οὗτος γάρ ἐστιν ὁ ῥηθεὶς διὰ Ἡσαΐου τοῦ προφήτου λέγοντος. With the exception of a reference to 'fulfilment' (which is reserved for the story of Jesus), all the elements of Matthew's introductory formula are here. As in those ten formulae, ὁ ῥηθείς and διά point to God's attestation, for he has spoken through the prophet. In Mark (and in Luke) the quotation from Isa. 40:3 is linked to John's baptising activity in the wilderness, but in Matthew the emphasis falls squarely on the person of John the Baptist: his proclamation is attested by God. This is in line with the changes Matthew has made to Mark in the preceding verse: there he takes pains to make the message of John correspond exactly with the proclamation of Jesus (cf. 3:2 and 4:17). John and Jesus both herald the coming of the kingdom; both are attested by God in Scripture, but Jesus alone is its fulfilment.

Since Matthew usually follows his sources closely, it is no surprise to find that he takes over with little modification many of the Old Testament citations found in his sources, principally Mark and Q. By and large they are septuagintal, so he retains them in that form. But in numerous passages Matthew does abbreviate, expand and modify Mark and Q in line with his own stylistic and theological concerns. As we have seen, he treats the OT quotations found in these sources in the same way as he treats the sources themselves.

## MATTHEW'S FORMULA QUOTATIONS

If Matthew's own hand can be traced so clearly in the modifications he has made to citations of Scripture in his sources, is this also the case with the formula quotations with their mixed text form which sometimes seems to reflect use of the LXX, sometimes the MT? Or should they be set aside as a quite distinct group? Their very different mixed text form seems to point in that direction. But we have tried to show that Matthew's primary allegiance is to the textual form of the quotations in his sources rather than to the LXX as such. So if the LXX was not necessarily the evangelist's own Bible, it is at least possible that he himself is responsible for the text form of some of the formula quotations.

It has become customary to assume that the formula quotations must all have originated in the same way: scholars have debated keenly whether they were all taken from a source or from earlier tradition, or whether the evangelist himself is responsible for them all. But the evangelist's own phraseology and emphases are so pervasive in his gospel that if we did not have Mark and Luke we should find it difficult or even impossible to unravel his sources. Some of his formula quotations have probably been taken by the evangelist from earlier tradition and fitted into his story with little or no adaptation. But perhaps he himself is responsible for some (such as the citation of Isa. 9:1f in Matt. 4:14–16 and of Isa. 42:1ff in Matt. 12:17–21) where the quotation and the context have more clearly been adapted to one another.

If there is still some uncertainty about the origin of the formula quotations, there is no doubt at all about the origin of the introductory formulae. As we have seen above, two of the three elements of the formulae can be seen in Matthew's redaction at 26:54, 56 of Mark 14:49c: as in numerous other passages, Matthew has taken a Marcan phrase and developed it considerably. Both Rothfuchs (1969) and Soares Prabhu (1976) have examined the individual words and phrases of the formulae meticulously and have shown that Matthew himself is responsible for the 'basic formula' which he has adapted slightly to fit individual contexts. In two cases, 1:23 and 2:15, the introductory formula mentions explicitly that it is God's word spoken through the prophet which has been fulfilled in Jesus, but this is clearly implied by the use of τὸ ῥηθὲν διὰ τοῦ προφήτου in all the formulae.

The formula quotations are not spread evenly throughout the gospel. Four are in the infancy narratives and a fifth quotation, 2:5–6, functions in a very similar way. Four more occur in the central chapters, 4:14–16; 8:17; 12:17–21; 13:35. The final two are linked with the 'triumphal' entry of Jesus into Jerusalem (21:4–5) and the death of Judas (27:9). Why is there such a concentration of quotations in the infancy narratives and why are there so few in the passion narratives? There is no obvious answer, though it has been suggested that the evangelist was well aware that whereas Mark had already set the passion narratives against the backdrop of Scripture, traditions concerning the birth and infancy of Jesus had not yet been interpreted in this way.

Nearly all the evangelist's distinctive themes are found in chaps. 1 and 2: the infancy narratives form a theological prologue to the gospel as a whole. Three factors strongly suggest that the formula quotations have been added by the evangelist himself to earlier traditions to which he had access. (1) Matt. 1:18–2:23 can be read without the formula quotations – indeed, the story line flows rather better! Only in the (marginal) formula quotation at 2:5–6 is the scriptural reference woven into the plot. (2) Five of the six formula quotations outside the infancy narratives have clearly been added to Marcan traditions by the evangelist. So this is also likely to have happened in chaps. 1 and 2, even though we cannot trace with certainty the extent of earlier traditions. (3) The OT passages referred to are not quoted elsewhere in the NT. With the exception of the citation of Isa. 7:14 in Matt. 1:23 (and, perhaps, of Micah 5:1 + 2 Sam. 5:2 in the 'marginal' formula quotation in Matt. 2:5–6), it is difficult to envisage just how these passages might have been used by earlier Christians. It seems likely that Matthew himself was the first to see their relevance in a christian setting.

As in all the formula quotations, the text form is puzzling. There seem to be signs of dependence on both Greek and Hebrew textual traditions, and perhaps also of Aramaic targumic traditions. Given the evangelist's penchant for the text form used by his sources, the fluidity of textual traditions in the first century, and the possibility that some passages have been quoted from memory or adapted to fit the context, perhaps this is not surprising. There is little doubt that in two cases Matthew himself has adapted the wording of the quotation to fit its context in his infancy narratives. (1) In Matt. 1:23, against all the textual traditions, the third person plural καλέσουσιν is used. Since Jesus was not literally called 'Emmanuel' and since Joseph had just previously been told to call Mary's son 'Jesus' (1:21), the evangelist has used this form of the verb in order to indicate that it is the 'people saved from their sins' (1:21) – Christians in his own day – who will call Jesus 'Emmanuel'. (2) By the addition of οὐδαμῶς in 2:6, the original sense of Micah 5:1 has been transformed: an unimportant village has now become (from Matthew's perspective) supremely important on account of the birth of the Messiah.

To what extent have the formula quotations led to the adaptation or even the creation of the traditions to which they have been attached? This seems to have happened only on a limited scale. Perhaps the phrase καὶ ἐν πᾶσι τοῖς ὁρίοις αὐτῆς has been added in Matt. 2:16 in order to make the reference to Ramah in 2:18 just a little less awkward. In fact the quotations in 2:15, 2:18 and 2:23 all fit their present contexts so awkwardly that it is difficult to suppose that the traditions have been created on the basis of the quotations.

In two cases, however, the quotations chosen seem to have encouraged the evangelist to modify his own introductory formula. In two of the ten formula quotations the word υἱός occurs (1:23 and 2:15): in both verses (and only here) an explicit reference to the Lord (κύριος) as the one who has spoken through the prophet has been added to the introductory formula. Since this can hardly be a coincidence, Matthew intends to make a christological point: Jesus is the Son of God.

At first sight the quotations in chap. 2 seem to have been chosen to give scriptural undergirding to the geographical places mentioned: Bethlehem (2:6), Egypt (2:15), Ramah (assumed to be near Bethlehem, 2:18) and Nazareth (2:23). But the evangelist's concerns are primarily christological. Jesus is to be called Emmanuel – God with us (1:23), a theme echoed in the closing verse of the gospel where the risen Christ promises to be with his disciples (μεθ' ὑμῶν) until the close of the age. At 2:6 Jesus is portrayed as the one who will shepherd God's people Israel. As we have seen, at 2:15 Jesus is God's Son. Although the final two quotations in chap. 2 have long baffled exegetes, there is little doubt that in 2:17–18 Matthew intends to link the story of Jesus with the exodus and the exile experiences of Israel: just as the machinations of the opponents of God's people were thwarted of old, so too will Herod fail to overturn God's purposes. In 2:23 Jesus is called Ναζωραῖος; the most likely explanation of this apparently odd designation is that Jesus is seen as the messianic *nēṣer* or 'branch' and the *nāzîr* or 'holy one' of God.

The quotation of Isa. 9:2 in 4:15–16 also functions similarly. The opening of the ministry of Jesus in Galilee, and in Capernaum in particular, is seen as the fulfilment of Scripture. But the evangelist's choice of this quotation is dictated by other considerations: in numerous passages in his gospel he stresses that the 'story' of Jesus is ultimately of significance for Gentiles as well as Jews. The reference (albeit indirect) to the coming of the φῶς is also related to Matthew's concerns. Jesus is here called (indirectly) φῶς for Γαλιλαία τῶν ἐθνῶν; his disciples will shortly be called to be τὸ φῶς τοῦ κόσμου (5:14). As elsewhere, the evangelist draws attention to the ways in which the disciples (and Christians in his own day) continue the ministry of Jesus.

Two further formula quotations, 8:17 and 13:35, are linked to summary passages and stress that both the healing activity and parabolic teaching of Jesus are to be seen as fulfilment of Scripture. The longest quotation, of Isa. 42:1–4 in 12:17–21, is also linked to a summary. Although the attempts of Cope (1976) and Neyrey (1982) to show that this quotation has influenced the themes and structure of the whole of Matthew 12 are only partly successful, there is little doubt that the quotation and its context have influenced one another to a greater extent than in the other formula quotations. There is also little doubt that once again Matthew's concerns are primarily christological:

Jesus is the servant who exercises his ministry in obedient lowliness and mercy. Even if he has overstated his case, Neyrey has shown that this lengthy quotation is also related to Matthew's apologetic concerns – to the conflict of Jesus with the Pharisees which dominates this part of Matthew's gospel.

Van Segbroeck (1972) has noted that four of Matthew's formula quotations are introduced with an explicit reference to Isaiah – and they all fall within chaps. 4–13, chapters which Matthew has redacted particularly strongly. This may be a coincidence, but van Segbroeck believes that Matthew is especially interested in Isaiah since no prophet is as preoccupied with the salvation of Israel, even though Isaiah underlines in his preaching that his work is fruitless.

Zech. 9:9 is the only one of Matthew's formula quotations which is cited elsewhere in the NT. Although this passage is linked to the 'triumphal' entry of Jesus into Jerusalem both at Matt. 21:4–5 and at John 12:14–15, the form of the quotation differs so markedly that a direct link between the two gospels is most unlikely. The Zechariah quotation seems to have led Matthew to introduce two animals into the Marcan tradition and to have supposed that Jesus rode on both at the same time. Although exegetes have been forced to exercise great ingenuity in their explanations of this passage, once again Matthew's concern is primarily christological. Jesus enters Jerusalem as the humble (πραΰς) king, a theme which has interested the evangelist at 5:5 and 11:29.

By a curious coincidence there are also ten 'fulfilment' quotations in John's gospel. But the differences are more striking than the similarities. The introductory formulae in John (listed in the chapter of this book treating John and the Johannine Epistles) are much more varied. Whereas only one of Matthew's formula quotations is found in his passion narratives (27:9, the burial of Judas), the first does not occur in John until 12:38. Only half the Johannine quotations are comments of the evangelist. Rothfuchs (1969, p. 176) has correctly noted that whereas the Johannine citations set the 'world's' hostile reaction to Jesus and his work in the light of prophecy, the Matthean quotations portray the person Jesus and the nature of his sending.

In this brief chapter we have tried to show just how closely Matthew's use of the OT is related to his distinctive theological themes. Although the evangelist usually retains with little modification OT quotations in his main sources, Mark and Q, some have been carefully adapted in line with his own concerns. But his most distinctive contribution is his use of ten OT passages with their carefully phrased introductions: they all comment on the story of Jesus and draw out its deeper significance by stressing that all its main features are in fulfilment of Scripture. While some of his quotations may have been used and transmitted orally by earlier Christians, Matthew himself is almost certainly responsible for the choice and adaptation of many of them.

BIBLIOGRAPHY

R. E. Brown *The Birth of the Messiah* (New York, 1977).

J. M. van Cangh 'La Bible de Matthieu: Les citations d'accomplissement', *EThL* 6 (1975), 205–11.

O. L. Cope *Matthew: A Scribe Trained for the Kingdom of Heaven*, CBQMS 5 (Washington, 1976).

R. T. France 'The Formula Quotations of Matthew 2 and the Problem of Communication', *NTS* 27 (1981), 233–51.

B. Gärtner 'The Habakkuk Commentary (DSH) and the Gospel of Matthew', *ST* 8 (1954), 1–24.

M. D. Goulder *Midrash and Lection in Matthew* (London, 1974).

R. H. Gundry *The Use of the Old Testament in St. Matthew's Gospel with Special Reference to the Messianic Hope*, SNT 18 (Leiden, 1967).
*Matthew: A Commentary on His Literary and Theological Art* (Grand Rapids, 1982).

L. Hartman 'Scriptural Exegesis in the Gospel of St. Matthew and the Problem of Communication', in M. Didier (ed.) *L'Évangile selon Matthieu, Rédaction et Théologie*, BEThL 29 (Gembloux, 1972), pp. 131–52.

D. Hill 'Son and Servant: An essay in Matthean Christology', *JSNT* 6 (1980), 2–16.

G. D. Kilpatrick *The Origins of the Gospel According to St Matthew* (Oxford, 1946).

J. D. Kingsbury *The Parables of Jesus in Matthew 13* (London, 1969).

U. Luz *Das Evangelium nach Matthaus*, EKK I/1 (Zürich and Neukirchen-Vluyn, 1985).

R. S. McConnell *Law and Prophecy in Matthew's Gospel* (Basel, 1969).

E. Massebieau, *Examen des citations de l'Ancien Testament dans l'évangile selon saint Matthieu* (Paris, 1885).

J. N. Neyrey 'The Thematic Use of Isa. 42.1–4 in Matthew 12', *Bib* 63 (1982), 457–83.

R. Pesch 'Der Gottessohn im matthäischen Evangelienprolog (Mt 1–2). Beobachtungen zu den Zitationsformeln der Reflexionzitate', *Bib* 48 (1967), 395–420.

W. Rothfuchs *Die Erfüllungszitate des Matthäus-Evangeliums*, BWANT 88 (Stuttgart, 1969).

A. Sand *Das Gesetz und die Propheten: Untersuchungen zur Theologie des Evangeliums nach Matthäus*, BU 11 (Regensburg, 1974).

D. M. Smith 'The Use of the Old Testament in the New', in J. M. Efird (ed.), *The Use of the Old Testament in the New and Other Essays* (Durham, NC, 1972), pp. 3–65.

G. M. Soares Prabhu *The Formula Quotations in the Infancy Narrative of Matthew*, AnBib 63 (Rome, 1976).

G. N. Stanton 'The Origin and Purpose of Matthew's Gospel. Matthean Scholarship from 1945 to 1980', *ANRW* II.25.3 (Berlin, 1985), pp. 1890–1951.

K. Stendahl *The School of St. Matthew and its Use of the Old Testament*, 1st ed. (Lund and Copenhagen, 1954); 2nd ed. (Philadelphia, 1968).

G. Strecker *Der Weg der Gerechtigkeit*, FRLANT 82, 1st ed. (Göttingen, 1962); 3rd ed. (Göttingen, 1971).

W. Trilling *Das Wahre Israel*, SANT 10, 2nd ed. (Leipzig, 1961); 3rd ed. (München, 1964).

F. Van Segbroeck 'Les Citations d'Accomplissement dans l'Évangile selon Matthieu d'après trois ouvrages recents', in M. Didier (ed.), *L'Évangile selon Matthieu. Rédaction et Théologie*, BEThL 29 (Gembloux, 1972), pp. 107–130.

# 13 · Mark

## MORNA D. HOOKER

I T is perhaps understandable that the editors assigned a mere 4,000 words to this chapter, for at first sight Mark seems to make little appeal to the Old Testament. In contrast to Matthew and Luke, who in their different ways emphasise the fulfilment of scripture, Mark includes only one explicit editorial quotation, in 1:2f, and gives that a wrong attribution.

But appearances are deceptive. Mark handles the material in his own distinctive way, and the opening quotation is significant: his story is good news precisely because it is the fulfilment of scripture.[1] Thereafter, Jesus' words and activities constantly echo OT scenes and language, until what is 'written' of the Son of Man (9:12; 14:21) is finally fulfilled. There is no dearth of references: one recent article (Kee, 1975) listed 57 quotations and approximately 160 allusions (not counting passages which had possibly 'influenced' Mark) in chapters 11–16 alone! But they do not all fit into the pattern of 'fulfilment', for in some cases Jesus appears to take issue with Scripture, notably in discussions about the law.

To deal adequately with the use of the OT in Mark's gospel in one chapter is clearly an impossible task. In order to reduce the problem to manageable proportions, we shall confine our attention to those quotations and allusions which can be traced to the Pentateuch.[2] Inevitably, this will raise the crucial question of Mark's attitude to the law, even though that particular term is never used by Mark: does he believe that the law has been abrogated by the gospel?[3]

## I QUOTATIONS

Turning first to those passages from the Pentateuch which are introduced specifically as quotations, we leave aside the possible use of Exod. 23:20 in 1:2 – since Mark himself attributes the quotation to Isaiah and is apparently unaware of the source of these particular words[4] – and move on to 7:10, where Jesus appeals to what 'Moses said' in Exod. 20:12 and 21:17. The context of this appeal to Scripture is an argument between Jesus and a group of Pharisees and scribes arising from the lax behaviour of his disciples, who eat with 'unclean' hands. Throughout this section, Mark emphasises that the issue in dispute is not one of the provisions of the Mosaic law, but part of 'the tradition of the elders'. At the beginning of the pericope he explains that the Pharisees

220

do not eat without washing their hands, so observing the tradition of the elders – and he goes on to list some of the other traditions that they observe.⁵ The challenge of the Pharisees and the scribes in v. 5 concerns the fact that his disciples do not observe these traditions; in reply, Jesus complains that his opponents abandon the commandment of God, while maintaining the tradition of men (v. 8). As an example of their 'hypocrisy', he contrasts what 'Moses said' – the commandment of God – with what 'you say' (v. 11). The clear commandment to honour father and mother is thus annulled by the tradition which allows a man to declare his goods 'corban'.

In this first example, therefore, we find that though the story begins with Pharisees and scribes challenging the behaviour of Jesus' disciples, it is Jesus who appeals to the torah and who in turn, on the basis of torah, challenges the practice of the Pharisees and scribes; the accusation of failure to keep the law is brought, not against Jesus, as we might have expected, but against the Pharisees and scribes. Thus far Mark has presented Jesus as a loyal son of Moses. This is the more remarkable, since the argument in vv. 9–13 might well have been conducted in terms of the relative weight to be given to different parts of the law, for the inviolability of an oath is affirmed in the law itself (Num. 30:2; Deut. 23:21–3), and Jesus' opponents would presumably have argued that in this particular instance of 'corban' they were maintaining the divine command. Nevertheless, this example is both introduced and concluded with an accusation by Jesus that they maintain their own traditions and make void the word of God. Again and again throughout vv. 1–13 Mark insists that this is the real issue.

The situation becomes more complex when we move on to the 'parable' in vv. 14–16 and its explanation in vv. 17–23. On its own, the saying in v. 15 might seem compatible with the story so far: in declaring that it is what comes out of a man (i.e. evil thoughts and desires, vv. 21f) rather than what enters him that defiles him, Jesus could well be summing up his position in the previous dispute: it is not the failure to observe traditions about the washing of hands or utensils which defile a man, but the failure to honour father or mother. But the issue in vv. 2ff concerns the ritual preparation of hands and utensils, not the food itself, whereas v. 15 is most naturally interpreted as referring to the food which is eaten; certainly this is the way it is understood in the private explanation to the disciples which follows. To be relevant to the dispute in vv. 1–5, we must assume that the Pharisees believed that cultic impurity could be passed from unwashed hands to food to eater.⁶ Moreover the radical nature of the saying – 'not this but that' – fits uneasily into a context where the issue has so clearly been a conflict between human tradition and divine command, for the prohibition of certain foods as unclean certainly belongs to the law. We might perhaps interpret v. 15 as a declaration of priorities, and understand it to mean: 'You must not be so busy with ritual cleanliness that you ignore moral cleanliness.' But this interpretation becomes impossible when we come to v. 19, where Mark spells out what he understands to be the significance of the saying with the comment: 'making all foods clean'.

This second section thus introduces a new idea into the question of Jesus' relationship with the law: whereas in vv. 1–13 we found Jesus appealing to the law, he now appears to be dismissing it! Having attacked the Pharisees for setting the tradition of men over the commandments of God, we now find him apparently abandoning another of the commandments altogether: the comparison is no longer between the tradition of men and the commandments of God, but between the teaching of Moses and that of Jesus. We can, of course, explain this inconsistency in terms of the different traditions used by Mark, but this hardly explains his own position. On the one hand, he sees Jesus as obedient to the commandments of God given through Moses and attacking the tradition of men; on the other, as setting his own authority above that of Moses. We must return to this problem later.

The next quotations from the Pentateuch occur in chap. 10, once again in a debate with the Pharisees, this time on the question of divorce. Here too, the argument is initiated by the Pharisees, and once again Jesus responds by appealing to the teaching of Moses. But here he invites his opponents to quote the law, and on this occasion 'what Moses said' proves to be inadequate, not because it was 'the tradition of men', but because it was adapted to human weakness. So in contrast to Moses' concession in Deuteronomy 24, Jesus appeals to Gen. 1:27 and 2:24, where the ideal for marriage is set out. This time we are clearly comparing one part of the law with what is understood to be a superior command. The logical outcome of this argument is set out in v. 9, which in effect annuls the provision of Deuteronomy 24. We have therefore reached a conclusion very similar to that in 7:19: the authoritative pronouncement of Jesus takes priority over that of Moses. But once again, the argument which leads up to this pronouncement affirms the inviolability of God's decree in Scripture.

On this occasion also, Mark adds a private scene between Jesus and his disciples in which the implications of his teaching are brought out. And once again this private teaching takes matters a further step, since Jesus' pronouncement in vv. 11–12 declares that those who take advantage of the Mosaic provision are guilty of adultery. As in 7:19, the authoritative teaching of Jesus is now challenging the law itself.

Later in this chapter, in vv. 17–22, Mark records the incident of a man who comes to Jesus asking what he must do to inherit eternal life. Once again, Jesus appeals to the torah; this time he quotes the last six commandments (Exod. 20:12–16/Deut. 5:16–20) – those concerned with human relationships. When the man protests that he has kept all these from his youth, he is told to sell all his possessions, give them away, and follow Jesus.

In the first part of this incident, Jesus is portrayed as loyally upholding the law, but in the second part, loyalty to the law proves to be insufficient: the one thing that the man lacks can be found only by abandoning all his possessions and becoming Jesus' disciple. As in the previous incidents, therefore, we find that the law is first upheld, but that the authority exercised by Jesus is then shown to be even greater than that of the law.

In chap. 12, Mark presents a series of incidents in which Jesus engages in dialogue with various groups. In vv. 18ff he is challenged by Sadducees, who mock the notion of resurrection by appealing to Moses' provision for levirate marriage in Deuteronomy 25. Since the Sadducees regarded the Pentateuch alone as authoritative, the argument here is quite different from the dispute with the Pharisees in chap. 7. Jesus protests that in fact they do not understand the Scriptures to which they appeal: nor do they understand the power of God, which can raise the dead. Scripture itself bears witness to this power, as is seen 'in the book of Moses' – namely, in the words of God at the burning bush.

In this incident, one passage of Scripture is played off against another: the quotation from Exod. 3:6 overthrows the conclusion which had been drawn from Deuteronomy 25. Yet how does Mark establish that Jesus' interpretation is correct, and the Sadducees' is wrong? As before, the matter is decided by the authoritative pronouncement of Jesus himself, who in effect gives the verdict in favour of his own position. In order to underline this authority, Mark has Jesus introduce and conclude his response with the declaration that the Sadducees are in error: this 'enclosure' is parallel to the one used in 7:9, 13, where Jesus sets out the error of the Pharisees. There is, however, another hint as to why Jesus' position should be accepted as correct: Mark sets the incident in the temple, where Jesus has just told the parable of the vineyard, ending with a proof text which points forward to his own resurrection; following the teaching in and concerning the temple, the story moves on to tell of Jesus' passion, death and resurrection. If the Sadducees do not know the power of God, therefore, is it because they do not recognise that power at work in the resurrection of Jesus himself? Jesus appeals to Moses as a witness to the power of God to raise the dead to life, but for Mark and his readers, that power has been seen in the risen Jesus, and this is why his words have authority.

The final pericope in which the torah is appealed to is 12:28–34, where a scribe questions Jesus about the commandments, and he replies by quoting Deut. 6:4f and Lev. 19:18. This is an unusual story, since encounters between Jesus and the representatives of official Judaism normally take the form of conflict stories, whereas in Mark's account (in contrast to those of

Matthew and Luke) the questioner is friendly. Nevertheless, the story represents a struggle: the scribe presents a challenge, and Jesus responds. The scribe – the official teacher of the Mosaic law – then approves and endorses that response. Mark tells us that Jesus, in turn, approved the scribe's wise reply – a somewhat surprising comment, since this reply consisted of little more than a repetition of Jesus' own words.[7] It is possible that Mark has adapted a story in which the scribe himself was challenged to make the reply – as in Luke 10:25–8 – and that he has clumsily retained Jesus' commendation of the scribe's words, but the story as it stands makes good sense. The scribe naturally assumes that he has the authority to vet Jesus' teaching, and he gives it his approval: he acknowledges Jesus as a true son of Moses. But Jesus turns the tables, by giving his *imprimatur* to the scribe: 'You are not far from the kingdom of God.' It is Jesus who has the authority to judge, not the representative of Moses. 'After that,' comments Mark, 'no one dared to ask him any question.'

It should be noted that both the original question as to which is the first commandment, and the scribe's comment on Jesus' reply, assume that it is proper and necessary to compare one part of the law with another, and to decide which should have precedence over the other.

In these five passages Mark presents us with a picture of Jesus as one whose teaching is in accordance with that of Moses, but who does not merely repeat the Mosaic teaching, since his authority goes beyond that of Moses. As Mark expressed it in 1:22: 'he taught them as one with authority, and not as the scribes'. It is notable that in three of these five passages Jesus makes specific appeal to Moses, while the other two refer to the decalogue; four of the five use the word ἐντολή.[8]

## 2 ALLUSIONS

It is notoriously difficult to decide what is and what is not an allusion to another text: some echoes of the Pentateuch may be accidental, and not the result of influence at all; others may be unconscious, and not due to any deliberate association with the OT on Mark's part, but they could nevertheless be important in betraying what was going on in his subconscious mind; others may well indicate that a link with the OT has been seen, either by Mark or by someone else before him, and that this link is important for the interpretation of the particular passage. The first reference noted in the margin of NA[26] is a good example. If the statement in 1:6 that John ate locusts is simply part of the tradition, then the link with Lev. 11:21f may be accidental; but Lev. 11:21f reminds us that locusts – unlike other insects – are 'clean' and may be eaten. Did it occur to Mark that John's diet was in accordance with the law? And if so, is this significant? Was it important enough to lead to the inclusion of this detail in the narrative? It seems more probable that the reference to locusts was included because it indicated that John's diet was desert food.

Another problem in this opening section occurs in v. 11. The voice from heaven uses words which are reminiscent of Ps. 2:7, and possibly also of Isa. 42:1, but the phrase υἱὸς ἀγαπητός is used by the LXX in Gen. 22:2, 12, 16 of Abraham's only son Isaac. It is used again by Mark in 9:7, and in the parable of the vineyard in 12:6. Whether or not the parallel with Isaac occurred to Mark, it was not long before other christian writers saw its relevance.

It is hardly surprising that many of the allusions to the Pentateuch in Mark concern what is lawful. Several of these occur in the two stories about the sabbath in 2:23–3:6, where the accusation of doing what is not lawful is brought first against the disciples, then against Jesus himself.[9] It is important to realise that the behaviour of the disciples does not necessarily contravene the law: plucking ears of corn is clearly distinguished from reaping in Deut. 23:25, so that it is questionable whether their action could properly be described as 'work'. The dispute thus concerns the interpretation of the Mosaic command to 'remember' the sabbath. So, too, in the second incident, where Jesus declares that it is proper to do good on the sabbath, not evil, and to save life, not kill. Since at the end of the story the Pharisees 'immediately' (i.e., on the sabbath), plot to destroy him, the implication seems to be that they are doing precisely what Jesus declares to be contrary to sabbath observance: as in chap. 7, it is not Jesus but his opponents who are shown to be guilty of breaking the law.

In the first incident, Jesus responds to his opponents in a way which is by now familiar to us, by quoting Scripture – though not, on this occasion, the Pentateuch: he justifies the behaviour of his disciples by appealing to the precedent set by David. But the analogy will hardly work unless Jesus is in some way comparable to the figure of David, so that already the argument depends on the authority of Jesus, as well as on the appeal to Scripture, and it is the declaration of this authority – that of the Son of Man – which clinches the argument in 2:28. In the second incident, his authority to pronounce is demonstrated in the healing of the man with a withered hand. Jesus does not merely interpret the law, but fulfils it in a uniquely authoritative way, by doing good and saving life. Once again we are reminded of the earlier scene in the synagogue in chap. 1, where Mark links together Jesus' authoritative teaching and healing in the comment of the congregation in v. 27.

Jesus' loyalty to the torah has already been demonstrated in an earlier allusion to the Pentateuch in 1:44. On this occasion, he sends the leper whom he has just healed to the priest, instructing him to make the offering for his cleansing which Moses commanded, 'as a proof to them'.[10] Are we to understand this as a proof of the man's healing? If so, why has Mark used the plural αὐτοῖς when only one priest has been mentioned? Or is he thinking of this command as a demonstration of the way in which Jesus himself kept the law? In this case, we must presumably understand the αὐτοῖς as referring to all those who might question his loyalty to Moses – those who later in the gospel emerge as Jesus' opponents. Whatever the explanation, we find here the same combination of ideas which we have already met in several other passages: Jesus is shown at one and the same time as upholding the law, and yet exercising a far greater authority than Moses. In this particular instance he does this by healing the man of his leprosy, where the law could make provision only for what should be done once the disease has been cured: when the law is fulfilled, it is seen to bear witness to the authority and power of Jesus.

It is perhaps worth noting that a similar theme will be spelt out in Mark's next story, where Jesus forgives sins – something which no man can do – though there is, of course, provision in the law for dealing with sins which have already been forgiven, just as there is provision for dealing with a leper. It is possible that Mark himself made this connexion between the two stories, and understood them both as examples of the superiority of Jesus to the law.

The next three passages containing allusions to the Pentateuch are of a somewhat different kind: each recalls an incident in the story of Moses. The first is the story of the feeding of the five thousand, in which we are told that the crowds were 'like sheep without a shepherd'; these words in 6:34 are reminiscent of a phrase used in Num. 27:17, where Moses requests Yahweh to appoint someone to lead the people after his death, and is instructed to commission Joshua.

The second passage is the story of the transfiguration, and in this instance there are several reminiscences of the story of Moses: the introductory 'after six days', together with the setting on the mountain, point us to Exod. 24:15f, and this association is confirmed by the presence of the cloud and the voice which speaks from it; the story alluded to on this occasion is the giving of the two tables of the law. The words of command addressed to the disciples from the cloud echo another passage, Deut. 18:15, in which Moses is again looking ahead to the time following his death, and promises that God will raise up for the people another prophet like himself. But the most remarkable feature of Mark's story as far as our present theme is concerned is the appearance of Moses himself on the mountain, conferring with Jesus and Elijah. It is impossible to consider Mark 9:2–13 here in the detail it deserves,[11] but already we have seen that the chief parallel to the story is the account of the giving of the law to Moses, and that when Moses vanishes from the scene, the divine voice commands the disciples to heed Jesus in words that demonstrate that he is Moses' successor. On the other hand, we must note that Jesus is singled out as God's beloved Son – a clear indication of his superiority to both Moses and Elijah. The summit conference signifies agreement between the parties, but not equality.

The third passage occurs later in this chapter (9:38–40), when one of the disciples reports that they have attempted to stop someone casting out demons in Jesus' name, 'because he does not follow us'. The parallel here is found in Num. 11:26–9, where Moses is told that two men who had not been included among the seventy elders whom he has just appointed as his helpers are nevertheless prophesying; Joshua asks him to stop them, but Moses recognises that Yahweh has put his spirit on these men, as well as on the chosen seventy. Though Mark does not refer here to the spirit, we know from 3:22–30 that he understands exorcism to be the work of the spirit. Unlike the other stories we have considered, this particular incident is not concerned with the position of Jesus himself, but with that of men and women who claim to act in his name. But in their case, too, the 'mighty works' they do is of vital significance in demonstrating who they are.

With the arrival of Jesus in Jerusalem in 11:1, the story becomes dominated by the approaching death of Jesus, and references to all parts of the OT multiply. Some possible allusions are tenuous: the colt which is tied in 11:2 (but not specifically to a tree!) may echo Gen. 49:11; the plot in 12:7 to kill the favourite son is similar to that against Joseph in Gen. 37:20. But the echo of Exod. 22:22 in 12:40, following closely after the conversation with the scribe in vv. 28–34, appears deliberate: in condemning those scribes who oppress widows, Jesus once again accuses those who claim to be the guardians of the law of doing, themselves, what the law forbids.

Mark 13 is full of OT allusions, and several of these come from the Pentateuch. The promise of v. 11 echoes Num. 22:35, and the language of v. 19 is reminiscent of Deut. 4:32. The warning against false prophets working signs and wonders in v. 22 may well be based on Deut. 13:1–3, and the promise that the elect will be gathered from the corners of the earth reminds us of the promise to gather the scattered people of God in Deut. 30:4. In the passion narrative, the majority of allusions can be traced to the psalms and prophets, but there are several echoes of the Pentateuch. The saying about the poor in 14:7 is reminiscent of Deut. 15:11; the reference to the blood of the covenant in v. 24 recalls Exod. 24:8. The problem in 14:55–9 arises from the need for two witnesses set out in Deut. 17:6 and 19:15, and the speed of burial in 15:42 is based on Deut. 21:22f.

## SUMMARY

Many of the passages we have referred to in section 2 support the picture derived from those in section 1. Mark's attitude is surprisingly consistent, and if we find his material confusing, this results from the inherent tension in the position that he maintains. For he presents us with a picture of Jesus who both upholds the Mosaic law, and yet exercises an authority which is greater than that of Moses. In spite of all attempts by his opponents to fault him, Jesus cannot be faulted in his loyalty to the law; on every occasion it is they who are shown to be the law-breakers, not he. The many references to Moses, both direct and allusive, serve to show that Jesus is Moses' successor, but again and again the successor is shown to be superior.

Obvious tensions arise if the actions and teachings of Jesus appear to challenge those laid down in the law. Sometimes, as in 3:1–6, this is resolved by showing that the vital issue is the way in which the law is interpreted. Elsewhere, as in 10:2ff, one part of the law is shown to be more fundamental than another; but in this particular instance the tension cannot be resolved, for Jesus' authoritative interpretation of one command leads to the annulment of another in the follow-up to the incident in vv. 10–12. So, too, in the scene in chap. 7, where Mark attempts to solve the problem by insisting that the debate is really about the conflict between God's commands and human tradition; but once again, the tension cannot be resolved in this way, and this emerges in the evangelist's comment in v. 19 that Jesus made all food clean, a statement which certainly cannot be reconciled with Mosaic regulations![12] It is perhaps significant that both these developments are said by Mark to have been private revelations to the disciples: the challenge of Jesus to the law itself is something that emerged as the christian community thought out the implications of his teaching.

If there are anomalies in Mark's picture, this was inevitable. They reflect the tensions of a christian community which attempted to reconcile the traditions of the past with their new experiences in Christ. His evidence supports the belief that neither Jesus himself nor the earliest generation of Christians regarded the teaching of Moses as abrogated: his commands were indeed those of God himself. But interpretation and adaptation led inevitably to the point of rupture – a point which had not yet been reached when Mark wrote, but which must eventually come. The problem reflected in Mark is one which in one form or another has continued to exercise the church ever since. The way in which he addressed the problem in his own day may perhaps offer some guidance to those who seek to meet it in our own.

## NOTES

1 *Contra* Suhl (1965), who denies that the theme of fulfilment is important for Mark.
2 Problems of space also compel us to leave on one side the question of the particular form of text which Mark has used. We shall concentrate here on the theological significance of Mark's handling of the Pentateuchal texts.

# Mark

3 See the discussion by Schulz (1961) and Hübner (1973), pp. 213–26. The question is more often posed in terms of Jesus' own attitude to the law.

4 If not Exod. 23:20, then Mal. 3:1.

5 It is clear that the story in its present form is being told for the benefit of Gentiles; the fact that the quotation from Isa. 29 follows the LXX, not the Hebrew text, suggests that the conversation reflects a debate between Jews and Christians, rather than between Jesus and his contemporaries, *pace* Thomas (1977).

6 Booth (1986) argues for this belief: see chaps. 4 and 5.

7 There is perhaps also an echo of Deut. 4:35 in the first part of his summary.

8 The word is used only six times by Mark – all of them in these four passages: 7:8, 9; 10:5, 19; 12:28, 31. The word νόμος does not occur at all.

9 The accusation in 2:24 refers to the command set out in Exod. 20:8–11 and other passages; cf. 34:21. The prohibition in v. 26 refers to Lev. 24:5–9. The reaction of the Pharisees in 3:6 could presumably be justified by appealing to Exod. 31:14.

10 The regulations for this offering are set out in Lev. 14:2ff.

11 I have discussed the role of Moses and Elijah in the transfiguration narrative in Hooker (forthcoming).

12 Matthew avoids this tension in his version of these two stories. He omits the comment in Mark 7:19 from the first story (Matt. 15:1–20), so that the issue remains that of eating with unwashed hands, not that of eating unclean food. In the second (Matt. 19:3–12), Matthew's arrangement of the material is such that he avoids the impression that Jesus is attacking the law; moreover, Jesus himself allows divorce 'for unchastity' (v. 9) and concedes that the ideal cannot be kept by all (v. 11). In neither story, therefore, is there any suggestion that the law itself is under attack. Luke has no parallel to either story.

## BIBLIOGRAPHY

H. Anderson 'The Old Testament in Mark's Gospel', in J. M. Efird (ed.), *The Use of the Old Testament in the New and Other Essays* (Durham, NC, 1972).

R. Banks *Jesus and the Law in the Synoptic Traditions*, SNTSMS 28 (Cambridge, 1975).

K. Berger *Die Gesetzesauslegung Jesu, Teil 1: Markus und Parallelen*, WMANT 40 (Neukirchen, 1972).

R. P. Booth *Jesus and the Laws of Purity* (Sheffield, 1986).

B. H. Branscomb *Jesus and the Laws of Moses* (London, 1930).

M. D. Hooker 'What doest Thou Here, Elijah?', in L. D. Hurst and N. T. Wright (eds.), *The Glory of Christ in the New Testament: Essays in memory of G. B. Caird* (Oxford, 1987), pp. 59–70.

H. Hübner *Das Gesetz in der synoptischen Tradition* (Witten, 1973).

H. C. Kee 'The Function of Scriptural Quotations and Allusions in Mark 11–16', in E. E. Ellis and E. Grässer (eds.), *Jesus und Paulus* (Göttingen, 1975), pp. 165–88.

E. P. Sanders *Jesus and Judaism* (London, 1985).

S. Schulz 'Markus und das Alte Testament', *ZThK* 58 (1961), 184–97.

A. Suhl *Die Funktion der alttestamentlichen Zitate und Anspielungen im Markusevangelium* (Gütersloh, 1965).

K. J. Thomas 'Torah Citations in the Synoptics', *NTS* 24 (1977), 85–96.

S. Westerholm *Jesus and Scribal Authority* ConB NT Series 10 (Lund, 1978).

# 14 · Luke/Acts

## C. K. BARRETT

I F the scope of this chapter is not carefully defined and the definition strictly observed it will far exceed the limitations of space imposed upon it. It is not intended to deal with the influence, whether literary or theological, of the OT upon the Lucan writings. This is profound and pervasive. It is safe to say that there is no major concept in the two books that does not to some extent reflect the beliefs and theological vocabulary of the OT; and it is a familiar fact that Luke's style often (though by no means always) bears a semitic stamp which suggests to some (notably Torrey) that he is translating Hebrew or Aramaic sources and to others (e.g. Sparks) that he deliberately imitated the style of the LXX. To explore these phenomena, interesting as it would be, does not fall within the range of this essay. It is arguable that references to OT characters, such as Abel or Lot's wife, are specific enough to be included among citations, but they will have to be set aside in the interests of what may legitimately be described as Scripture citing Scripture, that is, of passages where an Old Testament text is introduced by a citation formula and quoted literally (though not necessarily of course in complete agreement with any form of the OT text otherwise known to us).[1] Such citations imply beliefs about the authority of the text cited, and play a different part in argument and exposition from that which allusions, however clear and in their own way weighty, can play.

It is most probable that the two books under consideration were written by the same author; they are however different from each other and differ, if not in the kind of source used, at least in the accessibility to us of the sources used. In the gospel Luke shared sources with Matthew. Each used Mark; and each used in addition what is often described as a single sayings source but was in all probability a group of sources, some written, some oral, some possessed by Matthew and Luke in virtually identical forms and some in widely different forms. That Luke used sources in writing Acts is also probable, but since we lack documents corresponding to Matthew and Mark they stand on a much more hypothetical footing, and the study of Lucan redaction, of primary importance in the study of the gospel, becomes a very different process. This observation determines the lay-out of this chapter. The two books must be studied separately, the gospel first, in the light of a comparison with Matthew and Mark, then Acts, where anything learned about Luke's editorial methods in the gospel may be applied. This in fact will not amount to much, and to a great extent Acts will have to be taken as it stands and considered independently.

## LUKE

### (a) Marcan based passages

*3:4* It is a familiar observation that Mark (1:2) opens his account of John the Baptist with a reference to what is written 'in Isaiah the prophet' but before coming to his quotation of Isa. 40:3 inserts a quotation of Mal. 3:1. Luke alters the citation formula, referring specifically to a book: ὡς γέγραπται ἐν βίβλῳ λόγων Ἡσαΐου τοῦ προφήτου, and to Isaiah as a person, who uttered oracles, rather than as a mere book label. This will prove to be characteristic. Luke also drops the words of Malachi, which he uses in 7:27 (see below). There is no need to look long for an explanation of the omission: not only did Luke spot the error, he had readily available another, preferable, context for the quotation, whose importance he did not question.

*3:5f* In Luke's text this is simply a continuous piece with the preceding quotation, and naturally there is no fresh citation formula. It suited Luke's purpose (for his eye is already on the gentile mission to be described in Acts) to include the words, 'All flesh shall see God's salvation'.

*10:27* This passage is of doubtful standing in the present list. The probability is that Luke is not here using Mark. The Marcan parallel (12:29–33) occurs in a different context, and in Luke the question and answer are reversed, the OT quotations from Deut. 6:5 and Lev. 19:18 being run together and placed on the lips not of Jesus but of the lawyer. The whole is given more briefly than in Mark and is followed by the parable of the Good Samaritan, which is not in Mark. It is not surprising that this jewish answer to a jewish question should occur in more than one early christian source. We have no evidence here that Luke is reading the OT for himself. The quotations are an essential part of the discussion.

*18:20* Here the context is undoubtedly Marcan. Luke is using Mark, but there are signs that he is checking the OT reference, for he omits μὴ ἀποστερήσῃς (which is not one of the ten commandments) and changes the order of μὴ μοιχεύσῃς and μὴ φονεύσῃς so as to agree with that of both Exodus 20 and Deuteronomy 5. These editorial changes call for no further comment.

*19:31* Here a negative observation may be made. The context is Marcan (the entry into Jerusalem). Matthew (21:4f) adds a specifically cited (τὸ ῥηθὲν διὰ τοῦ προφήτου) reference to Zech. 9:9. This may be implicit in Mark; it is certainly not made explicit by Mark or Luke.

*19:38* Mark's ὡσαννά (11:9, 10) makes an allusion to Ps. 118:26 almost certain, though he has no citation formula. Luke is more remote from the OT text, but this may be due to his editorial work: he may have dropped ὡσαννά as unintelligible to his readers and inserted βασιλεύς in order to make the meaning of ὁ ἐρχόμενος clear. Again, a negative observation.

*19:46* Here at least is a clear reference to the OT. Luke changes Mark's rhetorical οὐ γέγραπται...; into the statement, γέγραπται. Against the LXX of Isa. 56:7 he has ἔσται for Mark's κληθήσεται, and drops πᾶσιν τοῖς ἔθνεσιν, probably in view of the destruction of the temple. It was now clear (to Luke) that the temple would never be a religious centre for all nations (cf. 21:21-4). Neither Mark nor Luke shows any clear awareness that σπήλαιον λῃστῶν is a quotation from Jer. 7:11.

*20:17* Luke reproduces exactly the quotation of Ps. 118:22 contained in Mark 12:10. Both evangelists introduce the quotation in rhetorical style, thereby integrating it into their narrative. There is no essential difference between Mark's οὐδὲ τὴν γραφὴν ταύτην ἀνέγνωτε; and Luke's τί οὖν ἐστιν τὸ γεγραμμένον τοῦτο; Mark goes on to add further words from Ps. 118:23. These are omitted by Luke, possibly because he had a verse of his own to add, though it is not easy to see why he should not have used both sayings. Ps. 118:22 is clearly alluded to in Acts 4:11, but without specific citation.

*20:28* Luke here takes over Mark's citation formula, Μωυσῆς ἔγραψεν ἡμῖν; again, the formula is one that fits into the argumentative narrative style of the paragraph. Notwithstanding the formula Luke gives a summary rather than a quotation of Deut. 25:5f. He varies Mark's wording slightly in the first part of the verse, but from ἵνα λάβῃ agrees identically. The ground of the argument, however, is not the wording of a law or prophecy but the existing practice of levirate marriage; it suffices to evoke this.

*20:37* Again, both Mark and Luke adopt a narrative style, but Luke, though referring to a specific text, goes further in integrating it into his own sentence. Mark (12:26) uses the question, οὐκ ἀνέγνωτε ἐν τῇ βίβλῳ Μωυσέως ἐπὶ τοῦ βάτου...; to introduce a quotation of Exod. 3:6, 15, 16; Luke states the argument, ὅτι δὲ ἐγείρονται...καὶ Μωυσῆς ἐμήνυσεν ἐπὶ τῆς βάτου, ὡς λέγει... The fact that Luke changes the gender of βάτος shows that he is here exercising a watchful editorial eye. He goes on to give the sense of Mark's quotation. What is important is that in a particular passage of Scripture

Moses, a trustworthy guide, spoke of God as the God of men who had died.

*20:42, 43* Luke conforms the quotation of Ps. 110:1 to the LXX, substituting ὑποπόδιον for Mark's ὑποκάτω. The argument is the same in the two gospels, and implies the belief that every word of Scripture is significant. If a verse refers to two κύριοι it is necessary to distinguish and identify them. Anyone to whom David the Psalmist refers as κύριος must be greater than he: one κύριος will therefore be God, the other the Messiah. The citation formulas in Mark and Luke differ. Where Mark (12:36) has αὐτὸς Δαυὶδ εἶπεν ἐν τῷ πνεύματι τῷ ἁγίῳ, Luke has αὐτὸς γὰρ Δαυὶδ λέγει ἐν βίβλῳ ψαλμῶν. Mark thinks of David as uttering words under the influence of divine inspiration, Luke of David's words as contained in an inspired book. Both of course accept them as authoritative, but it is characteristic of Luke to think of words in a book.

## (b) Passages shared with Matthew only

*4:1–13* The Q temptation narrative, contrasting sharply with the Marcan, is conducted mainly in terms of scriptural debate, Jesus and the devil quoting verses of the OT at each other, more or less in the manner of a disputation between two rabbis. It may well have taken shape in such a debate: Why did not your (allegedly) miracle-working Jesus turn stones into bread? Because it is written,...The quotations are common to Matthew and Luke; the main difference is in the order of the temptations, Matthew giving Luke's 1–2–3 in the order 1–3–2.

(i) In response to the temptation to cause a stone to become bread Jesus replies (Luke 4:4) by quoting Deut. 8:3, οὐκ ἐπ' ἄρτῳ μόνῳ ζήσεται ὁ ἄνθρωπος. Matthew and Luke have the same citation formula, γέγραπται; Matthew adds to the quotation.

(ii) In the second (Lucan) temptation the devil offers Jesus the authority and glory of the kingdoms of the world if he will fall down and worship him. Jesus replies, in both Matthew and Luke (4:8), by quoting Deut. 5:9; 6:13; 10:20. Between Matthew and Luke there is an insignificant difference in the order of words. Again, in each gospel the citation formula is γέγραπται.

(iii) In the third temptation the devil challenges Jesus to test the promise of Ps. 91:11, 12. Matthew and Luke (4:10, 11) agree identically except that Luke continues the quotation with the words τοῦ διαφυλάξαι σε, a natural but perhaps unnecessary addition (already made in the psalm). The citation formulas are virtually the same: Matthew, γέγραπται γὰρ ὅτι...καὶ...; Luke, γέγραπται γὰρ ὅτι...καὶ ὅτι...

(iv) Jesus replies to this temptation (Luke 4:12) by quoting Deut. 6:16, in agreement with Matthew. This time the citation formulas are different. Matthew, recognising the repetition, writes πάλιν γέγραπται, Luke, avoiding it, εἴρηται. It seems clear that Luke took all this OT material from his source, with minimal editorial modifications.

*7:27* See above, 3:4. Matthew and Luke agree in their citation formula, οὗτός ἐστιν περὶ οὗ γέγραπται. Neither needed Mark's wrongly attributed quotation of Mal. 3.1 because another common source provided them with the quotation in a discussion which Luke placed at this point (cf. Matt. 11:10). The actual identification of John the Baptist with Elijah seems to have been more important for Matthew (see Matt. 11:14) than for Luke, who is content to say that John will act ἐν πνεύματι καὶ δυνάμει Ἠλίου (1:17), which could have been said of Elisha and is a long way short of identification. Controversy over the person and work of John was apparently keener in some places than in others; hence no doubt the fact that this OT passage is not quoted in Acts, though Acts more than once mentions the prophecy that whereas John baptised with water a later baptism would be with Spirit.

### (c) Material peculiar to Luke

There are few passages to be reviewed here, but it is clear that they will be of the greatest importance in the investigation of Luke's citations of the OT.

*2:22, 23, 24* In each of the verses there is a specific reference to the law (κατὰ τὸν νόμον Μωυσέως...καθὼς γέγραπται ἐν νόμῳ κυρίου...κατὰ τὸ εἰρημένον ἐν τῷ νόμῳ κυρίου), and though the quotations are not exact it is clear that Luke means to indicate that the characters in his story were obeying the written commandments. The prescription of Lev. 12:6, which looks to the cases of the future, becomes a definite past, referring to the occasion in question; the prescription is provided with a basis quoted from Exod. 13:2, 12, 15; Luke then returns to Lev. 12:8, showing that Mary was one of the poor who offered not a lamb but a couple of doves or pigeons. These verses provide part of the means by which Luke builds up the atmosphere of OT piety which pervades the infancy narratives. In verse after verse the OT is recalled. The great songs are, as regards language, little more than centos of OT words and phrases, and all act so as to fulfil OT prophecy. It is surprising that the OT, so often echoed, is quoted, with citation formulas, only here.

*4:18, 19* This, together with the next, is the most important OT citation in Luke.[2] Its context is the account of Jesus' visit to and rejection at Nazareth, a passage which for Luke not only brings out both who Jesus was and what was his message but also shows in advance what the outcome of his ministry was to be: he will be rejected by men but preserved by God. It corresponds with this setting that the citation formula is an extended piece of narrative. 'There was given him the book of the prophet Isaiah, and when he had unrolled the book he found the place where it was written (οὗ ἦν γεγραμμένον)…and he rolled up the book…Today this Scripture has been fulfilled (πεπλήρωται ἡ γραφὴ αὕτη)…' Later there are references to Elijah and Elisha without any attempt to cite passages, and there is no resemblance to the synagogue sermons of Acts (see below). Indeed, the words of Jesus, though they begin with a 'text', cannot be called a sermon. Isa. 61:1f is quoted but it receives no exposition and does not become the basis of argument. Jesus simply claims that the prophecy is fulfilled in him and his ministry. The paragraph is probably Luke's own construction. Like the partial parallels in Mark (6:1–6) and Matthew (13:54–8) it is based on the saying which occurs in *Gos. Thom.* 31 (POxy 1.6): No prophet is acceptable in his village, no physician heals those who know him (cf. Luke 4:23), but whereas Mark is content with a simple story that shows the prophet unable to secure acceptance in his native place and as working few cures there Luke develops the two themes of Jesus as prophet and teacher, and does so by means of the OT. Isa. 61:1f is not quoted elsewhere in the NT, but the Spirit is so often said to rest upon Jesus that it is unlikely that it was never used until Luke discovered it. Like most of his OT citations he probably found it in familiar use. It is not to be thought of as a sort of additional 'servant song' (but see Seccombe, 1981, p. 255). The word '*ebed* – παῖς does not occur in it. Luke uses it because it depicts the work of the Messiah (ἔχρισέν με) in the role of prophet and healer. It is this double theme that is developed in the references to Elijah and Elisha, prophets who also acted as physicians, and did so for the benefit of Gentiles, so that the allusions serve also to foreshadow the ultimate extension of the work of Jesus to Gentiles. Jesus is a great prophetic figure (cf. 7:16) who announces the fulfilment of the OT and embarks on a mission of world-wide significance, which will be fulfilled in the ultimate rejection of the cross and the ultimate vindication of the resurrection. This points forward to the last citation.

*22:37* Here the citation formula is unique and calls for special consideration. 'This that has been written (τοῦτο τὸ γεγραμμένον) must be completed (τελεσθῆναι) in me (ἐν ἐμοί), namely, And he was reckoned with transgressors (Isa. 53:12); for my affair (καὶ γὰρ τὸ περὶ ἐμοῦ) has an end (τέλος ἔχει).' τὸ γεγραμμένον is a Lucan expression. Luke introduces it at 20:17 in rewriting a Marcan citation formula; we may compare 4:17 (τὸν τόπον οὗ ἦν γεγραμμένον) and the use of τὸ εἰρημένον at 2:24 (cf. Acts 2:16; 13:40). The use of τελεσθῆναι is also Lucan. The verb τελεῖν occurs not at all in Mark, several times in Matthew, but never in relation to Scripture. In Luke, in addition to the present passage, the verb is used twice in relation to Scripture, at 2:39 (ἐτέλεσαν πάντα τὰ κατὰ τὸν νόμον κυρίου) and at 18:31 (τελεσθήσεται πάντα τὰ γεγραμμένα διὰ τῶν προφητῶν); it thus may suggest complete fulfilment. At 12:50 it is used in a closely related way: Jesus is under constraint until the 'baptism' foretold for him is accomplished (ἕως ὅτου τελεσθῇ). Cf. Acts 13:29, which points the way in which Luke's closing clause is to be understood. The only other passages in Luke where we have the article followed by περί and either the name of Jesus or a pronoun referring to him are 24:19, 27. In the latter of these 'the things concerning Jesus' are explained in terms of the Scriptures. What Clopas and his companion had been unable to understand had in fact been the fulfilment of the OT. Luke 22:37b thus probably has a double meaning: Jesus' career is about to end, in death; but this fulfils Scripture and is thus what God wills. There is no space here even to list the interpretations that have been given to the four words quoted from Isa. 53:12 (καὶ μετὰ ἀνόμων ἐλογίσθη). In the Lucan context, the simplest is probably the best. Jesus is about to be treated as an ἄνομος, a lawbreaker, is, or ought to be, treated.

In the gospel, Luke's contribution to the christian use of the OT is very small. He has little fresh to offer except at 4:18, 19; 22:37, though his readiness to take over OT quotations from his sources and the summary statements in 24:27, 44 show that he believed the whole of the OT to be quotable in a christian sense. There is hardly sufficient evidence for a discussion of the question whether his use of the OT should be described as proof from prophecy or apologetic (raised already by Cadbury, 1958, p. 304; see also Rese, 1979, pp. 68–72). In truth, these are hardly alternatives. If it is apologetic to argue that Jesus knew in advance that his ministry must end in rejection and death, in his being treated as a transgressor, so that none of these things took him by surprise or upset his plans, then indeed Luke presents us with an apologetic scheme. But Jesus knew these things because they had been prophesied in the OT, and that in due course they happened was the fulfilment of prophecy. Jesus therefore was the one to whom the prophets pointed, the Messiah. Prophecy was fulfilled in a prophetic, healing, dying, risen Messiah, through whom God had sent salvation not only to the Jews but to the world. This may be described as proof from prophecy or as apologetic; Luke would have called it εὐαγγέλιον.

## ACTS

Even if there were space in this essay for a full discussion of the sources of Acts it would be impossible to analyse the material before us in the way in which the OT references in the third gospel have been analysed. Instead it will be useful to set out the OT citations in terms of the purposes they serve. These are few. Explicit references to the OT occur in preaching (understood in a fairly broad sense), in prayer, and in discussion of the constitution of the church and the directions that determine its life.

## (a) Preaching

*2:17–21*   Joel 3:1–5 is adduced to explain the events of the day of Pentecost. Prophecy has been fulfilled. The quotation is introduced in 2:16 by the words τοῦτό ἐστιν τὸ εἰρημένον διὰ τοῦ προφήτου ᾽Ιωήλ (the name is omitted by D and some other Western authorities). With a few variations, to some extent obscured by textual variants in Acts, Acts follows the text of the LXX.

*2:25–8*   The resurrection of Jesus was foretold in Ps. 16:8–11, introduced by Δαυὶδ γὰρ λέγει εἰς αὐτόν. For David as author of the Psalms cf. Luke 20:42f; Acts 13:33–7.[3]

*2:34, 35*   The exaltation of Jesus was foretold in Ps. 110:1, introduced by λέγει δὲ αὐτός (David). The same quotation is used in Luke 20:42f.

*3:22, 23*   Two passages (Deut. 18:15; Lev. 23:29), linked by καί, are introduced by one citation formula, Μωυσῆς μὲν εἶπεν ὅτι. Moses foretold the coming of a prophet; all must give heed to him.

*3:25*   Gen. 22:18; 26:4; God makes a promise to Abraham. The verse is virtually a quotation, and the introductory words, ὁ θεός...λέγων πρὸς ᾽Αβραάμ, are virtually a citation formula; Luke characteristically uses narrative form.

*7:3*   '(God) said to Abraham,...' (Gen. 12:1). This is the first quotation in Stephen's speech, which, at least in parts, is a catena of quotations, not all of which are formally introduced. The following are quotations, though without citation formulas: v. 5 (Gen. 48:4); v. 18 (Exod. 1:8); vv. 27, 28 (Exod. 2:14); v. 32 (Exod. 3:6, 15f); v. 33 (Exod. 3:5); v. 34 (Exod. 3:7f, 10); v. 35 (Exod. 2:14); v. 40 (Exod. 32:1, 23). These, with less precise allusions, sketch the story of the patriarchs and of Moses. At vv. 6, 7 (Gen. 15.13f), ὁ θεὸς εἶπεν is partly citation formula, partly narrative; similarly v. 37 (Deut. 18:15), with Μωυσῆς...ὁ εἴπας. Full formulas are found at the end of the speech. Amos's attack (5:25–7) is introduced (vv. 42, 43) with καθὼς γέγραπται ἐν βίβλῳ τῶν προφητῶν (that is, of the twelve minor prophets), and Isaiah's (apparent) rejection of a permanent temple (66:1f) with καθὼς ὁ προφήτης λέγει.

*8:32, 33*   The Ethiopian was reading Isa. 53:7f. This quotation may be

238

classed as occurring within preaching since though in form the event was a private conversation Luke himself describes it as preaching (v. 35, εὐηγγελίσατο). The passage is described as ἡ περιοχὴ τῆς γραφῆς ἣν ἀνεγίνωσκεν. It has often been pointed out that the verses quoted from Isaiah 53 contain neither the word *servant* nor any reference to the bearing of suffering in the place of others.

*13:22* is the first of a number of quotations in Paul's sermon in the synagogue of Pisidian Antioch (Ps. 89:21; cf. 1 Sam. 13:14). It has a narrative introduction, εἶπεν (ὁ θεὸς) μαρτυρήσας. Unlike those in chap. 7 the remaining quotations are introduced by their own citation formulae, and these are of some interest.

*13:33* quotes Ps. 2:7, introduced as follows: ὡς καὶ ἐν τῷ ψαλμῷ γέγραπται τῷ δευτέρῳ. Not only a book but a division of the book is given.

*13:34* quotes Isa. 55:3. It is integrated into the argument with οὕτως εἴρηκεν (the subject must be God) ὅτι...

*13:35* quotes Ps. 16:10 (cf. 2:25–8, above). The citation formula is διότι καὶ ἐν ἑτέρῳ λέγει... With ἑτέρῳ we must presumably supply ψαλμῷ; the subject of λέγει is probably God, though comparison with chap. 2 suggests David.

*13:41* is Paul's final warning, drawn from Hab. 2:5, described as τὸ εἰρημένον ἐν τοῖς προφήταις (see above on 7:42f).

The list of OT quotations used in preaching ends here; chaps. 14–28 have nothing to add.

## (b) Prayer

The one passage considered here might almost be included under *preaching*; the prayer opens with a recital of the nature and acts of God such as is used elsewhere in the sermons. Acts 4:24 reflects but does not cite a number of OT passages.

*4:25, 26* Ps. 2:1f. The introduction in v. 25 is a notorious linguistic puzzle, but the substance of it is clear. The words were spoken by God through the Holy Spirit by the mouth of David – a clear account of the utterance of an inspired man. Again Luke shows interest in David as the author of the Psalms.

### (c) Direction for the church's life

*1 : 16*  This verse refers explicitly to the fulfilment of the γραφή ἥν προεῖπεν τὸ πνεῦμα τὸ ἅγιον διὰ στόματος Δαυὶδ περὶ ᾽Ιούδα, but does not quote the γραφή or say where it is to be found – except of course that it is from the Psalms of David. The most probable passage is Ps. 41:10. What is important for Luke at this point is simply that Judas's treachery had been foretold; so far his concern is apologetic rather than constitutional.

*1 : 20*  Scripture did however specify the steps that were to be taken after Judas's departure and death. Pss. 69:26; 109:8 give the requisite instruction. Reference to the book is given: γέγραπται γὰρ ἐν βίβλῳ ψαλμῶν. The one introduction covers both quotations, which are simply linked by καί.

*13 : 47*  The quotation from Isa. 49:6 justifies the turn to the Gentiles. It is a command from God: οὕτως γὰρ ἐντέταλται ἡμῖν ὁ κύριος.

*15 : 16, 17, 18*[4]  James's composite quotation (of Jer. 12:15; Amos 9:11, 12; Isa. 45:21; see further below) serves the same purpose, and in addition is used to justify the terms on which the offer to the Gentiles is made. It appeals to οἱ λόγοι τῶν προφητῶν, καθὼς γέγραπται.

*23 : 5* may be included here if it is understood to mean that Christians, or at least jewish Christians, were expected to show respect to jewish authorities. Exod. 22:7 is formally introduced by γέγραπται γὰρ ὅτι.

*28 : 26, 27* like 13:47 points to the mission to the Gentiles, but whereas 13:47 does so in a positive sense (preachers are a light to the Gentiles) this passage does so negatively, Isa. 6:9, 10 (to which Luke at 8:10 omitted a Marcan allusion) being used as a prediction of the failure and unbelief of the Jews. The introduction is elaborate and draws special attention to the last OT quotation in the book: καλῶς τὸ πνεῦμα τὸ ἅγιον ἐλάλησεν διὰ ᾽Ησαΐου τοῦ προφήτου πρὸς τοὺς πατέρας ὑμῶν λέγων. On this see Bovon (1984).

It is natural to begin a general discussion of these passages with the many OT quotations that occur in speeches or sermons. Of the main speeches in the first half of Acts (1–14) only that in chap. 10 is without OT quotations. It cannot be said that this was because it was addressed to a Gentile, since Cornelius is represented as a God-fearing man, constantly engaged in prayer and probably as familiar with the OT as many Jews. It was probably therefore drawn from a different (Caesarean) source, and suggests that some early christian preachers made less direct use of the OT than others, though 10:43 contains a comprehensive reference to the witness of all the prophets. In this we may compare, in the later chapters of Acts, which contain so few quotations, a passage such as 26:22. Here Paul claims to say nothing but what is to be found in Moses and the prophets, but gives no detailed reference. Of the remaining speeches, those in chaps. 2 and 3 lay the christological and eschatological foundations of christian doctrine, and those in chaps. 7 and 13, which contain more OT quotations and allusions than any other, develop Luke's attitude to Judaism.

An important milestone in the study of the OT in the speeches in Acts is an article by Bowker (1967), who points out that synagogue homilies that have survived fall into two groups, the proem and the yelammedenu homilies. 'The proem homily is so called because it starts from a proem (introductory) text. The yelammedenu homily is so called because it derives from a request for instruction, *yelammedenu rabbenu*, let our teacher instruct us' (p. 99). The proem was not taken from either the seder or the haftarah of the day, but it had to contain at least one word that tallied linguistically with a word in the haftarah. The proem was interpreted by means of a further series of texts, which led eventually to a text taken from the seder. Yelammedenu homilies are similar in structure, apart from their starting-point, which is a question (usually of halakah). With this pattern in mind Bowker turns to Paul's synagogue sermon in Acts 13. It proves to contain 'certain clear indications of proem homily form. It suggests a *seder* reading Deut. iv: 25–46, a *haftarah* II Sam. vii. 6–16, and a proem text I Sam. xiii.14...On this analysis xiii. 17–21 is an introduction, linking the *seder* reading with the proem text, and xiii. 22–41 is a typical proem homily' (p. 104). A proem homily, then, but not in pure form. The Pentecost sermon in Acts 2 also looks like a proem homily, on the text Joel 2:32, the seder being Deut. 29:1–21 (alluded to in both Acts 2:36 and 2:39) and the haftarah Isa. 63:9–19. All this, however, is (so Bowker says) conjectural and open to doubt, as is a similar analysis of the speech in Acts 3. More probable, he thinks, is an analysis of Stephen's speech: proem, Gen. 12:1; seder, Exod. 33:12–34:9; haftarah, Isa. 65:22–66:5. A yelammedenu argument (which might have formed part of a yelammedenu homily) is found in James's words in Acts 15. A halakic question is raised: Must gentile converts be circumcised and required to keep the whole law? James's decision falls into four parts: (a) a summary of what has happened (v. 14); (b) a reference to Scripture which supports what has happened (vv. 15–18); (c) the decision (vv. 19, 20); (d) a comment (v. 21), which justifies the taqqanah (alleviation of torah) proposed in the decision.

This discussion, which should be read in all its detail, gives many valuable insights into the use of the OT in Acts, but, as its author says, it 'is to some extent inconclusive' (p. 111). It is; and it hardly seems possible to maintain (and Bowker does not maintain) that there is anywhere in Acts a straight transcript of a synagogue homily. This is in no way surprising; whatever sources Luke may have had he did not have verbatim reports of what his preachers said on the occasions he describes. He gives at best radically abbreviated versions of what was said. But again, whoever 'Luke' may have been, there was some kind of contact between him and the early christian synagogue preachers; indeed, Christians were still, in all probability, preaching in synagogues in his own day, and it would be surprising if, in the first place, they never used current synagogue methods, and if, in the second, these methods left no trace in Acts. Bowker's investigation is of real importance, but it remains open to criticism both in respect of its foundations in our knowledge of jewish lectionary and homiletical practice, which is less precise than could be wished (Rese, 1979, pp. 66–8), and in the agreement of the material in Acts with what we do know, or think probable. Some resemblances to proem and yelammedenu homilies could hardly be avoided. Given a belief that the OT mediated the word of God, and was therefore authoritative, was it not inevitable that christian preachers should sometimes begin with a text, and interpret it through other relevant passages, and sometimes begin with a pressing practical question, and seek an answer by means of a similar catena of passages?

Study of Luke's citation formulae in Acts might at first suggest little more than that Luke had an eye to variety. Parts of γράφειν are common: 1:20; 7:42; 13:33; 15:15; 23:5 (all γέγραπται); γραφή is used at 1:16; 8:32 (here with περιοχή, not used elsewhere). Parts of λέγειν are also common: 2:16; 13:40 (εἰρημένον); 2:25, 34; 7:48; 13:35 (λέγει; cf. 3:25, λέγων); 3:22; 7:3, 7 (εἶπεν; cf. 4:25, εἰπών; 7:37, εἶπας). In addition there are ἐντέλλεσθαι (13:47); ἐπαγγέλλεσθαι (7:5); λαλεῖν (7:6; 28:25, with λέγων). More frequently than in the gospel Luke in Acts records the name of speaker or writer: Isaiah (28:25); Moses (3:22; 7:37); David (1:16; 2:25, 34; 4:25); Joel (2:16); prophets unnamed (7:42, 48; 13:40; 15:15); a divine person (God: 3:25; 7:2–3, (5), 6, 7; the Lord: 13:47; the Holy Spirit: 4:25; 28:25). He also specifies the books from which his quotations are taken: the book of Psalms (1:20; 13:33 (the second Psalm), 35 (another Psalm)); the book of the prophets (7:42; 15:15 (the words of the prophets)). The variety, taken with the interest in persons and books, seems to mean that Luke thought of the OT less as a battery of texts than as a record that told of kings and prophets, but especially of a people, of Israel. This was the sort of thing he was himself writing: an account of a people, heir to Israel, told through the story of such men as Peter and Paul, and supplied with its meaning through their prophetic utterances, which were always in harmony with what the prophets of old had said.

This Lucan characteristic gives special significance to Stephen's speech in Acts 7 and Paul's synagogue sermon in Acts 13. These I have discussed elsewhere (Barrett, 1986) and may therefore pass over many details in order to make the point that the two speeches illustrate the two sides of Luke's attitude to Judaism and its Scriptures. Acts 13 manifests the positive side. The story of Israel is the story of God's election and providential care of Israel. He provided his people with a king, and when the first proved unsatisfactory removed him and replaced him with David, a man after his own heart. The story leads eventually to John the Baptist, and when Jesus appears to consummate it even his enemies are drawn into the process as by their opposition they fulfil the prophetic word. The reconstituted people that is now brought into being takes on its predicted role as light of the Gentiles; let Jews beware lest this leads to their exclusion! Acts 7 on the other hand shows a negative evaluation of the same story. God remains in control, but constantly has to exercise control by reversing the acts of his people, who reject Joseph and Moses and persecute and kill the prophets. They prefer their man-made house to the freedom of their tent-dwelling God.

These are fundamental Lucan themes but they do not cover the whole of Luke's use of the OT, which is co-extensive with most of the aims and interests that he has incorporated in his book. Thus in chaps. 2 and 3 he uses the OT as an essential element in his presentation of the gospel message that is the *raison d'être* of Acts. The gospel is not about a new God; it is about the God of Abraham, Isaac, and Jacob (3:13). The striking events of the gift of the Holy Spirit and the healing of a lame man are the fulfilment of purposes that this God had already declared in days of old: the prophecy of Joel of what should come in the last days (2:17–21) and the glorification of the servant of God (3:13; Isa. 52:13). This leads to christology, which is focused on the resurrection, which had been foretold by David (2:25–8; Ps. 16:8–11). Jesus was not only alive but exalted as κύριος (2:34f; Ps. 110:1). He was the promised Mosaic prophet (3:22; Deut. 18:15–20). God's fulfilment of his prophecies meant the offer of salvation to all, as had been promised to Abraham (3:25; Gen. 22:18; 26:4) and foretold by Joel (2:21; cf. 2:39). From the beginning this message had been destined for all the families of the earth. These of course included Israel, but the OT itself forecasts its rejection by those who should have received it most warmly (13:46f; 28:25–8). All this is not exactly either proof from Scripture or apologetic (see above). It is the interpretation of the life, death, and resurrection of Jesus, and of the life of the church, in terms drawn from and based upon the OT which constitutes Luke's only interpretative instrument.[5]

We have seen that the OT instructs christian preachers on occasion to leave the natural environment of their message within Judaism and take it out into the gentile world. The OT has other instructions for them, for example that Judas must be replaced (1:16, 20). It also provides the core of the argument by which the so-called Apostolic Decree is established. James's quotations and allusions provide some of the most difficult problems in Luke's use of the OT.

James appears to quote the LXX where this differs from the Hebrew. Is it conceivable that he would do this? All that can be said here is that Luke (or James?) has found a way of combining the restoration of Judaism (ἀνοικοδομήσω τὴν σκηνὴν Δαυίδ – or does this refer only to the resurrection?) with the call of the Gentiles (οἱ κατάλοιποι τῶν ἀνθρώπων); and this comes very near to the heart of Luke's faith. It is not unlike him to express it in a quotation.

## NOTES

1  In this paper there is no space for a discussion of textual questions. See the contribution by Wilcox, pp. 193–204. For general bibliography see in addition to commentaries and a few more recent works cited here Rese (1965 and 1978).
2  See also Seccombe (1981) and Albertz (1983).
3  On 2:30 see O'Toole (1983).
4  On 15:14 see Dupont (1985). The verse however is not a citation; James claims that the words of the prophets are in agreement with it.
5  Acts 14:15–17; 17:22–31 are not exceptions; here too the influence of the OT is apparent.

## BIBLIOGRAPHY

R. Albertz 'Die "Antrittspredigt" Jesu im Lukasevangelium auf ihrem alttestamentlichen Hintergrund', *ZNW* 74 (1983), 182–206.

C. K. Barrett 'Old Testament History According to Stephen and Paul', in Wolfgang Schrage (ed.), *Studien zum Text und zur Ethik des Neuen Testaments, Festschrift zum 80. Geburtstag von H. Greeven* (Berlin, 1986), pp. 57–69.

F. Bovon '"Schön hat der heilige Geist durch den Propheten Jesaja zu euren Vätern gesprochen" (Acts 28.25)', *ZNW* 75 (1984), 226–32.

J. W. Bowker 'Speeches in Acts: A Study in Proem and Yelammedenu Form', *NTS* 14 (1967), 96–111.

H. J. Cadbury *The Making of Luke-Acts* (London, 1958).

J. Dupont 'Un Peuple d'entre les Nations (Actes 15.14)', *NTS* 31 (1985), 321–35.

R. F. O'Toole 'Acts 2.30 and the Davidic Covenant of Pentecost', *JBL* 102 (1983), 245–58.

M. Rese *Alttestamentliche Motive in der Christologie des Lukas* (Bonn, 1965).
   'Die Funktion der alttestamentlichen Zitate und Anspielungen in den Reden der Apostelgeschichte', in J. Kremer (ed.), *Les Actes des Apôtres*, BEThL 48 (Gembloux and Leuven, 1978), pp. 61–79.

D. Seccombe 'Luke and Isaiah' *NTS* 27 (1981), 252–9.

H. F. D. Sparks 'The Semitisms of the Acts', *JTS* 1 (1950), 16–28.

C. C. Torrey *The Composition and Date of Acts*, HTS 1 (Cambridge, MA, 1916).

# 15 · John and the Johannine Epistles

## D. A. CARSON

### INTRODUCTION

UNTIL fairly recently, John's use of the OT received relatively little attention. What little there was tended to serve other interests. For example, six decades ago Faure (1922) argued that the quotation formulae in this gospel provide evidence from which we may deduce the existence and extent of written sources used by the evangelist in the composition of his work – a suggestion vigorously contested by Smend (1925).[1] The classic exchange between Dodd (1952), who argued that the NT writers understood the kerygma in terms of the OT, and largely respected the contexts of the various passages on which they tended to concentrate, and Sundberg (1959), who argued against these points, obviously had its importance for the study of the fourth gospel (FG). Apart from some notable exceptions, however, the study of John was largely shaped by other agendas. Debates focused on various source theories and on the intellectual matrix from which the FG sprang, the dominant hypotheses being represented by Bultmann (ET 1971), who insisted on the priority of Mandaean Gnosticism, and by Dodd (1953), who defended the influence of the Hermetica on the FG. The 'notable exceptions' included the commentary by Hoskyns and Davey (1940), the most important feature of which was the many lines drawn between the FG and the OT, the second volume of Braun (1964), and a seminal essay by Barrett (1947).

More than any other factor, the discovery of the Dead Sea Scrolls served not only to awaken interest in the ties between John and Judaism, but also to stimulate detailed study of the broader question of jewish hermeneutics in the first century – a growing field of inquiry that has generated many fresh studies on John. In this short chapter it is clearly impossible to comment on all of these; but I shall draw attention to some of the major contributions, and argue that the cumulative evidence suggests more complex connexions between John and the OT than is sometimes appreciated. The complexity of these connexions compels us to consider not only direct quotations of the OT, but the themes drawn from it and the way in which they are taken up.

245

## DIRECT QUOTATIONS FROM THE OLD TESTAMENT

Useful summaries of the bare data abound, organised in various ways (e.g. Amsler, 1960, pp. 34–44; Hanson, 1983, pp. 113–32). Because of the paraphrastic nature of some of John's quotations,[2] it is not always clear which instances we should class as 'direct quotations' and which are mere allusions. But arguably there are thirteen such quotations introduced by a formula (1:23 [Isa. 40:3]; 2:17 [Ps. 69:9]; 6:31 [Ps. 78:24]; 6:45 [Isa. 54:13]; 10:34 [Ps. 82:6]; 12:14f [Ps. 62:11 and Zech. 9:9; cf. Isa. 35:4; 40:9]; 12:38 [Isa. 53:1]; 12:39f [Isa. 6:10]; 13:18 [Isa. 41:10]; 15:25 [Ps. 35:19 or Ps. 69:5]; 19:24 [Ps. 22:18]; 19:36 [Exod. 12:46 or Ps. 34:21 or Num. 9:12]; 19:37 [Zech. 12:10]). Two more direct quotations from the OT appear without introductory formulae (1:51 [Gen. 28:12 – though some see this as an allusion, not a quotation]; 12:13 [Ps. 118:25f]. To these fifteen, four passages must be added where an introductory formula clearly refers the reader to the OT, but no OT text is cited (7:38; 7:42 (some find sufficient connexion with 2 Sam. 7:12 and Mic. 5:2 to warrant inclusion of this entry in the first list); 17:12;[3] 19:38 (cf. Ps. 22:15)). Finally, mention must be made of the six passages where 'the Scripture' or some OT person or persons are said to speak or write of Jesus or of some aspect of his teaching or mission (1:45; 2:22; 3:10; 5:39, 45f; 20:9).[4]

Restricting ourselves now to the direct quotations, whether introduced by a formula or not, five are attributed to Jesus (1:51; 6:45; 10:34; 13:18; 15:25); six others are editorial (12:14f, 38, 39f; 19:24, 36, 37), or perhaps seven if we include 2:17, where the remembering of Scripture is performed by the disciples, but in John's presentation that includes the Beloved Disciple. One quotation is found on the lips of John the Baptist (1:23); the other two are ascribed to crowds (6:31; 12:13).

It is difficult to discern any principle of discrimination that associates certain kinds of OT texts with certain speakers. What stands out is not which party in the FG appeals to the OT, but what is accomplished in each instance. The OT citations in one way or another point to Jesus, identifying him, justifying the responses he elicits, grounding the details of his life and death in the Scriptures. When the Baptist identifies himself as the one crying in the wilderness, 'Make the way for the Lord straight!' (1:23), the purpose of the quotation is as much to remove John from competition with the messiah as it is to identify his proper role. Jesus' cleaning of the temple and his entry into Jerusalem on a donkey are messianic actions understood to be anticipated in the OT (2:17; 12:14f). If the crowds cite Scripture to associate Moses and manna, reflecting perhaps the tradition that the messiah would provide a similarly lavish supply (6:31),[5] it is so that Jesus can be presented as the one who not only fulfils such expectations but outstrips them. The FG's christology and eschatology can both be grounded in the OT (1:51). If some people are judicially hardened so that they cannot respond to Jesus, if others hate him and Judas Iscariot betrays him, it is all foreseen and predicted by Scripture (12:38–40; 13:18; 15:25). Conversely, those who respond positively to Jesus do so in fulfilment of Scripture that predicts a time when 'all your sons will be taught by Yahweh' (Isa. 54:13; John 6:45). If Jesus can appeal to Scripture in what appears to be an *ad hominem* fashion, it is only to prove that he has every right to be called the Son of God (10:34). The crowds of enthusiastic supporters waving palms praise God in scriptural terms because those terms recognise Jesus as the one who comes in the name of the Lord (12:13). The details of Jesus' death are particularly tied to OT passages (19:24, 36, 37).

Moreover, it must be recognised that the evangelist does not think of these citations as an exhaustive list of the connexions he could make between the life and death of Jesus the messiah and the Scriptures revered both by himself, as a Christian, and by the non-christian Jews he wished to confront. They are a mere sample. After all, he insists, the Scriptures testify to Jesus (5:39, 45f); and after the resurrection, nothing is more important than that the disciples come to understand these Scriptures appropriately (20:9). Jesus' life, ministry, and death/resurrection/exaltation were mapped out by God's will. Insofar as that will is made known in Scripture, so far also must there be correlation between that Scripture and Jesus. Small wonder, then, to put the matter another way, that Jesus says and does *only* what the Father gives him to say and do, and *everything* the Father gives him to say and do, thereby pleasing him completely (5:19, 30; 8:29).[6]

When we turn from the rather unified purpose of the citations within the gospel as a whole to the formulae that introduce them, we find enormous diversity:

| | |
|---|---|
| 1:23 | ἔφη |
| 2:17 | ὅτι γεγραμμένον ἐστίν |
| 6:31 | καθώς ἐστιν γεγραμμένον |
| 6:45 | ἔστιν γεγραμμένον ἐν τοῖς προφήταις |
| 10:34 | οὐκ ἔστιν γεγραμμένον ἐν τῷ νόμῳ ὑμῶν ὅτε...; |
| 12:14f | καθώς ἐστιν γεγραμμένον |
| 12:38 | ἵνα ὁ λόγος Ἡσαΐου τοῦ προφήτου <u>πληρωθῇ</u> ὃν εἶπεν |
| 12:39f | ὅτι πάλιν εἶπεν Ἡσαΐας |
| 13:18 | ἀλλ᾽ <u>ἵνα</u> ἡ γραφὴ <u>πληρωθῇ</u> |
| 15:25 | ἀλλ᾽ <u>ἵνα πληρωθῇ</u> ὁ λόγος ὁ ἐν τῷ νόμῳ αὐτῶν γεγραμμένος ὅτι |
| 19:24 | <u>ἵνα</u> ἡ γραφὴ <u>πληρωθῇ</u> [ἡ λέγουσα] |
| 19:36 | <u>ἵνα</u> ἡ γραφὴ <u>πληρωθῇ</u> |
| 19:37 | καὶ πάλιν ἑτέρα γραφὴ λέγει |

We may add to this list the four passages where formulae are used in connexion with an OT allusion, even where there is no specific quotation:

7:38   καθὼς εἶπεν ἡ γραφή
7:42   οὐχ ἡ γραφὴ εἶπεν...;
17:12  ἵνα ἡ γραφὴ πληρωθῇ
19:28  ἵνα τελειωθῇ ἡ γραφή

The sheer diversity is striking. Other NT writers often prefer a simple γέγραπται, but John never uses that expression. Freed (1965, p. 126) finds in the list nothing more than a reflection of John's stylistic penchant for slight variations. But the clustering of some form or other of ἵνα πληρωθῇ (or in one instance ἵνα τελειωθῇ) in the second half of the book has not gone unnoticed. Hanson (1983, pp. 113ff) suggests that OT texts cited with the explicit 'fulfilment' formulae were commonly held by Christians to point to Christ, whereas those without the 'fulfilment' group were discovered by John, and had not yet achieved community endorsement. To Hanson's credit, this theory is entered as conjecture; it appears very difficult to prove, and suffers from some awkwardness over what is admitted as an introductory 'formula'.[7] By contrast, Evans (1982) offers a theological explanation for the clustering of the 'fulfilment' formulae. Even the two instances after 12:38 where a fulfilment formula is *not* used are linked to a preceding fulfilment formula through the use of 'again' (πάλιν); so the clustering is well-nigh absolute. It appears as if the evangelist particularly wishes to stress the fulfilment of Scripture in connexion with the passion of Jesus and the obduracy motif with which he links it. This does not mean that earlier passages without πληροῦν must not be understood as links between events in Jesus' life and the Scriptures, as fulfilment to prophecy (see especially 1:51; 2:17; 6:45; 12:14f); it does mean that the fulfilment motif is more forcefully stressed the closer one gets to the rejection of Jesus culminating on the cross. And this in turn suggests an audience that needs to be provided with a rationale, a biblical rationale, for the substantial rejection of Jesus by his fellow Jews.

The direct quotations in the FG come from all three divisions of the Hebrew canon; but another pair of clusters can be observed. Moses is mentioned by name about a dozen times – all in the first nine chapters, and sometimes as an equivalent to 'the law' or 'the Scripture'. In these chapters, the question of Jesus's *authority* vis-à-vis 'Moses' is particularly prominent. Of other OT personalities, only Isaiah receives multiple mention: he appears three times (1:23; 12:38, 39). The first of these passages does not now concern us; the other two occur in the chapter that Smith (1976) identifies as the crucial transition between what have sometimes been called 'the book of signs' (John 1–11 or John 1–12) and 'the book of glory' (John 13–21), where the glorification of Jesus is virtually synonymous with his passion, resurrection and exaltation. Here Isaiah is introduced, not only to ground the obduracy motif in Scripture (John 12:38–41), but for a deeper reason. In a still unpublished paper, Evans (n.d.) has listed the numerous links between John 12:1–43 and Isa. 52:7–53:12, suggesting that the former is a midrash on the latter. He notes, for instance, that between Isa. 53:1 and Isa. 6:10, which are cited back to back in John 12:38–40, there is not only the thematic link of obduracy (which justifies bringing them together by the principle of גזרה שוה, 'equivalence of expression'), but shared themes of exaltation and glory (compare Isa. 6:1, 3, 5, 7, 9 with Isa. 52:12, 13, 15), themes of obvious importance to the FG (Dodd, 1953, p. 247, made somewhat similar observations). Evans then lists a dozen features in John 12 that seem to reflect tight linguistic or thematic links with Isa. 52:7–53:12; and he concludes, against some recent treatments, that John may well be trying to identify Jesus with the suffering servant of the Lord.

When we ask more narrowly what kind of hermeneutical axioms and appropriation techniques (to use the categories of Moo, 1983, pp. 5–78) John adopts when he cites the OT, the answers prove complex and the literature on each quotation legion. At the risk of oversimplification, the dominant approach is that of various forms of typology (cf. the brief summary in Goppelt, ET 1982, pp. 179–95), which is itself based on a perception of patterns of continuity across the sweep of salvation history. The Davidic typology that surfaces repeatedly in the NT may well stand behind some of the Psalm quotations in the FG (2:17; 15:25; 19:24, 28). Ps. 69 offers the lament of the righteous sufferer: how much more appropriately does it fit the messiah who is on the way to the cross. If the psalmist's suffering is related to zeal for the temple (Ps. 69:9), then opposition to Jesus is likewise opposition to one whose zeal for the temple is remarkable (John 2:17; the close connexion between zeal and death is conveyed by καταφάγεται, as Moo, 1983, pp. 233f n. 4, points out). Indeed, granted the undergirding Davidic typology, the connexion is not merely analogical: the righteous sufferer of Ps. 69 prefigures, and thus predicts, the one in whom righteous suffering would reach its apogee.

Something similar may be argued with respect to the use of Ps. 22:18 in John 19:24. The psalmist, afflicted both by physical distress and by the mockery of his opponents, apparently uses the symbolism of an execution scene, in which the executioners have the right to distribute the victim's clothes amongst themselves. It is unlikely that John creates his 'fulfilment' out of whole cloth. The seamless garment episode is found in all three synoptic gospels, so is a staple of early christian tradition. The alleged symbolic value of such a creation is debatable: the seamless garment probably does not suggest Jesus is the new high priest, since this theme is but weakly attested in the FG, and χιτών is not in any case the normal word for the high priest's robe. Still less likely is the suggestion that the seamless robe is a symbol for the seamless unity of the church (cf. Schnackenburg, 1970, III, p. 274). Moreover, if this is a creation by the evangelist, it is hard to see why he should have used χιτών and λάχομεν, instead of the psalm's ἱματισμός and ἔβαλον κλῆρον (cf. Brown, 1966–71, II, p. 920). It is sometimes argued that John misunderstands the Hebrew parallelism, and consequently relates the distribution of some of Jesus' garments to the first stich of Ps. 22:18, and the gambling for the seamless garment to the second. But as Lindars (1961, p. 91) points out, 'John must not be held ignorant of the most constant characteristic of Hebrew poetry.' Moo (1983, pp. 256–7) suggests that 'John is aware of the application of Ps. 22:18 in the crucifixion narrative' and 'has access to a tradition which mentions a seamless tunic that was gambled for. Not unnaturally, he sees in this incident a fulfilment of the other half of the psalm verse and accordingly records it.' Consequently, this is 'a case in which the text has been re-oriented by the situation.' By contrast, Hoskyns and Davey (1940, II, p. 629) point out that the psalm verse itself allows the possibility of being divided into two parts, since the LXX switches from the plural to the singular, which conceivably could be taken to indicate outer and inner clothes respectively. In any case it is not entirely clear that the appeal to Ps. 22:18 is tied to *both* the distribution of the garments *and* to the gambling: it *may* be tied only to the latter. If he had been trying to make the connexion with both incidents, John could have made the dual link more explicit by using διεμερίσαντο in 19:23, rather than ἐποίησαν τέσσαρα μέρη. However the details be resolved, there can be little doubt that John understands the event to fulfil prophecy; for although ἵνα plus the subjunctive can have ecbatic force in the FG, it is difficult to imagine anything other than the more customary telic force when the verb in the subjunctive is πληρόω. Once again, however, the undergirding hermeneutical axiom is probably Davidic typology.

This does not mean that every OT quotation is utilised in some typological fashion. On balance, it seems best to see in John 12:37–41 a fairly direct appropriation of the OT texts cited (Isa. 53:1; 6:10), coupled with the cardinal assumption of Christians that Jesus is the messiah. Detailed discussion in this brief essay is not possible; but the main lines of a plausible interpretation are as follows. If the links developed by Dodd and Evans (discussed *supra*) are valid, then the pair of Isaiah quotations are linked not only by the obduracy theme but also by the exaltation/glory theme; and Jesus is understood to be the suffering servant prophesied by Isaiah.[8] In that case, the appropriation of the OT text, so far as the evangelist is concerned, is quite direct. The second quotation, from Isa. 6:10 (John 12:40), ends with the editorial explanation, 'Isaiah said this because he saw his [i.e. Jesus'] glory and spoke about him' (12:41). In the context of Isaiah 6 (LXX), the vision Isaiah saw was focused on Yahweh of hosts, the King. Given his understanding of the pre-incarnate nature of the Logos, John makes the obvious connexion and concludes that what Isaiah really saw was Jesus Christ in his pre-incarnate glory (cf. Barrett, 1978, p. 432; Hanson, 1965, pp. 104–8).[9] In this case the appropriation of the OT text depends not only on the 'obduracy' link with the previous citation from Isaiah, but on the governing christology. If God has revealed himself to us, it is by means of Logos, his self-expression: that is what Isaiah saw. But then both OT quotations refer to Jesus Christ – one in terms of the suffering servant, and one in terms of the glory of God reported in Isaiah 6. The two themes come together, for John, in the term 'glory': Jesus' glory is supremely displayed in the cross, the path to his return to the glory he had with the Father before the world began (17:5). This, then, is why John connects the two texts from Isaiah, and concludes that Isaiah said these things (ταῦτα, probably referring to *both* quotations) because he saw Jesus' *glory*.

In short, the reasons behind the appropriation of this or that text, and in particular the reasons why the evangelist can conclude that some of these texts are *fulfilled* in the ministry and death of Jesus, can usually be discerned, provided we focus attention not only on the appropriation techniques utilised in each instance, but also on the hermeneutical and theological axioms that guide his thought.

## APPARENT QUOTATIONS FROM AND ALLUSIONS TO THE OLD TESTAMENT

It is impossible to draw a strict line between this section and the ones that precede and succeed it; its purpose, however, is to draw attention to passages where there is neither direct quotation from the OT, nor the treatment of some major OT theme, but something in between.

As we have seen, there are four places where the evangelist, using a quotation formula, alludes to the OT without actually quoting it (7:38, 42; 17:12; 19:28), and one instance in 12:34 where the crowds testify to their understanding of what the 'law' taught concerning the messiah. These have been discussed at length in commentaries and journal articles; each instance is fraught with complex questions. For instance, in 19:28, there are three principal foci for debate: (a) Should the ἵνα clause be read with what precedes ('Jesus, knowing that all things had been accomplished in order to fulfil Scripture, said "I thirst"') or with what succeeds ('Jesus, knowing that all things had been accomplished, in order to fulfil Scripture said "I thirst"')? The former permits us to see a general reference to the OT; the latter requires us to look for a text that speaks specifically of thirst. Almost certainly the latter is correct (cf. Moo, 1983, pp. 275–278). (b) What OT text is in view? In part the answer to this question is related to the first question; for only if we agree that the fulfilment clause is tied to the exclamation 'I thirst' must we specify some particular text. But agreement has not been reached on which text that might be. Some have promoted Ps. 22:15: since the psalmist's tongue is cleaving to his jaws, presumably he is thirsty. Others advocate Ps. 42:2 or 63:2 ('My soul thirsts for God'); but that means John 19:28 must be taken in a highly symbolic way not clearly warranted by the context, since Jesus' thirst is for water, not for God. The best suggestion seems to be Ps. 69:21. Not only has this psalm been used twice before in the FG (2:17; 15:25), but this particular verse, Ps. 69:21, is apparently alluded to in John 19:29–30 (ὄξος). Moreover, Psalm 69 is a staple in the synoptic accounts of the crucifixion, and includes specific reference to 'thirst'. (I am not here presupposing a specific literary relationship between John and the synoptics, but merely pointing out that the latter demonstrate that frequent appeal to this psalm was a common feature of the earliest passion traditions.) (c) Why then the verbal form τελειωθῇ in the fulfilment clause, instead of the expected πληρωθῇ? Both verbs preserve the emphasis on fulfilment, the bringing to pass of God's design announced earlier; but it is likely that the choice of the verb was a self-conscious attempt to draw attention to the cognate ἤδη πάντα τετέλεσται (19:28), and the climactic τετέλεσται two verses later (19:30). John 19:28 represents the final instance of Jesus's *active, self-conscious* fulfilment of Scripture in the FG; and thus, tied to τετέλεσται, the cry 'I thirst' represents 'not the isolated fulfilling of a particular trait in the scriptural picture, but the perfect completion of the whole prophetic image' (Westcott, 1908, II, p. 315; cf. Lindars, 1961, p. 100; Reim, 1974, p. 49). These details converge to provide a further instance of an essentially typological appropriation of the OT by the evangelist.

There are other kinds of allusion to the OT Scriptures. Hanson (1980, pp. 166–71; 1983, pp. 126–9) shows that John sometimes permits the words of Scripture to influence the shaping of his narrative, and adduces several examples of greater or lesser plausibility, in which words or concepts seem to be transferred from the OT to the FG: 1:30f, 43–51 (Gen. 28); 10:24 (Ps. 118:10); 11:41 (Ps. 118:21); 11:11–14 (Job 14:12–15); 12:1–8, 20, 28f (Hag. 2:6–9); 12:19, 32 (Job 21:32f).

More striking yet is the list of passages in which it is either presupposed or argued that the OT Scriptures speak of Christ, and therefore *ought* to be interpreted christologically (1:45; 2:22; 3:10; 5:39, 45f; 20:9). Parallels are found elsewhere in the NT (e.g. Luke 24:44ff); but they are frequent in John, and not only orientate the reader to the hermeneutical axioms that govern the evangelist's reading of the OT, but sometimes carry a stinging suggestion that Jesus' followers or would-be followers should have understood how to read the OT from his stance earlier than they did.

The point is made not only to opponents (5:39, 45f), but also to Nicodemus. He is 'the teacher of Israel' (3:10 – presumably a title) and yet, incredibly, does not know 'these things'. This orientation to the OT provides the clue to the right interpretation of what it means to be born of water and spirit (3:3, 5). To find in 'water' a reference to baptism is not only needlessly anachronistic, it is to forfeit the grounding of the reference in the OT, which 3:10 leads us to expect. Nor will it do to see in 'water' a reference to natural birth: so far as we know, 'being born of water' is not an expression John's contemporaries used in this regard. And contrary to suggestions tentatively advanced by Odeberg (1929, pp. 48ff) and Morris (1971, pp. 216), evidence that water here stands as a symbol for semen is tangential and late. Still less satisfactory is Bultmann's famous excision of ὕδατος καί (1971, pp. 138f, n. 3). The most satisfactory approach is that of Belleville (1980), who looks for collocations of 'water' and 'spirit' in the OT, examining the symbolic component of the semantic range of 'water' both in the OT and in the FG. Passages such as Ezek. 36:25-7 may be suggested as providing the background: in John 3, then, 'water' refers to the eschatological cleansing accomplished through God's Spirit, and 'spirit' to the imparting of God's nature (i.e. what is born of the Spirit is spirit). Water and spirit together define the nature of the second birth that characterises the promised new covenant; and this, Jesus tells Nicodemus in 3:10, his interlocutor should have known.

## OLD TESTAMENT THEMES AND THE REPLACEMENT MOTIF

If explicit quotations and rather subtle allusions constituted the only kind of use of the OT made by the FG, the connexions would be impressive, but scarcely overwhelming. In fact, the FG is replete with OT themes and motifs, most of which have called forth voluminous discussion. One thinks of such themes as the vine and the branches, sheep and the shepherd, the serpent in the wilderness, the lamb of God, the jewish feasts, the Sabbath, Abraham and his sons, repeated references to the law and to the Spirit, mention of the temple, christological titles grounded in the OT (however shaped by intervening tradition), and more. The precise line of connexion with the OT is sometimes difficult to determine, not because of a want of OT evidence, but because of an overabundance: does 'lamb of God' primarily relate to the paschal lamb, the horned ram of jewish apocalyptic, the lamb led to the slaughter in Isaiah 53, or to the *Akedah* (Genesis 22)? A clear consensus has not yet been reached (in addition to the commentaries, cf. Vermes, 1961, pp. 224–5; Evans, n.d.; Dodd, 1953, pp. 233ff; Bruce, 1978, pp. 147–9; Reim, 1974, pp. 178f; Moo, 1983, pp. 312–14). The line of connexion is also made difficult to discern on occasion because the evangelist is not only drawing a line from the OT but simultaneously attempting to rule out one or more of the contemporary jewish exegeses. To mention but one instance, it is fairly clear that in John 3:13–14 the evangelist is providing, among other things, a polemic against the ascents of Moses and all others who are said to have ascended into heaven (cf. Odeberg, 1929, pp. 72–89; Meeks, 1967, p. 141; Borgen, 1977).

There are many other themes. Reim and Lindars especially stress the influence of wisdom motifs on John's christology. The themes of law and spirit have received substantial treatment (e.g. Pancaro, 1975, and Johnston, 1970, respectively); other themes, such as Abraham and his sons, have still been inadequately probed (though cf. Grässer, 1985, pp. 154ff). Moreover, Barrett (1947) has demonstrated that certain testimonia in the synoptic gospels reappear in the FG not as testimonia but as integral parts of the drama – although it should be said that, conversely, John can also provide explicit quotations of the OT where there are only hints in Mark (cf. Smith, 1972, pp. 162f).

The growing number of passages being labelled 'midrash' in the FG attests profound dependence on the OT – profound not only in terms of the knowledge of the evangelist, but also of his self-conscious dependence upon the authority of those Scriptures to justify his theological presentation, since midrash, unlike the Mishnah which is apodictic, projects the idea that justification of teaching is necessary (cf. Halivni, 1986). Following the influential work of Borgen (1965) on the treatment of manna in John 6:31–58, we find, among others, the suggestion that John's Logos doctrine is informed by Isa. 55:10–11, where God's word is sent into the world and then returns to heaven (Lausberg, 1979; Dahms, 1981); the argument that John 1:14–18 is a midrash on Exodus 34 (Hanson, 1980, pp. 97–109); a case for the view that John's affirmation of Jesus' deity is based on a midrash of Psalm 45, possibly in the text form of an emerging targum (Reim, 1984); and, as we have already noted, the suggestion that John 12 is a midrash on Isa. 52:7–53:12 (Evans, n.d.).

Part of the problem inherent in these discussions is the ambiguity regarding what 'midrash' really is. To say that it is interpretative commentary of an antecedent sacred text is inadequate, if it includes material as diverse as John 1:14–18, John 6:31ff, and the theme of the deity of Jesus in the FG. Moreover, interpretative comment cast in the form of, say, a story raises the question as to whether the story has historical referents. Is the comment 'midrashic' regardless of the answer to that question? If not, by what criteria can one decide if a narrative is 'midrashic' (i.e. without its own historical referent) comment on another text, or alternatively an historical account (or a mixture of the historical and the non-historical!) determinatively shaped by the categories of an antecedent sacred text? There is little consensus on these points, and insufficient work done on them to admit much of an answer.

What is perhaps most noteworthy is not how many of the themes and institutions converge on Jesus, but how they are so presented as to make Jesus 'fulfil' them and actually *replace* them. The only jewish feast the synoptists mention is the Passover; but John mentions it ten times, and also refers to Tabernacles (7:2), Dedication (10:22), and once simply ' a feast of the Jews' (5:1). But these are presented in contexts where Jesus' activity or utterance shows where the true significance of that feast now lies. Thus in John 7, at the festival of Tabernacles, he proclaims himself to be the one who gives living water (related to the water-pouring ceremony); and in John 8, still at the same feast, he calls himself the light of the world, outstripping the symbolic lighting of the candelabra. 'Interwoven into his festal pattern is the presentation of Jesus as the true Temple, the antitype of the brazen serpent, the true manna, the true water-giving rock, the true fiery pillar, the eschatological Moses, the new Torah, and the true Paschal Sacrifice' (Longenecker, 1975, pp. 153-4).

The replacement motif can coalesce with other approaches to the OT. Thus when Jesus proclaims himself the good shepherd (John 10), the reader cannot forget that in the OT Yahweh (Ezck. 34:11) or the messiah (Ezek. 34:23) is the shepherd who cares for his flock: Jesus identifies his ministry with theirs, and the appropriation of Ezekiel 34 is fairly direct. But the entailment, for the church, is that it is the new messianic community that 'fulfils' Israel's role in the Ezekiel passage; and that connexion is unavoidably typological, and bound up with replacement of the type. The same sort of connexion is made in John 15. The vine imagery cannot fail to recall Isa. 5:1ff; Jer. 2:21; Ps. 80:8-16; but now the true vine is not Israel, but Jesus himself, and the branches that are 'in' him. Unlike the vine that did not bear satisfactory fruit (Isaiah 5), Jesus, the true vine, produces lasting fruit to God's glory (15:8) through the 'branches' that remain in him (15:5, 16).

Doubtless the most studied replacement motif is that of Moses (cf. Glasson, 1963; Meeks, 1967; Haacker, 1972; Saito, 1977, pp. 109-21); and this is related to Jesus as the teacher of *law* (Pancaro, 1975; cf. Böcher, 1965, pp. 162f). But there are many others. Davies (1974, pp. 288ff) has creatively drawn attention to the way Jesus in the FG replaces various forms of *holy space*. This includes not only obvious references such as the temple (Jesus speaks of the temple of his body, 2:21) and the pool of Siloam (which, John 9:7 carefully points out, means 'Sent' – but Jesus is the Sent One *par excellence*), but also numerous others, some of them subtly presented. If the angels of 1:51 ascend and descend on the Son of Man, this does not make the Son of Man equivalent in role to Jacob's ladder, but to Bethel, the house of God. Jewish and samaritan holy places alike are transcended in the one who bequeaths his Spirit and insists that those who worship the Father do so in spirit and truth (4:21ff).

Thus again and again the typologies the evangelist develops do not *simply* interpret the OT, or *simply* utilise the categories of the OT to explain Jesus and his gospel, but become as well the vehicles by which Jesus and his gospel effectively *replace* those institutions, events and themes that have anticipated

## D. A. CARSON

him (cf. Goppelt, ET 1982, pp. 185ff). If they anticipate him, they point to him, prophesy of him; and he fulfils them and thus replaces them. This does not mean, for the evangelist, that they are discarded so much as fulfilled: they find their true significance and real continuity in him who is the true vine, the true light, the true temple, the one of whom Moses wrote.

In this light, the difficult expression in 1:16, χάριν ἀντὶ χάριτος, should probably be understood as 'grace instead of grace' or 'grace in exchange for grace': that is, the grace of God in the person and work of Jesus replaces the grace of God that was manifest in the earlier revelation. Barrett (1978, p. 168) objects that 'the point of the passage is that grace did not come by Moses; nor is the grace of God available in two grades'. But neither objection is weighty. John forcefully insists that salvation is from the Jews (4:22). He does not treat the OT with scorn or rejection; he views it with reverence, treating it as the 'given' of revelation that anticipates the new revelation occurring in Jesus. God's grace may not come in two grades; but it may come in degrees, the gracious revelation that anticipates what is yet to come, and the gracious revelation that fulfils the anticipation, the very epitome of grace and truth. Thus 1:17 *explains* 1:16 (ὅτι): from the fulness of the Logos's grace we have received one grace in substitution for, in exchange for (the most natural meaning of the preposition), another grace; *for* the law was through Moses, grace and truth through Jesus Christ.[10]

### THE JOHANNINE EPISTLES

The most striking feature relevant to our subject in these epistles is the absence not only of OT quotations but even of many unambiguous allusions to the OT. The only OT person named is Cain (1 John 3:12). Partly because of this mention of Cain, some have seen in δίκαιος (1 John 2:1) a reference to Abel; but the connexion is speculative, since this adjective is commonly applied to the messiah in jewish literature. The suggestion of Smith (1972, p. 58) to the effect that these epistles, and perhaps the farewell discourse as well, represent the progressive attenuation of the Johannine church's entanglement in a jewish matrix, is not very convincing. After all (as Smith himself points out), other NT writings normally considered late (e.g. Hebrews, Revelation), not to mention a non-canonical work like 1 Clement, are steeped in OT quotations and allusions; so if the alleged attenuation has taken place, it is certainly not a function of mere passage of time from the resurrection. More important, the most likely reason for the dramatic reduction of OT quotations and allusions lies elsewhere. If we adopt the majority view that holds that the epistles were written after the FG, and join with those who argue that the epistles are sparked off by growing disputes, grounded in incipient Gnosticism, concerning the correct interpretation of the FG (not to mention also the problem of travelling preachers – cf. discussion in Schnackenburg, 1968; Brown, 1982; Smalley, 1984), the solution is at hand. These circumstances demanded many allusions to the FG (which we find), not to the OT. The disputes represented by the epistles have to do with the church's relation with incipient Gnosticism, not with the OT. Although some gnostics appealed to the OT, John's quarrel with his opponents has less to do with their treatment of the OT than with their treatment of the FG.

## CONCLUDING REFLECTIONS

I shall attempt to apply these findings to a number of related issues, allowing scope at points for a little more speculation.

1. The appropriation techniques in John may be similar to those found in contemporary Judaism, but the underlying hermeneutical axioms are distinctively Christian. These relate not only to christology and the way the OT is read as a prefigurement of Jesus Christ, but even to the eschatological stance of the evangelist. NT writings, not least the FG, have often been compared with the DSS in this regard. Thus Black (1986, p. 4) writes: 'Like the primitive church, the Qumrân Essenes believed they were living in the End-Time, so that many pesharim or pesherised texts are apocalyptic and eschatological.' But the understanding of 'End-Time' in the two corpora is quite different. As Fitzmyer (1960–1, p. 331) noted twenty-five years ago, the Qumran sectarians believed they were in the end times such that they emphasised the *coming fulfilment of the OT Scriptures*. The NT writers, especially John, hold they are in the end times such that they emphasise *the fulfilment of the OT Scriptures that has already taken place* – even if their perception of the tension between the 'already' and the 'not yet' also leaves them anticipating the future. If 1 John 2:18 concludes that it is the last hour, it is because many antichrists *have come* and are opposing the Christ who *has already* come. That eschatological stance becomes a hermeneutical axiom unique to Christianity; but it is especially strong in the FG, where realised or inaugurated eschatology predominates.

2. The FG, as we have seen, not only interprets the OT christologically, but presents such interpretation as a moral obligation (e.g. 5:39f, 45f); yet at the same time it acknowledges in the strongest terms that even the disciples came to a correct understanding on many points of the Scriptures only after the resurrection (e.g. 2:22; 20:8f; cf. Carson, 1982). The tension between these perspectives has three results: (a) It confirms that even the disciples who come to a correct understanding *after* the resurrection were not party to a corpus of esoteric information *before* the resurrection; nor were they gifted

with peculiar intelligence or insight. If they were chosen, they were chosen out of the world. (b) It focuses attention on Christ 'full of grace and truth'; for while the Scriptures testify to him, it transpires that those same Scriptures cannot properly be understood apart from him. It is thus a way of shifting the focus of primary revelation from the text to the person. (c) Misunderstandings in the FG whose resolution turns on the resurrection thus *cannot* be misunderstandings in John's day. For instance, the identification of Jesus' body as the real temple (John 2:19ff) and the correlative belief in the Scripture (2:22) may not be *accepted* by jewish opponents in John's day; but if they are in dialogue with the Johannine community at all, these matters will not be *misunderstood*. This opens up a fruitful avenue for approaching difficult questions of historicity in the FG (Carson, 1982).

3. The cumulative evidence for the importance of the OT to the FG supports the view, now common enough, that the latter was written in some sort of dialogue with the synagogue. But was it written to support the church in its interaction with Judaism, or as a direct attempt at evangelism? Can John's use of the OT help us answer that question? The dominant voices of contemporary scholarship on John hold that the evangelist is strengthening the church. With some hesitation I am attracted to the theory of van Unnik and Robinson that the FG is designed primarily to evangelise diaspora Jews; and elsewhere I have argued that syntactically 20:31 must be rendered '...in order that you may believe that the Christ is Jesus', not 'that Jesus is the Christ' (Carson, forthcoming), thereby forcing us to conclude that the underlying question John is answering is not, 'Who is Jesus?' but 'Who is the Christ?' The latter question Christians would not ask: they already knew the answer. But it is precisely the question that Christians would seek to answer in their evangelism of Jews. Barrett (1975) has strongly objected to the view that the FG is a missionary tract for the Judaism of the diaspora, largely on the ground that there are not only jewish but some hellenistic and gnostic overtones in this book as well. But that is just the point: diaspora Judaism was nothing if not diverse and frequently syncretistic. The presence of other overtones is not surprising; and even the translation of Semitic terms (e.g. 1:41f) reminds us that the Judaism with which we are dealing is not Palestinian. Moreover, this general line of thought can be strengthened if we suppose that John is not limiting himself to Jews, but is also deeply interested in the evangelism of proselytes and God-fearers, who would also be likely to have some knowledge of the OT Scriptures of which Christians claimed to be providing the true interpretation. Certainly the use of the OT in the FG is congruent with either a missionary and evangelistic *Sitz im Leben*, or with one more narrowly aimed at providing Christians with apologetic materials; but it is hard to see how it decisively favours either position.

4. Since Dodd (1952), scholars have commonly argued that the kerygma came first, and the exegesis of the OT within the church came later. Lindars (1961) went further, and argued that the Christians' choice of texts and their handling of them were decisively shaped by their apologetic concerns, i.e. by the experiences they faced in the promulgation of the kerygma. Wilcox (1979) and Black (1986) have argued in response that the OT and the interpretative traditions regarding it were the matrix out of which the kerygma sprang. The church began with the exegetical traditions of Judaism regarding the messiah and end time events, and argued that these traditions had found their fulfilment in Jesus of Nazareth. But the evidence sketched in throughout this chapter suggests we are not shut up to a simple 'either/or'. On the one hand, the evangelist's frank confession that even the disciples did not understand the Scriptures until after the resurrection demonstrates that christian theology was not simply manufactured out of pieces of the OT. The decisive impact of Jesus' ministry, death and resurrection/exaltation triggered the reflection that made sense of the OT under the revised hermeneutical axioms that nascent Christianity generated. In that sense, Dodd is right: the kerygma came first. And Lindars is right: doubtless apologetic concerns in the articulation of the kerygma triggered further exegetical reflection on the OT. But on the other hand, the same evidence insists there were teachings of Jesus regarding the OT that were there to misunderstand. Inevitably, therefore, although the cross and exaltation proved to be the decisive turning point in the disciples' understanding, the Scriptures served to shed light on a messiah who could be both king of Israel and lamb of God, every bit as much as the cross and exaltation provided a fresh perspective from which to re-think the Scriptures. Thus 'the scriptures to a large extent guided the process of thought, and created many of the theological issues which were taken up in the New Testament' (Borgen, 1976–7, p. 70). If Moo (1983, esp. pp. 392ff; cf. also France, 1971) is right in arguing that the actual history and teaching of Jesus shaped the church's choice and handling of OT texts, in particular the passion texts, then as soon 'as the early Christians began to think and preach about the significance of Jesus' death, they must have utilised categories provided by the OT-sacrifices, the atoning death of the Servant, the innocent sufferer' (Moo, p. 394). After all, the earliest Christians were Jews before they were Christians: they needed *biblical* categories to make sense of the shattering event of the cross. Fundamental reflection on the OT was therefore necessarily generated *within* the church before it was further stimulated by apologetic needs. John's gospel, because of the interplay between its use of the OT and its handling of the theme of misunderstanding, provides particularly good access to these points.

# D. A. CARSON

## NOTES

1 The idea has been taken up more recently by Reim (1974), who argues that except for the three quotations from Ps. 69 (John 2:17; 15:25; 19:28[?]) the evangelist found all of his OT quotations in various written sources. This view depends on a complex source-critical theory that has failed to win wide approval.

2 Cf. the detailed discussion of textual matters in Freed (1965), who shows that when John agrees exactly with an OT text it is always with the LXX (four occurrences only). In no place does John agree with the Hebrew against the LXX, with the possible exception of 19:37 [Zech. 12:10, some MSS only]. In the other instances, certainty regarding textual affinity is difficult to achieve. Other essays have suggested, however, that when theological reasons can be advanced for this or that divergence in John's quotation, the divergence is from the LXX.

3 Freed (1965) and others argue that ἡ γραφή in 7:42 and 17:12 refers not to the OT but to the synoptic tradition in the former case and to Jesus' words (John 6:70f) in the latter. But connexions with the OT are more plausible in both cases: cf. Bernard (1928) *in loc.*; Hanson (1983), pp. 115f.

4 One might add 12:34. I am not here including passages in John that draw attention to some explicit OT *event* or *theme* (e.g. 3:14; 6:32; 7:22f), which are discussed elsewhere in this chapter. For the sake of completeness, I should note the two instances where a formula introduces a quotation *not* from the OT but apparently from an antecedent teaching of Jesus (18:9 [6:37?]; 18:38 [3:14? 8:28?]).

5 The manna story is found in Exodus 16, but references to this 'manna' are scattered through the OT (Num. 11:6; Deut. 8:3; Josh. 5:12; Neh. 9:20; Ps. 77:24). In three of these passages (viz. Deut. 8:3; Neh. 9:20; Ps. 77:24), even though the reference is to the Exodus 16 story, 'manna' has become something of a symbol for the Lord's blessing. In Judaism of the NT period, this symbolism is enriched. Philo repeatedly allegorises the manna account; in *Leg. All.* iii. 169–76 the food of the soul is God's word (λόγος θεοῦ). In 2 Baruch, roughly contemporary with the FG, we are told that at the end of the age the 'treasury of manna' will again descend from on high, and those who come to the consummation of time will eat it in those years (29:8). Later rabbinic tradition spells out the connexion more clearly: *Mekilta* Exod. 16:25 (וַיֹּסַע, §5) tells us: 'You shall not find it [the manna] in this age, but you shall find it in the age to come'. Cf. also *Ecclesiastes R.* 1:28. But whether these later sources reflect jewish tradition in the first century it is impossible to say with certainty.

6 For full discussion of this point, cf. Carson (1981), pp. 146ff.

7 Under the rubric 'Scripture is explicitly cited, but without any introductory formula', Hanson (1983, pp. 117–21) includes six examples, viz. 2:17; 3:14; 6:31, 45; 7:37f; 10:34–6. But although John 3:14 includes no formula, neither is it a citation; it merely makes reference to Num. 21:8f. John 7:38, a problem passage, I have included in the list of places where John 'quotes' the OT, using a quotation formula, without it being very certain what passage or passages he has in mind. All of the other four references listed by Hanson are introduced by one formula or another, but none using πληροῦν. His category seems misnamed.

8 The Isaiah connexions are strengthened if we accept the proposal of McNeil (1977), who argues that when the Jews claim they have heard that the law insists the messiah will live forever (12:34) they are alluding to a targumic rendering of Isa. 9:5, in which the child born to the house of David is not only called 'wonderful counsellor, mighty God' but also 'he who lives forever, the anointed one' (מְשִׁיחָא, the messiah). The importance of Isaiah to the FG was stressed by Young (1955) thirty years ago. The links

between the servant songs and John are well developed by Moo (1983), esp. pp. 79ff.

9 It is possible that John was thinking of some such rendering of Isa. 6:5 as that found in the targum: Isaiah sees not 'the King, the Lord of hosts' but 'the glory of the *shekinah* of the King of the ages' (יקר שכינת מלך עלמיא). There would then be a greater *verbal* tie with John 1:14, 'we have seen his *glory*'; but there would be no difference in the *referent*, which must still be the pre-incarnate Logos.

10 The absence of any connecting conjunction between the two clauses of v. 17 is probably to be explained by the explanatory value of the verse for v. 16: the realities behind the two clauses are neither merely additive nor adversative.

# BIBLIOGRAPHY

S. Amsler *L'Ancien Testament dans l'église* (Paris, 1960).

G. Bampfylde 'John xix. 28: A Case for a Different Translation', *NovT* 11 (1969), 247–60.

J. Barr *Old and New in Interpretation* (London, 1966).

C. K. Barrett 'The Old Testament in the Fourth Gospel', *JTS* 48 (1947), 155–69.

*The Gospel of John and Judaism* (London, 1975).

*The Gospel According to St John*, 2nd ed. (London, 1978).

L. Belleville '"Born of Water and Spirit": John 3:5', *Trinity Journal* 1 (1980), 125–41.

J. H. Bernard *A Critical and Exegetical Commentary on the Gospel according to St John* (Edinburgh, 1928).

M. Black 'The Theological Appropriation of the Old Testament by the New Testament', *SJTh* 39 (1986), 1–17.

O. Böcher *Der johanneischee Dualismus im Zusammenhang des nachbiblischen Judentums* (Gütersloh, 1965).

P. Borgen *Bread from Heaven: An Exegetical Study of the Concept of Manna in the Gospel of John and the Writings of Philo*, SNT 10 (Leiden, 1965).

'The Place of the Old Testament in the Formation of New Testament Theology: Prolegomena and Response', *NTS* 23 (1976–7), 59–75.

'Some Jewish Exegetical Traditions as Background for Son of Man Sayings in John's Gospel (Jn 3, 13–14 and context)', in M. de Jonge (ed.), *L'Evangile de Jean: Sources, rédaction, théologie*, BEThL 44 (Gembloux, 1977).

F.-M. Braun *Jean le théologien* vol. 2 *Les grandes traditions d'Israël et l'accord des écritures selon le quatrième évangile* (Paris, 1964).

E. Brown *The Gospel According to John*, AB, 2 vols. (London, 1966–71).

*The Epistles of John*, AB (New York, 1982).

F. F. Bruce *The Time Is Fulfilled* (Exeter, 1978).

R. Bultmann *Das Evangelium des Johannes* (Göttingen, 1941); ET *The Gospel of John: A Commentary*, tr. G. R. Beasley-Murray (Oxford, 1971).

D. A. Carson *Divine Sovereignty and Human Responsibility: Biblical Themes in Tension* (London, 1981).

'Understanding Misunderstandings in the Fourth Gospel', *TynB* 33 (1982), 59–91.

'The Purpose of the Fourth Gospel: John 20:31 Reconsidered', *JBL* (forthcoming).

J. V. Dahms 'Isaiah 55:11 and the Gospel of John', *EQ* 53 (1981), 78–88.

W. D. Davies *The Gospel and the Land* (Berkeley, 1974).

C. H. Dodd *According to the Scriptures: The Substructure of New Testament Theology* (London, 1952).

*The Interpretation of the Fourth Gospel* (Cambridge, 1953).

C. A. Evans 'On the Quotation Formulas in the Fourth Gospel', *BZ* 26 (1982), 79–83.

'Obduracy and the Lord's Servant: Some Observations on the Use of the Old Testament in the Fourth Gospel' (not yet published).

A. Faure 'Die alttestamentlichen Zitate im 4. Evangelium und die Quellenscheidungshypothese', *ZNW* 21 (1922), 99–121.

J. A. Fitzmyer 'The Use of Explicit Old Testament Quotations in Qumran Literature and in the New Testament', *NTS* 7 (1960–61), 297–333.

R. T. France *Jesus and the Old Testament: His Application of Old Testament Passages to Himself and His Mission* (London, 1971).

E. D. Freed *Old Testament Quotations in the Gospel of John*, SNT 11 (Leiden, 1965).

T. F. Glasson *Moses in the Fourth Gospel* (London, 1963).

L. Goppelt *Typos: Die typologische Deutung des Alten Testaments im Neuen* (Gütersloh, 1939); ET *Typos: The Typological Interpretation of the Old Testament in the New*, tr. Donald H. Madvig (Grand Rapids, 1982).

E. Grässer *Der Alte Bund im Neuen: Exegetische Studien zur Israelfrage im Neuen Testament*, WUNT 35 (Tübingen, 1985).

K. Haacker *Die Stiftung des Heils: Untersuchungen zur Struktur der johanneischen Theologie*, Arbeiten zur Theologie 47 (Stuttgart, 1972).

D. N. Halivni *Midrash, Mishnah, and Gemara: The Jewish Predilection for Justified Law* (Cambridge, MA, 1986).

A. T. Hanson *Jesus Christ in the Old Testament* (London, 1965).

*The New Testament Use of Scripture* (London, 1980).

*The Living Utterances of God* (London, 1983).

E. C. Hoskyns and F. N. Davey *The Fourth Gospel* (London, 1940).

G. Johnston *The Spirit-Paraclete in the Gospel of John*, SNTSMS 12 (Cambridge, 1970).

John and the Johannine Epistles

H. Lausberg 'Jesaja 55, 10–11 im Evangelium nach Johannes', in *Minuscula Philologia*, Nachrichten der Akademie der Wissenschaften im Göttingen 7 (Göttingen, 1979), pp. 131–44.

B. Lindars *New Testament Apologetic* (London, 1961).

*The Gospel of John*, NCB (London, 1972).

R. N. Longenecker *Biblical Exegesis in the Apostolic Period* (Grand Rapids, 1975).

B. McNeil 'The Quotation at John xii 34', *NovT* 19 (1977), 22–33.

W. A. Meeks *The Prophet-King: Moses Traditions and the Johannine Christology* (Leiden, 1967).

M. J. J. Menken 'The Quotation from Is 40.3 in Jn 1.23', *Bib* 66 (1985), 190–205.

D. J. Moo *The Old Testament in the Gospel Passion Narratives* (Sheffield, 1983).

L. Morris *The Gospel according to John* (Grand Rapids, 1971).

H. Odeberg *The Fourth Gospel* (Uppsala, 1929).

S. Pancaro *The Law in the Fourth Gospel*, SNT 42 (Leiden, 1975).

G. Reim 'Jesus as God in the Fourth Gospel: The Old Testament Background', *NTS* 30 (1984), 158–60.

*Studien zum alttestamentlichen Hintergrund des Johannesevangeliums* (Cambridge, 1974).

T. Saito *Die Mosevorstellungen im Neuen Testament*, Europäische Hochschulschriften XXIII.100 (Bern, 1977).

E. P. Sanders *Jesus and Judaism* (London, 1985).

R. Schnackenburg *The Gospel according to St John*, English translation of HTKNT, 3 vols. (London, 1968 [vol. 1]; New York, 1982 [vols. 2–3]).

*Die Johannesbriefe*, HTKNT XIII.3, 4th ed. (Freiburg, 1970).

S. S. Smalley *1, 2, 3 John*, WBC (Waco, 1984).

F. Smend 'Die Behandlung alttestamentlicher Zitate als Ausgangspunkt der Quellenscheidung im 4. Evangelium', *ZNW* 24 (1925), 147–150.

D. Moody Smith, Jr. 'The Use of the Old Testament in the New', in James M. Efird (ed.), *The Use of the Old Testament in the New and Other Essays: Studies in Honor of William Franklin Stinespring* (Durham, NC, 1972), 3–65.

'The Setting and Shape of a Johannine Narrative Source', *JBL* 95 (1976), pp. 231–41.

A. C. Sundberg, Jr. 'On Testimonies', *NovT* 3 (1959), 268–81.

G. Vermes *Scripture and Tradition in Judaism: Haggadic Studies*, Studia Post-Biblica 4 (Leiden, 1961).

B. F. Westcott *The Gospel According to St John*, 2 vols. (London, 1908).

M. Wilcox 'On Investigating the use of the Old Testament in the New Testament', in E. Best and R. McL. Wilson (eds.), *Text and Interpretation: Studies in the New Testament presented to Matthew Black* (Cambridge, 1979), pp. 231–50.

F. W. Young 'A Study of the Relation of Isaiah to the Fourth Gospel', *ZNW* 46 (1955), 215–33.

# 16 · The Pauline literature

D. MOODY SMITH

### PRELIMINARY CONSIDERATIONS

THE question of the use of the Old Testament in the Pauline literature is broader than that of Paul's use of the Old Testament, for when we inquire about the Pauline literature we have all thirteen letters of the traditional Pauline corpus (Hebrews excepted) in view. As is well known, only seven of these are uncontested in modern criticism (Romans, 1 and 2 Corinthians, Galatians, Philippians, 1 Thessalonians, and Philemon). The significance of the distinction between the Pauline literature and Paul himself is, however, considerably lessened by the fact that the explicit Old Testament quotations are not spread evenly through the Pauline corpus, but appear mainly in the *Hauptbriefe*, whose authenticity no one questions. Such quotations are missing from Philippians, Colossians, 1 and 2 Thessalonians, Titus and Philemon. Explicit quotations are, however, found in Ephesians and 1 and 2 Timothy. For purposes of convenience, I shall speak of Paul's use of the OT when referring to the entire Pauline corpus, but in most cases it will be clear I am referring to Paul himself.

Our attention will be directed primarily to Paul's explicit quotation of the OT, and hence largely to Romans, the Corinthian letters, and Galatians. Before proceeding further, we must give attention, however briefly, to two matters of definition: (1) What is meant by explicit quotation? (2) What OT are we talking about?

(1) Explicit quotations in Paul are almost always easily identified. Rarely do we find an OT quotation which is not introduced by an introductory formula or some sign that clearly identifies it as such. Unlike the book of Revelation, which reflects the language and phraseology of the OT without explicit citation, Paul characteristically signals his use of Scripture. The underlying reason for this difference is not far to seek. The book of Revelation purports to be exactly what the name implies, revelation from God; whereas, while Paul vests his letters with his own apostolic authority, by citing Scripture he appeals to a higher authority, a word that is divine revelation in a sense that he does not take his own words to be. We shall return to Paul's manner of citing the OT as we consider his understanding of its meaning and authority.

265

Despite Paul's practice of citing Scripture explicitly, it is nevertheless the case that (as Hays has argued) his language sometimes significantly echoes that of the OT. (See the table of OT allusions and parallels in Ellis, 1957, pp. 153–4, and, of course, the marginalia of NA[26].) A good specimen illustrating the fact that the line between allusion and explicit quotation is not hard and fast is Rom. 10:6–8, where much of the language of Deut. 9:4 (or 8:17) and 30:12–14 is used verbatim. Yet Paul seems to exercise great freedom as well, to delete whole phrases, to change words, and indeed to change the subject. Whereas Deut. 30:12–14 is spoken about the commandment (ἐντολή, i.e., the law), Rom. 10:6–8 has to do with the righteousness of faith made available through Christ. (Interestingly enough we find in Bar. 3:29–30 another paralleling of Deut. 30:12–14, in this case applied to wisdom.) The switch from Law to Christ is certainly surprising, but not capricious or arbitrary, as Cranfield (1975, p. 524f) has rightly pointed out. That Paul should present Christ as torah, or its replacement, is in itself exceedingly significant. Paul understands Christ as torah in the general sense of God's revelation of his righteousness, whether or not a more specific, Jewish expectation lies behind his statements (Davies, 1952). Although Rom. 10:6–8 is usually reckoned as an instance in which Paul is citing Scripture, and Paul was no doubt conscious of his use of the language of Deuteronomy, it nicely illustrates how explicit use of Scripture can shade over into the appropriation of the revelatory language of Scripture to describe God's new revelation. Probably Paul's choice of a unique introductory formula ('the righteousness of faith says') indicates his awareness that he is departing from his normal use of Scripture.

(2) As to the nature and definition of the OT Paul cites, several points require making at the outset. Obviously Paul knows our OT only as Scripture (γραφή, usually singular), for there is no *Old* Testament apart from a *New*. Whatever he may have meant by παλαιὰ διαθήκη in 2 Cor. 3:14, it was not the OT as a collection of writings in contrast to the new (3:6). Rather Paul is speaking of an old covenant in contrast to the new. Nevertheless, it is easy to see how and why this text has been construed anachronistically, inasmuch as Paul speaks of *reading* the old covenant and in the immediate context contrasts letter with spirit (3:6–8). Moreover, when Paul cites Scripture he is clearly referring to a corpus of sacred literature closely resembling, if not identical with, the Hebrew Bible. Perhaps significantly, he does not cite as Scripture apocryphal or pseudepigraphical books. In the rare instance in which Paul's citation is not clearly identifiable from our OT (e.g., 1 Cor. 2:9), its source remains unknown or obscure. Sundberg's case (1964) against the existence in the first century of an Alexandrian jewish canon more or less identifiable with the Septuagint known from the great christian codices of the fourth century (i.e., a canon including the apocryphal or deutero-canonical books) seems to

be confirmed by Paul. Although Sundberg himself believed the boundary of the canon had not been firmly or finally drawn in Paul's day, in his more recent study, Beckwith (1985) finds otherwise. His contention that the lines of the Hebrew canon had already been drawn before the beginning of the christian era is at least not contradicted, and to all appearances is confirmed, by the evidence of Paul and the other NT writers.

Modern investigation of Paul's use of the OT perhaps begins with Kautzsch (1869). In 1884 Toy published *Quotations in the New Testament*, displaying Greek and Hebrew parallels to all the appropriate NT quotations; and in 1903 Dittmar published a more elaborate apparatus showing septuagintal and masoretic parallels to allusions and echoes, as well as obvious OT quotations. In this century the chief monographs are by Michel (1929), Bonsirven (1939), and Ellis (1957; cf. also Ellis, 1978). Longenecker (1975, pp. 104–32) presents a succinct and useful treatment of the subject (cf. Smith, 1972). Several doctoral dissertations on Paul and the OT have apparently remained unpublished. The existence of those of Boney (1956), Ulonska (1964), and most recently Aageson (1983) is known to me.[1] Harnack (1928) and Vielhauer (1969) have devoted significant essays to the subject; both regard Paul's use of the OT as something less than germinal or central to the interests and substance of his thought. On the other side one finds in the work of Hanson (especially 1974; cf. also Hanson, 1980, pp. 21–96; and 1983, pp. 44–62), Luz (1968), and Aageson (1983) a vigorous insistence that Paul's understanding and use of the OT is ingredient to his theology. Via makes a similar point from a structuralist perspective (1974). From the standpoint of the OT and OT theology, von Rad (1965, pp. 319–409) offers proposals and reflections which are still germane. Goppelt's treatment (1982, pp. 50–62) of Paul's use of the OT is an admirably succinct statement of the main topics and issues regarding the significance of the OT for Paul's theology.

## THE EXPLICIT QUOTATIONS, THEIR ORIGIN AND DISTRIBUTION

In order to provide a basis for reference and discussion, a table of Paul's OT quotations based on a comparison of those found in Ellis (1957, pp. 150–2) and Longenecker (1975, pp. 108–11), as well as the italicised material in NA[26] (1979) is set out below. None of the half-dozen or more putative quotations italicised in NA[26] but not listed by Ellis and Longenecker (marked*) has an introductory formula with one possible exception, 1 Cor. 9:10, which may not be intended as a quotation at all, depending on whether one construes the ὅτι as causative or recitative. In the latter case its source is obscure. While these quotations by no means exhaust Paul's use of the OT, any consideration of the subject must begin with them.

## Table A

Key to Agreements

LXX/MT = agrees with Septuagint which apparently agrees with underlying Hebrew (masoretic text).

LXX = agrees with Septuagint only.

MT = agrees with masoretic text only.

N = agrees with neither Septuagint nor masoretic text.

N (LXX) = agrees exactly with neither, but is close to Septuagint.

| NT | OT | Introductory Formula | Agreement with |
|---|---|---|---|
| Romans | | | |
| 1:17 | Hab. 2:4 | 'as it is written' | N (LXX) |
| 2:24ᵃ | Isa. 52:5 | 'as it is written' | N (LXX) |
| 3:4 | Ps. 51:4 (MT = 51:6; LXX = 50:6) | 'as it is written' | N (LXX) |
| 3:10–12 | Eccl. 7:20 Ps. 14:1–3 (LXX = 13:1–3) | 'as it is written' | N |
| 3:13a | Ps. 5:9 (MT&LXX = 5:10) | | LXX/MT |
| 3:13b | Ps. 140:3 (MT = 140:4; LXX = 139:4) | | LXX/MT |
| 3:14 | Ps. 10:7 (LXX = 9:28) | | N |
| 3:15–17 | Isa. 59:7–8 | | N |
| 3:18 | Ps. 36:1 (MT = 36:2; LXX = 35:2) | | N (LXX) |
| 4:3(9, 22) | Gen. 15:6 | 'What does the Scripture say?' | LXX |
| 4:7–8 | Ps. 32:1–2 (LXX = 31:1–2) | 'as David also says' | LXX |
| 4:17 | Gen. 17:5 | 'as it is written' | LXX/MT |
| 4:18 | Gen. 15:5 | 'according to that which was said' | LXX/MT |
| 7:7 | Exod. 20:17 (Deut. 5:21) | 'the law said' | LXX/MT |
| 8:36 | Ps. 44:22 (MT = 44:23; LXX = 43:23) | 'as it is written' | LXX/MT |
| 9:7 | Gen. 21:12 | 'but' | LXX/MT |
| 9:9 | Gen. 18:10, 14 | 'this is the word of promise' | N |
| 9:12 | Gen. 25:23 | 'it was said to her' | LXX/MT |
| 9:13 | Mal. 1:2–3 | 'as it is written' | N (LXX) |
| 9:15 | Exod. 33:19 | 'to Moses he said' | LXX/MT |
| 9:17 | Exod. 9:16 | 'the Scripture said to Pharoah' | N |

## Table A (cont.)

| NT | OT | Introductory Formula | Agreement with |
|----|----|----|----|
| 9:25 | Hos. 2:23 (MT = 2:25) | 'as he [God] said also in Hosea' | N |
| 9:26 | Hos. 1:10 (MT = 2:1) | | N |
| 9:27–28 | Isa. 10:22–23 | 'Isaiah cried out concerning Israel' | N |
| 9:29 | Isa. 1:9 | 'as Isaiah said before' | LXX |
| 9:33 | Isa. 28:16; 8:14 | 'as it is written' | N |
| 10:5 | Lev. 18:5 | 'Moses wrote' | N (LXX) |
| 10:6–8 | Deut. 30:12–14 | 'the righteousness by faith speaks in this manner' | N |
| 10:11 | Isa. 28:16 | 'the Scripture says' | N |
| 10:13 | Joel 2:32 (MT&LXX = 3:5) | 'for' | LXX/MT |
| 10:15 | Isa. 52:7 | 'as it is written' | N |
| 10:16 | Isa. 53:1 | 'Isaiah says' | LXX |
| 10:18 | Ps. 19:4 (MT = 19:5; LXX = 18:5) | 'yes indeed' | LXX |
| 10:19 | Deut. 32:21 | 'Moses says' | N (LXX) |
| 10:20 | Isa. 65:1 | 'Isaiah is so bold as to say' | N (LXX) |
| 10:21 | Isa. 65:2 | 'but to Israel he says' | LXX |
| *11:2 | 1 Sam. 12:22 | | N |
| 11:3 | 1 Kings 19:14 | 'the scripture says of Elijah' | N |
| 11:4 | 1 Kings 19:18 | 'What was the divine response to him?' | N |
| 11:8 | Isa. 29:10; Deut. 29:4 (MT = 29:3) | 'as it is written' | N |
| 11:9–10 | Ps. 69:22–23 (MT = 69:23–24; (LXX = 68:23–24) | 'David says' | N |
| 11:26–27$^b$ | Is. 59:20–21; 27:9 | 'as it is written' | N (LXX) |
| 11:34 | Isa. 40:13 | 'for' | N (LXX) |
| 11:35 | Job 41:11 (MT&LXX = 41:3) | | MT |
| 12:19 | Deut. 32:35 | 'as it is written... says the Lord' | N |

*Table A* (*cont.*)

| NT | OT | Introductory Formula | Agreement with |
|---|---|---|---|
| 12:20 | Prov. 25:21–22 | | LXX |
| 13:9 | Exod. 20:13–17; Deut. 5:17–21 | 'for the [commandments]' | LXX/MT |
| 13:9 | Lev. 19:18 | 'and if there is any other commandment, it is summed up in this word' | LXX/MT |
| 14:11 | Isa. 49:13; 45:23 | 'it is written' | N (LXX) |
| 15:3 | Ps. 69:9 (MT = 69:10; LXX = 68:10 | 'as it is written' | LXX/MT |
| 15:9 | Ps. 18:49 (MT = 18:50; LXX = 17:50) | 'as it is written' | N (LXX) |
| 15:10*ᶜ* | Deut. 32:43 | 'again he says' | LXX |
| 15:11 | Ps. 117:1 (LXX = 116:1) | 'and again' | N (LXX) |
| 15:12*ᶜ* | Isa. 11:10 | 'and again Isaiah says' | LXX |
| 15:21*ᶜ* | Isa. 52:15 | 'as it is written' | LXX |
| 1 Corinthians | | | |
| 1:19 | Isa. 29:14 | 'it is written' | N (LXX) |
| 1:31 | Jer. 9:24 (MT = 9:23) | 'as it is written' | N |
| 2:9 | (Source not clearly identifiable) | 'as it is written' | N |
| 2:16 | Isa. 40:13 | 'for' | N |
| 3:19 | Job 5:13 | 'it is written' | MT |
| 3:20 | Ps. 94:11 (LXX = 93:11) | 'and again' | N (LXX) |
| *5:13 | Deut. 17:7 | | N (LXX) |
| 6:16 | Gen. 2:24 | '...for, said he' | LXX |
| 9:9*ᵈ* | Deut. 25:4 | 'in the law of Moses it is written' | N (LXX) |
| *9:10(?) | Sir. 6:19 | 'because of you it was written that' | N (LXX) |
| 10:7 | Exod. 32:6 | 'as it is written' | LXX/MT |
| 10:26 | Ps. 24:1 (LXX = 23:1) | 'for' | LXX/MT |
| 14:21 | Isa. 28:11–12 | 'in the law it is written' | N |

*Table A (cont.)*

| NT | OT | Introductory Formula | Agreement with |
|---|---|---|---|
| *14:25 | Isa. 45:14, Zech. 8:23 | | N |
| *15:25 | Ps. 110:1 (LXX = 109:1) | | N |
| 15:27 | Ps. 8:6 (LXX = 8:7) | 'for' | N |
| 15:32 | Isa. 22:13 | | LXX |
| 15:45ᵉ | Gen. 2:7 | 'so it is written' | N (LXX) |
| 15:54 | Isa. 25:8 | 'then shall come to pass the work that is written' | N |
| 15:55 | Hos. 13:14 | | N |
| **2 Corinthians** | | | |
| 4:13 | Ps. 116:10 (LXX = 115:1) | 'according to what is written' | LXX/MT |
| 6:2 | Isa. 49:8 | 'for he [God] says' | LXX/MT |
| 6:16 | Lev. 26:11–12 | 'as God said' | N |
| 6:17 | Isa. 52:11–12 | | N |
| 6:18ᶠ | 2 Sam. 7:14, 7:8 | | N |
| 8:15 | Exod. 16:18 | 'as it is written' | MT |
| *9:7 | Prov. 22:6 (LXX = 22:8a) | | LXX |
| 9:9 | Ps. 112:9 (LXX = 111:9) | 'as it is written' | LXX/MT |
| *9:10 | Isa. 55:10 | | N (LXX) |
| 10:17 | Jer. 9:24 (MT&LXX = 9:22–23) | 'but' | N |
| 13:1 | Deut. 19:15 | | N (LXX) |
| **Galatians** | | | |
| 3:6 | Gen. 15:6 | 'as' | LXX |
| 3:8 | Gen. 12:3 | 'the Scripture announced beforehand' | N |
| 3:10 | Deut. 27:26 | 'it is written' | N |
| 3:11 | Hab. 2:4 | 'because' | N (LXX) |
| 3:12 | Lev. 18:5 | 'but' | N (LXX) |
| 3:13 | Deut. 21:23 | 'it is written' | N |
| 3:16 | Gen. 22:18, 13:15, etc. | 'it does not say... but...' | LXX/MT |
| 4:27 | Isa. 54:1 | 'it is written' | LXX |
| 4:30 | Gen. 21:10 | 'What does it [Scripture] say?' | N (LXX) |

*Table A (cont.)*

| NT | OT | Introductory Formula | Agreement with |
|---|---|---|---|
| 5:14 | Lev. 19:18 | 'all the law is fulfilled in this one word' | LXX/MT |
| Ephesians | | | |
| 4:8 | Ps. 68:18 (MT = 68:19; LXX = 67:19) | 'therefore it says' | N (LXX) |
| *4:25 | Zech. 8:16 | | N (LXX) |
| *4:26 | Ps. 4:4 (MT&LXX = 4:5) | | LXX/MT |
| 5:14 | (source not clearly identifiable) | 'therefore it says' | |
| 5:31 | Gen. 2:24 | | N |
| 6:2 | Exod. 20:12 (Deut. 5:16) | | N |
| 1 Timothy | | | |
| 5:18 | Deut. 25:4 | 'the Scripture says' | LXX |
| 2 Timothy | | | |
| 2:19a | Num. 16:5 | 'having this seal' | MT |
| 2:19b | Sir. 17:26, Isa. 26:13 (cf. Lev. 24:16) | 'and' | N (LXX) N |

a   Paul's point is possible only on the basis of LXX. Gentiles are not mentioned in MT.
b   Only Paul, neither MT nor LXX has the deliverer coming *from* Zion (ἐκ Σιών).
c   Paul's point, the justification of the gentile mission, can best be made on the basis of LXX versions of these testimonies.
d   p. 46 of 9:9 agrees exactly with LXX.
e   Paul inserts πρῶτος and 'Αδάμ into a clause of six words that agree exactly with LXX.
f   6:18c reproduces λέγει κύριος παντοκράτωρ from LXX of 2 Sam. 7:8.

We have above a total of about a hundred OT quotations (cf. Aageson, 1983, pp. 64–5). The exact count may vary slightly. Only when there is an introductory formula can one be absolutely certain that Paul intends to quote the OT and is not simply falling into its language. In the vast majority of cases one finds a formula such as 'as it is written', 'as Isaiah said', or 'Moses says', which makes it clear beyond doubt that Paul intends to quote Scripture.

In Paul's quotation of the OT there are remarkable affinities with the LXX (Ellis, 1957, p. 12). Incidence of agreement with the LXX is highest in Genesis and Psalms, lowest in Kings, Job, Jeremiah, and Hosea. In only four cases does one find agreement with the MT against the LXX: Rom. 11:34, citing Job 41:3; 1 Cor. 3:19, Job 5:12–13; 2 Cor. 8:15, Exod. 16:18; 2 Tim. 2:19,

Num. 16:5. Paul's use of the OT agrees with or approximates our LXX more often than not, and when it does not, it usually agrees with no known OT text or version. Where Paul quotes a cluster or catena of OT passages, the variance with the LXX and with any known text, is at its greatest. Probably it is better to conclude that Paul's usage is septuagintal than to say that he uses the LXX, since the latter comes to us only through christian hands in manuscripts no earlier than the fourth century. Nevertheless, the agreement of Paul's letters, and other NT writings, with the LXX is remarkable.

The extent to which Paul reflects the Septuagint, together with his minimal agreement with the Hebrew, raises the question of his knowledge of the Hebrew text and language. Discussion of this question cannot presuppose a dichotomy between (Hebrew-speaking) palestinian Judaism and (Greek-speaking) hellenistic Judaism. The two entities are identifiable but intermingled, as Davies long ago pointed out (1948, pp. 1–16). Thus we should not ask whether Paul was a palestinian, rabbinic, or normative Jew who knew Hebrew, or a hellenistic Jew who did not. There is, however, a significant correlation between a decision on this matter and what one makes of the evidence of Acts, as well as Paul's own biographical statements. In Acts, Paul speaks to the crowd 'in the Hebrew dialect' (21:40; 22:2). If Paul had been a student of Gamaliel in Jerusalem (Acts 22:3), he would, of course, have studied the Scriptures in Hebrew. What he says about being a Hebrew (2 Cor. 11:22; Phil. 3:5) and a Pharisee (Phil. 3:5) certainly squares with the Acts narrative, if it does not require all that Acts claims. The increasing appreciation of Paul's Jewishness in scholarship since the Second World War bespeaks the likelihood that he knew Hebrew, as does the fact that his biblical exegesis has closer affinities with Qumran monastics and rabbis, who knew Hebrew, than with Philo, who did not. However that may be, Paul draws upon the LXX, or at least the tradition of Greek translation, when he cites Scripture. That he wrote and spoke primarily to people who knew only Greek, and no Hebrew, seems to be a sufficient explanation of this fact. Such usage would also be commensurate with Paul's own experience and background as a native of Tarsus.

The distribution of Pauline quotations within the OT itself is significant. There are about three dozen quotations from the Pentateuch, and at least two dozen from Isaiah and twenty from the Psalms. In other words, fully eighty per cent of Paul's OT quotations are from those three sources. Yet it is clear from his quotations that he is familiar with Jeremiah, the Twelve, probably Ezekiel (although 2 Cor. 6:16 also reflects the language of Lev. 26:11f), the books of Samuel and Kings, Proverbs, and Job. Perhaps significantly, Daniel is not cited explicitly, nor are Ecclesiastes, Song of Solomon, Esther, Lamentations, Ezra and Nehemiah, the books of Chronicles, and Ruth. But neither are Joshua and Judges. The absence of the latter two books shows how hazardous it would be to draw conclusions about the status of the OT canon in the first century from any lack of reference in Paul.

The distribution of explicit quotations within the Pauline corpus is as striking and disproportional as the distribution of their sources in the Old Testament itself. Not only are they confined to the *Hauptbriefe* among the uncontested letters, but fully half are found in Romans alone! In all the instances in Romans cited by Ellis (1957) and Longenecker (1975) Paul leaves no doubt of his intention to cite Scripture, usually by a more or less stereotypical introductory formula. In comparison with Romans (and Galatians) Paul seems a bit less careful in the Corinthian letters always to make clear that he is citing Scripture. Those instances without introductory formulae of any sort which NA[26] italicises (but Ellis and Longenecker omit) are mostly in the Corinthian letters, with a couple each in Ephesians and the Pastorals (1 Tim. 5:18; 2 Tim. 2:19).

The reasons for Paul's heavy use of the OT in Romans and Galatians are obvious enough. Paul must counter arguments advanced by Judaisers directly, or must give an account of his understanding of the gospel that will do justice both to it and to his own jewish heritage and tradition, which he is not of a mind to repudiate. In this regard the distribution of the OT quotations in Romans in particular is significant and telling. After the long catena (3:10–18) which serves to confirm Paul's view of human sinfulness before God, he begins to expound the manifestation of the righteousness of God apart from the law, although the law and prophets (i.e., Scripture) bear witness to it (3:21). This latter, programmatic clause recalls his use of Hab. 2:4 in 1:17b to support his thematic assertions of 1:16–17a. The succinct, closely packed statement which follows (3:22–31) is replete with traditional and OT language, although it contains no scriptural citations.

The question about Abraham, raised in 4:1, is more than incidental. Paul takes up again the continuing topic of the righteousness of God, which is the letter's theme (cf. 1:17; 3:1–8). One might equally well say the justice of God, because God's justice is a prominent concern in Romans. Abraham is not, however, merely an example of faith or even of the basis of God's dealing with humanity. Rather the promise to him vindicates God's righteousness and consistency in dealing with his people in their history. That Scripture says that 'Abraham believed God and it was reckoned to him as righteousness' (4:3) is of fundamental and indispensable importance for Paul's argument throughout Romans. Not surprisingly, as Paul gives his initial answer to the question about God's righteousness and justice that he raised in 3:1–8, he has recourse to this Genesis account, on which he gives a sort of midrash in 4:9–25. Throughout the chapter the explicit quotations of Scripture provide the firm pegs on which he hangs his argument. It is to this leading question of the righteousness and faithfulness of God that Paul returns in chaps. 9–11. Not surprisingly, those chapters contain fully half the OT quotations in Romans. His use of the OT in Galatians answers to similar issues and needs.

Compared to the use of the OT in Romans and Galatians, its use in the Corinthian correspondence is limited. In 1 Corinthians Scripture is, however, again cited in connexion with Paul's characterisation of the human condition (1:19, 30; 3:19–20), or is applied to the present situation of the christian community (6:16; 9:9; 10:1–13), usually for purposes of ethical instruction or exhortation. Paul's general reference to Scripture as supporting a christian interpretation of Christ's death and belief in his resurrection in 15:3–4 (κατὰ τὰς γραφάς) shows that he knows a primitive christological testimony tradition (Lindars, 1961, pp. 59–60, 78ff). Perhaps this fact is confirmed by Paul's use of Ps. 110:1 in 15:25 and Ps. 8:7 in 15:27, although in those instances testimonies that may have applied originally to Christ's exaltation/resurrection are now applied to the eschatological culmination of his present reign. Nevertheless, Vielhauer (1969, p. 43) has correctly observed that Paul's use of the OT is mainly soteriological rather than christological. That is, he uses the OT to set forth or confirm that the saving righteousness of God has been manifested in Jesus Christ on the basis of faith rather than the law. Paul does not adduce Scripture to prove that Jesus is the Christ. As Lindars (1961) had already pointed out, 'It is striking that he does not reproduce the christological texts nor argue that Jesus is the Messiah' (p. 247). Of course, a significant explanation of this fact is that in his letters Paul is arguing basic matters of soteriology to justify his *praxis*, and can assume belief in Jesus as the Christ. Precisely at the point at which he harks back to his original preaching (15:3ff) he mentions the christological testimony tradition. Interestingly enough, in his missionary speech in the synagogue at Pisidian Antioch Paul is portrayed as speaking of the fulfilment of prophecy in the death of Jesus (Acts 13:27, 29; cf. Aageson, 1983, pp. 100–1). Such christological use of the OT would have been appropriate on that occasion.

In 2 Corinthians Paul's use of the OT is if anything more incidental, and even casual, than in 1 Corinthians. Three of the quotations occur in the alleged 'fragment' of 6:14–7:1 and are hortatory (cf. also 9:7, 9, 10). Paul adduces Jer. 9:24 against boasting in 10:17 as he has in 1 Cor. 1:31 (cf. Rom. 5:11). On the whole the use of Scripture is not basic to Paul's arguments, as it is in Romans and Galatians and even at some points in 1 Corinthians, for much of 2 Corinthians is concerned with Paul's own plans, the collection for Jerusalem, and his defence of his apostleship. Yet the role and function of Scripture are not far from Paul's mind, as the important discussion of chap. 3 (see below) indicates.

Interestingly, in the part of Romans in which Paul sets forth the new character and conditions of distinctively christian life (chaps. 5–8) there are only a couple of explicit citations of Scripture (7:7; 8:36). Yet the theme of

5:13–21 is Christ and Adam; that of chap. 6, sin; and of chap. 7, the law. There is a sense in which each is a given that Paul must deal with because of the Bible and jewish tradition. That Paul does not more frequently adduce the OT is less remarkable when one considers that it is precisely the new element, Jesus as messiah, that necessitates Paul's dealing with these basic issues in an unprecedented way. Not the advent of any messiah, but precisely the claim that the messiah has come as Jesus the crucified, necessitates dealing with these issues *de novo*. Thus the OT sets the agenda, so to speak, but does not resolve the theological problems which Paul must here treat.

The non-occurrence of explicit citations in the remaining uncontested letters may be less significant than at first appears. Initially, there is the question of whether we are talking about only Philippians, 1 Thessalonians, and Philemon, or about those plus 2 Thessalonians and Colossians. (1 and 2 Timothy, as well as Ephesians, have such quotations, so their absence in Titus is relatively insignificant, even if one considers the Pastorals as Paul's work.) Philemon scarcely comes into question, so if we are considering the undisputed letters there are really only two, Philippians and 1 Thessalonians. The latter is hardly representative of Pauline style and thought, and deals mainly with specific issues or practical problems. Moreover, if in any letter the possibility of actual joint authorship (1:1) is to be taken seriously, it may be a factor in this the earliest of Paul's letters. Philippians is by any reckoning much more characteristically Pauline, but it is also personal, practical, and admonitory. The theological gems which Paul tosses off do not occur in the context of sustained argument, but almost incidentally. In any event, it is worth observing that the *Hauptbriefe* occupy almost ninety-five pages of NA[26]. By way of comparison, Philippians is eight pages long, and 1 Thessalonians seven, for a total of fifteen. It is remarkable, therefore, that a scholar like Vielhauer (who would not have regarded Colossians and 2 Thessalonians as Pauline – much less Titus – 1969, p. 33) seemingly attached much importance to the fact that Paul did not cite the OT outside the *Hauptbriefe* (1969, p. 35).

## PAUL'S EXEGESIS, HIS BACKGROUND, METHOD, AND PERSPECTIVE

If Paul adopts the jewish canon of Scripture native to him and received by the church as the OT, what methods of interpretation does he apply? That Paul was a Jew is clear enough. That he was in some meaningful sense a rabbi has increasingly come to be regarded as true and significant, particularly since the work of Davies (1943). Already the similarities between Paul's exegesis and the rabbinic had been pointed out by Bonsirven (1939). It should therefore not be surprising that Paul's methods of interpretation find precedent in rabbinic and intertestamental jewish literature. Since the discovery of the Qumran Scrolls, the affinities between NT and essene exegesis have been apparent. Not surprisingly, Paul shares in these affinities (Fitzmyer, 1960–1). Like the Essenes, Paul and early Christians generally believed that their own sect or community was the goal of God's activity in history and somehow the focus of scriptural prophecy (1 QpHab. 7:1–5, 7–8). Paul's occasional allegorical use of the OT, particularly in Gal. 4:21–31, but perhaps also in 1 Cor. 9:9, has raised the question of what he may owe (or, better, how he may relate to) his jewish contemporary Philo. Obviously both are consummate theologians for whom Scripture is exceedingly important, although Paul never wrote biblical commentaries as Philo did.

While Paul clearly shares certain presuppositions about the authority of Scripture and exegetical methods with the rabbinic tradition as it is represented in much later written sources, he differs from the rabbis in at least two important respects. First, he is not primarily concerned with casuistry, the understanding and appropriation of Scripture as injunction and prohibition (cf. Furnish, 1968, p. 33, esp. n. 11; Sanders, 1983, p. 14). Although Paul can invoke the specific injunctions or prohibitions of the law as commands to christian communities, for him law is predominantly an abstraction, indeed, a way of regarding Scripture and God's dealing with humanity that is, for Paul at least, provisional and temporary. Second, Paul emphasises the historic, prophetic dimension of Scripture. It is an oversimplification to say that the rabbis regarded Scripture as law, while for Paul it was fundamentally prophecy. Yet that generalisation does not badly mislead us. Although Paul can call Scripture νόμος (Rom. 3:19), by no means does he equate the two.

When we turn to Qumran, there is in that respect at least a closer affinity with Paul, although members of the Qumran community were strict legalists. As Fitzmyer (1960–1, pp. 329, 331) has observed, however, the emphasis of Qumran is relatively more on the element of future, unrealised, expectation and less on accomplished fulfilment than is the case in the exegesis of the early church, insofar as we can understand it from the NT. 'At Qumran many of the Old Testament texts were applied to events in the recent history of the sect; in this respect there is some similarity to the backward glance of the NT writers. But the messianic hope at Qumran put the emphasis much more on a *coming fulfilment* of the Old Testament Scriptures' (1960–1, p. 331). Fitzmyer points out that the Hebrew equivalent of the NT fulfilment formulae (πληροῦν) is not found in Qumran (1960–1, pp. 303, 331). (Moule, 1967–8, p. 311, makes a similar observation about Philo as well.) This is doubtless a corroboration of his point about present and future application of Scripture. Nevertheless, it is worth observing that the fulfilment motif in relation to Scripture, especially in the introductory formula, so typical of Matthew, and found in all the gospels and Acts, is not common to Paul either. If this raises a question about the extent to which we should speak of prophecy and fulfilment in describing Paul's use of the OT, we may nevertheless be confident that he thought the gospel had been promised in Scripture (Rom. 1:2; 2 Cor. 1:20).

Paul and Philo share a consuming interest in Scripture, and, indeed, in making Scripture intelligible to those outside the jewish orbit. If, occasionally Paul seems to border on the allegory that is Philo's stock in trade (Gal. 4:21–31) or uses a jewish midrashic tradition shared also by Philo (1 Cor. 10:1–13; Conzelmann, 1975, p. 167), the differences are nevertheless enormous. Obviously, Paul does not write commentaries on Scripture as does Philo (as well as the Qumran sectarians). Paul's interest is much more historical, less philosophical or mystical, than Philo's. As much as Paul's understanding of, and interest in, history may differ from our own, the event-character of the episodes he relates and the reality of the persons he describes are important to him. Thus even as he appears to share an Exodus midrashic tradition with Philo (1 Cor. 10:1–13) he understands the narrative as historical, not just in assuming that it happened, but in maintaining that 'these things happened τυπικῶς'. This word is variously translated, but one is tempted to render it 'typologically', as in fact Bauer suggests. Typology becomes for Paul as for other NT authors, a way of understanding Scripture's relation to the events of Christ and the christian church (Goppelt, 1982b). Not just the texts, but the events and persons of which the texts speak are prototypes of God's revelation in Christ.

Philo and the rabbis have methods of interpretation which they apply with some consistency or regularity. They are far different from modern historical-critical or literary-critical methods, and were certainly not conceived of as means of getting at the original meaning of texts, if by that is meant a meaning intended by an historical author. By way of contrast, there is a kind of unpredictability about Paul's use of the OT, except that he almost always reads it in light of the events of christian revelation. In this respect there is an analogy with the exegetical slant of the Qumran community. It may be that Paul is simply eclectic in exegetical method (Vielhauer, 1969, p. 51). On the other hand, Paul shows signs of having, or developing, an exegetical perspective on the OT. This perspective is not the product of a new method, but of a theological, christological presupposition (Luz 1968, p. 91; Hanson, 1974, p. 202). To the degree that he has such an exegetical perspective, Paul shares it with the primitive church of which he is a part. Yet there are unmistakable signs of his originality as his own exegetical work develops (cf. Aageson, 1983, pp. 129–30). To the best of our knowledge, there is nothing quite comparable to the scope of Paul's exegesis of Genesis 15 in Romans 4 or of a whole skein of OT texts in Romans 9–11. The discussion of Abraham in Galatians 3 and Romans 4 is, of course, echoed in Jas. 2:18–26, but that discussion is almost certainly based upon knowledge of Pauline letters or at least tradition. Only the epistle to the Hebrews can match Romans 9–11 for sustained exegetical argumentation, but even in Hebrews the typological pairing of old and new is more predictable than in Paul. The structures of promise and fulfilment and typology, which were to predominate in later christian exegesis, are clearly developing in and with Paul's theological arguments (Luz, 1968, pp. 47–51 on promise/prophecy and fulfilment; pp. 52–60 on typology). Yet they do not adequately comprehend Paul's use of the OT in these instances. Here Paul attempts to interpret the history of God's people as the history of election, with a view to defending the righteousness, justice, and faithfulness of God.

Ulrich Luz has pointed out that the category of typology is inadequate to comprehend Paul's achievement in Romans 9–11 (1968, pp. 30–3; cf. Aageson, 1983, p. 279). The fundamental point is not that the Scriptures present types of persons or events to which antitypes of the christian revelation correspond (e.g., Paul to Elijah in 11:2–6). Rather, Paul understands the history of Israel as the arena where God has really spoken and in which, by election, he has been working out his purpose. (In this connexion, however, Fishbane, 1985, p. 352, has underscored the indispensability of history for typology: 'For if legal and other aggadic exegeses emphasize the verbal aspects of ongoing divine revelation, typological exegesis reveals its historical concreteness.') If that purpose could only be understood later from the standpoint of faith in Jesus Christ, it was, in Paul's view, no less real. Although Luz declines to speak of *Heilsgeschichte*, because of the undesirable connotations and implications of the term (1968, pp. 14–15), he nevertheless finds it necessary and important to speak of history despite the fact that the term ἱστορία does not appear in Paul or the NT (ἱστορεῖν appearing only in Gal. 1:18). But Paul's use of the OT in Romans 9–11 is indissolubly wedded to his own concept of history as the arena of God's salvation, whether past or present. It is, in fact, just in his appropriation of the OT that his understanding of history is worked out. Conversely, his appropriation and understanding of the OT necessitates a *Geschichtsverständnis*. To say that Paul understands the OT historically is, of course, not to say that he understands it as an historically trained exegete would, nor that he understands history as a modern, secular person would. But it is to say that he appreciates its pastness, temporality and successiveness and that these dimensions cannot be resolved into theological principles or points without fundamental distortion of the apostle's thought. If Christ is not to be understood as the latest in a series of saving acts of God, he nevertheless appears in the same history as the word of the same God whose will and purpose cannot be apprehended apart from it.

As far as Paul's use of the OT is concerned, he engages in ethical application, typology, and allegory, and thinks in the categories of promise and fulfilment. But none of the above exhausts or gets at the essence of his use of the OT in crucial passages such as Romans 9–11, Romans 4, or Galatians 3. Precisely at such points Paul's understanding of history and appropriation of the OT, stand in mutually supportive relation. Ethical application, typology, allegory and promise/prophecy and fulfilment do not necessarily negate or deny history, but neither do they take its distinctive character and uniqueness into account as ingredient, essential, and indeed indispensable to the meaning of the OT. If Paul intends to do that, he cannot be satisfied to stay within those methods, and he does not.

If we are to inquire about Paul's use of the OT, and particularly now about his own understanding of Scripture and how he appropriates it, we should also ask how his use of the OT related to that of the primitive church generally. Doubtless Paul took up methods and modes of scriptural interpretation already practised in the early church (Lindars, 1961, pp. 222, 226–7). The exact form of that OT tradition in christian communities at the time Paul wrote is, however, a question that eludes resolution. Apart from uncertainties about the OT textual tradition, we do not know in what form the OT was accessible to christian authors. Rendel Harris's proposal (1916–20) of a primitive christian testimony book that antedates our NT clearly went farther than the evidence would allow. Yet several important facts make his proposal the subject of continuing fascination. Not only do certain OT testimonies occur more or less independently in different NT books (e.g., Ps. 110:1), but, for example, in Rom. 9:33 Paul (or his source) combines Isa. 28:16 and 8:14 while 1 Pet. (2:6–8) juxtaposes the same Isaiah testimonies in close proximity. It is difficult to explain the similarities by direct literary dependence (Luz, 1968, p. 96). Moreover, would christian missionary preachers like Paul have had ready easy access to the Bible? The Bible was a collection of scrolls, not a single volume, and was possibly not accessible outside a synagogue. The utility of such collections of testimonies is obvious. The discovery of a set of messianic testimonies at Qumran (4 QFlor) while falling far short of justifying Harris's hypothesis, at least keeps alive the possibility of less ambitious collections in the primitive church (Fitzmyer, 1957, pp. 536–7). Dodd's more modest effort (1952) to accommodate the pattern of the NT usage of the OT, in particular certain parts of the Pentateuch, Isaiah, and the Psalms by proposing an early traditional consensus in the use of certain parts (or plots) of the OT, rather than a testimony book, has a certain plausibility (but cf. Sundberg, 1959, pp. 268–9, as well as Aageson, 1983, pp. 109–10). Yet as confident as we may be that Paul stood in a tradition of christian use of the OT, we do not know enough about the state of that tradition before, or apart from, Paul to base an interpretation of Paul's usage on any assessment of how he used, or departed from, that tradition. The safest procedure is simply to observe how Paul actually uses the OT and what he says, or implies, about his understanding of the Scriptures and their authority (similarly Aageson, pp. 129–30).

It is frequently, and correctly, said that for Paul, Scripture, our OT, is the word of God. In introducing an OT quotation Paul can say simply, 'as God said' (2 Cor. 6:16), and there are a few other places at which God is the likely subject understood of the verb (Rom. 9:25; 2 Cor. 6:2, especially). Scripture is God's word. Thus, for Paul to say 'as it is written', implies it stands in the Scriptures that are regarded as the word of God. A quotation from the OT may have binding force for the community's practice. Paul cites the law of Moses generally and then Deut. 25:4 in 1 Cor. 9:8–9. In 1 Cor. 11:7–12 his argument that a woman should keep her head covered in church is based on the creation narrative of Genesis 2. The silence of women in church (if 1 Cor. 14:34–36 be genuine) is said to be enjoined by the law, although Paul might have helpfully indicated what commandment he had in mind. Paul's appeal for the Jerusalem collection is supported from Scripture (2 Cor. 8:15). Perhaps most important, his citation of Lev. 19:18 in Rom. 13:9 and Gal. 5:14 seems to presume that the (scriptural) law is to be fulfilled by Christians. In short, there is no dearth of passages to support the fact that Paul, like any other Jew of his time, believed that Scripture contained the word of God. Moreover, he was capable of applying Scripture for the regulation of any specific situation, as any rabbi or sage of his day might have.

Yet for Paul Scripture as God's word has a new and peculiar importance in the light of the coming of the messiah. Paul's initial statement about the gospel of God in Romans is typical and telling: it was 'proclaimed beforehand through his prophets in the holy Scriptures'. So when Paul quotes Hab. 2:4 in 1:17 he has already prepared the reader to understand that the truth of the gospel is to be found in the OT. As Luz (1968) has aptly put it: 'Für Paulus ist Alte Testament nicht in der erster Linie ein zu Verstehendes, sondern es selbst schafft Verstehen' (p. 134 'For Paul, the OT is not primarily something to understand; rather, the OT itself creates understanding.'). For Paul there is no 'problem' of interpreting the OT in light of the gospel. It is the OT that now makes the gospel clear. Nevertheless, the meaning of the OT was not discernible until the fulness of time had come and God sent forth his son (Gal. 4:4). For in Jesus 'the righteousness of God was revealed apart from the law, although the law and the prophets bear witness to it' (Rom. 3:21). One could perhaps paraphrase Paul to say that the righteousness of God was revealed apart from the law, although the Scriptures that contain the law bear witness to it. Obviously, for Paul law and Scripture overlap, but they are not to be identified. Whether Paul would have conceded that no one could have understood what Scripture had to say about the messiah until he came is a moot point. Probably so, but Paul would have regarded it as an academic question. Now that the messiah has come Scripture rightly understood clearly speaks of him. But there is no reason to doubt that Paul believed that God's dealings with Abraham were real and effectual historically, that is that the historical Abraham really did believe God and it really was reckoned to him for righteousness.

That Paul sees in the coming of Jesus Christ not only the turning of the ages but the turning point for understanding Scripture is apparent from 2 Corinthians 3. This is a very complex passage, to say the least. Clearly one should avoid interpreting γράμμα to mean Scripture. The letter–spirit dialectic is not a key to Paul's hermeneutics, but to his ethics (Westerholm, 1984, p. 241). Nor can Paul mean by 'old covenant' (παλαιὰ διαθήκη) the OT (3:14). That would be an obvious anachronism. Nevertheless, Paul is evidently talking about the reading of some part of what one could call the OT. Paul apparently understands the veil over Moses' face (3:13) to have been removed by Christ (3:14). This means that the veil over the Mosaic Scriptures (3:15), whether the law or the whole of Scripture, is in principle taken away. Yet when the Scriptures are read (3:14–15), presumably in synagogue, the veil remains if the hearers have not (yet) turned to the Lord. Paul is loath to say that the veil lies over Moses any longer, so he says it lies over the readers' (or hearers') minds (actually καρδία). When one turns to the Lord, to Christ, the veil is removed (v. 16; cf. v. 14). Conversion makes the Scriptures plain. Thus Paul is not hesitant to claim the Scriptures for Christ. (This reading of 3:14–16 presumes that what is done away with (καταργεῖται) in v. 14 is the veil rather than the old covenant, although the latter interpretation is grammatically possible [cf. Furnish, 1984, pp 210, 233f, in agreement with Lietzmann, Bultmann, and Hanson].) Hooker states the matter succinctly: 'For him it is axiomatic that the true meaning of scripture has been hidden, and is only now made plain in Christ' (Hooker, 1981, p. 305). Interestingly enough, when Paul is cataloguing the possessions of Israel in Rom. 9:4 (sonship, glory, covenants, giving of the law, the worship, the promises, the patriarchs, and finally the Christ), he does not mention the Scriptures per se. Whether this is merely an oversight we shall never know, but even if it is, Paul makes a telling omission. The Scriptures are now the province of believers, not unbelievers.

Thus at a number of points Paul simply asserts that the Scriptures were written with the christian church in view. 'But the words, "it was reckoned to him", were written not for his sake alone, but also for ours' (Rom. 4:23). After quoting Ps. 69:9 ('the reproaches of those who reproached thee fell on me.') Paul adds: 'For whatever was written in former days was written for our instruction, that by steadfastness and by the encouragement of the Scriptures we might have hope' (Rom. 15:4). Such general statements of the character or purpose of Scripture fit rather well with Paul's use of Scripture to exhort or comfort the Christians of his churches. The personages and episodes of the OT can be explicitly described by Paul as types not only of Christ (e.g. Adam in Rom. 5:14), but of the temptations faced by the members of Paul's churches (e.g., the apostasy of the wilderness generation in 1 Cor. 10:6, 11). In the latter case the connotation of 'warning' is doubtless present. Quite possibly the obscure injunction of 1 Cor. 4:6 'not beyond the things that are written', reflects Paul's estimate of the importance of Scripture in ordering life within their community. (Hooker, 1963, pp. 127–32, suggests that Paul here refers to the testimonies of 3:19–20, and indeed of chaps. 1 and 2, which are in effect warnings to the Corinthians who pride themselves on wisdom.) All in all Paul's use of the OT to instruct, encourage, or admonish the churches does not fit too badly the general statement attributed to him in 2 Tim. 3:16: 'All scripture is inspired by God and profitable for teaching, for reproof, for correction, and for training in righteousness'. Of course, 2 Tim. 3:16 touches upon the hortatory function of Scripture only. What is missing is the prophetic, promissory understanding of the OT word, which for Paul is the undergirding structure of everything else and allows him to say of Christ, in an almost incidental way, 'For all the promises of God find their yes in him' (2 Cor. 1:20).

## PAUL'S USE OF SCRIPTURE AND HIS THEOLOGY

That Paul regards Jesus the crucified messiah as the fulfilment of the promises of Scripture and the recognition of him as the lynchpin for the interpretation of Scripture is clear enough. But to what extent is Paul's own theology actually rooted in Scripture? Doubtless, if asked, Paul would aver that it was. Indeed, Romans can reasonably be viewed as a strong effort to make just that point. Yet for as influential, and representative, an interpreter of Paul as Bultmann (1951) the OT was not the beginning point for Paul, and is not a proper basis for the interpretation of Paul's theology. Or so it seems. As is well known, Bultmann treats Paul's theology as his doctrine of man; first, man prior to faith; then man under faith (1951, p. 191). Bultmann, however, makes clear the interrelatedness of all Paul's statements about man to his understanding of God, and vice versa. Probably because of the time in which he wrote, and because he did not want to subsume theology under psychology or biography, Bultmann did not make much of the relation of Paul's conversion to his theology. Yet his statement about the meaning of Paul's conversion is not only interesting, but full of theological significance (1951, p. 188):

His was not a conversion of repentance; neither, of course, was it one of emancipating enlightenment. Rather, it was obedient submission to the judgment of God, made known in Christ, upon all human accomplishment and boasting. It is as such that his conversion is reflected in his theology.

Such an understanding of Paul's conversion has rich and far-reaching implications for the exposition of his theology, and, indeed, offers some justification for the anthropological starting point that Bultmann has chosen.

Given that starting point, the OT as theological interpretation of the experience and history of Israel does not come into consideration as the positive basis of Paul's theology, nor does it supply his framework (Bultmann, 1964, pp. 72–5). Thus Hanson, whose own perspective is quite different, is understandably critical of Bultmann, particularly of his efforts to derive elements of Paul's basic conceptuality from non-scriptural, indeed, non-jewish, sources (Hanson, 1974, pp. 211–12). Yet precisely Bultmann's anthropological starting point makes some significant contact with the OT. He firmly rejects, for Paul, any gnostic (or hellenistic) dualistic anthropology in which the body (σῶμα) is a prison of the real self (Bultmann, 1951, p. 199), or any identification of the flesh (σάρξ) with the purely physical (Bultmann, 1951, pp. 201, 203). Soul (ψυχή) and spirit (πνεῦμα) are to be understood like *nepeš* and *ruaḥ* in the OT. In fact, for Bultmann's presentation of Paul's anthropology OT terms and concepts turn out to be quite important. This does not mean, however, that Paul's anthropology is free of gnostic motifs. For example, 'in describing the curse that lies upon Adamic mankind (Rom. 5:12–19), Paul is unquestionably under the influence of the Gnostic myth' (1951, p. 251). Yet precisely at the point of defining the salvation-event as it affects a person, Bultmann sharply delineates Paul's understanding from Gnosticism (1951, p. 269). Thus he maintains that what is rescued is not – 'as the Gnostic myth maintains – a fully inconceivable and only negatively describable self, the preexistent spark of light, but precisely the sinner, the innerly divided and self-misunderstanding human self'. Moreover, in describing Paul's understanding of how God 'rightwises' the sinner, Bultmann draws heavily on OT terminology. It is arguable (although it cannot be argued here) that Bultmann's understanding of Pauline anthropology is wholly inconceivable apart from the OT. In fact, one could go farther and argue that the concept of man (*Mensch*) upon which Paul bases himself is not so much that of contemporary Judaism, whether palestinian or hellenistic, as of the OT as it has been understood through historical criticism in the modern period. Statements such as the following, from Eichrodt's *Man in the Old Testament* (1951) have, in this regard, a quite familiar ring:

...the fundamental datum of Israel's view of life is that the individual is summoned to a responsibility which demands to be taken as absolute. The man to whom God's demand comes is recognized as a person, an I, who cannot be represented or replaced by any other. Even his belonging to the nation cannot provide him with a cover behind which he might retreat from the divine demand. He is summoned before God as the man he is, and placed before a decision (pp. 23–4).

When reasonable discount is made for the common cultural and theological influences upon Bultmann and Eichrodt, the similarities are nevertheless remarkable.

The consideration of Bultmann is germane to our subject if for him Paul is to a remarkable degree, and in a fundamental (i.e., anthropological) sense, an OT man. On his terms, Paul is closely aligned with OT anthropology. But, of course, this is an observation about a fundamental outlook rather than about Paul's explicit use of the OT. The latter is admittedly not so fundamental or crucial in Bultmann's view, and it is on that point that we propose to offer some observations about the relationship of Paul's use of the OT to his theology, and particularly, to recent developments in its exposition.

The question to put to Bultmann, and to a broad tradition of Pauline exegesis, is whether the OT has some further and theologically indispensable significance for Paul. Is it promise as well as law? It is promise only from the standpoint of fulfilment? (Any exegete must grant that Paul himself thought it was promise, after he had, so to speak, made the fulfilment his own.) To adopt and adapt Sanders's (1977) terminology, is the Pauline pattern of religion simply imposed upon the OT, or is it in any meaningful sense derived from the OT? There probably is an important sense in which it is imposed on the OT, in that Paul could never have thought of it apart from Christ, indeed, apart from his own experiential appropriation of Christ, his conversion. The question might then be: Does Paul's understanding of the OT really make sense, that is, on his own terms? This need not be the question of whether it makes sense to us, or to the modern interpreter, but whether it makes sense to Paul, and within Paul's implied or explicit theological frame of reference. More precisely, is it essential to the integrity of Paul's theology that he should endeavour, and succeed, in making sense of the OT as prophecy or promise? (For an illuminating discussion of how and why Paul's appropriation of the OT makes sense on structuralist grounds, i.e., because of basically congruent structures in Paul and in parts of OT, see Via, 1974, 201–20, esp. 212–13 and 218–20.)

To answer this question would naturally take us far beyond the scope of this chapter, but to raise it is entirely appropriate and necessary, for in doing so we are only pressing on with the question of Paul's use of the OT. Probably the best test case for this question is again Romans 9–11, which as we have seen contains a disproportionate number of Paul's scriptural quotations. For obvious reasons Paul draws heavily upon Scripture in this section. If Paul cannot here make his case on the basis of Scripture, it cannot be made. Scripture and the promises it contains constitute the reason for Paul's needing to make the case, as well as the only means by which that case could be made. Paul feels a responsibility to Scripture, and to his own understanding of it as promise that is correlative with his passion for his people Israel.

The way in which Paul makes that case might not have convinced an unbeliever, particularly a Jew, of its validity. But that would not have been Paul's primary purpose or concern. He was writing for Christians like himself, and in Romans in all probability with jewish Christians (like himself!), for whom Scripture had a continuing validity, in view. He was obviously concerned to make a case that would at once do justice to the crucial significance of Christ, but at the same time portray the coming of Christ as the fulfilment rather than the negation of biblical promise, especially in view of his recognition that his fellow Jews generally had not come to belief in Jesus (Rom. 9:2–3; 10:1–3). The biblical conception of election, which can be clearly established in the OT, as Paul's argument shows, allows him to make this case. The logic of 9:1–11:10 is clear enough, and as Paul makes his argument its conclusion is obvious: on the basis of the principle of election most of Paul's Jewish contemporaries will be excluded from the realm of God's future salvation.

It is, however, an interesting and important fact that Paul was not satisfied to leave matters where they stood at Rom. 11:11. The remainder of the chapter apparently has at least two foci or purposes. One is a hortatory one, insofar as Paul is addressing and warning gentile Christians. At the same time he is addressing himself to the question of the future and destiny of empirical Israel, which is obviously a matter of genuine concern to him. That Paul leaves that question open and unresolved is not surprising, nor is it surprising that his quotation of Isa. 40:13 and Job 41:11 rounds out his discussion of the matter, which appropriately ends with a doxology. Paul's interpretation of Scripture might be characterised as the history of promise and fulfilment by means of election. But Paul is unwilling to follow the hard logic implicit in his retelling and distillation of the story of God's dealing with his people. That logic would lead to the conclusion that the number of Israel who inherit the promised salvation would be small indeed. Even though Isaiah (10:22–3) can be invoked in favour of that version of history, Paul is not finally satisfied to leave matters there. He wants to see, and envisions, an ampler fulfilment of the promise in which the entire people will be included. It is not enough that there should be fulfilment in principle.

The importance of the reality of fulfilment of promise for Paul's theology has frequently been observed in recent exegesis (e.g., Müller, 1964; Luz, 1968; Cranfield, 1979; Käsemann, 1980; Beker, 1980; Hübner, 1984; also Sanders, 1983, p. 197, who sees a major tension within Paul's theology at this point). Paul has a vital interest in being able to argue that God will indeed fulfil his promises to his historic people, not just to Christians or the church (Cranfield, 1979, p. 448). This interest is not only personal (9:1–5; 10:1), although it is also that. The integrity of his theology is at stake. Davies (1977–8, p. 13) has put the matter with utter succinctness and accuracy:

But the very validity or efficacy of the gospel which he preached was...challenged for Paul by the refusal of his own people to accept it. Their rejection of Jesus as Christ called into question for Paul and for his readers what must have sounded like exaggerated claims for the power of God unto salvation through Christ.... If God who had made the promise to the Jewish people had failed to bring his salvation in Christ to them, what guarantee was there that he would complete the work of the believers' salvation? The failure of the mission to the Jews raised acutely the question of the faithfulness or the reliability of the very God who, Paul has claimed, justified even the ungodly. And so Paul devotes Rom. ix–xi to this question.

The integrity of Paul's theology cannot, on these terms, be established against the horizon of the individual's existence only. 'Although Paul's message of justification undoubtedly takes concrete form in the justification of the individual, God's grace wants the world. If not, we end up with a Christian mystery religion.... It is impossible to deny that the apostle's message of justification has the dimension of salvation history' (Käsemann, 1980, p. 255). This last assertion, aside from marking the watershed of Käsemann's break with his mentor Bultmann, means that for Paul the issues raised by the OT for the understanding of the gospel are not peripheral, but integral and germane to its theological explication. 'Only when the emphasis is shifted from the operative word to the contrast of faith and unbelief, i.e., to anthropology, does it make no sense to talk of salvation history. For then *the material link between the OT and the NT is snapped* [emphasis mine], the world simply becomes the theater of individual decisions, the Creator no longer reaches out for his world....' (Käsemann, 1980, pp. 255–6). Thus on Käsemann's reading the material link between OT and NT belongs to the essence of Paul's theology.

A judgement about the place of the OT in Paul's theology is then intimately, although not wholly, tied to the question of the place and importance of the argument in Romans 9–11. Galatians 3 and Romans 4 are, of course, also very significant in this regard. The question of whether such scripturally based arguments are fundamental or only secondary or ancillary is tied to a judgment about where the centre of Paul's theology lies, and what factors should come into play in determining the locus of such a centre. All of which is to say that hermeneutical decisions about where to begin and what horizon to keep in focus cannot be avoided, and that such decisions loom as very important in the reconstruction or interpretation of Paul's theology. We are in a sense faced with the question of whether historical conditioning and authorial intention – insofar as the latter can be inferred from the former – are allowed to play a decisive role in determining the much sought after centre of Paul's theology. If they are – or to the extent they are – one must take seriously Paul's appropriation of the OT and his understanding of it as providing the framework, if not the root, of his theology. Paul's Jewishness and immersion in biblical thought would have rendered him incapable of not developing his theology in the context of his traditional and biblical heritage. That being the case, the crucial question then becomes whether the interpreter must make central what Paul himself understood to be central. If understanding of existence is the determinative question that guides the exegesis of Pauline texts and the construction (or reconstruction) of Paul's theology, the putting of the question will guarantee a Pauline theology in which Paul's arguments from Scripture about salvation history and election will have at best a secondary role. Thus, Bultmann's magisterial construal of Paul's theology draws a clear and comprehensible line from a certain understanding of his conversion to a presentation of human existence prior to faith (in which OT perspectives admittedly play an important role) to the actualisation of the salvation event itself in human existence. The prior question determines the character of the outcome, as Bultmann himself would acknowledge. The horizon of meaning is implicit in the question that is put. If the horizon of meaning is allowed to be what Paul himself took it to be, that is, a scripturally conceived framework of history over which God rules, and within which his revelation of his purpose may be perceived, the outcome of the effort to construct, or reconstruct, Paul's theology will be somewhat different. The latter course takes more seriously the historically conditioned presuppositions of Paul's own thought. It is to be hoped that this chapter will make a modest contribution in the direction of clarifying the issues involved in the presentation of Paul's theology, including the choice of a beginning point, and particularly the basis on which such a choice is made. Basic to such a clarification is the recognition that the issues are integrally related to the subject of Paul's use of the OT, as is the question of the centre of Paul's theology.

## NOTE

1 Aageson has kindly allowed me to see his dissertation. Although this article was near completion by the time it reached me, I have been able to incorporate some helpful references to it. I am also grateful to my student Frank Thielman and to Dr Richard B. Hays of Yale Divinity School, who have read this paper and offered many helpful observations. Any deficiencies are, of course, my own responsibility.

## BIBLIOGRAPHY

J. W. Aageson 'Paul's Use of Scripture: A Comparative Study of Biblical Interpretation in Early Palestinian Judaism and the New Testament with Special Reference to Romans 9–11', Ph.D. Dissertation (Oxford, 1983).
'Scripture and Structure in the Development of the Argument in Romans 9–11', *CBQ* 48 (1986), 268–89.

# The Pauline literature

R. Beckwith *The Old Testament Canon of the New Testament Church and its Background in Judaism* (London, 1985).

J. C. Beker *Paul the Apostle: The Triumph of God in Life and Thought* (Philadelphia, 1980).

M. L. Boney 'Paul's Use of the Old Testament', Ph.D. Dissertation (Columbia University, NY, 1956).

J. Bonsirven *Exégèse rabbinique et exégèse paulinienne* (Paris, 1939).

R. Bultmann *Theologie des Neuen Testaments* (Tübingen, 1948–53); ET *Theology of the New Testament*, vol. 1 (New York, 1951).

'Prophecy and Fulfillment', in C. Westermann (ed.), *Essays on Old Testament Hermeneutics* (Philadelphia, 1964); ET of *Probleme alttestamentlicher Hermeneutic* (Münich, 1960)), pp. 50–75.

H. Conzelmann *Der erste Brief an die Korinther* (Göttingen, 1969); ET 1 *Corinthians: A Commentary on the first Epistle to the Corinthians* (Philadelphia, 1975).

C. E. B. Cranfield *The Epistle to the Romans*, vol. 20, ICC (Edinburgh, 1979).

W. D. Davies *Paul and Rabbinic Judaism: Some Rabbinic Elements in Pauline Theology*, 4th ed. (Philadelphia, 1980; 1st ed., London, 1948).

*Torah in the Messianic Age and/or the Age to Come*, JBLMS 7 (Philadelphia, 1952).

'Paul and the People of Israel', *NTS* 24 (1977–8), 4–39 (= *Jewish and Pauline Studies* (Philadelphia, 1984), pp. 123–52).

W. Dittmar *Vetus Testamentum in Novo: Die alttestamentlichen Parallelen des Neuen Testaments im Wortlaut der Urtexte und der Septuaginta* (Göttingen, 1903).

C. H. Dodd *According to the Scriptures: The Substructure of New Testament Theology* (London, 1952).

W. Eichrodt *Das Menschenverständnis des Alten Testaments* (Zurich, 1944); ET *Man in the Old Testament*, SBT 4 (London, 1951).

E. E. Ellis *Paul's Use of the Old Testament* (Grand Rapids, Michigan, 1957).

*Prophecy and Hermeneutic in Early Christianity: New Testament Essays*, WUNT 18 (Tübingen, 1978).

M. Fishbane *Biblical Interpretation in Ancient Israel* (Oxford, 1985).

J. A. Fitzmyer '"4Q Testimonia" and the New Testament', *TS* 18 (1957), 513–37 (= *Essays on the Semitic Background of the New Testament* (London, 1971), pp. 59–89).

'The Use of Explicit Old Testament Quotations in Qumran Literature and in the New Testament', *NTS* 7 (1960–1), 297–333 (= *Essays on the Semitic Background of the New Testament* (London, 1971), pp. 3–58).

## D. Moody Smith

V. P. Furnish *Theology and Ethics in Paul* (Nashville and New York, 1968).
*II Corinthians*, AB23A (Garden City, NY, 1984).

L. Goppelt *Theologie des Neuen Testaments* (Göttingen, 1976); ET *Theology of the New Testament*, vol. 2: *The Variety and Unity of the Apostolic Witness to Christ* (Grand Rapids, Michigan, 1982) (= 1982a).
*Typos: Die Typologische Deutung des Alten Testaments im Neuen* (Gütersloh, 1939); ET *Typos: The Typological Interpretation of the Old Testament in the New* (Grand Rapids, 1982) (= 1982b).

A. T. Hanson *Studies in Paul's Technique and Theology* (Grand Rapids, 1974).
*The New Testament Interpretation of Scripture* (London, 1980), esp. 'A Quasi-Gnostic Midrash: I Corinthians 2.6–16', pp. 21–96.
*The Living Utterances of God: The New Testament Exegesis of the Old* (London, 1983), esp. pp. 44–62 on Paul.

A. von Harnack 'Das Alte Testament in den Paulinischen Briefen und in den Paulinischen Gemeinde', *Sitzungberichte der preussischen Akademie der Wissenschaften zu Berlin: Sitzung der philosophischhistorischen Klasse vom 19. April 1928*, pp. 124–41.

R. B. Hays 'Effects of Intertextual Echo in Romans: Preliminary Soundings' (a paper read before the Pauline Epistles Section of SBL, Anaheim, November, 1985).

M. D. Hooker 'Beyond the Things which are Written: An Examination of I Cor. iv. 6', *NTS* 10 (1963–64), 127–32.
'Beyond the Things that are Written? St. Paul's Use of Scripture', *NTS* 27 (1980–1), 295–309.

H. Hübner *Das Gesetz bei Paulus. Ein Beitrag zum Werden der paulinischen Theologie* (Göttingen, 1982); ET *Law in Paul's Thought* (Edinburgh, 1984).
*Gottes Ich und Israel, zum Schriftgebrauch des Paulus in Römer 9–11*, FRLANT 136 (Göttingen, 1984).

E. Käsemann *An die Römer*, 4th ed. (Tübingen, 1980); ET *Commentary on Romans* (Grand Rapids, 1980).

E. F. Kautzsch *De veteris testamenti locis a Paulo apostolo allegatis* (Leipzig, 1869).

D.-A. Koch *Die Schrift als Zeuge des Evangeliums: Untersuchungen zur Verwendung und zum Verständnis der Schrift bei Paulus*, Beiträge zur historischen Theologie 69 (Tübingen: Mohr, 1986).

B. Lindars *New Testament Apologetic. The Doctrinal Significance of the Old Testament Quotations* (London, 1961).

R. N. Longenecker *Biblical Exegesis in the Apostolic Period* (Grand Rapids, 1975).

U. Luz *Das Geschichtsverständnis des Paulus*. BEvTh 49 (Munich, 1968).

290

O. Michel *Paulus und Seine Bibel*. BFChrTh 18 (Gütersloh, 1929).

C. F. D. Moule 'Fulfillment-Words in the New Testament, Use and Abuse', *NTS* (1967–8), 293–320.

C. Müller *Gottes Gerechtigkeit und Gottes Volk: Eine Untersuchung zu Römer 9–11*, FRLANT 86 (Göttingen, 1964).

G. von Rad *Theologie des Alten Testaments*, vol. 2: *Die Theologie des prophetischen Überlieferungen Israels* (Munich, 1960); ET *Old Testament Theology*, vol. 2: *The Theology of Israel's Prophetic Traditions* (Edinburgh and London, 1965).

H. Räisänen *Paul and the Law*. WMANT 29 (Tübingen, 1983).

E. P. Sanders *Paul and Palestinian Judaism: A comparison of Patterns of Religion* (Philadelphia, 1977).

*Paul, the Law and the Jewish People* (Philadelphia, 1983).

D. M. Smith, Jr. 'The Use of the Old Testament in the New', in J. M. Efird (ed.), *The Use of the Old Testament in the New and Other Essays: Studies in Honor of William Franklin Stinespring* (Durham, North Carolina, 1972), pp. 3–65.

A. C. Sundberg 'On Testimonies', *NovT* 3 (1959), 268–81.

*The Old Testament of the Early Church* HTS 20 (Cambridge, MA, 1964).

C. H. Toy *Quotations in the New Testament* (New York, 1884).

H. Ulonska 'Paulus und das Alte Testament', Ph.D. Dissertation (Münster, 1964).

D. O. Via, Jr. 'A Structuralist Approach to Paul's Old Testament Hermeneutic', *Int* 28 (1974), 201–20.

P. Vielhauer 'Paulus und das Alte Testament', in *Studien zur Geschichte und Theologie der Reformation, Festschrift für Ernst Bizer* (Neukirchen, 1969), pp. 33–62.

S. Westerholm 'Letter and Spirit: The Foundation of Pauline Ethics', *NTS* 30 (1984), 229–48.

# 17 · Hebrews

## A. T. HANSON

I T is a distinction to be asked to contribute to a *Festschrift* in honour of
Barnabas Lindars. As well as knowing him personally as a colleague for some
years, I have always admired his scholarship and ability in the study of both
the OT and the NT, not least in the area with which this volume is particularly
concerned.

In 1983 I published a book called *The Living Utterances of God* in which I
devoted eight pages (104–12) to the subject of 'The Use of Scripture in
Hebrews'. Since I did not wish to offer merely a rehash of this material, I
decided to approach the topic of this chapter in a slightly different way. I have
instituted a comparison between the author of Hebrews and his contemporaries
or near-contemporaries as far as concerns their exegesis of common or similar
passages of Scripture. I believe that this will achieve the object intended by the
editors of this book without running the risk of unnecessary reduplication. I
have not included a consideration of rabbinic exegesis of Scripture, since the
nature of the materials for this hardly allows one to regard the rabbis as
contemporary with the author of Hebrews.

### I

We begin with that figure who has always been used as a foil to the author of
the epistle to the Hebrews, Philo of Alexandria.[1] The method pursued will be
to observe some of the most significant of those passages in Scripture which
are used by both authors. This should bring out clearly the relation between
the two as far as scriptural exegesis is concerned.

In Heb. 6:7–8 our author refers to Gen. 3:17–18 in an exhortation to his
readers not to apostatise but to go forward in the faith: 'land which has drunk
the rain...and brings forth vegetation...receives a blessing from God. But if
it bears thorns and thistles, it is worthless and near to being cursed' (RSV; the
quotations from Philo are my own translation). Philo in *Leg. Alleg.* III.222–3
uses the same passage as an analogy for what happens when mind (νοῦς) listens
to sense-perception (αἴσθησις) rather than the other way round (cf. also *Leg.
Alleg.* III.246–7).

In Heb. 6:13–14 occurs one of the most remarkable coincidences between
our author and Philo, his reference to God swearing by himself. See *Leg. Alleg.*

III.203. This oath was taken at the time of the sacrifice of Isaac (Gen. 22:16). But the author of Hebrews pays no attention to the context, whereas Philo does: cf. *Leg. Alleg.* III.209. In another passage, *De Abrahamo* 273, Philo represents this oath as being an indication of God's intimacy with Abraham: God was conversing with him as a friend with an acquaintance (ὡς φίλος γνωρίμῳ διαλεγόμενος). It is remarkable that when in 11:17–19 our author refers to the *Aqedah* he sees it not as a type of Christ's sacrifice but of Christ's resurrection. Philo, besides understanding the incident in a perfectly straightforward way as a test of Abraham's faith (*De Somniis* 1.195), also allegorises it. In *De Cherubim* 31 we learn that the taking of the knife to kill Isaac signified the cutting away from him all that was mortal, leaving the immortal soul; and in *De Fuga et Inventione* 132f Isaac's question and Abraham's reply really convey information about the mind, the senses, and the machinery of perception.

For the author of Hebrews Melchizedek was important because he represented an eternal priesthood, distinct from Levi's lineage. For Philo he represents the δίκαιος νοῦς that does not tyrannise over the soul and body (*Leg. Alleg.* III.78–84). Then in *De Congressu* 89f Philo refers to a list of tithing passages. Abraham giving tithes to Melchizedek means that the right mind brings peace and calm, instead of the passions and the senses being at variance. Melchizedek is described (*De Congressu* 99–100) as having received the 'self-learned and self-taught priesthood' (τὴν αὐτομαθῆ καὶ αὐτοδίδακτον ἱερωσύνην). His receiving the tithes from Abraham means that Abraham 'perceived rightly what comes by perception, spoke well what belongs to reason, and thought well as far as concerns the mind.'

In Heb. 9:1–10 there is a description of the furniture and the use of the tabernacle: it was intended to show the impermanent and ineffective nature of the old dispensation. For Philo the golden altar was 'a material symbol of God's propitious power'. The cherubim signify by etymology ἐπίγνωσις and ἐπιστήμη πολλή; they represent the kingly and creative powers of God; the lamp signifies the movements of the stars etc. (Cf. *De Vita Mosis* II/III. 95–100). In *Quis Rev. Div. Heres* 216f he gives us a more elaborate allegorisation of the lamp, using considerable number symbolism.

In Heb. 9:20–2 the author refers to Exod. 24:3–8 and Lev. 17:11 to show that blood was necessary for a covenant and that without shedding of blood there is (within the Levitical system at least) no remission of sin. Philo holds that Moses' action in Exod. 24:3f was done in order to teach that 'the holy race of wisdom is two-fold, one part divine and the other human'. It also signifies the mind (νοῦς) and perception (αἴσθησις); cf. *Quis Rev. Div. Her.* 182–4. In *Quod Det. Potiori* 79–83 he uses Lev. 17:11 to teach that we have a double nature, a vital and a rational. It would be difficult to imagine a greater contrast with Hebrews.

We next consider the treatment by the two writers of three patriarchs, Enoch, Noah, and Abraham. In 11:15 our author claims that Enoch's translation is an indication of his faith. Philo does indeed understand Gen. 5:24 as meaning that Enoch was transferred from the mortal life to the immortal; but he also understands it as meaning that the good man does not wish to associate with the evil, and hence he is not noticed by inferior men (*De Mutatione Nominium* 34–8; cf. also *De Abrahamo* 18–20; *De Praemiis et Poenis* 16–20). In Heb. 11:7 Noah manifests his faith by obeying God's command to build the ark and becomes 'an heir of the righteousness that is by faith', very like Abraham in Paul's writings. In *De Vita Mosis* ii.60 Philo tells us that Noah knew that even if God destroyed τὰ εἴδη, that which was incorruptible because it was like God's nature would remain. In Heb. 11:8–10 Abraham shows his faith by obeying God's call to set out from his native land not knowing whither he went. The same passage in Scripture, Gen. 12:1–3, is explained by Philo thus: 'God, wishing to purify the soul of man, first gives him as an inducement towards complete salvation a translation from three places, from the body, from perception, from utterance of the word (λόγου τοῦ κατὰ προφόραν; cf. *De Mig. Ab.* 1–2).

In 11:21 the author of Hebrews sees in Jacob's children in Gen. 20:27 an example of the patriarch's faith. Philo finds in this incident a reference to the existence of two faculties, memory and recollection, of which memory is the better (*Leg. Alleg.* iii.91ff).

Our author devotes several verses to a description of the giving of the torah, quoting a wide variety of Scripture passages drawn from Exodus 19–20; Deuteronomy 4–5; 19; cf. Heb. 12:18–29. He wishes to show that, fearful as was this occasion, the coming *parousia* will be still more fearful. Philo refers to the law-giving in several passages: see *De Spec. Leg.* ii, 188f; *Quis Rev. Div. Her.* 16–21; *De Mig. Ab.* 48–9; *De Decalogo* 48. Generally speaking he takes the details of the law-giving literally, since they redound to the glory of Moses (Moses spoke much more freely to God than we would dare to speak with an earthly king). But of course the people did not literally hear God's voice or see any form. What they saw, they saw with the eye of the soul.

Finally, we observe that our author sees in the slaughter and burning of the goat and the bullock on the day of Atonement a foreshadowing of the cross (13:10–11 interpreting Lev. 16:27). Philo does not refer to this verse, but in *De Plantatione* 61f he allegorises the two goats, and in *De Posteritate Caini* 71 he gives us an allegory of the scapegoat.

One must conclude that really as far as exegesis of Scripture is concerned Philo and our author have very little in common. Despite the impression of an acquaintance with the Alexandrian jewish tradition on the part of the author of Hebrews, the two writers differ very widely indeed. The author of Hebrews was interested in a christocentric, eschatological scheme of interpretation. He uses allegory very occasionally. Philo accepted the literal interpretation for the most part as a basis, but for him an allegorical interpretation that provided the philosophical, ethical and psychological teaching that he desired to find was of far greater importance.

## II

We turn now to a comparison with the other major non-Christian interpretation of Scripture that is nearly contemporary with Hebrews, that of Qumran. An obvious parallel at once presents itself: both the Qumran sectaries and the author of Hebrews believed that Jeremiah's prophecy of the new covenant in Jer. 31:31–4 applied to their group and they quote the passage. But this belief is not peculiar to Hebrews. Indeed it was shared by all the main writers of the NT.

An interesting contrast occurs with respect to Leviticus 16, the account of the ritual of the day of Atonement. Hebrews finds in this ritual a type of the rejection and death of Jesus (13:11–13). P. Wernberg-Møller points out an apparent implication of 1QS 2:2–4, where there is a reference to God's blessing on the elect and his curse on 'the men of Belial's lot'. He says that the juxtaposition of 'the men of God's lot' and 'the men of Belial's lot' probably refers to Lev. 16:8–10, where the lots are to be cast over the two goats. He suggests that 'our author may by some peculiar interpretation have taken (this passage) as referring to the two irreconcilable groups'. Where the author of Hebrews saw a reference to the reconciling death of Christ, the Qumran writer saw his favourite doctrine of double predestination.

There is however one notable text in the prophets which is used by both the author of Hebrews and the Qumran sectaries. This is Hab. 2:3–4, cited in Heb. 10:37–8 and in 1QHab. Hebrews, following the LXX, interprets the MT ולא יכזב לקץ ויפח (RSV 'it hastens to the end, it will not lie') as ὁ ἐρχόμενος ἥξει καὶ οὐ χρονίσει, 'the coming one shall come and shall not tarry'. Hebrews has emphasised what was undoubtedly a messianic reference in the LXX by adding the definite article, 'the coming one'. Our author has also transposed the next two lines. He did this in order to make it clear that the subject of ὑποστείληται was ὁ δίκαιος and not 'the coming one', as is the case with the LXX (cf. Michel, 1960, in loc.). The verb ὑποστείληται represents a mistranslation of the MT עפלה on the part of the translator of the LXX, but we need not enquire how that came about. Hebrews also reads ὁ δίκαιός μου. LXX has ἐκ πίστεώς μου and MT באמונתו. In Hebrews the phrase refers not to the Messiah (as I believe is the case in Paul's citation in Rom. 1:17; Gal. 3.11), but to the faithful Christian.

The Qumran commentator is more faithful to the Hebrew, since he does not have the LXX translation to come between him and the original. He fastens on the phrase which the LXX and Hebrews interpret in a messianic sense and finds in it the message that the end will be long in coming. His words are פשרו אשר יארוך הקץ האחרון (Lohse, 1971, pp. 236–7; 'the interpretation is that the last time will be long in coming' [my translation]). The rest of the passage he understands as follows, 'Interpreted, this concerns all those who observe the Law in the House of Judah, whom God will deliver from the house of judgment because of their suffering, and because of their faith in the Teacher of Righteousness' (Vermes, 1962, p. 239). It is interesting that this is also the way in which the Targum of Jonathan understands v. 3b: 'If there is a long period of waiting for the event, keep looking out for it' (quoted by Bruce, 1964, *in loc*.). And of course we notice that the faithful in Qumran live by their faith in the teacher of righteousness.

There is a certain resemblance between the usage in Qumran and in Hebrews; both use it to encourage faith in the time of waiting; both associate the period with suffering (see Heb. 10:32–4). But whereas Qumran quotes it in order to show that the end time is delayed, Hebrews quotes it in order to show that the end time (by which of course the author means the *parousia*) is imminent. The text is not as important for Hebrews as it is for Paul; Bruce (1964, *in loc*.) describes it as 'the principal *testimonium* for the doctrine of justification by faith'. For the author of Hebrews it serves as a useful text with which to introduce his great catalogue of the heroes of faith in the course of Israel's history. It is a text which would appeal to all, including the Qumran writer, Hebrews, and Paul, who approached Scripture with strong eschatological assumptions.

Another point of contact between Hebrews and Qumran as far as Scripture interpretation is concerned lies in their treatment of the figure of Melchizedek. We now know that the Qumran sectaries regarded Melchizedek as a superior angel. De Jonge and van der Woude in their magisterial article (1966) describe him as an archangel. In 11QMelch, Melchizedek is called אלהים, a word never used of God, but only of angels, in this fragment. He executes the judgment of God against Belial; and they acutely compare Heb. 2:14, where there is a reference to Christ's victory over Satan. They suggest that the phrase ἀφομοιώμενος δὲ τῷ υἱῷ τοῦ θεοῦ in 7:3 indicates Melchizedek's subordination to Christ. He is a 'copy' of the Son of God (see pp. 305, 316–7, 321). Much of this is admirably said, but is seems rather to confirm my theory that Hebrews saw Melchizedek as an appearance of the pre-existent Son, but did not have the scope or perhaps the nerve to say so (see 5:11f). The more closely Melchizedek's position in Hebrews approximates to that which he has in Qumran, the less likely it is that Hebrews viewed him as an angel. Our author would have had to have made absolutely clear Melchizedek's subordination to Jesus, as he does in the case of the angels (1:5–14). In fact he never uses any word of Melchizedek that suggests a copy, still less does he view him as a 'type', as Schröger (1972, pp. 313–29) implies.[2] I agree therefore with van der Woude and de Jonge that 'the Melchizedek conception of Hebrews was influenced by notions which are also to be found in Qumran' (p. 322), but maintain that Hebrews accorded to Melchizedek a still higher role than that which he holds in Qumran.

One more text treated by both Qumran and Hebrews must be mentioned, 2 Sam. 7:14: this is quoted in 4QFlor[3] and in Heb. 1:5b. The text is interpreted thus in Qumran: 'That is the sprout of David who will stand up with the searcher of the law...in Zion at the end of the days' (my trans.). The phrase rendered 'searcher of the law' is דורש התורה. Does it refer to the teacher of righteousness, expected to return when the messiah comes? Bruce well describes the Teacher as 'not only a spiritual leader but a figure of eschatological significance'.[4] The words which the Qumran writer applies to the Davidic messiah and possibly to the teacher of righteousness, both in the future, the author of Hebrews applies to the messiah who has already come in the person of Jesus.

In his exegesis of Scripture the author of Hebrews is much closer to the Qumran sectaries than he is to Philo, because both he and they approach Scripture with a strongly eschatological emphasis, something which was not at all central in Philo's thought. Hebrews differs from Qumran chiefly in the fact that for him the Messiah had already come. Hence his exegesis is more christocentric than is that of the Qumran writers. Just because it was the community that existed in the present time and not the messiah, the Qumran writers tended to find references to their community in Scripture in a way which was not necessary for the author of Hebrews.

## III

In comparing Hebrews's attitude to Scripture with Paul's we begin with the point of closest convergence:

2 Cor. 3:11:
εἰ γὰρ τὸ καταργούμενον διὰ δόξης, πολλῷ μᾶλλον τὸ μένον ἐν δόξῃ.

Heb. 8:13:
ἐν τῷ λέγειν καινήν, πεπαλαίωκεν τὴν πρώτην. τὸ δὲ παλαιούμενον καὶ γηράσκον ἐγγὺς ἀφανισμοῦ.

Paul and Hebrews agree that the old dispensation is obsolete and has been superseded by the new and better dispensation in Christ. By what respective routes have the two writers reached the same point? Paul contrasts with the old dispensation the new dispensation based on faith in Christ. Hebrews contrasts the old with the new which has been inaugurated by Christ's sacrifice. Paul is thinking in terms of knowing and serving God; Hebrews in terms of worshipping and serving God. Paul thinks of the torah as a system, a way of life alternative to the way of faith. Hebrews thinks of it as a system of worship, preparatory to the sacrifice of Christ whereby Christians can obtain forgiveness and cleansing from their sins. Faith does not play the same role in Hebrews that it does in Paul. It is not something revealed in Abraham and then suspended by the coming of the torah, only to be taken up again by Christ, as it is in Paul. On the contrary, for Hebrews all the great characters of the OT exhibited faith. The coming of the torah made no difference to this. In his list of the heroes of the faith he goes serenely on from Joseph to Moses, and from Moses to Joshua, Rahab, and Gideon, without any suggestion that the torah inaugurated an epoch where faith was displaced by works (11:22–3, 30–2).

There are however two passages in Hebrews where a superficial reading might give the impression that Hebrews holds the same faith-versus-works doctrine as Paul does. These are 6:1 and 9:14, where the author refers to 'repentance from dead works' as part of the rudiments of Christianity (6:1), and describes the blood of Christ as 'cleansing our conscience from dead works' (9:1). Does the phrase 'dead works' mean 'the works of the law', the attempt to approach God by means of strict observance of the torah? On the whole it seems unlikely. It is true that Westcott (1892) understands the phrase to mean 'all the works corresponding with the Levitical system not in their original institution, but in their actual relation to the Gospel'. But this seems unduly complicated. Windisch (1913) takes it to mean 'wirkliche Sünden, die zum Tode führen' ('real sins which lead to death'), and well compared Col. 2:13; Eph. 2:1,5. Likewise Strathmann (1963) says the phrase does not mean the jewish external works-righteousness.[5] It means the life of unregenerate man. Even Paul does not suggest that one should *repent* of the works of the law.

Would Paul have recognised in the prescriptions of the old dispensation a foreshadowing of the new, as Hebrews does? It seems unlikely. Paul does not anywhere specifically refer to any of the ritual or cultic ordinances in the torah. He was not interested in the torah's prescriptions about sacrifice, as the author of Hebrews is. Professor Otto Betz (1985) has recently suggested that Paul's citation of Ps. 69:22–3 in Rom. 11:9 may be an implicit condemnation of the temple cult: 'May their table become a snare to them'. He may well be right.

There is another point at which Hebrews to some extent converges with Paul in the exposition of Scripture, and that is in the treatment of Abraham. The author of Hebrews agrees with Paul in seeing Abraham's coming out from Mesopotamia at God's call as a sign of his faith (11:8). Likewise Abraham's believing that God could give him offspring despite his advanced age is regarded as an indication of his faith (11:11 – unless indeed we adopt the reading that attributes this act of faith to Sarah). But unlike Paul (Rom. 4:17–21), he does not connect this with belief in the resurrection. He does however see the sacrifice of Isaac as a type (παραβολή) of the resurrection, whereas Paul is remarkably silent on the subject of the *Aqedah*.

There are one or two Scripture citations that are common to the two writers: Hab.2:3–4 is one of them (see Rom. 1:17; Gal. 3:11; Heb. 10:38). Paul probably uses this citation in a messianic sense: the Righteous One when he came was to live by faith. Hebrews, as we have seen, uses the citation in order to encourage his readers to endure until the *parousia*. Hebrews makes great use of Psalms 8 and 110 in connexion with the priesthood and exaltation of Christ. Paul certainly uses both these psalms in Rom. 8:34; 1 Cor. 15:25–8, in much the same context. And both authors make use of the concept of the new covenant from Jer. 31:31–4. But all these passages were no doubt part of the Scripture testimones used by all well-instructed christian evangelists.

Certainly of all the expositors of Scripture with which we are comparing the epistle to the Hebrews, the nearest to the author of this epistle is Paul. But this is because they are both early Christians learned in the Scriptures who accept a christocentric interpretation. The author of Hebrews is not a disciple of Paul's and there is no evidence to suggest that he had read any of Paul's works. He is remarkably independent as an exegete. Granted a common determination to find Christ in Scripture, in other respects his interests are different to those of Paul. This is why there are relatively few passages from Scripture which they quote in common. Those parts of Scripture which mean much to one hold little significance for the other. The author of Hebrews does not quote very much from Isaiah, and Paul shows no interest at all in the ritual prescriptions of Leviticus. Where they do coincide it is in references to Scripture passages which were widely used by all early christian exegetes.

When we turn to the other great theologian of the NT, the author of the fourth gospel, we find even less in common between him and the author of Hebrews. This is partly because John is writing a gospel, not a λόγος παρακλήσεως, but it is also due to the different circumstances in which John was writing. In John's day the separation between Jews and Christians had become more marked: one could no longer attend the synagogue and continue to be a Christian. John is estranged from the torah: it is 'your law' (8:17; 10:34 *s.v.l.*). As in Paul, the law is contrasted with grace (1:17).

We can however point to two places in the FG where there is a certain convergence with Hebrews. The first is John 19:36, the episode of the soldier piercing the side of the dead Jesus. John sees in this a fulfilment of some passage in the law, probably Exod. 12:46.[6] John is here doing what Hebrews does, interpreting a ritual prescription in the torah as prophesying the mode of Christ's death (cf. Heb. 13:11–13). Paul never does this. The other place is John 7:17–24, 37–9. I have suggested (1980, pp. 161–2) that, among other

Scripture passages lying behind the mysterious citation in 7:38, is Ps. 40:8b 'thy law is in my heart'. LXX renders 'heart' with κοιλία. In 7:17–24 there is much talk about doing God's will. It looks as if Psalm 40 lies behind the whole passage. Psalm 40 is of course profoundly applied to the work of Christ in Heb. 10:5–10. We may be sure that the author of the FG would have heartily endorsed the author of Hebrews's interpretation of this psalm.

IV

When we try to assess the worth of the epistle to the Hebrews as a piece of scriptural exegesis, we must at all costs avoid making the mistake of judging the author by the standard of our methods of scriptural exegesis today. If we were to do so, we would have to say that he did not seriously consider the original text and setting of his citations, altered the text to suit his convenience, and made no attempt to establish original authorship. Most scholars have realised this by now, though a hankering after an attempt to present the writer as a reasonable exegete by our criteria may perhaps be traced in the mistaken efforts of commentators to prove that the author did not mean his scriptural quotations to be taken as proofs but rather as a suitable mode of expressing what he meant; see Kuss (1966) on Heb. 10:37f, and Hughes (1979, pp. 60–61). We must accept that the author believed he was providing striking proof from Scripture for what he was saying, strange though it may seem to us.

We must judge the writer of Hebrews by the standards of exegesis of his own day. As such, he must be described as a very able and imaginative exegete. Scripture is more central in his work than in any other book of the NT, except the Apocalypse (and the scriptural technique of John the Divine is quite different). Our author sets out to interpret the work of Christ in terms of the cultus as recorded in Scripture; in this he is remarkably successful. Both in his clear indication of what is obsolete, and in his christianised use of scriptural terms, his work has been of the greatest value to the christian church down the ages. If indeed the theologians of the early Middle Ages in the West had paid more attention to his theology they would have avoided much unsatisfactory exposition of the significance of Christ's sacrifice.

There is however one basic point at which Christians today can agree with the writer to the Hebrews in his exposition of Scripture. It is in the point of what Hughes calls 'revelation' and Schröger 'Heilsgeschichte'. Both these scholars rightly emphasise that what the writer was trying to do was to interpret Scripture in terms of the revelation of God in Jesus, and that must mean in terms of salvation history (see Hughes, p. 157, n.4; Schröger, p. 314). He approached Scripture, as did all the writers of the NT, with christocentric assumptions. Christians also must understand the OT in this sense. Not that

# Hebrews

we are thrown back on the traditional method of allegorical interpretation so as to bring in a reference to Christ by means of a violent distortion of the original meaning of the text; nor by the old-fashioned 'prophetical proofs' in the OT (cf. Schröger, p. 325). But we must see the event of Christ in the light of all God's dealings with his people. In the last analysis the God who is revealed to us in Jesus Christ is the same God as he who made himself known πολυμερῶς καὶ πολυτρόπως to the fathers by means of the prophets. Our method of tracing the activity and revelation of that God in the OT must be widely different from that of the author of Hebrews, and indeed of all the writers of the NT. But our aim in interpreting Scripture is the same as his. And, at a very basic level, his assumptions about Scripture are the same as ours, that is, that all that is true and valuable in the revelation that is recorded in the OT finds its completion and justification in Jesus Christ.

## NOTES

1 All quotations from Philo are from L. Cohn and P. Wendland (eds.), *Philonis Alexandri Opera Omnia Quae Supersunt* (Berlin, 1896).
2 He actually calls Christ 'der Antityp des Melchisedech' (319) – a most unhappy phrase! In Heb. 9:24 the ἀντίτυπα describe the imperfect, temporary furnishings of the tabernacle, made obsolete by the coming of Christ.
3 See Brooke (1985): Fragment 1:11; Hebrew text on p. 87. Cf. also Lohse (1971), p. 257.
4 Bruce (1964), *in loc*. Heb. 10:37–9. Brooke (1985), p. 92, Brooke (op. cit. 92) renders דורש התורה with 'the interpreter of the law'.
5 A reference to the works of the law is also rejected by von Soden, Moffat, Bruce, Kuss, Braun (this last would associate the phrase with the worship of pagan gods). Michel gives both views, and Spicq thinks it could include the works of the law.
6 I rule out the possibility that the reference is to Ps. 34:20. In this psalm the devotee is promised immunity from pain and disaster in this world: to apply this to Christ, who had just been barbarously executed with the maximum of suffering, would have been too painfully ironical.

## BIBLIOGRAPHY

O. Betz *Die Menschensohnwörte Jesus und die Zukunftserwartung des Paulus (Daniel 7.13–14)*, vol. 2 of O. Betz (ed.), *Jesus und das Daniel Buch* in *Arbeiten zum Neuen Testament und Judentum* (Frankfurt, 1985).
H. Braun *An die Hebräer* (Tübingen, 1984).
J. G. Brooke *Exegesis at Qumran* (Sheffield, 1985).
F. F. Bruce *Commentary on the Epistle to the Hebrews* (Edinburgh, 1964).
L. Cohn and P. Wendland (eds.) *Philonis Alexandri Opera Omnia Quae Supersunt* (Berlin, 1896).

A. T. Hanson *The New Testament Interpretation of Scripture* (London, 1980).

*Living Utterances of God* (London, 1983).

G. Howard 'Hebrews and the Old Testament Quotations', *NovT* 10 (1968), 208–16.

G. Hughes *Hebrews and Hermeneutics*, SNTSMS 36 (Cambridge, 1979).

M. de Jonge and A. S. van der Woude 'II Q Melchizedek and the New Testament', *NTS* 12 (1966), 301–26.

O. Kuss *Der Brief an die Hebräer* (Regensburg, 1966).

E. Lohse *Die Texte aus Qumran* (Münich, 1971).

O. Michel *Der Brief an die Hebräer* (Göttingen, 1960).

J. Moffatt *A Critical and Exegetical Commentary on the Epistle to the Hebrews*, ICC (Edinburgh, 1924).

F. Schröger *Das hermeneutische Instrumentarium des Hebräerbriefverfassers*, in J. Ernst (ed.), *Schriftauslegung* (Münich, Paderborn, Vienna, 1972), pp. 313–29.

H. von Soden *Hebräerbrief, Briefe des Petrus, Jakobus, Judas* (Freiburg, 1890).

S. G. Sowers *The Hermeneutics of Philo and Hebrews* (Zürich, 1915).

C. Spicq *L'Épitre aux Hébreux*, 2nd ed. (Paris, 1952).

H. Strathmann *Der Brief an die Hebräer* (Gottingen, 1963).

K. J. Thomas 'The Old Testament Citations in Hebrews', *NTS* 11 (1965), 303–25.

G. Vermes *The Dead Sea Scrolls in English* (London, 1962).

P. Wernberg-Møller *The Manual of Discipline* (London, 1957).

B. F. Westcott *The Epistle to the Hebrews*, 2nd ed. (London, 1892).

E. C. Wickham *The Epistle to the Hebrews* (London, 1910).

R. Williamson *Philo and the Epistle to the Hebrews*, ALGHJ 4 (London, 1970).

H. Windisch *Der Hebräerbrief* (Tübingen, 1913).

P. S. M. Zarb *De Historia Canonis Utriusque Testamenti*, 2nd ed. (Rome, 1934).

# 18 · James, 1 and 2 Peter, Jude

RICHARD BAUCKHAM

THESE four letters contain a wide variety of types of use of the Old Testament, some of them, as we shall see, indistinguishable from contemporary jewish use of Scripture, and most of them heavily indebted to traditions of jewish exegesis. In order to keep the discussion within bounds, I shall select some important types of use of the OT: formal exegesis akin to the Qumran pesharim, in Jude and 1 Peter; OT figures as ethical and religious models, in James and 2 Peter; paraenetic use of Scripture, in 1 Peter; and interpretation of the Mosaic law, in James.

In my view (argued for Jude and 2 Peter in Bauckham, 1983), Jude and James derive from early palestinian jewish Christianity, and 1 and 2 Peter from Roman Christianity just before and not long after the death of Peter. I therefore discuss them in that order, which I think likely to be the order in which they were written, but the discussion is largely independent of these views of date and provenance, though it may help to confirm them.

## JUDE

The short letter of Jude contains perhaps the most elaborate and carefully composed piece of formal exegesis in the style of the Qumran pesharim to be found in the NT, though it has only recently been recognised as such (Ellis, 1978; Bauckham, 1983). This passage, which I shall call a midrash (using the word loosely to refer to a passage of formal exegesis, not necessarily in the form of the rabbinic midrashim), is vv. 4–19, of which v. 4 forms the introductory statement of theme. Though it has usually been regarded as a mere stream of undisciplined denunciation, the passage is in fact a detailed exegetical *argument*, designed to show that the false teachers who are active in Jude's churches have been foretold in prophecy, which condemns their libertine behaviour and predicts their judgment at the parousia.

The midrash can be analysed thus:

| | |
|---|---|
| 4 | Introductory statement of theme |
| 5–7 | 'Text' 1: Three OT types |
| 8–10 | + interpretation |
| 9 | including secondary 'text' 1a: Michael and the devil |

11      'Text' 2: Three more OT types
12–13   + interpretation
12–13   including secondary allusions (Ezek. 34:2; Prov. 25:14; Isa.
        57:20; 1 Enoch 80:6)
14–15   'Text' 3: The prophecy of Enoch (1 Enoch 1:9)
16      + interpretation
17–18   'Text' 4: The prophecy of the apostles
19      + interpretation.

The midrash consists of four main 'texts' each followed by a commentary identifying the false teachers as those to whom the 'text' refers. The 'texts' – although for convenience I shall call them this, since they function as such – are not all scriptural quotations. The first pair, texts 1 and 2, are not verbal prophecies but historical types, to which Jude refers in summary form rather than by quoting Scripture. However, v. 5a (indicating dependence on paraenetic tradition; and see also Bauckham, 1983, pp. 46–7) and the fact that v. 11 is a prophetic woe-oracle in form, suggest that 'texts' 1 and 2 may already have been known to Jude in the form he gives them. They are clearly a pair, being each a set of three types, and texts 3 and 4 form a second pair, this time of verbal prophecies of the false teachers, one ancient and one modern. They are both quotations, but the introductory formulae (vv. 14a, 17–18a) indicate the differences between quotations from a written and an oral source. The written source is 1 Enoch, a work with which (or with parts of which) Jude was very familiar (Bauckham, 1983, p. 7), but the fact that he sets it alongside a quotation from an oral prophecy means that we cannot deduce his view of the canon of Scripture from this. However, it is certainly odd that none of Jude's four main 'texts' is an actual quotation from the canonical OT.

Despite this peculiarity, the midrashic *structure* of 'text' + interpretation is plain. The transition from 'text' to interpretation is in each case marked in two ways: by a change of tense, from verbs in the past or future in the 'texts' to present tenses in the interpretation, and by phrases with οὗτοι used in a formulaic way at the beginning of each section of interpretation. These phrases, which are intended to identify the false teachers as the people to whom the prophecies refer, resemble exegetical formulae used in the Dead Sea Scrolls for the same kind of purpose, and in particular the form used in vv. 12 and 19 corresponds in wording and function to the Qumran usage (see Bauckham, 1983, p. 45).

As well as the four main 'texts' a secondary 'text' (1a) is introduced in v. 9 to help the interpretation of 'text' 1. This is a reference, with close verbal allusion, to an apocryphal account of the death of Moses (for details, cf. Bauckham, 1983, pp. 65–76). Again the 'text' is marked off by change of tense and by οὗτοι at the beginning of v. 10, but v. 10 also continues the interpretation of 'text' 1 begun in v. 8. Moreover, v. 9 is not a type or prophecy of the false teachers, but an example with which they are contrasted. It should therefore be seen as part of the commentary on 'text' 1. Such use of a secondary quotation can be paralleled in the Qumran pesharim, which also, to the same effect, incorporate implicit allusions to other texts in the interpretation of a given text (see Horgan, 1979, p. 95; Brooke, 1985, pp. 130–3, 145–7, 304–5). Jude adopts the latter practice in vv. 12–13, where a series of scriptural allusions are worked into the commentary on 'text' 2 (for these and the structural role of 1 Enoch 2:1–5:4; 80:2–8 in these verses, see Bauckham, 1983, pp. 78–9, 87–91; Osburn, 1985).

Certain features of Jude's midrash we have already compared with the Qumran pesharim. Though the comparison cannot be pressed in every detail, it is an illuminating one, especially if we think of Jude's midrash as comparable with the 'thematic pesharim' (4QFlor, 11QMelch, 4Q 176, 177, 182, 183), which are commentaries on a collection of texts on one theme. With the pesharim, Jude shares the hermeneutical *presupposition* that prophetic Scripture refers to the last days in which the commentator is living, though Jude's use of typology as well as prophecy is not characteristic of the Qumran pesharim. He also uses exegetical *formulae* similar to those in the pesharim (see above on οὗτοι phrases; and Bauckham, 1983, p. 93 on v. 14a). Finally, he shares with the pesharim exegetical *principles and techniques* which we have yet to mention. Although such techniques are by no means unique to Qumran (see, e.g., Brooke, 1985, pp. 284–8), the full range of resemblances we have noted aligns Jude's midrash more closely with the Qumran pesharim than with other examples of jewish exegesis.

Exegetical techniques in Jude include the deliberate modification of a text to suit its interpretation (vv. 14–15: see Bauckham, 1983, pp. 93–7; Osburn, 1977), but the most prominent feature is the use of catchword connexions. Some instances of this are examples of *gezera šawa*: the association of texts by means of common words. Thus 'texts' 1 and 2 are linked by ἀπωλ- (vv. 5, 11) and 'texts' 3 and 4 by ἀσεβ- (vv. 15, 18). Similarly, the secondary 'text' 1a is linked to 'text' 1 by κρίσιν (vv. 6, 9), and one of the secondary allusions in v. 13 is connected with 'text' 2 by the link between πλάνη (v. 11) and πλανῆται (v. 13, alluding to 1 Enoch 80:6).

Catchwords also link the introductory statement of the theme of the midrash (v. 4) to the 'texts': κρίμα (v. 4) to κρίσιν in 'texts' 1, 1a, and 3 (vv. 6, 9, 15), and ἀσεβεῖς (v. 4) to the four occurrences of this word-group in 'text' 3 (v. 15) and the one in 'text' 4 (v. 18). These links establish v. 4 as an anticipatory, summarising interpretation of all four 'texts', while the especially close links with 'text' 3 reinforce the impression which is in any case given by v. 4 (πάλαι προγεγραμμένοι) that 'text' 3 is really Jude's key text.

Finally, catchwords link interpretation to 'text'. Thus σάρκα and κυριότητα in v. 8 pick up σαρκός and κύριος in vv. 7, 5, while βλασφημίας (v. 9) is picked up by the words of interpretation which both precede and follow this 'text' (βλασφημοῦσιν: vv. 8, 10). Sometimes, as in the Qumran pesharim (Horgan, 1979, pp. 245–6, n. 70), catchwords refer not to the 'text' under immediate interpretation but to a following 'text' (κατὰ τὰς ἐπιθυμίας... πορευόμενοι: vv. 16, 18) or to an earlier text (ζόφος... τετήρηται, v. 13; ζόφον τετήρηκεν, v. 6).

## JAMES

Lacking the space to study all uses of Scripture in James (for the fullest listing and discussion of possible allusions, see Chaine, 1927, pp. xli–lxiv; cf. also Mayor, 1897, pp. lxix–lxxvii), we shall deal with the two most important aspects. These are James's use of OT figures as ethical and religious paradigms and his treatment of the Mosaic law.

OT figures – Abraham (2:21–3), Rahab (2:25), the prophets (5:10), Job (5:11) and Elijah (5:17) – play an important role, as examples of righteousness, in James's argument, but they are very much the OT figures as *interpreted* in current jewish haggadah. James's Abraham, for example, is much closer to the contemporary jewish image of Abraham than is Paul's radical reinterpretation of the patriarch. (For the jewish features of James's treatment of Abraham, see Ward, 1968; Davids, 1974, pp. 121–2, 129–33; Dibelius, 1976, pp. 168–74; Jacobs, 1976; Davids, 1982, 127–30.) In the light of the jewish image of Abraham, it is probable that for James Abraham's faith (2:22) is not faith in Paul's sense, but the monotheistic faith of the *shema* – as in 2:19 – for which Abraham was famous, as the man who renounced idols and pioneered monotheism (e.g. Jub. 12:1–21; Apoc. Abr. 1–8; Josephus, *Ant.* 1.154–7). Relying on his readers' familiarity with Abraham's reputation for faith, James can presuppose it in 2:22–3, in which he adduces his primary scriptural evidence, the *Akedah* (Gen. 22:1–14), even before he adds, as a secondary supporting text, Gen. 15:6 (Jas. 2:23), in which Abraham's faith is explicitly mentioned. That Abraham's faith was complemented by his works is proved by the *Akedah*, because this was the greatest (Philo, *Abr.* 167; Jub. 17:16), the most difficult and the most important of the 'tests' to which God subjected Abraham to prove his faithfulness and obedience (the tests usually reckoned as ten: Jub. 17:15–18; 19:8; *Aboth* 5:3; other references to Abraham's testing are Jdt. 8:25–7; Sir. 44:20–21; 1 Macc. 2:52; Heb. 11:17). Abraham was 'justified' on this occasion in the sense that God declared that he had proved righteous under severe testing (Gen. 22:12; Jub. 17:16; 18:11, 16). Gen. 15:6 can then be adduced to confirm the point, even though in Genesis it precedes the account of the *Akedah*, because in Jewish usage this text had been detached from its context and become 'a motto for the whole of Abraham's life'

(Dibelius, 1976, p. 170). Moreover, in Jewish interpretation the 'righteousness' of this verse was connected with the trials in which Abraham proved faithful to God and therefore with the *Akedah* as the climax of these (1 Macc. 2:52). Thus, for James, Gen. 15:6 means that Abraham was 'justified' not by his monotheistic faith alone, but by the acts of difficult obedience to God in which he proved faithful under trial. Finally, James's use of the title 'friend of God' for Abraham is not loosely but closely connected with this argument. James knew it, not from the LXX (in which Isa. 41:8; 2 Chron. 20:7 are not translated in this way), but perhaps from the MT and certainly from jewish haggadic tradition in which it was closely connected with Abraham's testing. In remaining faithful to God under trial Abraham proved his *love* for God (Jub. 17:18; *Aboth* 5:3) and *as a result* 'he was recorded as a friend of the Lord in the heavenly tablets' (Jub. 19:9; cf. 1 Clem. 10:1; CD 3:2; Jub. 30:19–20). Especially this was true of the *Akedah*, in which Abraham proved his love of God in his willingness to sacrifice his beloved son (Jub. 17:16; Philo, *Abr.* 271; and cf. Jacobs, 1975–6, 458–61).

The haggadic background to 2:21–3 suggests that Abraham was relevant to James, not simply as the obvious biblical example of faith and works (which it would certainly not have needed Paul's theological use of Abraham to suggest to James), but also in more specific ways. In the first place, the theme of Abraham's *testing*, which was not only in Gen. 22:1 but also so prominent a feature of the haggadic tradition that in 2:21–3 James does not have to use the word in order to suggest the theme. This relates the Abraham material to the letter's more general theme of πειρασμός (1:2–4, 12–15) which 'forms the thread which ties the whole epistle together' (Davids, 1982, p. 35). The 'perfecting' (ἐτελειώθη) of Abraham's faith by works (2:22) therefore represents the 'perfect work' (ἔργον τέλειον) of steadfastness under the trials which are testing the faith of James's readers (1:2–4).

Secondly, practical charitable activity is a major feature of the 'works' which James expects of his readers (1:27; 2:15–16), and some have therefore seen in Abraham's 'works' (2:21) a reference to his hospitality, for which he was well known in jewish haggadah (Ward, 1968; Davids, 1982, p. 127). This is less convincing (see Laws, 1980, 134–5), because, in spite of the proximity of 2:15–16, it is most natural to interpret the 'works' of 2:21 as Abraham's obedience in the tests which culminated in the *Akedah* and which did not include his hospitality. The tradition that Isaac was spared as the reward of Abraham's hospitality seems to be attested only in late sources. On the other hand, since it is 'faith and hospitality' which link Abraham and Rahab in 1 Clem. 10:7; 12:1, it may be that a traditional pairing of Abraham and Rahab as instances of faith demonstrated in hospitality accounts for James's introduction of Rahab in 2:25 (Davids, 1978, 116–17).

As examples (ὑπόδειγμα, 5:10, a technical term in citations of OT examples) of faithful endurance under the trials of affliction, James cites the prophets (5:10) and Job (5:11). The persecution of the prophets, not especially prominent in the OT itself, was a major theme in later haggadah (T. Levi 16:2; Lives of the Prophets; Matt. 5:12; 23:29–37; Mark 12:2–5; Heb. 11:36–7; Asc. Isa. 1–5). James does not mention the martyrdom of the prophets, on which the tradition focused, no doubt because his readers did not face martyrdom, but only less severe hardships in which their need was for endurance until the parousia (5:8). From this point of view, the example of Job is more precisely to the purpose, in that Job endured testing, but not martyrdom, until God in his compassion produced the outcome (τέλος κυρίου) of blessing. Job's ὑπομονή is not the most obvious feature of the OT book, but it receives more emphasis already in the LXX of Job (2:9–10, on which see Heater, 1982, 31–6) and much more emphasis in the Testament of Job, which frequently uses the term and its cognates (1:5; 4:6; 5:1; 27:4, 7) and also ascribes Job's eventual blessing to God's compassion (σπλαγχνισθείς) and mercy (26:5; 47:4). It is possible that James and his readers knew the Testament of Job (Rahnenführer, 1971, pp. 86–7; and cf. Jas. 1:12 with T. Job 4:6–5:1). In any case, James is dependent on the kind of haggadic tradition which the Testament of Job reflects (Davids, 1978, p. 119), focusing on the Job of the prologue and epilogue to the canonical book.

Finally, the account of Elijah in 5:17–18 does not depend directly on 1 Kings, which ascribes neither the beginning nor the end of the drought to Elijah's prayer (though 18:42 might be interpreted as prayer) and gives it a shorter duration (18:1). But the tradition behind James is reflected in 4 Ezra 7:109 and Lives of the Prophets 21:5, which, except for the time period, corresponds closely with Jas. 5:17–18. (Though this verse in the Lives of the Prophets is probably an addition to the text, it is more likely to depend on Jewish tradition than on James.) The period, paralleled in Luke 4:25, is the symbolic time of judgment (cf. especially Rev. 11:3, 6). It seems likely that this traditional interpretation of the Elijah story reflects the practice of Jewish charismatics, such as Honi the Circle-drawer and Hanina ben Dosa, who were famous for their prayers for rain. Unfortunately, Epiphanius's story (*Haer.* 78:14), which would make James himself one of these, is only a legendary development of Jas. 5:18 (against Eisenman, 1986, p. 34).

Thus James's references to OT figures reveal a wide acquaintance with and, in some cases, quite subtle use of traditional haggadah, which places James quite firmly within a Jewish context (*contra* Laws, 1980, pp. 4, 10–11), so much so that no distinctively christian interpretation emerges in this material at all. A christian emphasis, at least, will be more apparent in the second main area of James's use of the OT: his treatment of the Mosaic law.

James's concept of the 'whole law' seems to focus on the decalogue (2:11) and on the law of love of neighbour (Lev. 19:18b), which he calls 'the royal law' (2:8), probably because it is the law of God's kingdom (2:5). But 2:9 shows that partiality (the theme of 2:1–7) is transgression of the law of love, because the law against partiality in Lev. 19:15 is one of the implications of love. In other words, James understands Lev. 19:18b as a summary of the Mosaic law, and he understands it in its immediate context in Leviticus 19, where the other commandments are examples of the application of the general principal of love of neighbour. For this reason it is not possible to obey Lev. 19:18b without obeying Lev. 19:15. L. T. Johnson (1982) has convincingly shown that the whole section Lev. 19:12–18, which ends with the summarising law of love of neighbour, lies behind James's work:

| Lev. 19:12 | Jas. 5:12 |
|---|---|
| 19:13 | 5:4 |
| 19:15 | 2:1, 9 |
| 19:16 | 4:11 |
| 19:17b | 5:20 |
| 19:18a | 5:9 |
| 19:18b | 2:8 |

This focus on the decalogue and the ethical requirements of Leviticus 19 as the essence of the Mosaic law is by no means un-jewish. It is paralleled, for example, in the Sentences of Pseudo-Phocylides, which begins with a summary of the decalogue (3–8) and a paraenetic passage based especially on Leviticus 19 (9–21), though without reference to the love commandment. But it is also true that this focusing of the law on its moral requirements, crystallised in the decalogue and the love commandment, is typical of the Jesus tradition (Mark 10:9; 12:31; Matt. 5:21, 27, 43; 19:18–19). Thus James's notion of keeping the 'whole law' reflects Jesus' interpretation of the law, which makes the love commandment the law of the kingdom (2:8) and means that the specific commandments of Leviticus are to be read in the light of the teaching of Jesus (Jas. 4:11; cf. Matt. 7:1; Jas. 5:12; cf. Matt. 5:33–7; Jas. 5:20; cf. Matt. 18:15). James's is a jewish-christian attitude to the law, which accepts its authority but also accepts Jesus as its interpreter (cf. 2:1).

## 1 PETER

The lavish use of OT quotations and allusions in 1 Peter falls into two main categories: prophetic interpretation and paraenetic application, although, as we shall see, these two categories are not wholly distinct. We shall confine ourselves here to studying one major example of each (for other aspects and examples of the use of the OT in 1 Peter, see, besides the commentaries, Dalton, 1965; Adinolfi, 1967; Hanson, 1980, pp. 122–35; Osborne, 1981; Hanson, 1983, pp. 140–6; Manns, 1984).

1 Pet. 1:10–12 is a fine statement of the early christian view of the OT ('prophets' should not be understood too narrowly: they include the psalmists, cf. Acts 2:30; 1 Pet. 2:7) as prophecy now fulfilled and being fulfilled in Jesus Christ and his people, and consequently as prophecy which is fully understood only now that the gospel is preached under the inspiration of the same Spirit who inspired the prophecies. The passage has often been compared with 1QpHab 7:1–8, and it is therefore not surprising that our author's methods of scriptural exegesis, like Jude's, also bear comparison with those of the Qumran pesharim. This can be seen most clearly in 2:4–10, which stands out in 1 Peter as a particularly complex and studied piece of exegesis, resembling both the thematic pesharim of Qumran and Jude 4–19.

Elliott's (1966) full discussion of the structure and meaning of this passage seems to me largely to carry conviction, despite the criticisms of Best (1969; cf. Elliott, 1982, pp. 240–1; also the independent study of the use of the OT in this passage by Danker, 1967). But the exact status of the introductory verses 4–5 in relation to the rest of the passage (a point in debate between Elliott and Best) can be clarified when we notice that these verses play a role analogous to that of Jude 4. In other words, vv. 4–5 briefly state the theme which is then both supported and expanded by the OT citations and their interpretation in vv. 6–10. The introductory statement of the theme in vv. 4–5 has been carefully composed to introduce vv. 6–10, and so (like Jude 4) it already echoes the texts to be quoted and provides a basic framework for their interpretation. It divides into two parts, so that v. 4, on Christ the 'living stone', introduces the three texts and their interpretation in vv. 6–8, while v. 5, on the readers as 'living stones', introduces the three texts in vv. 9–10. The link between Christ and believers, established in vv. 4–5, is also the link between the two parts of the midrash: vv. 6–8 and vv. 9–10.

Thus the structure of the passage 2:4–10 is:

| | | |
|---|---|---|
| 4–5 | Introductory statement of theme | |
| 4 | A | Jesus the elect stone |
| 5 | B | The church the elect people of God |
| 6–10 | Midrash | |
| 6a | Introductory formula | |
| 6–8 | A¹ | The elect stone |
| 6b+7a | | Text 1 (Isa. 28:16)+interpretation |
| 7b+7c | | Interpretation+Text 2 (Ps. 118:22) |
| 8a+8b | | Text 3 (Isa. 8:14)+interpretation |
| 9–10 | B¹ | The elect people |
| 9 | | Text 4 (Isa. 43:20–21)+Text 5 (Exod. 19:5–6) conflated, the expansion of Text 4 |
| 10 | | Text 6 (Hos. 2:23) paraphrased (cf. Hos. 1:6, 9; 2:1). |

As in Jude 4–19, catchwords are used to link the texts together (*gezera šawa*), to link the introductory statement to the texts, and to link the interpretations to the texts. Thus, for example, in A (v. 4), λίθον is the catchword which links together all three texts in A¹ (vv. 6b, 7c, 8a), ἐκλεκτόν and ἔντιμον pick up the same words in text 1 (v. 6b), and ἀποδεδοκιμασμένον picks up ἀπεδοκίμασαν in text 2 (v. 7c). In the interpretation of text 1 (v. 7a), τιμή and πιστεύουσιν echo ἔντιμον and πιστεύων in the text (v. 6b). The words ἅγιον and ἱεράτευμα, the latter highly distinctive, link B (v. 5) to B¹, while the three texts in B¹ are linked together by the catchword λαός (*contra* Elliott, 1966, pp. 138–41). This is true in spite of the fact that the word occurs only once in v. 9, because λαὸς εἰς περιποίησιν in v. 9 represents *both* λαόν μου ὃν περιεποιησάμην in Isa. 43:21 LXX *and* λαὸς περιούσιος in Exod. 19:5 LXX. (In Mal. 3:17 LXX the phrase εἰς περιποίησιν translates *segullâ*, which is translated λαὸς περιούσιος in Exod. 19:5 LXX.) It was this coincidence between Isa. 43:20–1 and Exod. 19:5 which suggested and made possible the conflation of these two texts in v. 9.

This last point already indicates another pesher-type feature of the midrash: selection and adaptation of the text form to suit the interpretation. A striking example is the way in which ἐκλεκτόν is both the first adjectival description of the stone in A¹ (v. 6b) and the first adjectival description of the people in B¹ (v. 9). This has been achieved by the omission of πολυτελῆ from the quotation of Isa. 28:16 in v. 6b, and by placing the phrase γένος ἐκλεκτόν from Isa. 43:20 before the epithets from Exod. 19:6 in v. 9. This gives the idea of election the prominence which the introductory statement in v. 4 has already given it, and serves to link together the elect stone (Christ) in A¹ and the elect people in B¹. Hence the form in which the texts are quoted is governed by the intention of the whole midrash: to show how the election of Christ leads to the election of those who believe in him as the holy people of God.

The use of τίθημι in v. 6b, where Isa. 28:16 LXX has ἐμβαλῶ, is probably an example of the selection of a text form. This form of the text was also known to Paul (Rom. 9:33) and to the author of Barn. 6:2–3, who in the manner of the pesharim in fact makes use of both text forms (Harris, 1916, p. 31; cf. Kraft, 1960, pp. 344–5). τίθημι is a natural word to use for laying a foundation, and so probably simply a variant translation, not originally designed for any special interpretative purpose. But the author of 1 Peter has *selected* it for *his* purpose, because it can also mean 'appoint', and so again stresses the theme of election at the outset of his series of texts. The use of the same verb in this sense at the end of v. 8 (ἐτέθησαν) forms an *inclusio* with τίθημι in v. 6, and so marks the theme of election as the overarching theme of section A¹. The same theme is played up in B¹ by the interpretative expansion of Isa. 43:21 in v. 9b (καλέσαντος).

The association and christological interpretation of 'stone' testimonia was already traditional in Christianity (cf. Luke 20:17–18; Rom. 9:33; Barn. 6:2–4; and see Lindars, 1961, pp. 169–86), following jewish precedent (Black, 1971, pp. 11–14). The association of Hos. 2:23 with the 'stone' texts may also have been traditional (Rom. 9:25–6, 33). But, as Elliott has shown, the exegetical skill of our author appears in the way he builds on the tradition in order to create a midrash specifically designed for its context in 1 Peter (cf. also Snodgrass, 1978, pp. 103–6). The passage 2:6–10 provides the scriptural grounding both for the previous part of the letter, in which the election of Christ (1:20) and the election of christian believers (1:1–2) to be the holy people of God (1:15–16) are key themes, and also for the succeeding part of the letter, in which the relation of believers to unbelievers is the major topic. The priestly service, in both word and conduct, of a holy people, to the glory of God and as a witness to the world (2:5, 9), is the scriptural concept which undergirds all the paraenesis from 2:11 onwards. Thus 2:4–10 plays a key foundational and transitional role in the whole letter, for which its carefully studied composition is designed.

Another type of scriptural exegesis in 1 Peter is the use of paraenetic material from the OT to support the christian paraenesis of the letter. In some cases, this amounts to no more than reproducing a quotation or allusion as it already occurred in the paraenetic tradition. For example, the quotation of Prov. 3:34 in 5:5 is certainly of this type, since it not only agrees in its text form with Jas. 4:6; 1 Clem. 30:2; Ign. Eph. 5:3, but also occurs in the context of a cluster of parallels with James 4 which indicate a common paraenetic tradition (cf. Selwyn, 1946, pp. 417–18; Dibelius, 1976, p. 226). But the author's use of Psalm 33(34) is more interesting. This psalm was traditionally used in christian paraenesis, as is sufficiently demonstrated by Heb. 12:14 (alluding to Ps. 33[34]:15, quoted in 1 Pet. 3:11); 1 Clem. 22:1–7 (= Ps. 33[34]:11–17, which includes the quotation in 1 Pet. 3:10–12; cf. also Barn. 9:2) and 1 Clem. 23:1 (alluding to the same phrase of Ps. 33[34]:5 as appears in 1 Pet. 2:4), though I am not convinced by Selwyn's argument (1946, pp. 413–14) for this psalm's influence on Pauline paraenesis. However, it appears that our author has done his own exegetical work on the psalm.

The passage 3:8–12, in which Ps. 33(34):12–14 (LXX with minor rephrasing) is quoted, is a studied composition. Verses 8–11 are chiastic in structure, so that each element in vv. 8–9 corresponds, in reverse order, to an element of the quotation from Ps. 33(34):12–14, thus:

$$\begin{array}{lll} \text{v. 8} & = & \text{v. 11b} \\ \text{v. 9a} & = & \text{v. 11a} \\ \text{v. 9b} & = & \text{v. 10b} \\ \text{v. 9c} & = & \text{v. 10a.} \end{array}$$

The terminology of vv. 8–9 does not derive from the psalm but from the paraenetic tradition: it has simply been arranged in the order suggested by the psalm. The psalm then serves to give a scriptural basis for the paraenesis, and to supply the additional element of motivation in v. 12. The phenomenon of dominical teaching (v. 9) supported not by explicit citation of gospel tradition (which rarely occurs in early christian paraenesis) but by an OT quotation may seem odd, but is paralleled in Rom. 12:19–20.

Further allusions in 2:3–4 (cf. Ps. 33[34]:8, 5) suggest careful attention to this psalm in the preparation of the letter (though I am less convinced by other echoes of the psalm suggested by Snodgrass, 1978, pp. 102–3). They also suggest that the psalm was of interest to our author not simply as a traditional text of christian paraenesis, nor simply for the sake of its general theme of the persecution of the righteous, but also because of the kind of midrashic links with his other texts which are of such importance in the jewish exegesis of the period. In 2:3–4 the pair of allusions to Psalm 33(34) serve to link the exegetical passage 2:4–10 to what precedes, but the appropriateness of Ps. 33(34):5 in this context goes beyond the opening three words which are echoed in 2:4. The next thought (φωτίσθητε) corresponds to 2:9b, and the final words of the verse (οὐ μὴ καταισχυνθῇ) are identical with the final words of the quotation from Isa. 28:16 in 2:6. Furthermore, Ps. 33(34):13, quoted in 3:10, corresponds materially and verbally (δόλον) to Isa. 53:9, quoted in 2:22. That our author saw this connexion is indicated by the fact that the terms in which he expounds each of these texts, drawing on the paraenetic tradition, also correspond (2:23; 3:9).

This link between a christological–prophetic interpretation of Scripture and a paraenetic use of Scripture is interesting (cf. Lindars, 1961, p. 97), but the two ways of using Scripture are in any case not completely distinct. From 2:3–4 it is clear that our author read the psalm christologically, taking the Κύριος to be Christ and perhaps intending the pesher-like wordplay χρηστός (= Χριστός) ὁ Κύριος (2:3 = Ps. 33[34]:8) (cf. Beare, 1970, p. 116). It follows that Κυρίου in 3:12 (= Ps. 33[34]:16) is also Christ, and this is confirmed by 3:14b–15a, with its christological gloss on Isa. 8:12–13 LXX. This latter quotation of verses immediately adjacent to the text quoted in 2:8 also helps to demonstrate, along with the allusions to Ps. 33(34), that the author of 1 Peter was by no means content to relay isolated scriptural texts which came to him in the tradition, but studied whole passages of Scripture (cf. Dodd, 1952, pp. 78–82, for early christian interpretation of Isaiah 8 as a unit) in a way which combined christological–prophetic interpretation and paraenetic application.

## 2 PETER

Again, it is necessary to be selective, since 2 Peter's allusions to the OT, though not as pervasive as in the other three works we have discussed, are many and varied (see the list in Bauckham, 1983, p. 138). Some derive from the sources the author used, but a brief study of his treatment of Noah and Lot in 2:5–9 will enable us to recognize his first-hand acquaintance with jewish haggadic traditions about OT heroes of the same kind as we have detected in James.

The passage 2:4–10a is based on Jude 6–8, but our author takes material out of Jude's midrashic structure in order to use it in a somewhat different way. Jude's two types (the apostate angels and the cities of the Plain) become, in 2 Peter, *proofs* that divine judgment does happen (2:9), contrary to the sceptical mockery of the opponents (cf. 2:3). But they do also continue, as in Jude, to function as *types* of the imminent eschatological judgment. This is clear from the way the author describes them in vv. 4 and 6 (note especially v. 6b: 'making them a warning example of what is going to happen to the ungodly,' i.e. to the author's contemporaries in the last days). It is also clear from the third 'warning example' which the author himself introduces: the Flood (v. 5b). As the only universal judgment in the past, the Flood was sometimes seen as a prototype of the eschatological judgment (e.g. 1 Enoch 93:4) and our author himself presents it as such in 3:6–7. Thus it appears that the OT material in 2:4–10a is subject to the same eschatological hermeneutic as Jude's, in line with the lively eschatological expectation which, contrary to common assertions, pervades the outlook of 2 Peter.

If 'the world of the ungodly' (2:5) and the cities of the Plain (2:6) represent typologically the ungodly of the last days, which are the author's own time, then Noah (2:5) and Lot (2:7–8) must be models for the righteous of the last times, among whom the author hopes to count his readers. By including Noah and Lot he has adapted Jude's material in accordance with a common jewish paraenetic scheme which listed examples of God's judgment on sinners along with counterexamples of righteous people delivered by God at the same time (details in Bauckham, 1983, pp. 46–7, 246–7). Precisely the Flood and the destruction of Sodom and Gomorrah were the classic illustrations of God's discriminatory judgment, in which the righteous, however few, are spared. Thus Noah and Lot are types of faithful Christians who hope for deliverance at the parousia (2:9a), but meantime must live righteously in the midst of an evil society doomed to judgment. It is significant that in his accounts of Noah and Lot the author does not focus on aspects of their deliverance, but on aspects of their previous life among their evil contemporaries. He must have intended these accounts to have existential relevance for his readers, living amid the pressures of a predominantly pagan society and tempted to compromise their moral standards accordingly.

Noah is presented as a man who proclaimed righteousness, Lot as a man who suffered for righteousness. At least in Noah's case this portrayal derives from haggadic tradition. 2 Peter's readers may well have known the long report of

Noah's preaching in the jewish Sibylline Oracle 1:125–99, written in Asia Minor around the turn of the era. The verb κηρύσσω was traditionally used of Noah (Sib. Or. 1:129; 1 Clem. 7:6; 9:4; Apoc. Paul 50; cf. Philo, *Quaest. Gen.* 2:13) and the noun κῆρυξ, used in 2 Pet. 2:5, even occurs as a loanword in rabbinic Hebrew, applied to Noah in *Gen. Rab.* 30:7. But traditionally it was repentance that Noah was said to have proclaimed (Sib. Or. 1:129; Josephus, *Ant.* 1:74; b. *Sanh.* 108; 1 Clem. 7:6; Apoc. Paul 50). Our author's substitution of 'righteousness' must belong to his desire to contrast righteousness and ungodliness throughout this section (cf. vv. 6, 7, 8, 9). Also traditional was the term 'eighth' for Noah (cf. 1 Pet. 3:20). In Sib. Or. 1:280–1 it is used of him as he emerges from the ark to found a new world (cf. 269–74), and probably there and here it is the eschatological symbolism of the number eight which is in mind. Noah the herald of righteousness and the most righteous man (Sib. Or. 1:280) prefigures the righteous of the last days who will survive the eschatological judgment and enter the new world in which righteousness will be at home (2 Pet. 3:13). (For Noah as both moral and eschatological model, see also Vanderkam, 1980.)

Lot's righteousness, which is so stressed in 2 Pet. 2:7–8, was also well known in haggadic tradition (Wis. 10:6; 19:17; Philo, *Mos.* 2:58; 1 Clem. 11:1), because, although it is not directly mentioned in Genesis, Abraham's plea on behalf of the righteous in Gen. 18:23–32 (note especially the singular in vv. 23, 25) was understood to refer to Lot (*Pirqe R. El.* 25; *Gen. Rab.* 49:13). Lot's righteousness was especially thought to have consisted in his hospitality (Gen. 19:1–3; see Alexander, 1985), but this does not seem to be in view in 2 Peter. Rather, the connexion is with the theme of Abraham's intercession: that God does not destroy the righteous with the wicked (Gen. 18:23). 2 Peter's threefold δίκαιος (vv. 7–8) echoes the fourfold δίκαιος of Gen. 18:23, 25 LXX. The extended picture of Lot's distress – the suffering of a man who loves righteousness and is pained by its absence from his society – may be based on no longer extant haggadic tradition or it may be an original haggadic development by our author. In either case it serves to make Lot a model of righteous suffering, with the same kind of function as the examples of the prophets and Job in Jas. 5:10–11.

## BIBLIOGRAPHY

M. Adinolfi 'Temi dell'Esodo nella I Petr', in Associazione Biblica Italiana, *San Pietro: Atti della XIX Settimana Biblica* (Brescia, 1967).

T. D. Alexander 'Lot's Hospitality: A Clue to His Righteousness', *JBL* 104 (1985), 289–91.

R. J. Bauckham *Jude, 2 Peter*, WBC 50 (Waco, TX, 1983).

F. W. Beare *The First Epistle of Peter*, 3rd ed. (Oxford, 1970).

E. Best 'I Peter II 4–10 – a Reconsideration', *NovT* 11 (1969), 270–93.

M. Black 'The Christological Use of the Old Testament in the New Testament', *NTS* 18 (1971–72), 1–14.

G. J. Brooke *Exegesis at Qumran: 4QFlorilegium in its Jewish Context*, JSOTSS 29 (Sheffield, 1985).

J. Chaine *L'Épitre de Saint Jacques*, 2nd ed. (Paris, 1927).

W. J. Dalton *Christ's Proclamation to the Spirits: A Study of 1 Peter 3:18–4:6*, AnBib 23 (Rome, 1965).

F. W. Danker 'I Peter $1^{24}$–$2^{17}$ – A Consolatory Pericope', *ZNW* 58 (1967), 93–102.

P. H. Davids '*Themes in the Epistle of James that are Judaistic in Character*', unpublished Ph. D. Dissertation (University of Manchester, 1974).

'Tradition and Citation in the Epistle of James', in W. W. Gasque and W. S. Lasor (eds.), *Scripture, Tradition and Interpretation: Essays presented to E. F. Harrison* (Grand Rapids, 1978).

*The Epistle of James*, NIGTC (Exeter, 1982).

M. Dibelius *James*, revised by H. Greeven, Hermeneia (Philadelphia, 1976).

C. H. Dodd *According to the Scriptures: The Sub-Structure of New Testament Theology* (London, 1952).

R. H. Eisenman *James the Just in the Habakkuk Pesher*, SPB 35 (Leiden, 1986).

J. H. Elliott *The Elect and the Holy: An Exegetical Examination of I Peter 2:4–10 and Phrase* βασίλειον ἱεράτευμα, SNT 12 (Leiden, 1966).

*A Home for the Homeless: A Sociological Exegesis of 1 Peter, Its Situation and Strategy* (London, 1982).

E. E. Ellis 'Prophecy and Hermeneutic in Jude', in *Prophecy and Hermeneutic in Early Christianity*, WUNT 18 (Tübingen, 1978).

A. T. Hanson 'The Scriptural Background to the Doctrine of the *Descensus ad Inferos* in the New Testament', in *The New Testament Interpretation of Scripture* (London, 1980).

*The Living Utterances of God: The New Testament Exegesis of the Old*, (London, 1983).

R. Harris *Testimonies Part I* (Cambridge, 1916).

H. Heater, Jr. *A Septuagint Translation Technique in the Book of Job*, CBQMS 11 (Washington, DC, 1982).

M. P. Horgan *Pesharim: Qumran Interpretations of Biblical Books*, CBQMS 8 (Washington, DC, 1979).

I. Jacobs 'The Midrashic Background for James ii.21–3', *NTS* 22 (1975–6), 457–64.

L. T. Johnson 'The Use of Leviticus 19 in the Letter of James', *JBL* 101 (1982), 391–401.

R. A. Kraft 'Barnabas' Isaiah Text and the "Testimony Book" Hypothesis', *JBL* 79 (1960), 336–50.

S. Laws *A Commentary on the Epistle of James*, BNTC (London, 1980).

B. Lindars *New Testament Apologetic: The Doctrinal Significance of the Old Testament Quotations* (London, 1961).

F. Manns 'Sara, modèle de la femme obéissante: Étude de l'Arrière-Plan Juif de l ᵗ ierre 3, 5–6', *BibOr* 26 (1984), 65–73.

J. B. Mayor *The Epistle of St. James*, 2nd ed. (London, 1897).

T. P. Osborne 'L'utilisation des citations de l'Ancien Testament dans la première épître de Pierre', *RThL* 12 (1981), 64–77.

C. D. Osburn 'The Christological Use of 1 Enoch i.9 in Jude 14, 15', *NTS* 23 (1976–7), 334–41.

'*1 Enoch* 80:2–8 (67:5–7) and Jude 12–13', *CBQ* 47 (1985), 296–303.

D. Rahnenführer 'Das Testament des Hiobs und das Neue Testament', *ZNW* 62 (1971), 68–93.

E. G. Selwyn *The First Epistle of St. Peter* (London, 1946).

K. R. Snodgrass 'I Peter ii.1–10: its Formation and Literary Affinities', *NTS* 24 (1977–8), 97–106.

J. C. Vanderkam 'The Righteousness of Noah', in J. J. Collins and G. W. E. Nickelsburg (eds.), *Ideal Figures in Ancient Judaism*, SBLSCS 12 (Chico, CA, 1980).

R. B. Ward 'The Works of Abraham: James 2:14–26', *HTR* 61 (1968), 283–90.

# 19 · Revelation

## G. K. BEALE

### 1 INTRODUCTION

IN comparison with the rest of the NT, the use of the OT in the Apocalypse of John has not been given a proportionate amount of attention: merely three books (Schlatter, 1912; Jenkins, 1972; Beale, 1984) and six significant articles have been dedicated to the topic (Vanhoye, 1962; Lancellotti, 1966; Trudinger, 1966; Gangemi, 1974; Marconcini, 1976; Goulder, 1981; cf. also Cambier, 1955 and Lohse, 1961, which are of more limited value).

Otherwise, important discussion of this subject can be found only in portions of books and commentaries, the more valuable of which are Swete (1911, *passim*, but esp. pp. cxl–clvi), Charles (1920, *passim*, but esp. pp. lxv–lxxxii), Vos (1965, pp. 16–53), Caird (1966, *passim*), van der Waal (1971, pp. 174–241), Ford (1982, pp. 243–306), Beasley-Murray (1981, *passim*), and to a somewhat lesser degree Delling (1959), Comblin (1965), Farrer (1964) and Holtz (1971).

There is general acknowledgement that the Apocalypse contains more OT references than any other NT book, although past attempts to tally objectively the total amount have varied.[1] The variation in statistics is due to the different criteria employed to determine the validity of an OT reference and the fact that some authors include 'echoes' and parallels of a very general nature (cf. the survey and evaluation of Vos, 1965, pp. 17–19 and Vanhoye, 1962, pp. 438–40). The range of OT usage includes the Pentateuch, Judges, 1–2 Samuel, 1–2 Kings, Psalms, Proverbs, Song of Solomon, Job, major prophets and the minor prophets. Roughly more than half the references are from the Psalms, Isaiah, Ezekiel and Daniel, and in proportion to its length Daniel yields the most (so Swete, 1911, p. cliii, where numerical statistics are also given for many of the OT books used).

The evaluation of Daniel as most used is supported by recent study (cf. Beale, 1984a). Among the allusions to Daniel, the greatest number come from Daniel 7. Proportionally Ezekiel ranks second as the most used OT book (cf. Vanhoye, 1962, pp. 473–5), although in terms of actual numbers of allusions Isaiah is first, followed by Ezekiel, Daniel and Psalms (although statistics cited by commentators differ; e.g. Swete cites Isaiah = 46, Daniel = 31, Ezekiel = 29, Psalms = 27). The OT in general plays such a major role that a proper understanding of its use is necessary for an adequate view of the Apocalypse as a whole.

## 2   THE TEXT FORM OF OT REFERENCES IN THE APOCALYPSE

The text form of the OT references in Revelation needs indepth discussion since there are no formal quotations and most are allusive, a phenomenon often making textual identification more difficult. Unfortunately, however, the scope of the present discussion precludes such important analysis (cf. further Trudinger, 1966; Beale, 1985; Beale, 1986) including criteria for discerning degrees of dependence (but see further Trudinger, 1966; Beale, 1984a, pp. 43–259, 306–13; Beale, 1985; Beale, 1986).

## 3   PRELIMINARY CONSIDERATIONS FOR STUDYING OT USAGE IN THE APOCALYPSE

*A   Problematic use of combined allusions and the issue of literary consciousness*

We have already acknowledged the non-formal character of the OT references in Revelation. Not only does this make OT textual identification more difficult but it also renders it problematic to determine whether or not the author is consciously or unconsciously referring to an OT text. This problem is compounded since many, indeed most, of the OT reminiscences are found in combination with one another. Sometimes four, five or more different OT references are merged into one picture. Good examples are the descriptions of Christ (1:12–20), God on the throne and the surrounding heavenly host (4:1–11) and the diabolic beast (13:1–8; for a thorough list of other examples, see Vos, 1965, pp. 39–40). How are such combined allusions to be studied? This phenomenon would be particularly hard to analyse if, as some contend, it is less intentional and more the result of a memory so saturated with OT language and ideas that they are unconsciously organized in the author's visions 'like the changing patterns of a kaleidoscope' (so Swete, 1911, p. cliv and Vos, 1965, pp. 38–9). In this case, the OT contextual meanings of the allusions need not be examined to comprehend better John's use, since he himself did not consciously reflect on such OT contexts. Indeed, many have concluded that the lack of formal citation in the Apocalypse points in the same direction.

However, Caird sees conscious effort in such allusive combinations for the purpose of expressing evocative and emotive power. Therefore, it is unnecessary to attempt to comprehend the meaning of each reference in its OT and NT context, since the whole picture must be kept together – without separating and analysing various strands – in order to evoke the desired emotional effect (1966, pp. 25–6). Of course, in these mosaics there is always the possibility of a mixture of conscious intention with unconscious activity.

But often a greater understanding is gained and emotive effect felt when the various allusive parts of these visionary amalgamations *are* studied separately in their OT contexts. Vos cites Rev. 4:2–9 as a fitting illustration of unconscious mixing of OT allusions. However, when the OT context of each allusion is studied one finds that, without exception, they are all from descriptions of theophany scenes, which function as introductory sections to an announcement of judgment either upon Israel or the nations (cf. Vos's parallels: Rev. 4:2 = Isa. 6:1 and/or 1 Kgs 22:19; Rev. 4:3f = Ezek. 1:28; Rev. 4:5a = Ezek. 1:13 and/or Exod. 19:16; Rev. 4:5b = Ezek. 1:13 and Zech. 4:2, 6 [omitted from Vos]; Rev. 4:6a = Ezek. 1:22; Rev. 4:6b = Ezek. 1:5 and 1:18; Rev. 4:7 = Ezek. 1:10; Rev. 4:8a = Isa. 6:2; Rev. 4:8b = Isa. 6:3; Rev. 4:9 = Isa. 6:1). This common denominator of theophany–judgment is enhanced when one notes also the dominant influence of Dan. 7:9–13 throughout Revelation 4–5 (see below). This clearly common motif in all the OT allusions points toward a more intentional thematic formation of texts to describe a similar theophany scene in Revelation. This seems even more likely when one considers that in the immediate contexts of three of the OT allusions there appears the image of a 'book' associated with judgment, as in Rev. 5:1 (cf. Dan. 7:10; Ezek. 2:9–10; Zech. 5:1–3). All of the common scenes and themes of these OT contexts intensify the cognitive and emotive aspects of the picture in Rev. 4:2–9.

The same thing can be illustrated through Rev. 1:12–20, 13:1–8 and 17:1ff, other examples cited by Vos to support his proposal of unconscious clustering (see Beale, 1984, pp. 154–270).

Therefore, caution must be used in making claims of unconscious activity on the author's part, although this is a possibility. For example, it is possible, though speculative, to propose that the above-mentioned exegetical links were already intact in some previous tradition to which John makes unconscious allusion (e.g., a synagogue or christian liturgical tradition). Such unconscious activity is more likely to have occurred with the less clear or non-clustered allusions, although exegetical analysis must determine this in each case. Furthermore, as Vanhoye has concluded, it is not typical for John to use OT allusions in isolation but to fuse them together on the basis of their affinity with one another (Vanhoye, p. 467), as illustrated above in Revelation 4–5.

Although space does not permit, it would be helpful to discuss in this section whether or not the Apocalypse is a literary stereotype or if it can be traced to a visionary experience, or is a combination of both (cf. further L. Hartman, 1966, p. 106; Beale, 1984, pp. 7–9). If there was an experiential basis, descriptions of such visions were probably coloured both unconsciously and consciously by the traditions which had exerted a formative influence on the author's thinking. Furthermore, actual visions would have been experienced in the author's own thought forms, so that it might be difficult to distinguish description of a visionary experience from that of a retelling of the experience through unconscious or conscious appeal to various traditions (OT, jewish, etc.).

John's apparent self-identification with the line of OT visionaries implies that he would be conscious of developing the ideas of the earlier prophets and, therefore, that the *clearer* OT references in his work are the result of an intentional activity (cf. 1:1–3, 10; 4:1–2; 17:3; 21:10; Vos, 1965, p. 52). Furthermore, the chain of associated texts in Revelation 1, 4–5, 13 and 17 discussed above, and evident elsewhere, confirms an intentional activity on the author's part. This conclusion is enhanced by the remaining evidence considered below.

## B   A consideration of contextual and non-contextual use of the OT

Of course, if one concluded that John alluded to the OT only unconsciously, there would be little possibility of studying his method of allusion, since such study assumes conscious activity. In the light of our conclusion in favour of intentionality, however, we must first ask whether or not John uses the OT in harmony with its broader contextual meaning.

There is unanimous consensus that John uses the OT with a high degree of liberty and creativity. As a result, many conclude that he handles numerous OT passages without consideration of their original contextual meaning – even assigning meaning quite contradictory to it. This has been argued in a thoroughgoing way by Vos. Our comments will be focused on an evaluation of his discussion as generally representative of those who hold this viewpoint.

Vos restricts most of his survey to what he considers to be the clearest OT references in the Apocalypse (pp. 21–37, 41). He concludes that at least seven of the twenty-two passages discussed there show a 'disregard for [the OT] context'. Four of these concern references to heavenly beings. The first is the application of a description of Yahweh (Ezek. 43:2) to that of the Son of Man figure (Rev. 1:15). But this is more of a change of application than non-contextual use, since the Son of Man is clearly portrayed as a divine figure in Revelation 1. In Rev. 18:1 a description of Yahweh (Ezek. 43:2b) is applied to an angel descending from heaven, yet since angels in the OT and Revelation are mere conveyers of divine decrees, it is plausible that they would take on other theophanic characteristics besides that of the divine word. In addition, sometimes in the OT God appears in the form of a heavenly being, and this may be the case also in Revelation (e.g. Rev. 10:1–6, which is based on the heavenly being of Daniel 10–12 who may be divine). Therefore, in spite of a possible change of application, the broad OT idea of a heavenly being revealing a divine decree to a prophet remains intact. The same general conclusion can be reached with respect to the similar usage of Ezek. 37:3 in Rev. 7:14. In Rev. 4:8a descriptions of the Isaiah 6 seraphim are merged with those of the Ezekiel 1 cherubim, but again the primary OT framework of a heavenly being guarding God's throne is still retained.

Vos also argues for a disregard of context in the use of Ezek. 37:10b in Rev. 11:11. The Ezekiel text uses the idea of resurrection as a metaphor for the future ingathering of Israel from throughout the nations, while John applies it to the resurrection of the two witnesses, who probably are symbolic of the witnessing church as the true Israel (so Caird, Sweet, etc.). This kind of reference may fit into the analogical usage category (see below) because of the common idea of *Israel's resurrection*. The shift of application to the Church as the true Israel and the understanding of the Ezekiel language as apparently connoting a literal resurrection may represent eschatological escalation whereby the resurrection terminology now finds an eschatological – not merely historical – level. Although there is a possibility of disregard for context because of the different application and even somewhat changed meaning, a correspondence and sense of continuity can be discerned (note also in both passages that those 'resurrected' have previously been slain among the nations; cf. Ezek. 37:9–14, 21–2 / Rev. 11:7–10).

Vos also contends that the use of Isa. 22:22 in Rev. 3:7 is non-contextual, since Eliakim's authority over the Israelite kingdom is applied to Christ's authority over God's kingdom. But, this can also be viewed as an escalated analogy wherein the human, earthly, political and temporal rule over Israel by Eliakim finds a correspondence on a grander scale with Christ's divine, heavenly, spiritual and eternal rule over the whole world (cf. Revelation 1–5). Additional points of note in Isaiah 22 are: (1) the possible priestly connotations of Eliakim's rule (22:21a); (2) Eliakim was to be like a 'father' for the Israelites in the exercise of his office (22:21b); (3) apparently Eliakim's authority was to be equal to that of King Hezekiah's (22:22); (4) the exercise of his office would bring glory to his relatives (22:23–4); (5) Eliakim is referred to as the 'servant' of Yahweh (22:20). All of these elements, together with the messianic overtones of the 'house of David' (22:22) enhance the idea that John was quite aware of the context of Isa. 22:22 and intentionally escalated these aspects of Eliakim's reign to the grander scale of Christ's reign. Perhaps the correspondences were just too good to miss (cf. von Rad who argues cogently for a typological relationship between Isa. 22:22 and Rev. 3:7 [1965, p. 373]).

We may therefore viably speak about changes of applications but need not conclude that this means a *disregard* for OT context, since this is not a logically necessary deduction. It seems likely that Vos, and others, confuse disregard for context with change of application. That the above texts reflect disregard for OT context is possible but other explanations are equally satisfactory. The passages we have discussed are test cases, the conclusions of which are applicable to other OT references where it is probable that the author has made *intentional allusion*. Admittedly, it is sometimes difficult to know whether there has been conscious or unconscious activity. Non-contextual uses of the OT can be expected to occur in those places where there is unconscious allusion. No doubt the apocalyptist's mind was so saturated with OT language from the tradition he had learned that when he described his vision he sometimes spontaneously used this language without much forethought. For example, the phrase 'I turned *to see the voice which was speaking*' (Rev. 1:12a) is probably drawn from Dan. 7:11 (LXX), but there it refers to the 'boastful words' of the beast. This may have been drawn in unconsciously because of the clear influence of Daniel 7 in Rev. 1:7–14.

To clarify what is meant by 'context' is important. What is usually meant is *literary* context – how a passage functions in the logical flow of a book's argument. But there is also *historical* context. For example, the *historical* context of Hos. 11:1 is the Exodus and not the argument of the book of Hosea. A NT author might reflect on only one of these contexts, he could focus on both or entirely disregard both. In the light of the passages discussed above, the author appears to display varying degrees of awareness of literary context, as well as perhaps historical context, although the former is predominant. Those texts with a low degree of correspondence with the OT literary context can be referred to as semi-contextual, since they seem to fall between the opposite poles of what we ordinarily call 'contextual' and 'non-contextual' usages. The categories of use to be considered below should further clarify and illustrate these initial conclusions.

### 4 VARIOUS USES OF THE OT IN THE APOCALYPSE

#### (a)  *The use of segments of OT Scripture as literary prototypes*

Sometimes the author takes over large OT contexts or sequences as models after which to pattern his creative compositions (cf. Schüssler-Fiorenza, 1980, p. 108). Such modelling can be apparent (1) through observing a thematic-structure which is uniquely traceable to only one OT context or (2) by discerning a cluster of clear allusions from the same OT context. Sometimes both are observable, thus enhancing the clarity of the OT prototype. It has been argued in some depth that broad patterns from Daniel (especially chaps. 2 and 7) have been followed in Revelation 1, 4–5, 13 and 17, the former two sections in particular exhibiting both allusive clusters and structural outlines from segments of Daniel (Beale, 1984a, pp. 154–305, 313–20). Incidentally, this would show further design in these chapters and point further away from an unconscious use of the OT. The same use of Daniel as a midrashic *Vorbild* is also observable in jewish apocalyptic, indicating that this kind of use of the OT was not uncommon (e.g. 1QM 1; 1 En. 90:9–19; 4 Ezra 11–13; 1 En. 69:26–71:17; 2 Baruch 36–40; see Beale, 1984a, pp. 67–153). The suggestion is also made that this influence of Daniel may even extend to the structure of the whole Apocalypse, since the same Daniel 2:28–9 allusion punctuates the book at major divisional transitions (1:1; 1:19; 4:1; 22:6). Furthermore, the five apocalyptic visions in Daniel (2, 7, 8, 9, 10–12) cover the same time of the eschatological future, which may be the prototypical structure followed by Revelation in some of its purported synchronously parallel sections (Beale, 1984a, pp. 271–85; 1984b, pp. 413–23).

In a somewhat similar vein, Goulder has argued that broad portions of Ezekiel have been the dominant influence on at least twelve major sections of the Apocalypse (Rev. 4; 5; 6:1–8; 6:12–7:1; 7:2–8; 8:1–5; 14:6–12; 17:1–6; 18:9–24; 20:7–10; 21:22; cf. Goulder, 1981, pp. 343–9). Goulder observes that these uses of Ezekiel are a dominant influence on the structure of Revelation since they are placed to a marked extent in the same order as they are found in Ezekiel itself (pp. 343–54), a somewhat similar observation to that made earlier by Vanhoye (p. 442). However, Goulder proposes that a liturgical rather than literary explanation can be given to account better for the Revelation–Ezekiel parallel order. He attempts to demonstrate this by speculating that there is a general alignment of the Apocalypse with the jewish calendar, especially with respect to the year of festivals and holy days, and that this liturgical-calendrical pattern is even more formative on the structure of Revelation than Ezekiel (pp. 349–64).

Others have also recognised Ezekiel's broad influence, especially in Revelation 20–2, where the order of events appears to have been taken from Ezekiel 37–48 (Selwyn, 1902, pp. 332–4; Wikenhauser, 1932; Kuhn, 1933; Lust, 1980). And there are many commentators who, along with Goulder, see Ezekiel as the paradigm for Rev. 4:1–5:1 (e.g., Caird, Sweet).

In addition to Goulder's above liturgical view, others of paradigmatic significance for the book have also been proposed, which are based either on early jewish or christian liturgical tradition (cf. Carnegie, 1978; Läuchli, 1960 [see Carnegie's evaluation, 1982, p. 245]; Prigent, 1964, pp. 46–79 [see Beale's evaluation, 1984a, p. 184]).

There is consensus that the plagues of the 'trumpets' in Rev. 8:6–12 and those of the bowls in 16:1–9 follow the paradigm of the exodus plagues (Exod. 8:12), although creatively reworked and applied (e.g. Beasley-Murray, Caird, Sweet). Already this exodus model had been used by Amos (chaps. 8–10) and creatively amplified in Wisdom of Solomon 11–19, the latter usage perhaps also exerting influence on John's application (Sweet, 1979, pp. 161–2). Draper proposes that the eschatological scheme in Zechariah 14 'provides the basis for a midrashic development in Revelation 7' (1983, pp. 133–47), while Sweet more tentatively suggests the same thing for Revelation 20–2 (1981, p. 112).

Mention should also be made of the synthetic use of the end time woes from the synoptic eschatological discourse together with Lev. 26:18–28, Ezek. 14:13–23 and Zech. 6:1–8 (cf. 1:8–15), all of which have served as the compositional paradigm for Rev. 6:2–8. Likewise, Müller has argued that the Sinai theophany, 1 Kings 22, Isaiah 6, Ezekiel 1 and Daniel 7 have been synthesized to provide the *Vorbild* for Revelation 4–5 (1962 and 1963; for evaluation see Beale, 1984a, pp. 178–239).

All of the above proposed OT models have woven within them allusions from other parts of the same OT book and from elsewhere in the OT corpus, and many of these are based upon common themes, pictures, catch-phrases, etc. Often these other references serve as interpretative expansions of an OT prototype. On the reasonable assumption that these models were intentionally composed, two primary uses of them can be discerned. First, the OT patterns appear to be used as forms through which future (sometimes imminent) eschatological fulfilment is understood and predicted (cf. Revelation 13; 17. Also see the same employment of the Daniel models in 1QM 1; 1 En. 46–7; 69:26–71:17; 90; 4 Ezra 11–13; 2 Bar. 36:1–42:2). Second, the *Vorbilder* are utilized as a lens through which past and present eschatological fulfilment is understood (cf. Revelation 1; 4–5). It is not always clear whether or not these OT prototypes are the means or the object of interpretation, and perhaps there is an oscillation between the two.

## (b)  Thematic use of the OT

In addition to alluding to specific OT texts, the author of Revelation develops important OT *themes*. Many of these themes are delineated throughout the major commentaries. Some special studies of note are Ford's tracing of Daniel's 'abomination of desolation' theme (1979, pp. 243–314), Longman's study of the OT divine warrior concept (1982, pp. 291–302), Bauckham's article on the OT earthquake idea, recent articles on the employment of the ancient Near East/OT covenant form in Revelation 2–3 and throughout the book (Shea, 1983; Strand, 1983) and the OT concept of the 'day of the Lord' (Gray, 1974).

Carnegie has offered a most interesting study on the function of hymns in the OT and their re-use in Revelation. He shows that the various songs in Isaiah 40–55 come at the end of subsections and round them off, not only by offering a concluding thanksgiving, but also by giving an interpretative summary of the theme of the whole previous section (cf. Isa. 48:20ff; 52:9;

etc.). The series of hymns in Revelation are seen to have the same function under the inspiration of the Isaianic songs (cf. Rev. 4:11; 5:13ff; 7:9–12; 11:15–18; 19:1–8; so Carnegie, 1982, pp. 250–2).

## (c)   Analogical use of the OT

This use can be considered the most general description of OT usage in the Apocalypse, since the very act of referring to an OT text is to place it in some comparative relationship to something in the NT. However, here we have in mind specific well-known persons, places and events. The pictures undergo creative changes (expansions, condensations, supplemental imagery, etc.) and, of course, are applied to different historical situations (for a superb example of such alteration see Vos' discussion of the exodus plague imagery in Rev. 8:6–12 and 16:2–15, pp. 45–7). Nevertheless, a key idea in the OT context is usually carried over as the main characteristic or principle to be applied in the NT situation (so Vos, pp. 47–8). Therefore, even though John handles these OT figures with creative freedom, almost always these pictures broadly retain an essential OT association and convey principles of continuity between the OT and NT (so Cambier, 1955, pp. 116–20; cf. Gangemi, 1974, pp. 322–39).

For example, the image of the deceiving 'serpent of old' in Rev. 12:9 (cf. 20:2) evokes an episode of primitive religious history which maintains the same meaning for the final, eschatological phase of theological history (so Cambier, pp. 118–19). The author's theological basis for maintaining such continuities lies in his conviction that OT and NT history is but the working out of God's unified design of salvation and deals throughout with the unchanging principles of faith in God, God's faithfulness in fulfilling his salvific promises, the anti-theocratic forces attempting to thwart such promises and the victory of God's kingdom over that of Satan (Cambier, pp. 119–20).

The following is a sampling of these analogies with a brief description of the primary point of continuity: (1) *judgment*-theophanies introducing judgment (Isaiah 6, Ezekiel 1, Daniel 7/Revelation 4–5), books of judgment (Ezekiel 2, Daniel 7, Daniel 12/Rev. 5:1–5 and Ezekiel 2/Revelation 10), lion from Judah exercising judgment (Gen. 49:9/Rev. 5:5), 'Lord of lords and King of kings' exercising judgment (Dan. 4:37 [LXX]/Rev. 17:14; 19:16), horsemen as divine agents of judgment (Zechariah 1 and 6/Rev. 6:1–8), exodus plagues inflicting judgment (Exodus 8–12/Rev. 8:6–12; 16:1–14), locusts as agents of judgment (Joel 1–2/Rev. 9:7–10), prophets giving testimony through judgment (Exod. 7:17; 1 Kings 17:1/Rev. 11:6), 'Babylon' judged by God in 'one hour' (Dan. 4:17a [LXX]/Rev. 18:10, 17, 19); (2) *tribulation and persecution of God's people* – ten days of tribulation (Dan. 1:12/Rev. 2:10), three-and-a-half years of tribulation (Dan. 7:25; 12:7/Rev. 11:2; 12:1;

13:5), Sodom, Egypt and Jerusalem as infamous places where persecution occurs (Rev. 11:8), persecuting rulers symbolized as beasts (Daniel 7/Revelation 11–13, 17) and 'Babylon the Great' (Dan. 4:30, etc./Rev. 14:8; 16:19; 17:5; 18:2); (3) *seductive, idolatrous teaching* – Balaam (Num. 25; 31:16/Rev. 2:14) and Jezebel (1 Kgs 16:31; 2 Kgs 9:22/Rev. 2:20–3); (4) *divine protection* – the tree of life (Gen. 2:9/Rev. 2:7; 22:2, 14, 19), the 'sealed' Israelites (Ezekiel 9/Rev. 7:2–8) and the wings of the eagle (Exod. 19:4; Deut. 32:11/Rev. 12:14); (5) *victorious battle of God's people over the enemy* – Armageddon (Zech. 12:11/Rev. 16:16 [19:19]; cf. Gog and Magog in Ezek. 38–39:16/Rev. 20:8); (6) *apostasy* – the harlot (Ezek. 16:15; etc./Rev. 17); (7) *the divine Spirit as the power for God's people* – Zech. 4:1–6/Rev. 1:12–20; 11:4.

Some analogies are repeated in the book and creatively developed in different ways, though usually within the parameters of the OT context to some degree.

### (d) Universalisation of the OT

Vanhoye is apparently the only author to discuss this as a formal category of OT usage. The apocalyptist has a tendency to apply to the world what in the OT was limited in reference to Israel or other entities (cf. Vanhoye with reference to Ezekiel, pp. 446–67). There are several examples of this phenomenon. The title which Yahweh gave Israel in Exodus 19:6 ('kingdom of priests') is applied in Rev. 1:6 and 5:10 to the church, composed of kingly priests 'from every tribe and people and nation' (Rev. 5:9). Indeed, this very phrase of universality in Rev. 5:9 is most likely taken from Dan. 7:14, where it referred to the nations of the world subjugated to Israel's rule – now extended to the rule by all these very nations (cf. Rev. 5:10; Beale, 1984, pp. 214–19). The phrase in Rev. 1:7, 'and every eye will see him, even those who pierced him; and all the tribes of the earth will mourn over him', refers in Revelation to the peoples throughout the earth, although in Zech. 12:10 it is limited to the Israelite tribes. The same trend in this widening application of Zech. 12:10 is also given in John 19:31–7, where one of the gentile, Roman soldiers is viewed as a beginning fulfilment of this prophecy (so Michaels, 1967; Sweet, 1981, p. 112).

Another classic example of this tendency is the extension of the exodus plague imagery from the land of Egypt to the whole 'earth' in Rev. 8:6–12 and 16:1–14 (e.g. in 8:8 a third of the sea, including fish and ships, is affected instead of merely a river and fish; in 16:10 rather than the sun being darkened, it is the kingdom of the satanic beast which becomes darkened). The 'ten days of tribulation' experienced by Daniel and his friends (Dan. 1:12) and the three-and-a-half years of Israel's tribulation (Dan. 7:25; 12:7) are both extended to the tribulation of the church – the eschatological, true Israel –

throughout the world. And part of this tribulation is instigated by the eschatological 'Babylon the Great' (Dan. 4:30) who persecutes not merely ethnic Israelite believers, but also saints throughout the earth (Rev. 17:5–8; 18:24), and harmfully affects 'nations', 'kings of the earth' and the world's economy (18:1–23). Therefore, when 'Babylon the Great' falls, rather than the effect being provincial 'the cities of the nations' also fall (16:19). Likewise, the former persecutors of God's people in the OT (Sodom, Egypt and Jerusalem) are now defined as 'peoples and tribes and tongues and nations' (Rev. 11:8–10).

The Apocalypse concludes with references from the predicted eschatological temple reserved for Israel, although now its cultic benefits are extended to the Gentiles (cf. Ezek. 37:27, 44:9 and 48:35 in Rev. 21:3; cf. Rev. 22:2 where the 'leaves of healing' foretold in Ezek. 47:12 to be an aid to the Israelites are transformed into 'leaves...for the healing of the *nations*').

Sometimes the rationale for universalization is found already in the OT contexts (cf. Ezek. 14:12–21 in Rev. 6:8) from which the allusions are drawn, although the inspiration can also arise from combining a narrowly designed OT Israelite reference with another very similar OT text which, however, is universal. For example, the Israelite-orientated book of judgment from Ezek. 2:9 is given cosmic dimensions in Rev. 5:1 and 10:8–11 because it has been attracted to other OT judgment-book allusions which have a wider cosmic application (cf. Dan. 7:10; 12:4, 9 in Rev. 5:1–5 and Dan. 12:4–9 in Rev. 10:1–6). Nevertheless, the primary reason for the extended applications is the NT's and John's presupposition concerning the cosmic dimensions of Christ's lordship and death (cf. Rev. 1:5; 5:9–10; for other examples of universalization see Rev. 19:7 [bride], 17:1ff [harlot], 7:9, 15 [Ezek. 37:26], 18:9 [Ezek. 26:16ff; 27:29–35], 1:12–13, 20 [lampstands], 2:17 [manna], 3:12 and 21:2 [Jerusalem]).

It is tempting to conclude that John does not handle the OT according to its original contextual meaning when he universalises. But Vanhoye's evaluation is plausible. He says that while this universalisation is motivated by the christian spirit to explain redemptive fulfilment, it is not contrary to the OT sense. Although the author certainly makes different applications and executes developments beyond those of his OT predecessors, he stays within the same interpretative framework and is conscious of being profoundly faithful to the overall parameters of their message (Vanhoye, p. 467). This is a viable analysis since all of these universalisations can be considered sub-categories of the above-discussed analogical use of the OT, where it was proposed that, although John creatively reworks the OT and changes the application of it, his pictures retain significant points of correspondence with the OT context and express salvation-historical principles of continuity. All of the cited examples of universalisation appear to be harmonious developments of these principles as, for example, is the case with the OT texts pertaining to ethnic Israel's redemption and applied in Revelation to the world's redemption on the basis of defining the true people of God according to their faith in him. This is why the church comes to be viewed as the true Israel.

### (e) Possible indirect fulfilment uses of the OT

Although there are no formal OT quotations (with introductory formulae) used as prooftexts to indicate prophetic fulfilment, it is still possible that some OT texts were *informally* referred to in order to designate present or future fulfilment of OT verbal prophecy. The determination of whether a text refers to future or present fulfilment often depends on one's overall view of the book (e.g. preterist, historicist, idealist, futurist).

Of special note is the introduction to the book (1:1), where allusion is made to Dan. 2:28–9, 45: δεῖξαι...ἃ δεῖ γενέσθαι followed directly by ἐν τάχει (cf. Dan. 2:28, ἐδήλωσε...ἃ δεῖ γενέσθαι ἐπ' ἐσχάτων τῶν ἡμερῶν). John's 'quickly' has been substituted for Daniel's 'in the latter days' so that what Daniel expected to occur in the distant future – the defeat of cosmic evil and ushering in of the kingdom – John expects to begin in his own generation, and perhaps has already been inaugurated. Such imminence and even *incipient inauguration* is corroborated by the phrase – ὁ γὰρ καιρὸς ἐγγύς in 1:3, which elsewhere includes *both* the 'already' and 'not-yet' element (so Mark 1:15; Matt. 26:45; Lam. 4:18; cf. Matt. 3:2 with 4:17; cf. Beale, 1984b, pp. 415–20).

Dan. 12:4, 9 is used likewise in 22:10: whereas Daniel is commanded to 'conceal these words and seal up the book until the end of time' (12:4), John is given the consummatory command to 'not seal up the words of the prophecy of this book, for the time is near'. This use in 22:10 intensifies that of 1:1–3 since it is directly linked to a verbatim repetition of 1:1 in 22:6.

The reference to the Son of Man (1:13–14) probably indicates John's belief that Jesus had begun to fulfil the Dan. 7:13 prophecy of the Son of Man's exaltation, although the similar reference in 1:7 refers to a further phase of the same prophecy which still awaits realisation. The same kind of already-and-not-yet idea is found in 2:26–7 where Jesus says he has started to fulfil the Ps. 2:7 prediction but that his followers will also take part in the fulfilment at a future time (probably at death).

If the argument that Revelation 1 and 4–5 are each modelled on Daniel 7 can be sustained (cf. Beale 1984a, pp. 154–228), then John's intention may be to indicate that Jesus' death, resurrection and gathered church is the inaugurated fulfilment of Daniel.

There is also evidence of expectations of exclusive future fulfilment, of which only the clearest examples are listed (Zech. 12:10/Rev. 1:7; Isa. 25:8/

Rev. 7:17; Ps. 2:1/Rev. 11:18; Ps. 2:8/Rev. 12:5; 19:15; Isa. 65:17; 66:22/Rev. 21:1; Ezek. 47:1, 12/Rev. 22:1–2).

All of the illustrations so far have concerned fulfilments of OT texts which are clearly direct verbal prophecies. It also seems possible that there are texts which John understands as prophetic but which do not appear as such in the OT. It is worth considering whether parts of certain OT historical narratives are viewed as *indirect typological prophecies*. Many of the OT passages listed in our above discussion of analogical uses are potential candidates in this category. That is, are all of these texts merely analogies? We have already found that the essence of the analogies has to do with a basic *correspondence* of meaning between OT prophecy or *historical* narrative and something in the NT. Some of these OT historical elements have also undergone an escalation, even a universalisation, under John's hand. Perhaps there was a prophetic rationale in escalating these historical texts. At any rate, such uses are worth further inquiry in this regard, especially against the background of John's and the NT's awareness that the 'latter days' had been inaugurated, that the church was the latter-day Israel and that the whole OT pointed toward this climax of salvation history (for inaugurated eschatological language cf. Mark 1:15; Acts 2:17; Gal. 4:4; 1 Cor. 10:11; 2 Cor. 6:2; 1 Tim. 4:1; 2 Tim. 3:1; 1 Pet. 1:20; Heb. 1:2; 9:26; Jas. 5:3; 1 John 2:18; Jude 18; Rev. 1:1; 1:19; 4:1; 22:6, 10 – cf. Beale, 1984b, pp. 415–20). The precedent of overt typological-prophetic uses in Matthew, Hebrews and elsewhere in the NT should leave open the same possibility in Revelation.

### (f)   Inverted use of the Old Testament

There are some allusions which on the surface are distinctly contradictory to the OT contextual meaning. But further study again reveals the imprecise nature of such categories. The clearest example of this is Rev. 3:9, which collectively makes reference to the Isaianic prophecies that the Gentiles would come and bow down before Israel and recognize them as God's chosen people (Isa. 45:14; 49:23; 60:14). However, this jewish hope from Isaiah has been turned upside down, since it is the jewish persecutors of the Christians whom God will make to submit to the church. This reversal of Isaiah's language is most likely attributable to a conscious attempt to express the irony that the submission which unbelieving ethnic Jews hoped to receive from Gentiles, they themselves would be forced to render to the church (so also Vos, p. 25; Mounce, 1977, p. 118). John concludes that ethnic Jews had become as unbelieving Gentiles because of their rejection of Christ and persecution of Christians. In fact, this ironic element is intensified at the end of v. 9 through John's reference to the gentile church as the true Israel. This is accomplished by making a reverse application of Isa. 43:4, which originally spoke of God's love and honour for Israel above the nations. Vos is therefore inconsistent in recognising an irony in the first part of v. 9 but concluding with respect to the Isa. 43:4 citation that 'the context of the alleged quotation has been totally disregarded' (p. 26). This rather shows a consistent ironic understanding of some of the major themes in Isaiah 40–66. And while such a view arises out of a contextual awareness of the OT, the NT use is so diametrically opposite that it is best to categorise this as an inverted or ironic use.

The use of the cosmic universality terminology from Dan. 7:14 in Rev. 5:9 reveals an intended inversion. Whereas in Daniel the phrase refers to the nations subjugated to Israel's rule, now these very nations rule together with the messiah.

A sampling of other such uses is noteworthy. Dan. 7:21 refers to an anti-theocratic 'horn' which 'was waging war with the saints and overpowering them'. This is applied in reverse fashion in Rev. 12:7–8 to describe the overthrow of Satan by Michael and his angels. Such reverse application probably does not reflect unconscious activity or an atomistic exegesis, but polemical irony, expressed by portraying the theocratic forces' defeat of the cosmic enemy through the same imagery from Daniel 7 which was used to describe how this enemy began to defeat God's forces. This may be a figurative way of expressing a *lex talionis* irony whereby the point is to show that the same way in which the enemy will try to subdue God will be used by God himself to subdue the enemy. That this language is intentionally drawn in reverse manner from Dan. 7:21 is evident not only from the verbal likeness (cf. Theodotion) but also from the immediately following allusion to Dan. 2:35 (Rev. 12:8b) *and* from the same Dan. 7:21 reversal in Rev. 17:14, where the Danielic 'Lord of lords and King of kings' (= Dan. 4:37 [LXX]) is the subject of the polemical overthrow.

The same kind of retributive ironies can be observed elsewhere in the Apocalpyse: Dan. 8:10 in Rev. 12:4, 9, 10; Dan. 7:7ff in Rev. 5:6–7 (so 1 En. 90:9–13, 16; Test. Jos. 19:6–8; Midr. Rab. 99:2; 4 Ezra 13:1ff; cf. Beale, 1983); Dan. 7:14 in Rev. 13:7–8; Exod. 8:10 and 15:11, etc. in Rev. 13:4; Exod. 3:14 (esp. Midr. Rab. Exod. 3:14) in Rev. 17:8 (cf. 1:4, 8; 4:8; 11:17; 16:5; cf. also Ezra 9:14b in 1QM 1. 6b and Dan. 11:40, 44–5 in 1QM 1. 4).

There may be other examples of this reversal phenomenon but those discussed should alert one to caution in making facile statements about non-contextual, atomistic or straightforward contextual use, since the apocalyptic style is not always susceptible merely to such categories.

Nevertheless, all of the above cases studied here and throughout section 4 can be categorized as at least *broadly* contextual. Vanhoye has noted that John always employs OT references with a view to making them contribute to the unified argument of his work (1962, pp. 463–4), and that every page 'witnesses to a penetrating intelligence of the ancient prophecies and of a perfect familiarity with their mode of expression' (1962, p. 462). Gangemi observes that John does not choose OT allusions at random but in accord with the main themes of the Apocalypse: divine transcendence, redemption, Yahweh's servant, Babylon's judgment and new creation of the heavenly Jerusalem (1974, pp. 322–38). And it is clear that John drew these unifying themes of his work from the OT (in this case Isaiah 40–66). Indeed, John is continuing to develop fundamental lines of OT salvation history (Cambier, 1955, pp. 118–21; Gangemi, 1974, pp. 332–9).

### (g)   Stylistic use of OT language

This use represents the most general category so far discussed. It has long been recognised that the Apocalypse contains a multitude of grammatical solecisms. Charles claimed it contained more grammatical irregularities than any other Greek document of the ancient world (1920, p. cxliii). He accounted for this with his famous dictum '*while he writes in Greek, he thinks in Hebrew*, and the thought has naturally affected the vehicle of expression' (p. cxliii), a judgment which has met with subsequent agreement, especially recently (cf. Sweet, 1979, pp. 16–17, Collins, 1984, p. 47 and above all Thompson, 1985, *passim*).

But was this intentional on the author's part or an unconscious by-product of his semitic mind? It seems that his grammatical 'howlers' are deliberate attempts to reproduce semitic idioms in his Greek, the closest analogy being that of the LXX translations – especially Aquila (Sweet, 1979, p. 16; see especially Thompson, 1985, p. 108 and *passim*). The fact that most of the time the author does keep the rules further points to the solecisms being intentional.

Why did John write this way? His purpose was deliberately to create a 'biblical' effect in the hearer and thus to demonstrate the solidarity of his work with that of the divinely inspired OT Scriptures (Sweet, 1979, p. 16). A polemical purpose may also have been included. John may have been expressing the idea that OT truth via the church as the new Israel was uncompromisingly penetrating the gentile world, and would continue to until the final parousia (cf. somewhat similarly Collins, 1984, p. 47; Thompson, 1985, p. 108).

### 5   CONCLUSION

Perhaps one of the reasons for the high degree of OT influence in the Apocalypse is that the author could think of no better way to describe some of his visions which were difficult to explain than with the language already used by the OT prophets to describe similar visions. The present study, particularly of categories of usage in the Apocalypse, favours the evaluation of Fransen:

The familiarity with the Old Testament, with the spirit which lives in the Old Testament, is a most essential condition for a fruitful reading of the Apocalypse

(1956–7, p. 67; cf. likewise Sweet, 1981, p. 111).

This is a conclusion which runs counter to that of Barnabas Lindars's general evaluation of the primary role of the OT in the majority of the NT corpus:

The place of the Old Testament in the formation of New Testament theology is that of a servant, ready to run to the aid of the gospel whenever it is required, bolstering up arguments, and filling out meaning through evocative allusions, but never acting as the master or leading the way, nor even guiding the process of thought behind the scenes

(1977, p. 66).

However, Lindars appears to exclude the Apocalypse from his analysis (cf. 1961, *passim*; 1977, 63–4). He expresses apparent openness to discovering more respect for OT contextual meaning in the Apocalypse because he judges John's writing not to be the result of urgent, *ad hoc* apologetic concerns but to have arisen out of meditation worked out quietly in the study at a slightly later stage of christian apocalyptic (1977, p. 63).

Therefore, the conclusion of this investigation is that the place of the OT in the formation of thought in the Apocalypse is both that of a servant and a guide: for John the Christ-event is *the* key to understanding the OT, and yet reflection back on the OT context leads the way to further comprehension of this event and provides the redemptive–historical background against which the apocalyptic visions are better understood. Whether or not there is the same reciprocal relationship elsewhere in the NT is a question which cannot be addressed here. However, the observation that much of the NT was written not only with an apologetic motive but also in an apocalyptic atmosphere should cause us to be open to this possibility.

## NOTE

1 UBS³, pp. 901–11 = 394; NA²⁶, pp. 739–74 = 635; British and Foreign Bible Society Greek text, pp. 734–87 = 493; E. Hühn, 1900, pp. 269ff = 455; W. Dittmar, 1903, pp. 263–79 = 195; Swete, 1911, p. cxl = 278; Charles, 1920, pp. lxv–lxxxii = 226; C. van der Waal, 1971, pp. 174–241 = 1000 (approx.).

## BIBLIOGRAPHY

R. Bauckham 'The Eschatological Earthquake in the Apocalypse of John', *NovT* 19 (1977), 224–33.

G. K. Beale 'The Problem of the Man From the Sea in IV Ezra 13 and Its Relation to the Messianic Concept in John's Apocalypse', *NovT* 25 (1983), 182–8.

*The Use of Daniel in Jewish Apocalyptic Literature and in the Revelation of St John* (Lanham, 1984) (= 1984a).

'The Influence of Daniel Upon the Structure and Theology of John's Apocalypse', *JETS* 27 (1984), 413–23 (= 1984b).

'The Origin of the Title 'King of Kings and Lord of Lords' in Revelation 17.14', *NTS* 31 (1985), 618–20.

'A Reconsideration of the Text of Daniel in the Apocalypse', *Bib* 73 (1986), 539–43.

G. R. Beasley-Murray *The Book of Revelation*, NCB (Grand Rapids, 1981).

G. B. Caird *The Revelation of St John the Divine*, HNTC (New York, 1966).

J. Cambier 'Les images de l'Ancien Testament dans l'Apocalypse de saint Jean', *NRTh* (1955), 113–22.

D. R. Carnegie 'The Hymns in Revelation: Their Origin and Function', unpublished Ph.D Dissertation submitted to the Council for National Academic Awards (1978).

'Worthy is the Lamb: the Hymns in Revelation', in H. H. Rowden (ed.), *Christ the Lord: Studies Presented to Donald Guthrie* (Downers Grove, 1982), pp. 243–56.

R. H. Charles *A Critical and Exegetical Commentary on the Revelation of St John*, ICC (Edinburgh, 1920).

A. Y. Collins *Crisis and Catharsis. The Power of the Apocalypse* (Philadelphia, 1984).

J. Comblin *Le Christ dans l'Apocalypse*, in Bibliothèque de Théologie, Théologie biblique – Série III, 6 (Tournai, 1965).

G. Delling 'Zum gottesdienstlichen Stil der Johannes-Apokalypse', *NovT* 3 (1959), 107–37.

W. D. Dittmar *Vetus Testamentum in Novo* (Göttingen, 1903).

J. A. Draper 'The Heavenly Feast of Tabernacles: Revelation 7:1–17', *JSNT* 19 (1983), 133–47.

A. Farrer *The Revelation of St John the Divine* (Oxford, 1964).

D. Ford *The Abomination of Desolation in Biblical Eschatology* (Washington, 1979).

I. Fransen 'Cahier de Bible: Jésus, le Témoin Fidèle (Apocalypse)', *BVC* 16 (1956–7), 66–79.

A. Gangemi 'L'utilizzazione del Deutero-Isaia nell'Apocalisse di Giovanni', *ED* 27 (1974), 311–39.

M. D. Goulder 'The Apocalypse as an Annual Cycle of Prophecies', *NTS* 27 (1981), 342–67.

D. A. Gray 'The Day of the Lord and Its Culmination in the Book of Revelation', unpublished Ph.D. Dissertation (Univ. of Manchester, 1974).

L. Hartman *Prophecy Interpreted*, in CBNTS 1 (Uppsala, 1966).

T. Holtz *Die Christologie der Apokalypse des Johannes*, TU 85 (Berlin, 1971).

E. Hühn *Die alttestamentlichen Citate und Reminiscenzen im Neuen Testament* (Tübingen, 1900).

F. Jenkins *The Old Testament in the Book of Revelation* (Marion, IN, 1972).

K. G. Kuhn 'Gog-Magog', in *TWNT* 1 (Stuttgart, 1933), pp. 790–2.

A. Lancellotti 'L'Antico Testamento nell'Apocalisse', *RivistBib* 14 (1966), 369–84.

S. Läuchli 'Eine Gottesdienststruktur in der Johannesoffenbarung', *ThZ* 16 (1960), 359–78.

B. Lindars *New Testament Apologetic* (London, 1961).

'The Place of the Old Testament in the Formation of New Testament Theology', *NTS* 23 (1977), 59–66.

E. Lohse 'Die alttestamentliche Sprache des Sehers Johannes: Textkritische Bemerkungen zur Apokalypse', *ZNW* 52 (1961), 122–6.

T. Longman 'The Divine Warrior: The New Testament Use of an Old Testament Motif', *WTJ* 4 (1982), 290–307.

J. Lust 'The Order of the Final Events in Revelation and in Ezekiel', in J. Lambrecht (ed.), *L'Apocalypse johannique et l'Apocalyptique dans le Nouveau Testament*, BEThL 53 (Gembloux, 1980), pp. 179–83.

B. Marconcini 'L'utilizzazione del T. M. nelle citazione isaiane dell' Apocalisse', *RivistBib* 24 (1976), 113–36.

J. R. Michaels 'The Centurion's Confession and the Spear Thrust', *CBQ* 29 (1967), 102–9.

R. H. Mounce *The Book of Revelation*, NICNT (Grand Rapids, 1980).

H. P. Müller 'Formgeschichtliche Untersuchungen zu Apc 4F', unpublished doctoral dissertation (Univ. of Heidelberg, 1962).

'Die himmlische Ratsversammlung. Motivgeschichtliches zu Apc 5:1–5', *ZNW* 54 (1963), 254–67.

P. Prigent *Apocalypse et Liturgie*, CT 52 (Neuchâtel, 1964).

'Une Tradition Messianique relative à Juda', *MDB* 11 (1979), 46.

G. von Rad, *Theologie des Alten Testaments*, Bd 2, *Die Theologie des prophetischen Überlieferungen Israels* (Münich, 1960); ET *Old Testament Theology*, vol. 2, *The Theology of Israel's Prophetic Traditions* (New York, 1965).

A. Schlatter *Das Alte Testament in der johanneischen Apokalypse*, in BFChrTh 6 (Gütersloh, 1912).

E. Schüssler-Fiorenza 'Apokalypsis and Propheteia. The Book of Revelation in the Context of Early Christian Prophecy', in J. Lambrecht (ed.), *L'Apocalypse johannique et l'Apocalyptique dans le Nouveau Testament*, BEThL 53 (Gembloux, 1980), pp. 105–28.

E. G. Selwyn 'Dialogues of the Christian Prophets', *Expositor*, Sixth Series 5 (1902), 321–43.

W. H. Shea 'The Covenantal Form of the Letters to the Seven Churches', *AUSS* 21 (1983), 71–84.

K. A. Strand 'A Further Note on the Covenantal Form in the Book of Revelation', *AUSS* 21 (1983), 71–84.

J. P. M. Sweet *Revelation*, in SCM Pelican Commentaries (London, 1979). 'Maintaining the Testimony of Jesus: the Suffering of Christians in the Revelation of John', in W. Horbury and B. McNeil (eds.), *Suffering and Martyrdom in the New Testament. Studies Presented to G. M. Styler* (Cambridge, 1981), pp. 101–17.

H. B. Swete *Commentary on Revelation* (London, 1911).

S. Thompson *The Apocalypse and Semitic Syntax*, SNTSMS 52 (Cambridge, 1985).

P. Trudinger 'Some Observations Concerning the Text of the Old Testament in the Book of Revelation', *JTS* 17 (1966), 82–8.

C. van der Waal *Openbaring van Jezus Christus* (Groningen, 1971).

A. Vanhoye 'L'utilisation du livre d'Ezéchiel dans l'Apocalypse', *Bib* 43 (1962).

L. A. Vos *The Synoptic Traditions in the Apocalypse* (Kampen, 1965).

A. Wikenhauser 'Das Problem des tausendjährigen Reiches in der JohannesApokalypse', *RömQ* 40 (1932), 13–25.

# Index of passages cited

# Indexes

# Indexes

# Indexes

344

# Indexes

347

# Indexes

# Indexes

# Indexes

20:9   246, 247, 252
20:31   258, 262

*Acts*   17, 19, 203, 204, 231, 237, 244, 277
1–14   240
1:16   240, 242, 243
1:20   240, 242, 243
2   241, 243
2:16   236, 238, 242
2:17   330
2:17–21   238, 243
2:21   243
2:24   198
2:25   242
2:25–8   196, 238, 239, 243
2:25–31   196
2:26   197
2:30   244 n.3, 244, 310
2:30–31   196
2:31   196, 197, 198
2:34   238, 242
2:34f   243
2:35   238
2:36   241
2:39   241, 243
3   241, 243
3:13   243
3:22   238, 242, 243
3:23   238
3:25   238, 242, 243
4:8–12   195
4:10   196
4:11   195, 196, 233
4:22   196
4:24   239
4:25   239, 242
4:26   239
7   239, 241, 242, 243
7:2–3   242
7:3   238, 242
7:5   238, 242
7:6   238, 242
7:7   238, 242
7:18   238
7:27   238
7:28   238
7:32   238
7:33   238
7:34   238
7:35   238, 239
7:37   238, 242
7:40   238
7:42   238, 242
7:43   238
7:48   242
8:32   238, 242
8:33   238
8:34f   10

10   240
10:43   240
13   241, 242, 243
13:17–21   241
13:22   238
13:22–41   241
13:27   275
13:29   237, 275
13:33   239, 242
13:33–7   238
13:34   197, 198, 239
13:35   197, 239, 242
13:36   197
13:37   197
13:40   236, 242
13:41   125, 239
13:46f   243
13:47   240, 242
14–28   239
14:15–17   244 n.5
15   241
15:14   241, 244 n.4
15:15   242
15:15–18   241
15:16   240
15:17   240
15:18   240
15:19   241
15:20   241
15:21   241
17:22–31   244 n.5
21:40   273
22:2   273
22:3   273
23:5   240, 242
26:22   241
28:25   242, 244
28:25–8   243
28:26   240
28:26–7   207
28:27   240

*Romans*   265, 274, 275, 281, 289, 290
1:2   278
1:16–17   274
1:17   268, 274, 281, 295, 299
2:24   268
3:1–8   274
3:4   268
3:10–12   268
3:10–18   274
3:13   268
3:14   268
3:15–17   268
3:18   268
3:19   277
3:21   274, 281
3:22–31   274

# Indexes

# Indexes

## C. Apocrypha and Pseudepigrapha

# Indexes

# Indexes

# Indexes

# Indexes

# Indexes

# Indexes

# Indexes

# Indexes

# Indexes

# Indexes

# General index

# Indexes

# Indexes

# Indexes

# Indexes